BELLE COOLEDGE LIBRARY
5600 SOUTH LAND PARK DRIVE
SACRAMENTO, CA 95822

D0058276

Andersonville

Civil War America

 Gary W. Gallagher, editor

Andersonville

⧨ The Last Depot

William Marvel

The University of North Carolina Press

Chapel Hill & London

The paper in this book meets the guidelines for permanence

and durability of the Committee on Production Guidelines for

Book Longevity of the Council on Library Resources.

Library of Congress Cataloging-in-Publication Data

Marvel, William.

Andersonville : the last depot / by William Marvel.

   p. cm.—(Civil War America)

Includes bibliographical references (p.) and index.

ISBN 0-8078-2152-7 (cloth : alk. paper)

1. Andersonville Prison. 2. United States—History—Civil War,

1861–1865—Prisoners and prisons, Confederate. 3. Prisoners

of war—Confederate States of America. 4. Prisoners of war—

United States—History—19th century. I. Title. II. Series.

E612.A5M44   1994   93-40101

973.7′71—dc20

CIP

98 97 96 95 94   5 4 3 2 1

To

HARVEY KNIGHT

of Atmore, Alabama,

1947–1992,

the quintessential

army buddy

Contents

A map of Andersonville appears on pages 2–3,

and a section of illustrations follows page 112.

S Preface

ome 41,000 men shuffled into the prison stockade at Anderson Station, Georgia, between February of 1864 and April of 1865. Of these, perhaps 26,000 lived long enough to reach home. Theirs was undoubtedly the most unpleasant experience of the Civil War, but, almost without exception, those who wrote about Andersonville appear to have exaggerated their tribulations at that place. Some did so deliberately, for political reasons or simply because accounts of prison misery sold well in the postwar North. Others forgot personal acts of kindness, regurgitating tales of horrible cruelties that they never witnessed because, as one of them reasoned, they must have been true. In many cases they based their anecdotes on testimony from the trial of Henry Wirz, the transcript of which runs heavy with some of the most absurd hearsay that any American judge ever permitted to stand.

Literary demands may have driven former prisoners to enliven their recollections with grisly imaginings or borrowings, if only to avoid infecting their readers with the sheer tedium of Andersonville. Memories of their helplessness at the hands of their captors and crystallized suspicions that their deprivation was an act of conscious design may also have provoked a certain license with the truth. These men did not, however, have to embellish their accounts to produce a picture of immense suffering: the prison and the circumstances provided that without any infusion of malice.

Much effort has been expended by various partisans to prove that Southern spite against prisoners or Northern intransigence on the exchange question was responsible for this tragedy. Surviving documents seem to discredit any accusation of deliberate deprivation, unless one takes the position that the Richmond government should have devoted a greater proportion of its dwindling resources to its prisoners than to its own army, but thorough examination of the exchange question would require the better part of a book. This will not be that book. Clearly the breakdown of prisoner exchange was responsible for the lengthy imprisonments that allowed vitamin deficiency to kill and cripple so many, but the real cause of that breakdown is less certain.

It was the Federal government that suspended the exchange cartel, first in response to disagreement over numbers and then in protest of the Confederate refusal to repatriate black soldiers. At one point it appeared that the two sides might work that out, except perhaps for those prisoners who were recognized as former slaves, but the Federal government insisted on absolute equality for all black prisoners: it could do no less without appearing to foresake them. Conversely, as hungry for manpower as it was, the Confederacy could not comply without renouncing the very reason for its existence. Northern stubbornness on that point puzzled equally resolute Southerners, leading them to suspect that this was merely an excuse for keeping the large preponderance of prisoners held in Union prisons. In the summer of 1864 Ulysses Grant let it slip that there was at least a grain of truth to that argument: as hard as it was on those in Southern prisons, he contended, it would be kinder to those still in the ranks if each side kept what prisoners it had, since that would end the war sooner.

As important as the exchange question was to the prisoners, the finer points of the debate do not bear particularly on what actually happened at Andersonville. It may not even be possible to determine whether the issue of black soldiers was a pretense, or whether the more pragmatic motive evolved during the cartel's suspension, since intentions varied widely among those who held power. Grant's implied policy of attrition was just as legitimate as the administration's stated motive was high-minded: if it was adherence to such a policy that led to the deaths of thousands who might otherwise have lived, it probably saved even more lives that might have been lost, North and South, by prolongation of the conflict.

That would have been a tough bill of goods to sell in 1865, had Grant's reasoning been public knowledge. Even the principle of equal treatment for black prisoners held little sway with many in the North: Lincoln's own secretary of the navy privately denounced the obstinacy over former slaves. The inhabitants of Andersonville felt particularly bitter on that account. Prison officials played the card for all it was worth, prompting great numbers of prisoners to express contempt for the Lincoln administration, which they felt had abandoned them for the "confiscated contrabands."

Back home, many of the prisoners' families shared that sentiment. It therefore behooved the victors to establish that enemy malevolence had caused it all rather than a matter of lofty principle or a conscious practical policy of the victims' own government. That aim proved consistent with the politics of the bloody shirt, and military justice provided the requisite scapegoat. With that pronouncement one frail Swiss immigrant went to the gallows and Andersonville came to signify all that was evil in the hated Confederacy.

Andersonville

Only the winners decide

what were war crimes.

—Gary Wills

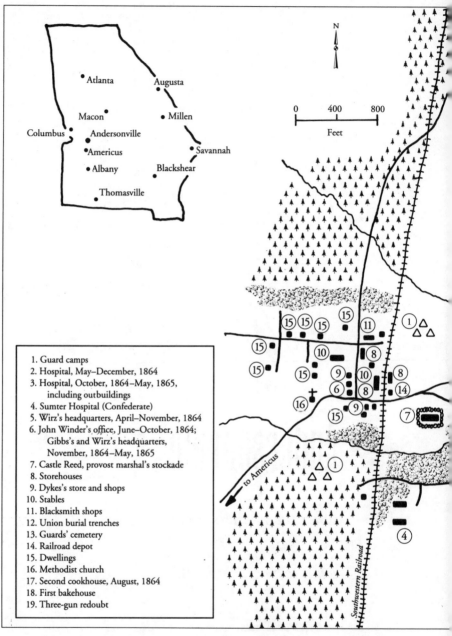

1. Guard camps
2. Hospital, May–December, 1864
3. Hospital, October, 1864–May, 1865, including outbuildings
4. Sumter Hospital (Confederate)
5. Wirz's headquarters, April–November, 1864
6. John Winder's office, June–October, 1864; Gibbs's and Wirz's headquarters, November, 1864–May, 1865
7. Castle Reed, provost marshal's stockade
8. Storehouses
9. Dykes's store and shops
10. Stables
11. Blacksmith shops
12. Union burial trenches
13. Guards' cemetery
14. Railroad depot
15. Dwellings
16. Methodist church
17. Second cookhouse, August, 1864
18. First bakehouse
19. Three-gun redoubt

Andersonville, Georgia, and Andersonville Prison, 1864–1865. Adapted from a map by Blake A. Magner.

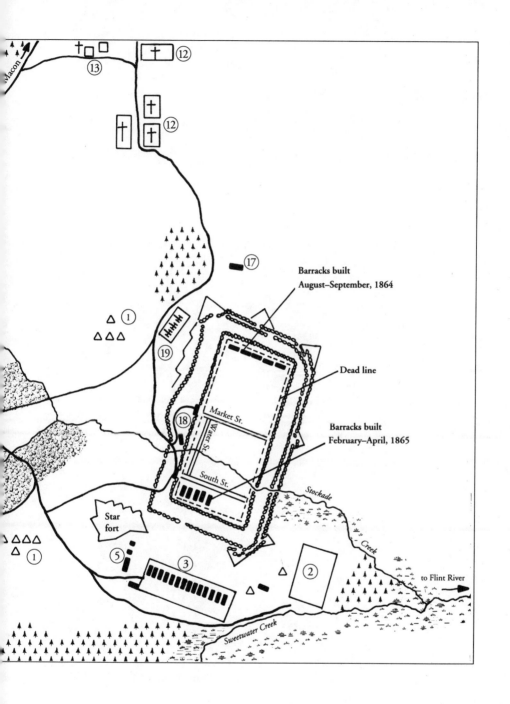

Barracks built
August–September, 1864

Dead line

Barracks built
February–April, 1865

Market St.

Water St.

South St.

Star fort

Stockade

Creek

to Flint River

Sweetwater Creek

Macon

1 ⤜ A I Find Me in a Gloomy Wood

s on any other day, the world spent Tuesday, November 24, 1863, spinning the thread of tomorrow's events from the flax of yesterday's. In Moscow a former political prisoner struggled to document the horrors of his experience; from Copenhagen a new Danish king evoked the wrath of the growing Prussian empire when he cast a covetous eye on two German duchies; at the mouth of the Seine a young artist who would help change the complexion of painting sketched the rugged coast of his native Normandy; off Japan a British frigate avenged the execution of a countryman with a surprise bombardment of the city of Kagoshima; in the wind-whipped autumn chill that reminded him of his Norwegian homeland, a laboring man in Winchester, Wisconsin, learned that his name—Knud Hanson—had been drawn that very day from a tumbler full of such names, and now he would have to fight in the war that raged across the American continent.[1]

That same evening George Templeton Strong attended a lecture by Henry Ward Beecher at the Academy of Music in New York. The address benefited the U.S. Sanitary Commission, to which Strong belonged. When the Reverend Beecher ran out of words—a rare enough event in itself—he and the more prominent members of his audience adjourned to the home of the Sanitary Commission's president. Beecher's sister, the author of *Uncle Tom's Cabin*, offered her presence at this soirée, impressing Mr. Strong as a "very bright and agreeable" lady.[2]

In the wee hours of November 24 an Iowa farmboy, George Shearer, clambered down the bank of the Tennessee River under the eerie glow of a full moon and joined his comrades in the flat bottom of a square-ended pontoon boat. With surprisingly little noise beyond the dull clunking of poles and an occasional cough or sneeze, Shearer's and many other boats glided across the shimmering water to a dark, indefinite shore, the passengers touched by the beauty and romance of the occasion in spite of their nervous anticipation. When the blunt prows grounded just below the mouth of East Chickamauga Creek, there came a hollow thudding of feet, like so many kettle drummers practicing the long roll, as the companies scrambled ashore and formed ranks in their azure, moon-painted overcoats. They marched to a stubbly cornfield in the shadow of a hill, where officers whispered that they might rest for a couple of hours. Their lines melted to the ground just behind the supine silhouette of the 5th Iowa Infantry, at the center of which lay Corporal John Whitten, clutching the furled red, white, and blue banner of the Hawkeye State. Shearer and Whitten curled on the cold earth and tried to sleep, for they had been awake all night now, but the thought of what was to come must have troubled their repose.[3]

Beyond the hill that hid the Iowans sat the extreme right flank of Braxton Bragg's Army of Tennessee. Six miles to the southwest, on the far side of Chattanooga, another Federal force waited to throw itself against Bragg's left, on Lookout Mountain, and in the morning they would all move forward to settle accounts for the Union army's humiliation at Chickamauga nine weeks before. The work would take two days; when it was over, George Shearer would lie in a field hospital with a bandage bound around the trough a bullet had plowed through his scalp, while John Whitten would no longer own either his flag or his liberty.[4]

Two hundred fifty miles south of Chattanooga, the citizens of Sumter

County, Georgia, still reveled in the news of Chickamauga; not since Chancellorsville had such a victory swelled Southern hopes. Thirty months of war had begun to wear on the population. Prices seemed out of control, and some items could not be had at any price. Eggs, corn, and wheat flour periodically disappeared from village markets as farmers speculated in more profitable crops. The *Sumter Republican*, of Americus, joked about the wasteful habit of eating three meals a day, and praised the patriotic farmer who turned his cotton fields over to corn. A year earlier Sumter County farmers had tried to force the price of corn up by cutting production. They had had some success in their conspiratorial venture, so the 1863 crop had been a little more plentiful, but discontent still simmered in southwest Georgia's piney woods. The farmers made plans to organize anew, and the *Republican*, which had just raised its subscription rate again, complained of hearing disloyal sentiments muttered on the dusty streets of Americus.[5]

One of the muttering men may have been Ambrose Spencer. Though he had been South many years now, Spencer was a genuine Yankee, born and bred in upstate New York. Always on the lookout for the main chance, he had come to Georgia hoping to join the planter aristocracy— perhaps as a means of restoring the dwindling dignity of the family name. His grandfather and namesake had been a prominent jurist, and his father had served as secretary of both the War and Treasury departments under John Tyler, but his brother had been hanged in the wake of the infamous *Somerset* mutiny and his father had resigned from the cabinet, never to hold public office again.[6]

Spencer had not done well in his Georgia enterprises, and his wife, a Sussex-born immigrant, owned the property on which they lived. At the outbreak of war he tried for a direct commission in the Provisional Army, but failing that he attempted to raise an artillery company. The Confederate War Department declined to accept his battery without muster rolls naming the scores of recruits he claimed to have enlisted, refusing him a commission even when he implied imaginary service in the Mexican War, and for a time the disappointed Spencer acted like a man who wished to retire from society: he put his wife's Starkeville Road home on the market, and when a Macon cleric bought that house Spencer moved his family out to a two-hundred-acre plantation he had convinced Mrs. Spencer to buy southwest of Americus. Through the Christmas season of 1862 the rebuffed patriot advertised that he wanted everyone who had borrowed books from him to return them. This November of 1863, however, he came out of his exile long enough to cast about, without success, for some sort of government sinecure that might support him better than the plantation did.[7]

November 24 found Shepherd Pryor, another Sumter County resident, in Richmond's Chimborazo Hospital. A bushy-bearded captain of the 12th Georgia Infantry, Pryor nursed an ugly purple scar on his right leg, six inches above the knee. He had been in the war from the start, and had won his brigade commander's praise at Gettysburg, but during the Bristoe campaign a piece of shell had laid him low as he led his skirmish line forward somewhere beyond Warrenton. Captain Pryor wanted to go home now, but his wound was nearly healed and he might soon have to return to duty: remembering that Georgia's civil officers were exempt from military service, he decided to run for sheriff of Sumter County. Deputy Sheriff William Wesley Turner and one other candidate, a speculator, had already announced for the seat in July, and the election was only a few weeks away, but Pryor wrote to his Sumter County friends in the 10th Georgia Infantry Battalion and Cutts's Artillery Battalion, asking for their support. As a battle-scarred veteran he had good reason to suppose that he could beat two men who had spent the war at home.[8]

Shepherd Pryor had sustained his wound in the last real offensive that Robert E. Lee's army ever undertook. The contending armies in Virginia sat much farther south now, along the Rapidan River, and now it was the Yankees who proposed taking the initiative. Ira Pettit, a twenty-two-year-old farm lad from western New York, passed November 24 resting in camp at Paoli Mills with his company of the 11th U.S. Infantry. Pettit, too, had fought at Gettysburg, though on the opposite end of the line from Captain Pryor, and his regiment had taken a fearful pounding. In a couple of days these Regulars would march south, for the Culpeper Ford of the Rapidan, bound for a place called Mine Run.[9]

At Morton's Ford, on the same river, Colonel Edward O'Neal waited for the long blue columns with which Ira Pettit would march. At forty-five, O'Neal commanded the brigade that included his own 26th Alabama: he had led that brigade since the spring, through Chancellorsville and Gettysburg, in the same division as Shepherd Pryor, but when this Thanksgiving offensive was over he would be displaced by a junior officer promoted over his head. Thus robbed of his general's stars, the proud Irishman would raise such a stink as to get himself and his regiment transferred elsewhere, but for now he rode conscientiously up and down his reach of the river, occasionally peering into the mists with his binoculars.[10]

That same day Hiram Jepperson, another Gettysburg veteran, walked a beat along a prison stockade on the mile-long spit of sand where the Potomac River emptied into Chesapeake Bay. Clam flats bordered either side of Point Lookout military prison, adding their saline pungency to the crowded peninsula where some eight thousand Confederates lived in drafty tents inside the pale; other prisoners, who had taken the oath of allegiance to the United States, populated a separate camp nearby. Jepperson's 5th New Hampshire was one of three Granite State regiments that had just arrived to guard these Southrons. It was a monotonous duty patrolling the prison, but presumably it was preferable to the bloody career the regiment had followed since Hiram joined it in August of 1862: he had seen four major battles in his first ten months of service. Still, he did not seem inclined to go home if he could, for there was little left for him there. The illegitimate son of a Lisbon farmgirl, Hiram had lived most of his life with neighbors, as a hired hand, especially after his mother married. His grandfather acted as his guardian, but the only time he seems to have exercised that office was when he signed a waiver for the boy to enlist. Swearing to the minimum age of eighteen years (he was only sixteen, and at five-foot-two he had a few inches yet to grow), Hiram scratched his laborious mark on an enlistment certificate and turned his back, apparently forever, on the Connecticut River valley. One more battle still lay ahead of him this November 24, but as he paced his beat he was probably more interested in the meal his company would enjoy for Thanksgiving, two days away.[11]

At that very moment another New Hampshire youth trod Morris Island, a similarly sandy outcrop about five hundred miles down the coast, at the entrance to Charleston harbor. Aaron Elliott plodded up and down and back and forth in the shadow of the abandoned Confederate bastion known as Battery Wagner, while his noncommissioned officers tried to imbue a new influx of recruits and substitutes with some basic notions of close-order drill. Each company of the 7th New Hampshire had drawn its share of 268 "fresh fish," some of whom were a rough-looking lot. The new men nearly outnumbered the old. Siege guns hammering at the city and at Fort Sumter and Fort Moultrie outplayed the beat of the drums, and the slippery sand threw even the most willing feet astray. Sergeants cursed, privates chuckled, and officers shook their heads.

More than two years before, on his sixteenth birthday, Aaron Elliott had left his Goffstown home for the abutting town of Manchester, where he enlisted in the regiment with which he now served. His father not only allowed him to go, but permitted his older brother Warren to join him when the 7th left the state. That deprived Mr. Elliott of his only two farmhands: of his other four children, two were too young to be of any help and the other two lived in the private, tragic world of deaf-mutes. For months Warren and Aaron supplemented their family's income with their army pay, but that source had been cut in half since July, when Warren was killed in the ill-fated assault on Battery Wagner.

At last the drill sergeants gave up for the day. Recruits and veterans alike found cool spots to sit, for even late November can be uncomfortably warm on the sea islands, and there they contemplated their empty pockets and the crates of canned chicken the sutlers had stocked for the holiday. The native Yankee that he was, Aaron Elliott would probably not go into debt for delicacies, so there would be no sutler's wares for him.[12]

While Elliott lounged on the Carolina sand, Thomas Genzardi writhed on his cot in a Richmond prison hospital along the James River, not far from Captain Pryor's ward. His intestines seemed alternately to twist and explode within him, curling him up like a caterpillar, and whatever nourishment he took soon came surging back up. The roving ward surgeon diagnosed it as cholera morbus, but by November 24 Genzardi had lain in the hospital twelve days and it was beginning to look as though he might pull through; he had begun to absorb at least some of the liquids the nurses fed him, and the doctor saw that as a good sign. Another week would say for certain whether he would live.

In the past two years Genzardi had nearly completed a broad circuit of the United States. His real name was Salvador Ginsardi, and he had been born in Boston in 1843, shortly after his family arrived from Italy. By 1850 his mother was dead, and his father supported him by playing a flute in a Charlestown band, but music made for a precarious living. Pedro Ginsardi eventually took his son to New York, and there they finally parted, but not before Anglicizing their names slightly: in August of 1861 Pedro enlisted in the 12th U.S. Infantry band as Peter Genzardi, leaving Salvador to drift into the American West as Thomas Genzardi. The son also played an instrument, but the frontier saw little call for orchestral woodwinds, and late in the autumn of 1862 the unemployed musician enlisted as a private in the 8th Kansas Infantry, at Fort Leavenworth.

Genzardi's company had served on detached duty at Fort Kearny, Nebraska, but more recently it had been fighting Confederate guerrillas. Three months after he enlisted, "Thomas" boarded a steamboat with four companies of the 8th Kansas, and in the spring the reunited regiment joined William Rosecrans's army in Tennessee. With that army the

Kansans marched into northern Georgia, and there, on September 19, Peter Genzardi's only child saw his first and last battle. Early that afternoon his brigade swept across the Lafayette Road and past a log schoolhouse, where several Georgia regiments battered the point of the Federal spearhead and drove it back, pinching off a couple of dozen of the foremost Yankees as prisoners. Thomas Genzardi huddled among those two dozen, and that is what had brought him to Richmond. A prisoner exchange and another hundred miles would have taken him to Washington, closing the missing length of his loop around the contiguous states.[13]

In the woods less than a mile north of the spot where Thomas Genzardi became a prisoner, the same Confederate onslaught nearly encircled a fought-out brigade in John Palmer's division. One by one the Union regiments ran out of ammunition and withdrew, until the 84th Illinois stood alone against a relentless tide of grey uniforms that washed inexorably around its right flank. At last the Illinois colonel pulled his regiment back, leaving behind his dead and a few of his wounded. One of those unfortunate few, a loquacious former gardener named Thomas Herburt, had fallen behind when a bullet clipped his right leg. The onrushing Confederates bounded over him, ignoring him for the present, but later the provost guards came along to gather him up. Confederate surgeons tried to save his leg, but infection set in after they transported him to Richmond. By November 24 he had begun to suffer great pain in the wound, but prison doctors were too overworked and their hospitals were too crowded for timely treatment. New patients could only be admitted as others died or were discharged, and not until December 20 would a bed open up in Hospital 21: a surgeon would put Mr. Herburt on his table while the steward wiped off the saw, and when the leg was gone they would carry him to a cot in the teeming wards, where he would spend the next seven weeks regaling his annoyed fellow prisoners with endless renditions of his last battle. The hooknosed Canadian never seemed to shut up, and the other patients might have wished for the return of Patrick Delany, the burly, bullying Irishman whose discharge from the hospital had made room for Herburt.[14]

Elsewhere in that same hospital lay a young German who had just arrived in America, only to be swept up by scavenging substitute brokers who dubbed him George Albert, enrolled him in the 52nd New York, and promptly relieved him of most of his substantial bounty. Barely two months had passed since he donned his uniform, but he had been six weeks a prisoner already. He fell ill early and often, and whenever he saw the doctors he tried to tell them his real name, which was something like

Albrecht but which the attendants took down as Allbeck or Ilbeck. On the morning of November 24 he complained of loose bowels.[15]

Genzardi, Herburt, Delany, and "Albert" typified the nine thousand Union prisoners within musket shot of the Confederate capitol building, most of whom occupied the sprawling camp on Belle Isle, in the middle of the James River. This hostile multitude worried Richmond authorities in more ways than one. Not only did they offer great danger if Yankee cavalry should raid the city, they were literally eating up tons of food in a community that had little to spare, diminishing civilian supplies and driving up prices. Of late the meat and bread rations had periodically failed to arrive in time to give the prisoners their daily allotment, and the commanders of the various prison buildings blanched at the prospect of hungry captives going on a rampage, especially when guards were so few. Heretofore the Richmond prisons had been relieved now and then by wholesale exchanges, where soldiers in blue or grey returned to their respective lines in an even trade, private for private and captain for captain. Thanks at least partly to the complicating factor of black men wearing Federal uniforms, the exchange system had broken down in the past few weeks, and that meant the Richmond dungeons would only continue to swell. Settling in along the Rapidan after his autumn feints at the enemy, Robert E. Lee suggested to the Richmond authorities that it was high time to start looking for another place to house their reluctant guests.[16]

Secretary of War James Seddon agreed, but suitable buildings were hard to come by. Owners of warehouses and factories hesitated to sell or lease their property, probably because their neighbors would surely protest, and Seddon had had no better luck looking for a more rural equivalent of Belle Isle in the Yadkin and Roanoke rivers. As a temporary expedient he had moved four thousand of Richmond's thirteen thousand prisoners to Danville in mid-November, but the people of Danville would not leave their complaints unvoiced for long. The solution that finally occurred to the secretary was a stockade prison in some isolated but productive region, somewhere near a railroad, and preferably in a warmer climate: in their flimsy tents the Belle Isle prisoners were already suffering terribly from the cold Tidewater nights. On November 24 Seddon detailed these general criteria in a note to Brigadier General John Winder, his chief prison keeper, sending the message down to the general's office by the hand of a War Department clerk.[17]

John Henry Winder was not the sort of fellow any child might have been glad to have for a grandfather. At sixty-three he was a dour, crusty old man. He raked his thinning white hair forward like a Roman senator, and affected those preposterous throat whiskers that cranky old men of his generation so often wore, shaving his face well below the jawline but allowing the rest of his beard to creep over his standing collar like chest hair gone wild: perhaps men of his disposition dared allow no barber near their gullets with a razor. Winder had worn a uniform all but seventeen years of his life—for forty-two of them the blue flannel of the U.S. Army. They had not been especially happy years, either. He had known too much of death, and too little of success. As the son of a Baltimore general blamed for allowing the British to burn Washington in 1814, he had suffered a good many unfriendly jokes in his career. Most of Winder's service had been in the Commissary or Quartermaster departments, where his accounts occasionally brought him to grief and where the monotony offered him no opportunity to distinguish himself. Despite a couple of brevets from the Mexican War he was still a captain when he turned sixty, and his promotion to major did not reach him until a few weeks before he relinquished his commission to join the Confederacy.[18]

Then, for a short time, Winder's star had seemed to be on the rise. A few days after resigning from the Federal army he accepted a commission as lieutenant colonel in the state forces of North Carolina; barely a week after that the governor there appointed him colonel of the 1st North Carolina State Troops, and on June 21 Jefferson Davis named him a brigadier general in the Provisional Army, with the job of inspecting the camps around Richmond. Four months later the secretary of war gave him his own department to command. It was a tiny department, to be sure, consisting only of Henrico County, but that essentially made him the duke of Richmond, for it gave Winder power over all the thousands of prisoners, common folk, and dignitaries who came to the capital; he might have likened his understated office to that of the bishop of Rome. Winder set himself up as chief of his own unofficial secret police, hiring a network of "detectives" from the meanest of Baltimore's refugee riffraff. He seemed to relish his unbridled authority, and people in the know said his henchmen would shake as much as two thousand dollars out of someone just to sign a pass. Those who could steer clear of him did so.[19]

The War Department messenger found Winder in his new office on Tenth Street, between Broad and Capitol. Sitting with the general were his son, William Sidney Winder, and his chief detective, a Baltimore barrel maker named Philip Cashmyer. Sidney, a thirty-year-old sometime lawyer, had served on his father's staff since the early days of the war, and the general thought of him as the right man for such a job as the secretary proposed; perhaps he considered his son the staff member he could best trust out of his own reach. Taking the memo in one hand and Sidney's arm in the other, he sauntered out of the office, turning toward the War Department. Cashmyer, the cooper-cum-sleuth, watched the backs of the two grey coats as they made the corner. He saw them return a little while later, whereupon a clerk scratched out an order for the younger Winder while the old man dictated.[20]

As they came from his father's desk, Sidney Winder's orders required him to find a prison site in Georgia, preferably in the vicinity of Fort Valley or Americus, on the Southwestern Railroad. In deference to the rare states' rights jealousy of Georgia's civil leaders, though, he was warned not to make the final decision until he had conferred with Governor Joseph Brown and Brown's foremost political opponent, Howell Cobb. Captain Winder made his way to Georgia as quickly as the cars could carry him (which, by this stage of the war, was not terribly fast), turning off to Milledgeville for the audience with Joe Brown before doubling back to Cobb's home in Macon. There seems to have been some talk of locating the prison below Albany, at the southern terminus of the Southwestern line, but President Davis feared that that location would invite a Federal raid from the Gulf Coast. Reverting to the limitations of his father's orders, Winder left Macon for Americus to begin snooping around.[21]

The captain arrived in Americus on Saturday afternoon, November 28, and straightway he looked up Uriah Harrold, who had been acting as the Commissary Department's agent in that region since the first year of the war. Harrold was not yet twenty-five, but he had already shown surprising business acumen and had won the respect of the town's leaders, several of whom he introduced to Winder. They agreed that a place called Bump Head might do well for a prison: it was an old camp meeting ground west of Americus, and had previously accommodated hundreds of people at one time. The next morning Winder and Harrold rode out there and found the locals going about their religious devotions. Like any people faced with a potentially obnoxious imposition on their lives, the Bump Head congregation objected, remarking how distant they were from the railroad and how much more abundant the water was at Anderson, a rail station eleven miles northwest of Americus. They seemed to make a good point, so the two officials returned to town to rent a buggy.[22]

They reached Anderson that afternoon. The depot consisted of a dozen log and plank buildings, their long roof shakes held down with poles for lack of nails. At the beginning of the war about seventy people had lived within a mile's radius of Anderson, most of them bachelor farmers: besides three newlywed couples, only four complete families resided there when the last census taker passed through. The people were as poor as the sour soil they worked, and few of them lived to the age of sixty; three of those four families were headed by widows—all of them, coincidentally, only thirty-eight years old. War had thinned the district out even more in the intervening three years, taking many of the twenty-seven men of military age. Surrounding these hardscrabble farms were whole forests of tall, straight southern yellow pines, growing over thickets of scrub oak, and through it all the Macon train rattled twice daily, once each way.[23]

Harrold and Winder made the acquaintance of Ben Dykes, who owned much of the village and the surrounding land. Dykes devoted himself almost exclusively to extinguishing the poverty of his childhood, and the war did not interrupt his chosen pursuit, for he was a little too old for the army and he was lame. He had come down to Sumter from Fayette County on the first day of 1861, taking possession of land he had bought four years previously. His brothers had preceded him, building houses on the property, and Dykes appropriated those, too; the brothers were gone now, anyway, fighting with the Army of Northern Virginia (where one of them had already been killed, serving under Shepherd Pryor). Mr. Dykes had discovered a talent for making money in barren places such as this: these past three years he had simultaneously held the positions of railroad agent, express agent, and postmaster, and he operated the local store. He had already begun the first of his two decades as a Sumter County land speculator, and when he divined Captain Winder's intent he may have steered the officer to one of his own unused parcels east of the railroad tracks.[24]

The captain and the commissary agent sauntered the quarter mile to the lot, where the tight pine canopy shut out most of the sunlight, locking in the sharp resin smell and the chattering challenge of resident squirrels. As Winder walked the soft carpet of amber needles he probably did not reflect on the eerie beauty of the darkened forest, so full was his head with practical considerations. He found no water on the land owned by Mr. Dykes, but a few hundred yards to the south a ravine collected the runoff of several springs, creating a respectable branch for Sweetwater Creek, a tributary of the Flint River. The trees did not grow so thick there, and nearby sat a clearing. This was the plantation of W. W. Turner, the deputy sheriff, who had bought it at an estate sale barely three months before. One of Shep Pryor's opponents for the high sheriff's seat, Turner had recently moved his wife and seven children into the house that graced the clearing—one of those small structures called a double pen, consisting of a pair of two-room cabins combined under one roof, with a hallway between, which usually housed two generations of an extended family. Turner was not well—he would be dead in less than six months, though he was just under forty—and he appears to have bought the place in the hope that his boys could support their mother and sisters upon it.[25]

In his pragmatic mood, neither did Captain Winder consider Turner's aspirations for the land. He saw only that this spot seemed to offer all that Secretary Seddon wanted: railroad service, isolation, and plenty of water and timber. A Macon paper praised the choice for those reasons, promising that a prison in that locale would be but "little annoyance." The *Sumter Republican* did not disagree, though the prison would be in its backyard. Less than a week after Winder visited the site the Americus editor published the news, running a shocking little filler warning that six thousand Yankees were coming. "Trot out your 'Home Guards,'" he teased—adding that he would rather not see a prison camp so near, but admitting that he could offer no argument against it.[26]

In order to have plenty of timber and water within his proposed prison, Winder leased both Dykes's land and Turner's. The two apparently made no complaint, for Winder asked for no authority to impress the property without permission. Almost immediately he began to stake out the perimeter of the projected stockade, which he envisioned as a square, with 750 feet to a side. The enclosure would occupy both slopes of the stream, giving each prisoner ample access to water. Winder notified his father of his accomplishment, then he sat back to wait for a quartermaster to come build the stockade for him.[27]

The quartermaster General Winder chose was another relative who worked in his office. Richard B. Winder shared a great-grandfather with the general, but while John Winder's father had gravitated to Baltimore from the old homestead on Maryland's Eastern Shore, Richard's father had drifted down the Delmarva Peninsula to Accomack County, Virginia. Because of its exposed position, Virginia's Eastern Shore provided relatively few loyalists for the Confederacy, but Richard Winder was one of them. He risked a large plantation and many slaves by his allegiance to the South, and he had already lost nearly everything. Elected captain of a company of the 39th Virginia in the summer of 1861, he sponsored a desperate petition to President Davis, asking the government to pay better attention to that vulnerable neck of the Old Dominion. That attention had not been paid, and the peninsula was lost. With it went the 39th Virginia, which disbanded and scattered at the approach of the Yankees early in 1862. That left Winder without a job until April, when a War Department assignment as a quartermaster brought him to Richmond and to his second cousin's staff.[28]

Richard Winder had just returned to the city from a furlough when he found the Andersonville orders on his desk. He was six years older than Sidney: though the younger captain held formal command of the post, it was the older one who took effective charge. He arrived after the middle of December, and with his fresh knowledge of the Richmond prison population he made the enlargement of the stockade boundaries his first goal. Rather than merely planning for the six thousand Federals Sidney had been told to expect, Richard proposed expanding the prison by more than a third, so it could hold ten thousand; that would allow him to use some of the flat shelf beyond the northern limit of Sidney's survey stakes, where the inmates could camp more comfortably and use the space more efficiently. Richmond agreed, so the linesmen trotted the stakes another eighty yards onto Ben Dykes's property. Lacking any professional survey equipment, they managed to throw the rectangle askew.[29]

General Winder had told Richard that the country would respond readily to his requests for labor, teams, and materials, but the quartermaster learned differently when the time came to ask. Part of his difficulty lay in continued local resistance, for no one really wanted a prison near his home—save, perhaps, opportunists like Ben Dykes. Then, too, there was that undercurrent of disloyalty, which had grown so thick by January that Howell Cobb felt it necessary to stop by Americus and deliver one of his thumping patriotic speeches, but economic circumstances also hindered Richard Winder's efforts. Slave owners ignored his appeals to hire their field hands at a time when crops were beginning to command high prices, and few draymen would rent him their horses, mules, or services. Lumber proved equally elusive because Winder could pay no more than the price fixed by the state impressment commissioners; he found himself in hopeless competition with navy and hospital contractors who were gladly paying half again that much. Christmas, New Year's Day, and Epiphany thus passed with the winter wind still soughing through the tall longleaf pines, and with the roughhewn stakes tilting, forlorn, in the soft, pungent forest floor.[30]

Governor Brown also visited Americus in January, exhorting the local gentry to support the army and the government—presumably the state government, given Brown's political predilections—but his appeal did nothing to relieve Richard Winder's plight. It appeared the only solution lay in the actual impressment of goods and services—taking them by force if necessary, while paying only official schedule prices. No government liked treating its own citizens in that manner, but at this stage of the game inflation was turning the free market squarely against the Confederate authorities. James Seddon reluctantly authorized Richard Winder to take what he needed: the capital had to be rid of the prisoners, come what may. That did the trick, and about the 10th of January Winder saw the first spadeful of umber earth turned, with an amateur engineer named Heys directing the project and a nearby overseer, J. M. McNealy, supervising the impressed slave gangs.[31]

First the woodchoppers began leveling pines, dragging the limbed trunks to a central location where teams of slaves armed with broadaxes and adzes scored and squared them into posts at least twenty feet long. They heaped a fraction of the pine and scrub-oak slash on bonfires or burned it in campfires on those long, cool winter nights, but they left tons of boughs. When they had cleared the footprint of the prison and a sufficient halo around it, the work gangs traded their axes and bucksaws for shovels, opening a five-foot-deep trench around the perimeter of those driven stakes, pulling or hacking out only those stumps that sat in the path of their planned trapezoid. Mr. Heys, the acting engineer, would have to divert the branch to run the stockade past it, so he probably saved these two sections for last. With the rest of the ditch completed, though, he turned his hewn beams upright, starting at one of the northern corners, while a separate crew followed along behind, filling and tamping.[32]

On the west wall, above and below the stream, Winder located a pair of gates, each of them surrounded on the outside with their own little stockade and another gate. That would allow one portal to always remain barred whenever prisoners or supplies entered; no one considered traffic in the other direction just now. At intervals of ninety feet around the enclosure carpenters perched six-by-four-foot pole platforms on the outside of the wall, about three feet beneath its upper edge. These "pigeon roosts," as the prisoners came to call them, sported sloping shed roofs made of rough boards. Here the guards would stand, or lean their elbows on the log ends, counting the minutes until they could climb back down the ladders.[33]

As construction commenced, captains Richard and Sidney Winder discovered that their remote location offered as many disadvantages as advantages. As commander of the post, Sidney had to call for a doctor whenever one of the workmen fell ill, and he could find none nearer than four miles from Anderson depot. He urged his father to send him a regular army surgeon; General Winder obliged him with another Eastern Shore Virginian, twenty-five-year-old Isaiah White. And while a post commissary officer would normally concern himself with the sustenance of the garrison, Richard Winder's position as post quartermaster left him responsible for feeding the prisoners when they arrived; he quickly saw that his distance from sources of supply would prove a great hindrance. The Confederate quartermaster general, himself a Georgian, told Winder to bake his own bread at the prison and gather beef on the hoof in southern Georgia and northern Florida, driving it up to Anderson for slaughter. Florida harbored the greatest herds of cattle in this portion of the Confederacy, but Chief Commissary P. W. White had had to beg civilians to sell him some in November. Even if Major White managed to collect enough cattle, though, that left Winder the problem of finding men to make the long stock drive. Late in January he appealed to the commander of the Macon conscript camp for a detail of drafted men, but that officer declined, so Winder tried to hire some of the local men who had been exempted from military service. Thanks to Governor Brown, Georgia was full of such men who held part-time public positions, but none came forward except a few cripples, whom Winder deemed incapable of enduring the journey even once, let alone regularly. The able-bodied exempts, he guessed, found government pay far less profitable than preying upon their fellow citizens as speculators, and that suspicion may have had a solid foundation: exempted officials frequently advertised quantities of such scarce commodities as salt and coffee for sale. At the last minute, though, the quartermaster found some cattle drivers in the form of five healthy individuals who had previously worked for the Commissary Department in that capacity. Their government jobs had come to an end, nullifying their exemptions, and at least one of them had already received his notice to report for military duty.[34]

Winder hoped to attract as much local fare as possible, authorizing Uriah Harrold to buy whatever provisions he could find and supplying him with large quantities of brown sugar to sweeten his deals. Harrold immediately began offering to trade the sugar for bacon, pound for pound. Despite his best efforts he could not meet the prison's anticipated requirements by half, so Winder called on the commissary at Columbus to forward him beef, bacon, flour, molasses, and rice. Even the Columbus depot could not supply him with all the necessary cooking equipment, though, and he had to send an appointed citizen nearly two hundred miles away, north of Atlanta, for half a dozen hundred-gallon boiling kettles; nowhere could Winder find suitable baking pans.[35]

In addition to the stockade, the new prison would need a cookhouse, a few headquarters and hospital buildings, and some big warehouses. According to the orders Richard Winder had received from his elder cousin, these had to be constructed of logs—General Winder obviously having concluded that sawn lumber would cost too much. Peeling, squaring, and notching logs consumed much time, however, and Quartermaster Winder's impressment authority over his work force already neared the midpoint of its sixty-day limit. He could not impress any sawmill material because most millowners immunized themselves from such enforcement by means of token, sacred contracts with the railroads. To avoid both these impediments and the greater part of the lumber's expense, Winder asked permission to use his own discretion in the choice of log or lumber construction, and he suggested using the refuse slabs from the railroad mills, which merely took the center of each log for ties and bridge timbers. In case that proposal failed, he persuaded a local entrepreneur to locate a sawmill (and a gristmill) about four miles from Anderson, promising him all the government work he could handle. In one way or another he began accumulating a stockpile of boards and framing material, but never enough to keep up with the demand. Giving priority to the prisoners' cookhouse, Winder postponed construction of both his own quarters and the storehouses, instead stashing the commissary supplies in the church near the depot; for now the headquarters buildings and the hospital would have to wait, and barracks for the prisoners stood at the bottom of the quartermaster's list. He did try to buy some tents owned by the state of Georgia, but Governor Brown refused to let them go, preferring to save them for the state militia he knew he would be called upon to mobilize in the spring.[36]

Up on the James River Samuel Cooper, the adjutant general of the Confederate army, pondered whom to choose as permanent commander of the new prison. Such a position would require great energy and ability; whether or not Cooper believed Sidney Winder was fit for the command, he knew that the right candidate would need more rank. Rather than deprive the army of the services of such a worthy officer, he began thinking of who might be disabled for field duty. The last consideration, but by no means the least important in light of regional rivalries, was that the man had to be a Georgian: Cooper asked Howell Cobb if he had anyone in mind.[37]

Cobb certainly did. He nominated Alexander W. Persons, a twenty-seven-year-old lawyer from Fort Valley, barely thirty miles up the rail line from Anderson. Persons was the lieutenant colonel of the 55th Georgia. He was in good health, but it might be said that he was disabled from field duty because he no longer had a regiment: the bulk of the 55th Georgia had surrendered at Cumberland Gap five months before. The 55th had never been in a real battle, and it enjoyed no great reputation, once having mutinied, but the blame for that shameful episode had apparently rested with its colonel, an unscrupulous ne'er-do-well. Joe Brown admitted as much, but he suspected Alex Persons might be the man to whip the troops back into shape. Persons had had little chance to prove that before leaving Cumberland Gap on a furlough just before Yankees surrounded the place, and now 541 of his men sat in the howling wind at Camp Douglas, Illinois. If Persons were given the assignment, it would occupy not only him but whatever convalescents he could collect from his regiment, who would constitute too small a unit for effective use in the field but who could certainly serve as guards.[38]

Camp Sumter, as Confederate authorities had begun to call this cantonment, consisted of three separate commands. One officer would serve as commander of the post, with jurisdiction reaching from the village of Anderson to the gates of the stockade. Below him, in one manner of speaking, would be the commander of whatever troops occupied the grounds, exclusive of support staff and detailed men. The commander of the actual prison would be virtually independent of those two, having charge of the stockade itself and its inmates, enjoying only enough authority to demand a daily guard detail from the commander of the troops and to requisition the necessary provisions and supplies from the post quartermaster. That is the complicated bureaucratic structure that evolved, at any rate, but with no prisoners and no troops except a few dozen of his own scattered Georgians, Colonel Persons quickly assumed all three titles at once.[39]

Even after Colonel Persons arrived, in the middle of February, Richard Winder remained the busiest man at Camp Sumter. The stockade lagged about half-finished and the cookhouse stood, framed but naked, on the left bank of the creek between the two gates; nearly everything else Winder had planned remained undone, awaiting materials for which he scoured the state. Then came a telegram from General Winder, informing him that the first of the ten thousand prisoners were on their way, with the rest following in daily contingents. Guessing that he had only two or three days in which to complete as much work as he had accomplished in the past month, the harried quartermaster dispatched all his clerks on urgent errands and began hounding both Richmond and his tardy local suppliers by mail. One of his complaints—though it concerned a topic beyond his responsibility—served to highlight the haphazard communications between Richmond authorities and the prison staff. Captain Winder wrote the general that when those prisoners arrived there would be fewer than one hundred guards to greet them, but that was not the worst of it: the post's entire armament, it appeared, would be whatever revolvers the officers carried in their holsters, for the few dozen out-of-practice enlisted men who had drifted in had not been issued so much as a shotgun.[40]

General Winder had little choice but to forward the prisoners from Richmond. To begin with, conditions at Belle Isle and the waterfront warehouse prisons had deteriorated abominably. Federal captives huddled cheek by jowl for lack of heat and space, and some of them had frozen to death. The Confederate Commissary Department failed more frequently now to receive its requisitions of meat, and all rations had to be stretched thin at times. Winder's desire to give his prisoners sufficient food may have sprung more from the practical fear of an outbreak than from any great compassion, but Richmond's busy railroad agents did not count Yankee bellies any great priority. On Belle Isle, at least, the starving inmates had begun to turn upon one another, with the healthier among them stealing food from the weak and the sick.[41]

During the winter Winder had tried to relieve the overcrowding by removing more prisoners to Danville. In mid-December Thomas Genzardi, the Kansan-Italian musician-soldier, suffered the jarring ride down there with one trainload; he had just begun to recover from his bout with cholera morbus when his intestines started to trouble him again, and he no sooner landed in the Danville warehouse than a prison doctor admitted him to a hospital in the middle of town. By now the buildings there were all bursting, too, and the mayor of Danville led a deputation of prominent citizens who asked the secretary of war to remove the malodorous and pestilential Lincolnites from their midst.[42]

Early in February Richmond shuddered at the alleged discovery of evidence revealing a plot to liberate all the Federal prisoners and assassinate President Davis. The suspect documents arrived at General Winder's office on February 7, and two days later the rumors of a wholesale escape earned a measure of credibility: Thomas Rose, a Pennsylvania colonel captured at Chickamauga, had spent much of the winter master-minding a tunnel out of Libby Prison, and after midnight on February 9 over a hundred officers slipped out. More than half of them made it back to Union lines, including the notorious cavalry raider, Abel Streight.[43]

An even more startling affair lay in the works, however. Judson Kilpat-rick, a rather reckless Union cavalry general, took a notion to lead two mounted columns against Richmond, circling the capital like a pair of calipers and entering from the south with one wing to free the prisoners on Belle Isle and along the waterfront. This was the raid Robert E. Lee had feared. It was a bold plan—too bold, as it turned out. A one-legged colonel by the name of Ulric Dahlgren led Kilpatrick's spearhead all the way from the army's camp above the Rapidan to Richmond's very door, while Kilpatrick hammered at the opposite side with the rest, but Dahl-gren's wing could not cross the James; poor communications and timing doomed the bifurcated attack. Dahlgren was killed, and a good many of his troopers joined the very captives they had intended to liberate. The most frightening aspect of the raid came after the repulse, though, in the form of some scraps of paper fished out of Dahlgren's pocket by a thirteen-year-old militiaman: one of them appeared to be the draft of an address to his troops, full of the requisite romantic seasoning, while the other gave flat, ungrammatical orders for the officers in command of Dahlgren's assorted details. Both these documents made it clear that the released prisoners should be cut loose on the city to burn it, while the cavalrymen would seek out Jefferson Davis and his cabinet officers for summary execution. No one knew for certain whether the papers were genuine, or if the zealous young colonel were not acting on his own misguided initiative, but the people of Richmond cringed.[44]

By the time Dahlgren's horsemen thundered up the Westham Road, most of the prisoners had already left Belle Isle. John Winder had been planning the exodus for more than three weeks, on the orders of Samuel Cooper. As early as February 7 he had mapped out their route, impelled perhaps by that first incriminating paper work, which reached his desk that day. The journey from Richmond to Camp Sumter involved no fewer than nine separate rail lines. Winder expected to dispatch four hundred prisoners each day, and he would need a full company of infan-try to escort the daily shuttle. The question of where those guards might come from was indirectly solved by the appointment of a new brigadier to the command of Edward O'Neal's brigade: having expected that posi-tion himself, O'Neal ranted high and low over the slight, invoking the influence of the Alabama legislature on his behalf. In protest, the Montgomery solons requested the return of O'Neal's regiment to its home state, and O'Neal asked independently for a transfer to another army. General Lee offered no objection, which may have said as much for his opinion of O'Neal as his failure to promote him had, and a few days later the 26th Alabama was ordered back from the Rapidan to Richmond, to guard the southbound Yankees.[45]

On February 17 the *Richmond Dispatch* pleaded for the removal of the prisoners, and by that evening everything was ready: provisions had been stockpiled at depots along the way, and cars had been reserved for each leg of the trip. Originally General Winder had arranged a complicated relay of guards from Richmond to Gaston, North Carolina, and thence to Augusta and Andersonville, but Edward O'Neal's petulance rendered that plan unnecessary, at least for the present: on their own way south—away from what their colonel perceived to be patrician favoritism—the ten companies of Alabamians could chaperone up to ten days' shipments of prisoners. That bitterly cold afternoon a couple of hundred selected Yankees gathered up their paltry belongings and marched, shivering, off Belle Isle, down the right bank of the James to Mayo's Bridge, and up to the Byrd Street depot of the Richmond & Petersburg Railroad. The rest of the island buzzed with speculation, perhaps fueled by guards' promises that they were all on their way to be exchanged. That rumor may have circulated spontaneously, or it may have been a deliberate ruse to discourage escape, but few of the men between the bayonets really believed it. They had heard tales of a new prison in the sunny South, and they pretty well knew that they were headed for Georgia. Still, one who watched that first lot depart doubted they could be going to a worse place than Belle Isle.[46]

The two hundred men crowded into four boxcars. Once the guards had counted heads they lurched out of the station and over the James, past the teeming island these men had been so glad to leave. So precariously did the cars creak along the overworked rails that by nightfall they had barely crossed the North Carolina border. Not until the next afternoon did the downcast travelers reach Raleigh, where Confederates handed out a day's food. Twenty-four long, cramped hours after Raleigh they made Charlotte, and two days after that they came to Columbia, South Carolina. Once or twice, when they had to change lines and wait for the cars, the guards herded them into adjacent fields to sleep, but lest the Yankees slip through the thin cordon of Alabamians the prisoners were warned not to even stand up during the night, on pain of death. A few tried to run for it anyway, but they found the guards true to their word.[47]

Richard Winder flew into a dither as the overoptimistic date of arrival neared. He still had collected no baking pans, no flour or meal, no beef, and only ten thousand pounds of bacon—enough to last only three days when the stockade was filled to capacity. He made a hasty contract with a miller twenty miles below Americus to grind meal for him, then he had to prevail upon the various district quartermasters to supply that miller with corn. Winder still had to look for beeves in Florida, probably supposing that he would be able to detail soldiers to drive them north if only he were lucky enough to find the steers. He even bought some pickled beef hearts, tongues, and other slaughterhouse refuse until he learned how outrageously the Albany shambles was overcharging him. Even if his commissary stores overflowed their little warehouse, he would have had no means of transporting them the quarter mile from the depot to the prison gate, for he lacked a single wagon, team, or harness. Slaves worked from dawn to dusk on the palisade, but it would not be ready. That made little difference, though, for Winder had no padlocks for the prison doors—nor any doors, for that matter, or nails with which to make them. He scrawled urgent requests, demands, and threats to all points of the compass, emptying his vocabulary of superlatives in the effort to prepare for his premature tenants.[48]

Even as the melancholy caravan lumbered down Southern railroads, one Confederate officer made his best effort to gain freedom for the Federal prisoners. Colonel Robert Ould, Richmond's commissioner of exchange, journeyed down to City Point to meet a flag-of-truce steamer bearing an agent for his Union counterpart. The two spoke earnestly of the difficulties thrown in the way of the exchange cartel. For nearly a year, until July of 1863, both sides had regularly paroled all prisoners and released them, pending exchange, and once that formal accounting had taken place the paroled men were free to fight again. The first sticking point was a provision requiring the capturing party to transport the paroled prisoners to either Aiken's Landing, on the James River, or to Vicksburg, on the Mississippi. In the autumn of 1862 Southern armies had surged into Kentucky and Maryland, sweeping up thousands of Yankees in isolated garrisons, and had paroled them on the spot, letting them march unarmed back to their own nearest lines without the arduous pilgrimage back to the points of exchange. Though there may have been a touch of humanity in this oversight it also served the captors well, relieving them of the expense of guarding and transporting the prisoners, but Federal authorities made no formal complaint, dutifully interning the returned men in parole camps until they were exchanged.[49]

Abraham Lincoln's secretary of war, Edwin Stanton, did not care for these irregular paroles, or even for the established cartel, supposing that many of his men surrendered just for a chance to go home for a few weeks, but he hesitated to interrupt the system until the preponderance of prisoners swung to his side. The battle of Gettysburg and the imminent capture of the Vicksburg garrison promised to shift that balance, and on July 3, 1863, Stanton issued an edict retroactively repudiating such paroles, ordering the remaining unexchanged prisoners back into the field. Among the Union soldiers released by this decree were hundreds of Gettysburg wounded whom Lee had paroled on both practical and humanitarian grounds.[50]

Refusing to recognize at least the retroactive aspect of Stanton's proclamation, Confederate authorities reciprocated by declaring many of the paroled Vicksburg garrison exchanged. Grant had paroled those troops for the same convenience that had prompted the objectionable paroles of Union prisoners captured the previous autumn, and many of the Vicksburg garrison helped to fight Grant at Chattanooga five months later. According to the original cartel, such differences of opinion were to be argued out separately, without disruption of the regular exchanges, but the Washington bigwigs immediately stopped all exchanges. Robert Ould labored mightily to iron out this rumple, but to him it seemed as though the Lincoln administration were intent on blocking any settlement. Ould's travails had only begun, however, for the United States government had produced an enormous impediment in the form of black soldiers. Not surprisingly, the president of a nation founded to preserve African slavery refused to respect the uniform worn by such men, initially promising to execute them and their officers and denying them exchange. Again overlooking the provision for separate settlement of such differences, Federal authorities declined any routine exchanges until the Confederacy promised equal recognition of black and white soldiers.[51]

The officer with whom Colonel Ould negotiated (as the Belle Isle prisoners made their uncomfortable way to Georgia) was an emissary from the most hated man in the South, Benjamin Butler—whom Stanton had recently appointed a special commissioner in the matter. Butler's fertile legal mind had contrived a seemingly acceptable means of resuming the cartel, however, and only two questions now presented themselves: did the South wish to exchange prisoners badly enough to treat with Butler, and was the North willing to budge at all? For his part, Ould urged his own secretary of war to recognize the Beast of New Orleans.[52]

Speculation about events like Ould's mission provided the major material of conversation to the Yankees in the rattling boxcars, but exchange had been a favorite topic through the winter—and so it would remain, regardless of the actual prospects. For further diversion they tried to track their route on mental maps from bits of information dropped by guards or gleaned from station signs glimpsed through cracks in the car siding. Boarding a fresh train in Columbia, they changed again at Augusta the next day. The 160-mile ride from there to Macon ate up more than twenty-four hours, partly because both the track system and the rolling stock gave way so frequently. Few who followed the path to Camp Sumter failed to suffer delays or injury from assorted breakdowns: only the previous Christmas season a freight train had run off the track just above Anderson Station, killing three of the engine crew.[53]

It was nearly a full week after their departure from Richmond before the bone-weary passengers felt the pressure of a sharp left turn as their wheezing locomotive eased onto the Southwestern Railroad at Macon. Several painful hours later the train came to another jolting halt, and after a time the guards prodded them out of the cars. Slowly the bedraggled forms creaked to their feet, glad to stretch their stiffened legs once more. They hopped, crawled, or were helped or carried down to a primitive platform, the more curious glancing at the rude cabins scattered about the station. After a lengthy wait for counting into squads of ninety, the column limped along over a quarter mile of spongy, sandy clay and passed under the pine portcullis north of the branch. With little fanfare the prisoners halted, fell out, and began looking for places to lie down.[54]

The sun that had risen on the morning of February 24, 1864, saw the first residents in the prison that would come to be known as Andersonville. A score of tall pines and a lot of scrubwood and saplings still stood, especially in the thick brake along the creek, and the rest of the ravaged ground lay dotted with unburned heaps of pine boughs; numbers of felled trees too twisted or thin for stockade logs littered the sixteen acres of their new home. For the moment a skirmish line of guards—probably Colonel Persons's Georgians, armed with muskets borrowed from the exhausted Alabamians—prohibited them from crossing the stream, where they might otherwise have simply waltzed through the missing lengths of the south wall. Those who ventured down to the stream found the water sprinkled with tiny green flakes of vegetable matter, and it smelled a tad sulfurous, but otherwise it looked amazingly clear and fresh, in pleasant contrast to Belle Isle. Quartermaster Winder's clerk, James Duncan, brought rations from the chapel in a couple of rickety, mule-drawn wagons rented from W. N. Pickett. Duncan handed out a pound of coarse corn meal to each prisoner, as well as some sweet potatoes, beans, and a ration of beef or pork. It was all raw, for none of the cookhouse supplies had arrived, but the quantity alone soothed stomachs still growling over the Richmond rations. Duncan also issued some buckets for drawing water, and a few dozen skillets that constituted the only cooking equipment Winder could find; some of the prisoners kept crude utensils of their own. As the stronger of them scrambled about collecting poles and boughs for huts, and cooking their rations over roaring fires, none of them could deny that this place beat their former camp all hollow.[55]

Richard Winder had impressed another five dozen slaves and free blacks to meet his accelerated schedule; they and the old gangs raised the lacking wall as quickly as their overseer could drive them. The young chief surgeon, Dr. White, erected a single tent to serve as the hospital, locating it inside the stockade near the north wall; twenty-five sick quickly filled it—more than a tenth of the first lot of prisoners. The bare ground or a lumpy cushion of pine boughs served them for beds; for cover they enjoyed only whatever shreds of blankets they had brought with them. Among them lay thirty-four-year-old Adam Swarner (another alumnus of Richmond's Hospital 21), his forehead ablaze with fever and his lungs rattling with pneumonia.[56]

The first day passed quietly, most of the prisoners using the time to dig in for a long stay while the inevitable few scanned the walls for the best way out. Their punishing week's journey still told on them, and the better part of that tattered battalion probably turned in early. In the forenoon of the next day five hundred more refugees from Belle Isle poured into the prison, taking up more of the polewood and branches for the shelters they built in the remaining open space. At least one of their number had perished on the way; many others among them steered straight from the gate toward the greying canvas hospital, supported by comrades on either side. On February 26—the day Sidney Winder yielded formal command to Colonel Persons and reverted to the role of his father's proxy—still more prisoners arrived, further straining the limits of the hospital. On the twenty-seventh Dr. White found room for at least one more patient when his paroled attendants lugged out the body of Adam Swarner: Andersonville had claimed its first victim. Of the twenty-four men who entered the hospital tent with Swarner, all but five would be dead in less than a month, and the last of them would linger only three weeks beyond that.[57]

Some amateur garrison carpenter tacked together a coffin for that first dead Yankee. Perhaps he used the lumber from an assortment of boxes that came down on the train that day from the Macon arsenal: that afternoon Colonel Persons equipped the remnant of his regiment with 125 ancient British smoothbores, with sixteen rounds of .75 caliber buckshot-and-ball cartridges per man.[58]

2 ⋘ E All Hope Abandon

ven before they learned that the first trainload of prisoners was on its way, the Winders of Camp Sumter had cause to doubt
the security of their secluded keep. For nearly two years the coast of
Florida had known Yankee forays, none of which had caused much
concern as far inland as Sumter County, and the probability of further
raids had not affected the selection of Anderson as a prison site. In
January local papers reported a platoon of Federals taken near Saint
Augustine, emphasizing the little victory of the capture rather than any
danger posed by the presence of the enemy. But the beginning of February saw a flotilla of eighteen gunboats and transports unloading eleven
Union regiments, three batteries, and two battalions of cavalry at Jack-

sonville. The size of the landing—perhaps seven thousand men—alarmed Confederates from southern Florida to Charleston, and it gave Southerners little comfort that a good third of those troops were black. A full division thrust into so feebly defended a region could only mean an expedition into the interior, and, sure enough, the last blue uniform had barely hustled down the gangplank before the skirmishers started forward.[1]

The Florida Federals stepped out briskly for Baldwin, eighteen miles west of Jacksonville, sending their advance guard on another twenty miles to Sanderson's Station. It seemed they intended to roll on past Lake City to Tallahassee, the capital, from which they might communicate with the Union navy in the Gulf of Mexico. Seizure of that line would seal off virtually the whole of Florida, depriving the Confederacy of all that state's resources: Richard Winder's best supply of beef would evaporate. Even more unsettling, a Northern army in Tallahassee would sit only ninety miles south of the railhead at Albany. All that lay between the enemy and the gulf just then was a single brigade of mixed infantry, cavalry, and artillery, dug in east of Lake City near a tiny railroad depot called Olustee.[2]

Among those Union regiments marched the 7th New Hampshire, staggering through the alien heat of a Florida winter in wool uniforms. Veterans like eighteen-year-old Aaron Elliott tried to set an example for the hundreds of recruits who answered half the names at the morning roll call, but the "fresh fish" nevertheless tended to fall behind as new troops will. The recruits represented Granite State boys who had been too young to enlist before the autumn of 1863 (or at least too childlike to fool the recruiters), as well as family men whose economic circumstances had made it attractive for them to sign up for the reasonably generous bounties towns had begun offering to meet their draft quotas. Also present was a class of soldier who would not be seen again in America when this war ended: the substitute. Anyone called up by the 1863 Conscription Act could, if he had the money, literally hire someone to go in his place, but his replacement must, himself, be somehow exempt from military service. Many possible exemptions might allow a man to enlist as a substitute. Anyone who was underage, who was the only son of a widow, or of aged parents dependent upon his support, or one who had two brothers currently in the ranks, could not be drafted, but he could enlist as a volunteer or as a substitute for his richer neighbor. By far the most common substitute, however, was the foreigner exempted by virtue of his citizenship. Most of the homegrown substitutes—and most of the foreign-born, for that matter—tried to live up to the bargains they had made, but a hefty percentage of Canadians and Europeans allowed their lack of natural allegiance to lead them astray. Having come largely for money, many shirked their duties or deserted altogether.[3]

On the morning of February 20, while the first trainload of Belle Isle prisoners climbed back onto the boxcars at Charlotte, Aaron Elliott stuffed his haversack with enough food to carry him three days. The commander of his division planned to make a spectacular (and unauthorized) raid on the Suwannee River railroad bridge, over sixty miles away. He doubted the pitiful Confederate force would stand in his way, but just in case he took along most of his troops.[4]

Unbeknownst to the Yankee general, the Confederates had juggled their forces precisely in time to meet him with nearly equal numbers. In more than eight hours the 7th New Hampshire covered almost eighteen miles from its morning bivouac without a sign of trouble, but at midafternoon the crackling of skirmish fire caused at least the untried privates to cock an ear. The sound grew louder and closer, and finally an officer came cantering back to order the New Englanders into the fight. Aaron Elliott's colonel put his men into a trot. A quarter of a mile farther on they saw the billowing smoke, like a forest fire in the barren. Just as they did a couple of hundred miles to the north, the yellow pines of Florida grew straight and rather tall, their canopy stunting the undergrowth to create the illusion of cultivation. The plush amber of fallen needles shone dark and distinct against the angry white fog in the distance.[5]

Perhaps some in the 7th New Hampshire worried about the unprepared recruits, for they owned little parade-ground savvy, and under fire they would need to know their maneuvers instinctively. The regiment's colonel should have been more concerned about that than anyone, had he not been too much of a politician and too little of a soldier. He had apparently not spent enough time with either his regiment or his drill manual: when his brigadier told him to fill a particular gap in the firing line, the colonel shouted an order to deploy on the first company. That would have thrown the regiment too far to the right, leaving an inviting hole, and the brigade commander bellowed over the rising din that he wanted the colonel to deploy on his eighth company. The bumbling New Hampshire colonel halted his men and faced them to the front, gave the corrected order, and watched his regiment's fragile formation disintegrate. Those who heard the order and understood it tried to shove and drag the rest of the men into place, but those in front began milling about in confusion. All the while bullets sang overhead and thudded into the muddled mass of men in blue, few of whom could return effective fire, and before long the unavoidable flurry of fugitives began darting to the rear. Both the errant colonel and his brigadier pitched into the throng to sort it out, but the damage was done. A few score of those who had kept free of the tangle began banging away at the Georgians opposite, but the rest of the 7th New Hampshire fell apart and vanished into the forest. As they fled they passed a battery of Napoleon smoothbore cannon—all that prevented the enemy from swallowing them whole. Some of the more unfortunate Yankees would see at least one of those guns again.[6]

New Yorkers came up to fill the void, but the 8th U.S. Colored on the Union left also collapsed under a furious fire that killed its colonel and dropped its major. Two more black regiments came up to bolster each wing, one from North Carolina taking the ground where the New Hampshiremen had broken; there it, too, lost the only two field officers it had. By dark the shattered Union juggernaut had turned in full retreat, weaker by one-third, and the jubilant Confederates swept over the field, scooping up half a dozen cannon, hundreds of wounded, and scores of cowering stragglers. Among the injured whom they sent to the rear were Major Archibald Bogle of the 1st North Carolina Colored Infantry and Private Aaron Elliott of Goffstown, New Hampshire. Bogle had both a body wound and a broken leg; Elliott suffered only from a great bruise that a spent bullet had raised on his ankle, but he could not walk.[7]

The Olustee rout ended any concerns the Andersonville staff may have entertained about trouble from the south. The only Yankees to reach Tallahassee came as prisoners, most of them wounded, while their overbold general scurried all the way back to Jacksonville with visions of fifteen thousand rebel demons on his heels. In order to cement that image, the commander of that Confederate department ordered reinforcements and a major general to Florida.[8]

Soon after learning that the Florida Yankees had been sent packing, Richard Winder found himself relieved of at least one other worry. The War Department notified him that prison quartermasters would henceforth not have to feed inmates; in a rare demonstration of bureaucratic logic, the responsibility had been shifted to the Commissary Department. Winder passed this news along to the beleaguered chief commissary in Florida, commenting that he would no longer need trail horses to drive cattle cross-country (as though someone else would not need them for that purpose). He still hoped to have ten freight wagons, though, and an ambulance, a light dray, and the appurtenant harness, all of which he had previously requested. None of those vehicles seem to have ever materialized, and Winder asked the sheriffs of six local counties—including Sumter's Shepherd Pryor—to impress a few farmers' wagons, but that also proved fruitless. For the present he would have to make do with Mr. Pickett's decrepit tumbrels.[9]

If he need not gather the actual food now, the quartermaster still bore the burden of providing nearly every other physical want for the post. The administrative change in the prisoners' sustenance meant an assistant commissary officer would have to come down from Columbus, so Winder had to build him a house; he had not yet scared up any great quantity of lumber, and had therefore decided to build the commissary warehouse out of logs, but the unfinished stockade currently demanded all of those that his workmen could hew. March began with the last gap in the palisade nearly closed, and on the fifth of the month Winder let his impressed laborers go, but none of the necessary hardware had arrived.[10]

While Richard Winder's travails increased, Alexander Persons's problems eased a little with the opening of March. True, every day brought a new trainload of prisoners, but each of the first ten of those days also saw the arrival of yet another company of the veteran 26th Alabama. Persons also needed fewer guards as the stockade walls closed, so the garrison knew a brief spell of relative ease. Ultimately nearly three hundred Alabama soldiers camped along the branch just upstream from the stockade, sleeping in lean-to huts improvised from forked sticks and misappropriated boards. The reunion of the regiment concluded with the appearance of Colonel O'Neal, still smarting from the slight he had endured in Virginia. His arrival caused a little trouble, because O'Neal ranked Persons by the measure of a third star on the collar, and he breezed into headquarters with the expectation that he would become the new commander of the post. Persons declined to surrender his desk, though, citing the division of duties old John Winder had outlined for him. As the inferior officer in linear rank Persons stood ready to yield command of the troops on the post to O'Neal, but the lieutenant colonel insisted on retaining command of the post itself. The sensitive Irishman protested to no avail, and his relations with Persons instantly began to fester.[11]

The secretary of war had decided to remove the stockade proper from Persons's control, too. On February 29 he assigned Major Elias Griswold, another of General Winder's Maryland cronies, to the command of the prisoners. Griswold was the former provost marshal of Richmond, and he had been chief jailer at the Tuscaloosa prison during the war's first winter. Seddon's order made Griswold subordinate to Colonel Persons, prompting General Winder to complain about the embarrassing administrative structure of his Andersonville and Danville responsibilities. As Winder explained it to Seddon, both the prisons lay outside his geographical department, in someone else's bailiwick, and Winder wielded no control over the commanders of those posts although he was accountable for the prisoners. Winder enclosed Major Griswold's order with his own letter to Seddon, and these two missives made the circuit of War Department offices during the next week, collecting endorsements at each stop until the original order came, unchanged, back to Winder. Winder returned the order a second time, and about March 12 some War Department official passed it to the major, who started for Georgia with it. He arrived just after the middle of the month to find that General Winder had created some confusion himself: the job for which Griswold had come had already been taken by a stooped, frail fellow named Henry Wirz.[12]

The forty-year-old Wirz bustled about the prison in a white linen shirt and white duck trousers, with a revolver strapped to his side and a grey army cap drawn squarely over his eyebrows as token uniform. He wore a full beard a little darker than his hair, which betrayed the first few strands of grey, and his hazel eyes darted restlessly about him, reflecting a nervous energy for which he was well known. Born Hartmann Heinrich Wirz in Zurich in November of 1823, he had married a girl slightly older than himself when he was twenty-one, and over the next four years she bore him two children. The second, a boy, was not yet born when Wirz left Switzerland for France: he boarded the brig *Sarah Boyd* at Le Havre in the spring of 1849, bound for America. Later he would deny allegations that he had fled to avoid a brush with the law, ascribing that rumor to a cousin with the same name who served a prison term. The only such cousin he had was August Heinrich Wirz, a Zurich wholesaler, and it seems it was the emigrant who assumed his cousin's name, arriving in New York on April 23 as "A. Wirz." He also claimed he had remained in New England for over a year, working as a weaver and as an attendant in a Massachusetts bathhouse, but less than eleven months after his arrival in the United States he turned up in New Orleans, living in a coffeehouse with an assortment of Germans and New Englanders, supporting himself as a bartender. His landlord's name was Webber—Wirz had relatives of that name in Zurich—and that landlord may have been the means of his introduction to another Webber, Dr. Augustus Webber, who lived in the western Kentucky town of Hopkinsville. Dr. Webber was apparently trying to shed his European roots and blend into Kentucky's backwoods society. He seemed to make a better living from speculating in land than from medicine, but he still spoke German and that appealed to the expatriate Swiss.[13]

All his life Wirz had wanted to be a doctor, and in 1854 he joined Dr. Webber as an apprentice, but after a couple of months he began to doubt Webber's competence as a physician, leaving him for Edward Caspair, a Prussian doctor practicing in Louisville. Wirz's first wife had divorced him for abandonment in the summer of 1853, and when he departed western Kentucky he took along a new one: on May 28, 1854, he married Elizabeth Wolf, née Savells, at the home of her widowed mother near Cadiz, the Trigg County seat. Though she could not read or write, Mrs. Wolf was a perfectly respectable Methodist lady whose husband had recently died, leaving her with two small girls; Wirz's stepdaughters stood by during the ceremony, under the wing of their new guardian, the bride's brother.[14]

Ultimately Wirz did find work as a doctor, of sorts. Returning to Louisiana about 1856, he set himself up as a homeopathic physician in Madison Parish, along the Mississippi River. Known best for the tiny pills they distributed, homeopathists believed that illness could be cured by administering minute doses of the very toxins that might have produced the original symptoms. It was not the sort of career that might last long in a more enlightened age, but for a few years Wirz wrung a meager living out of it. By the beginning of the Civil War he had fathered two more daughters (one of whom had recently died), but his personal fortune amounted to less than a thousand dollars. Either from the excitement of war fever or from the sense that he could do no better as a civilian, he enlisted within weeks of Fort Sumter in a local company styled the Madison Infantry.[15]

Wirz joined as a private. Arriving in Richmond with the 4th Louisiana Battalion just after First Manassas, the Madison Infantry stood a tour as guards over the prisoners from that fight. General Winder noticed Wirz, whom at least one distinguished Federal prisoner regarded as very kindly, and Winder asked for the Swiss as a permanent assistant. Henceforth Wirz acted more or less as an officer, having charge of records and prisoners. The North first heard of Wirz through one bitter Bull Run prisoner who, in keeping with the rabid sentiments of the war's early months, described Wirz and all other Southern prison keepers as raging, vicious beasts. He credited Wirz with both the authority and the inclination to starve recalcitrant Union prisoners, and to even send them to New Orleans as punishment if he chose. Nearly two years before anyone ever heard of Andersonville, this same Yankee prisoner recorded the

Swiss sergeant's ominous prediction that the U.S. government would kill him if he ever fell into its custody.[16]

Despite the opinions of Wirz's prisoners, his superiors thought highly of him, though a year would pass before he received a commission. Late in 1861 he accompanied Captain Elias Griswold—the same major he met at Andersonville—to Tuscaloosa, where his treatment of prisoners there also earned him their gratitude. When Griswold left Tuscaloosa, sixty-two citizens of that town asked that Wirz be given command of the prison, and though he was only a sergeant he did take charge of the place on several occasions, but by June he was back in Richmond with an appointment as captain on General Winder's staff. In the final hours of his life he told a story of being wounded in the right wrist at the battle of Seven Pines while serving as an aide-de-camp to Joe Johnston, but Wirz did not receive his commission until eleven days after that battle and the document specifically assigned him to Winder, for duty related to martial law in the city. It appears, besides, that Wirz could only have arrived from Tuscaloosa after the battle ended, and that his account of the wound represented another deathbed fabrication. Antagonists later insinuated that he broke the arm in a stagecoach accident, but whatever the nature of the injury, it never healed.[17]

In August of 1862 Wirz assumed command of all Richmond prisons, exerting a strict but reasonably humane authority over the Federal captives. He denied the Yankees any opportunity to communicate with their own officers, or to buy contraband from civilians, but he did not hesitate to arrest a guard for shooting one of the prisoners. That autumn his tenure in Richmond was interrupted by a mission to Alabama and Mississippi, where he went looking for the missing rolls of six thousand Union prisoners. After further search for them in Charleston, Savannah, Macon, Montgomery, Tuscaloosa, Mobile, and Vicksburg, Wirz telegraphed Colonel Ould that he could not find the records. The exchange commissioner responded that Wirz could go where he pleased to document the missing prisoners, but he wanted the matter cleared up. Wirz took Ould at his word, embarking on a quest of another four thousand miles, crisscrossing the Deep South from Columbus, Georgia, to Houston, Texas. It may have been during this marathon journey that Wirz sustained the injury to his arm: when his wandering ended, the week before Christmas of 1862, he received not only nearly seven hundred dollars in mileage allowances but a medical furlough of almost three months. He seems to have spent the time at his home, across the Mississippi from Vicksburg, reporting for duty finally at Jackson, Mississippi, the next March. After only a few weeks' service with the Ordnance Department in Louisiana, he was granted another sick leave, this time for four months, and with that he sailed for Europe—on an international errand for the Confederate government, as his daughter later told the story.[18]

After doing whatever it was he did across the Atlantic—and what that was will probably never be known—Wirz ran the blockade back to the Confederacy (and his doom) through Wilmington, North Carolina, probably coming in on the British steamer *A. D. Vance* in the predawn hours of January 20, 1864. By the time he had collected seven months of his back pay and made his way up to the War Department, it was February. General Winder greeted him gladly, remembering his earlier efficiency, and promptly sent him to Georgia, all before learning of Major Griswold's appointment. Winder gave Wirz a letter of introduction to Colonel Persons, describing him as an old prison hand who ought to be given control of the stockade.[19]

Wirz arrived early in March and went right to work. One of his first projects was the construction of a "dead line." With free access to the walls all around the stockade the prisoners would have little trouble undermining the logs, toppling them, and rushing the guard, or they could very easily tunnel under it and simply escape—especially in the stiffer clay north of the branch. Wirz's dead line might not solve those problems altogether, but it could hamper such attempts severely. He began by ordering stakes driven into the ground parallel to the stockade and fifteen feet inside it, but haphazard pacing brought some of those stakes several feet farther in. Pieces of scantling eventually connected the tops of those stakes, completing a fragile fence that defined the limits of the prisoners' range, and anyone who ventured across it was liable to be shot. The dead line was not a feature of Wirz's own invention: Camp Douglas, Illinois, and other Union prisons had such formal barriers, while at still others they were not marked at all, and the guards operated under nebulous instructions to shoot at prisoners who "approached" the stockade or stepped outside certain indefinite bounds at night. With the population of prisoners growing by hundreds each day, the outnumbered guards of an open pen needed some sort of strictly controlled buffer.[20]

Captain Wirz had only begun his duties when Major Griswold appeared with his own set of orders. Obviously Richmond authorities were working at cross-purposes, and an inquiry would have to be made; meanwhile both Griswold and Wirz remained at Camp Sumter, Wirz taking his board with the Anderson entrepreneur, Ben Dykes. Between his dry goods store, his postmastership, his sinecures as station and express agent, the lease of his land, and paying guests, Mr. Dykes seemed to be on the way to making a tidy profit.[21]

When Major Griswold first stepped off the Macon train he found that Camp Sumter (or Camp Anderson, as the locals called it) had become a scenic attraction. Dozens of citizens, many of them women who came to peddle baked goods, congregated daily on adjacent hillsides and stared by the hour at the milling Yankees. Their best view came from a rise southwest of the stockade, from which they could watch the activity at the branch and on the slope north of it; they could plainly see the prisoners standing or squatting at the impromptu sinks on the far end of the stream, and it galled certain Southern gentlemen that ladies should be permitted to witness such things. The ladies themselves seemed less offended, for they continued to visit all the same. Some of the burghers, like the editor of the Americus paper, tried to slip inside for an interview with the devils of their dreams, or spoke to them through the security of the gates. The editor reported that the prison still seemed nice and tidy, while the prisoners claimed to be happy enough.[22]

The prisoners might well have still considered themselves fortunate, compared with their Belle Isle circumstances, but those responsible for their welfare could already see things turning sour. Space was growing scarce, and deliveries of provisions failed to keep up with the swelling ranks. By the middle of March, less than three weeks after the first inmates entered the stockade, fifty prisoners had died. Most of these had perished from pneumonia or intestinal disorders they had carried down from Richmond, but the prison staff was horrified to learn that two of those men had succumbed to smallpox. Of all the diseases prevalent in 1864, perhaps none sparked so much fear as this one. A year earlier an outbreak had struck in the Plains of Dura, a settlement ten miles west of Americus, killing at least three people and electrifying the county: "Do not go into public," the newspaper had warned its readers; "stay where you are." Word of the Camp Sumter cases spread quickly, and civilians scorned army assurances that the virus would be contained within the prison. Indeed, there loomed an excellent chance of an epidemic, for the smallpox patients initially went straight into the open prison hospital, which remained inside the stockade. Prisoners with particular vocational skills were released from the pen each morning to work on the outside, on parole of honor not to escape, where they mingled with Confederate soldiers who could very easily carry the plague into the countryside. At first a dozen men came down with the symptoms of fever, headache, wracking spasms of vomiting, and the little red eruptions that gave variola its common name. A third victim died March 18, and for a week it looked as though that might be the end of it, but a second crop of patients appeared at the end of March. One died March 27, another on the 31st, and three each on April 4 and 6. This second wave spawned a third that was larger still.[23]

Andersonville's smallpox panic began with the diagnosis of Henry Gebhardt, an Ohioan who had just come down from Richmond when he was admitted on March 3. The outbreak seems to have originated with a case from East Tennessee, however. The Knoxville *Whig and Rebel Ventilator* of March 6 reported the disease "raging" in that city, and the vast majority of the Camp Sumter victims belonged to regiments assigned to that vicinity. The only unit reporting the recent loss of any prisoners there was the 11th Tennessee Cavalry, an entire battalion of which was surprised and captured five miles east of Cumberland Gap on February 22. The carrier, who perhaps brought the disease with him from a recent sojourn in Knoxville, naturally gravitated toward his own countrymen as soon as he entered prison; that would explain the high ratio of Tennesseeans among those who died. Since Richmond officials registered a short outbreak, the infected man may have stopped briefly in that city on his way to Andersonville. The first Andersonville fatality from smallpox was a Tennesseean who died on March 12, which would suggest he contracted the disease the last week in February—about the time the 11th Tennessee Cavalry prisoners came in. The third man to die of that ailment at Andersonville, James Guild, was himself a member of the 11th Tennessee. Guild seems not to have been the original carrier, though, because his death on March 18 indicates that he was probably infected after he was taken prisoner. Most likely Guild, too, caught the disease directly from that unwitting source of the contagion, who either died on the way to Georgia or—in the vigorous health of recent freedom—recovered.[24]

Within days after Gebhardt's ailment was identified, someone found a couple of spare tents for a pest hospital and Doctor White removed the smallpox patients to the woods outside the stockade, where an old (and probably immunized) surgeon cared for them. As an added precaution, White proceeded to vaccinate other prisoners by the thousands, but, as often happened with the nonsterile practices of the day, many of the vaccinations did more harm than the disease itself. Sores from the inoculation sometimes rankled for months, inviting infection and, finally, turning gangrenous. Numerous vaccinations concluded with an amputation, and many of those patients died anyway. Smallpox remained active at Camp Sumter well into the summer: the last victim succumbed on July 4, and the pest house remained occupied as late as August 9.[25]

The month of March saw yet another stir at Andersonville that carried, like the smallpox scare, into the citizen population. Confederates in Florida had kept the Olustee prisoners in Tallahassee for a few weeks, since so many of them were wounded, but once they could hobble around a little their guards started loading them into boxcars. Facilities for transport were even harder to secure in that region than in other parts of the Confederacy, so the captives came only two or three dozen at a time over the second half of the month. One railroad dropped them on the banks of the Appalachicola, where a flimsy little steamer chugged them up that river and the Chattahoochee to Fort Gaines. There sat the terminus of a branch of the Southwestern Railroad, which carried them east again to the town of Smithville and a junction with the main line. When the first of those cars stopped at Americus most of the people in that town caught their maiden glimpse of Federal soldiers, and therein lay the seeds of the great excitement, for among the groaning passengers on the floor of the closely guarded cars sat several black men in blue uniforms.[26]

These black soldiers represented everything the South was fighting against. Initially disavowing any inclination toward abolition, or even a belief in racial equality, Abraham Lincoln had nevertheless raised those very specters in 1862 by enlisting black troops, some of whom had gained freedom from slavery by running away. The very notion of slaves arming themselves against the white population had long struck such a chord of fear in the slave states that the standard punishment for encouraging an insurrection was summary execution. To Southerners, that was precisely what the officers of the U.S. Colored Troops had done, and some time previously the executive department had issued a proclamation threatening the mortal consequences prescribed by state law if any of them were captured. That proclamation, along with the provision that escaped slaves would be returned to their masters when taken in battle, offered the Federals their latest reason for declining any further exchanges.[27]

One of the first carloads of Olustee prisoners included Archibald Bogle, the major of the 1st North Carolina Colored Infantry. Judging from a camp order issued the next day prohibiting the practice, large numbers of off-duty soldiers must have crowded the railroad platform to see the black Yankees and their leader. Bogle's chest and leg wounds had hardly begun to heal, so his subordinates bore him on a litter. Camp Sumter had been intended solely for enlisted men, but the Confederates refused to acknowledge Bogle as an officer, and he had been sent from Tallahassee to the stockade deliberately. Colonel Persons treated him decently enough, but the medical staff would not attend to him, perhaps hoping he would die of his wounds. He survived, however, though for many weeks he seemed not to improve. Later, when he could get about on crutches, he swung himself over to the hospital, which had grown by several more tents and flies. A hospital steward—a prisoner like himself— bandaged his leg, but Surgeon White recognized the major by his shoul- der straps and told the steward to stop working on him and send him back outside "with his niggers." Bogle remained at Andersonville through most of 1864, despite Henry Wirz's personal efforts to have him exchanged or sent to an officers' prison.[28]

Major Bogle reached Camp Sumter on March 14, and shortly after- ward a civilian arrived among some other Olustee prisoners. David A. Cable, who had been a captain in a ninety-day Ohio regiment in 1861, had apparently dropped out of the conflict because of dissatisfaction with the political turn it had taken. Somehow he attached himself to the Federal army that penetrated Florida, and when he fell into Southern hands he introduced himself as what might have been called a minister extraordinary—very extraordinary. He said he had come representing Northern peace men who wished to work with the Confederates to see Lincoln defeated in the November election. From the Andersonville stockade he wrote the Confederate vice-president, Alexander Stephens, to propose a meeting; Stephens asked President Davis to grant Cable a parole for that purpose, but Davis and Stephens did not get on well and the arrangement was never made. The gate that had closed behind Mr. Cable would not reopen for him while he lived.[29]

Other Olustee contingents straggled in through the last of March. On the 22nd many of the 7th New Hampshire arrived, and toward the end of the month an Italian Swiss named Frederick Guscetti came in with his comrades of the 47th New York. Guscetti, like most of the Olustee wounded, had to be carried from the depot to the stockade in a wagon. Like every new trainload from Tallahassee, this one contained a few more black men: the Americus editor counted eleven of them on Sunday, March 27. Colonel Persons inquired what to do with them, in light of the president's proclamation on that subject, but General Winder told him to hold them as ordinary prisoners of war until the question was resolved at a higher level. Persons just marched them into the stockade, where they congregated in their own little encampment near the south gate—ignored by everyone, including the doctors.[30]

Assisted by his fellow New Yorkers, Frederick Guscetti settled into a rude shelter for his first night's sleep in the bull pen. At that very moment a steamer bearing a white flag started down the James River from Richmond. It was a stormy, foggy evening, and the captain finally hove his vessel to until morning, docking at Fort Monroe the next day. Colonel Robert Ould, still the Confederacy's commissioner of exchange, started down the gangplank to meet Ben Butler: apparently Southern authorities had pocketed their animosity toward the Beast long enough to talk about prisoners.

One by one, Ould and Butler covered the thorny issues: the paroles made in the field, the Port Hudson paroles (made after Washington had repudiated such arrangements), and the Vicksburg parolees' declaration of exchange. The Confederate emissary even expressed willingness to recognize free black soldiers and their officers as legitimate prisoners of war. That left only the matter of returning former slaves to their masters. Butler tried several arguments, ranging from the authority of the Emancipation Proclamation to the right of conquest, purporting that the United States government had taken ownership of them as prizes of war, and had then freed them before enlisting their services. Richmond would not budge on that issue—could not budge, without renouncing its raison d'être. Neither could the North appear to go back on its commitment to its black soldiers, but Butler was a Democrat of old, and seemed not to comprehend this, so the pair parted with the understanding that even this hurdle could be overcome. Ould suggested that, since runaway slaves constituted so tiny a fraction of the total prisoners, it would be inhumane to allow their status to derail the entire process. Supposing that few fugitives would even be recognized, he hit upon the plan of resuming the cartel while reserving the right to object to individual cases of enslavement—just as the belligerents had so often disputed the cases of alleged spies and war criminals who suffered execution or unusually severe confinement. In those relatively rare instances, the aggrieved government chose hostages for retaliation, and so the Union might do in the matter of any slave-soldiers who were returned to bondage.

This idea so pleased Butler that he filed a most optimistic report with his secretary of war, suggesting that they thrash out all the other disagreements and leave the issue of black prisoners as the sole obstacle to the general exchanges that the Confederacy seemed to want so badly. Word of a near agreement drifted south, winding its way through a snowstorm to the fourth floor of a cold Danville prison, where Private Jessie Hines dared hope for release if only his government did not "begin again to agitate the negro question."[31]

In Washington Butler's negotiations were not viewed as progress. There was still the old issue of the Vicksburg and Port Hudson prisoners, for which the Federal government continued to insist upon equivalents, and no agreement that distinguished between black and white soldiers would be acceptable. Ulysses Grant ordered Butler not to exchange another man.[32]

Jessie Hines would very soon find himself transported from the snow-covered Danville warehouse to the red mud and open sky of southwestern Georgia. There he and his friends would collect a promiscuous assortment of sticks and scraps for one of the hovels that prisoners called "shebangs," in corruption of an Irish term, and, as they scavenged or bargained for these materials, they heard others muttering their name for this new home—"Andersonville"—where it was going to be a very long summer.[33]

A telegram from Richmond finally sorted out the conflict between Major Griswold and Captain Wirz. Griswold returned to the capital, unaware just how lucky he was, and on March 29 Colonel Persons officially appointed Wirz commander of the interior of the prison, where he was already hard at work. Wirz had his new title etched on a little shingle, and he asked Richard Winder for a building to hang it from. Eventually the quartermaster put up a board shack on that rise just off the southwest corner of the stockade.[34]

Both the guards and prisoners at Andersonville found Henry Wirz an explosive and profane man, but the most credible testimony also paints him as fair, with an occasional glint of kindness. Even the friendliest of his Georgia acquaintances left an image of volatility that contrasts sharply with those of some who knew him in 1861. The change may have been born of the frustrating demands of his assignment, or it may have sprung from months of constant pain in his injured arm. A doctor who saw that wound a few months after Wirz took charge of the prison cringed at its condition, urging him to have it treated, but Wirz would not, keeping it wrapped in a towel in hopes it would heal on its own. His right forearm remained constantly swollen and inflamed, with ugly ulcers perched about the hole that exposed a pair of grey, dead-looking bones. Nerve damage had curled the two smallest fingers into his palm. He could eat and write with that hand, but that was about all: it hurt him even to ride a horse. Nevertheless, his renowned energy persisted. He came to the post early, took off his coat, and went straight to work. There was a good deal to be done when he first assumed his duties, and the chores multiplied with each passing month; as the only officer directly connected with the prison, he worked every day of the week and often into the night. From the first he did not like the job, largely because he lacked sufficient authority to demand the materials he needed to meet his responsibilities.[35]

One of the worst problems Wirz encountered was sanitation within the stockade. With more than seven thousand men confined in sixteen acres, a fetid odor hung over the entire pen. Latrines, like the two near the hospital, might have contained the excrement, where it could be periodically limed and buried, but Wirz could not get the loan of so much as a shovel. The prisoners consequently used the only portion of the interior in which they could not build shelters, where the branch—now unofficially dubbed Stockade Creek—had been somewhat dammed by the upright logs. This broad, swampy basin quickly evolved into the most obnoxious open sewer. At other places too distant from the creek for convenience, prisoners stricken suddenly by the call of nature scooped little pits with their bare hands, but those pits soon overflowed; those too lazy or ill to observe even such minimal sanitary concessions began to pollute the prison indiscriminately, some gouging little holes with their heels and fouling the interiors of their own shelters.[36]

Wirz worried the quartermaster for tools, and early in April Colonel Persons learned of a supply available in Augusta. He stopped by Richard Winder's quarters to apprise him of them, but the quartermaster lay writhing in bed with an acute attack of rheumatism. Persons's own quartermaster from the 55th Georgia, Captain James Wright, had gone to Atlanta looking for tents, and the 26th Alabama's quartermaster had also departed in search of uniforms for his ragged regiment. Taking a calculated risk, Persons left his post, without orders, to snag the tools before they disappeared. In a few days he returned with them, and Captain Wirz distributed shovels to two platoons of prisoners whom he assigned to clean up the ordure daily. They still had to dump the refuse in the extremity of the stream, but Wirz came up with an idea that might reduce that annoyance, too: he wanted to build two dams on the upper part of the creek, their elevations staggered like a pair of locks, both of which he planned to open each day to flush out the accumulated filth. The uppermost dam would provide a reservoir of clean drinking water, while the lower pool could be used for bathing. Filled with dry clay, the banks of such a flume could also be spanned by a footbridge, which would relieve the prisoners from having to wade through two feet of muck to collect water or visit across the creek.[37]

Cold rain fell during each of the last four days in March, driving home the need for some sort of general shelter within the prison. Richard Winder still planned to build barracks, but lumber continued to elude him. He complained to the Macon quartermaster that one whole train-load of materials destined for Camp Sumter had been sitting in central Georgia for nearly a fortnight, just waiting for cars to bring it down. Colonel Persons again interfered on behalf of his post quartermaster, contracting for a million board feet with a Macon sawyer, but that lumber only came in by driblets. The portion of it that did arrive found its way to the cookhouse, where Yankee carpenters on parole hammered the building together. Captain Winder considered this camp kitchen more important than barracks, and justly so, for while most of the prisoners yet owned some form of shelter, many of them had no means of cooking the raw rations issued to them.[38]

Another item of some importance to Winder, if not to the prison, was the establishment of a shoe factory outside the stockade. Shoes proved perpetually scarce in the Confederacy after 1863; few Southerners knew how to make them, for people in that region had generally either imported their footgear or gone barefoot. It occurred to Winder—or was suggested to him—that enough Yankee cobblers probably resided within the stockade to fill a good-sized shop. That happened to be a valid assumption, but Winder lacked both a loyal artisan to organize the shop and the barest essentials of shoemaking equipment. Early in April he started hounding the nearby department quartermasters for his various needs: from Atlanta he requested an "experienced shoe man"; from Columbus he asked for leather enough to supply 150 hands; after learning of a cargo of shoemakers' findings that had run the blockade into Mobile, he applied for the entire shipment.

Atlanta supplied the requisite shoemaker, one J. R. Smoot, and from Mobile came whatever tools had entered that port, while the Columbus quartermaster sent some rough leather suitable for soles. Guards took a descriptive list of the prisoners that revealed more than six hundred of them had some shoemaking experience, giving Winder such confidence that he hoped to have the factory in full operation by early May. Enough prisoners were willing to do the work if it would take them out of the stockade, but by late April Winder still could not find certain vital imple-ments, patterns, or upper leather.

The shoemaking project stalled there for a month while Mr. Smoot went looking for those items. Another snag developed when the Con-scription Bureau scooped up Winder's roving superintendent, but even after Winder won Smoot's freedom he could not procure all the equip-ment necessary for a factory, or enough of such simple items as shoe pegs. Still, on June 15 an optimistic Winder sent a recruiter—a paroled Federal—to look for experienced craftsmen in the stockade, but the other prisoners handled him rather roughly: they shredded the list of names he had compiled, held him down while someone shaved half his head, then hooted him back to his quarters near the gate, forcing him to pull off his hat now and then to display his humiliating punishment. In the end a number of cobblers did emerge from the prison on parole, but most of them appear to have been dispersed among the homes of officers living in the countryside, with whom they boarded while making custom foot-wear for those officers' families and friends—perhaps occasionally throwing together some brogans for the army. A week after the assault on his recruiter, Winder hired an agent to find a building suitable for a shop, but he could secure none. A few Yankee cordwainers eventually filled a tiny atelier up the line at Oglethorpe, but the great shoe factory Richard Winder envisioned at Andersonville never came to be.[39]

Hardly any work could have been accomplished had it not been for the paroled prisoners like those who built the cookhouse or offered to cover Confederate feet. Not only did experienced tradesmen reside in far greater proportions among the prison population than in the Southern ranks, the troops at Camp Sumter had more than they could handle with guard duty, even if they had possessed the manual skills. Every day Colonel O'Neal was asked to turn over a detail to Captain Wirz for manning the sentinel stations around the stockade; with forty-odd plat-forms on the perimeter and several posts on the ground, that daily levy could never have numbered fewer than 150 men. Four outlying picket stations also had to be patrolled constantly, and other details had to stand ready to escort prisoners from the depot, guarding them during the hours it sometimes required to record the newcomers' names and divide them into squads. O'Neal could mobilize barely four hundred men in the ranks of the 26th Alabama and the 55th Georgia combined, and as many as a third of those might be on the sick list at any given moment. The minimum daily details, exclusive of fatigue duty, thus called for more than half the available men in camp. That meant the same soldiers frequently had to pull guard two or three days in a row. A private who had turned four two-hour stints on the stockade over the past twenty-four hours might well be kicked out of his blankets at ten o'clock in the morning to meet a shipment of prisoners; after standing without food in the hot sun all afternoon he could rely upon having to wake up early the next morning for guard mount again, with another day of two hours on, four hours off, and little sleep in between. Except for better supplies of firewood and cooking utensils, the Confederate soldiers at Camp Sumter endured the same ration constraints as the prisoners. Many of them found it necessary to supplement their diets by foraging around the countryside, so the constant guard duties interrupted both their volume of food and their culinary efforts as well as their sleep.[40]

On their grocery expeditions the guards sometimes accumulated more food than they needed, and they traded the surplus with the prisoners, finding vegetables particularly marketable when they could get them. Prison officials strictly prohibited that sort of commerce, justly fearing too much intimacy between those thousands of Yankees and their outnumbered jailors. In order that the prisoners could buy the extra provisions they wanted, Quartermaster Winder offered one of his own clerks, James Selman, Jr., as a sutler for the stockade. Wirz so assigned Selman, who took some of the scrap cookhouse lumber to build himself a little shack from which to peddle his goods. He carted in vegetables, fruit, rice, beans, salt, tobacco, candles—just about everything but weapons and digging implements—and sold them for a substantial markup from the prices he paid his Americus suppliers.[41]

Selman had briefly held a commission early in the conflict, and, although his only present military attachment consisted of nominal membership in the militia, he had served for a time as acting adjutant of Camp Sumter. When some of the guards continued to trade with the prisoners, Selman used that dubious former authority to protect his monopoly. Suspecting an Alabama soldier of exchanging something with a Federal, Selman gave orders to have the Southron bucked and gagged: that is, to have his hands tied around his upraised knees, under which a stick was thrust, locking his elbows in a most uncomfortable position.

The victim's comrades threatened to tear Selman apart. Winder asked O'Neal for a guard to protect his clerk, and O'Neal sent one, probably snickering all the while. Colonel Persons had left for Augusta on his mission for shovels, which technically left Henry Wirz in command of the post, but neither Colonel O'Neal nor his battle-hardened veterans feared a crippled foreigner with no troops at his disposal, and the Alabamians went for Selman with blood in their eyes. Dismissing his guard by sheer force of numbers, they trussed up the sutler, perched him painfully on a rail, and paraded him all around their camp, right past Colonel O'Neal's quarters. Not an officer raised his voice to stop it, though the uniformed mob roared like demons. The mutiny affected three-quarters of the garrison. By the time the battered Selman broke free he was missing both his watch and his pocketbook.

The next day Selman ranted about the loss as he complained to Wirz, calling O'Neal a "damned old thief." An Alabama private standing nearby carried that slander back to his colonel, and O'Neal responded by sending over a guard detail to arrest Selman. Protesting O'Neal's usurpation of the post command, Captain Wirz observed that he had no force with which to resist, and he reluctantly surrendered the unhappy sutler. Colonel Persons returned after Selman had spent a couple of days in confinement, releasing him on the grounds that Selman was a civilian and therefore not subject to court-martial. Objecting that Selman had signed documents as adjutant of the post, a raging O'Neal insisted that Selman was a private soldier masquerading as a commissioned officer. Mr. Selman, meanwhile, remained free, returning to his captive market in the stockade.[42]

The flap between Persons and O'Neal left the Alabama troops more surly than ever: O'Neal's officers met in secret session to file a petition with the inspector general of the Confederate army, but nothing came of it. O'Neal remained at the camp in something like informal post arrest. That freed Persons momentarily from the conflict over rank, but henceforth he had to wonder whether the greater half of the garrison would support him in an emergency. Former prisoners who reminisced years later about what good fellows the Alabama soldiers were may have unwittingly recorded this hostility toward the post commander and his staff, whom the veteran Alabamians seem to have regarded as more objectionable than the Yankees.[43]

It only complicated the tight guard situation when the inmates finally used up all the wood left inside the stockade; by the end of March they had burned all the construction slash and had chopped down all but three of the trees that offered them shade. They could hardly cook their food without fuel, Persons knew, so he had to assign yet another detachment of guards to supervise prisoners in the gathering of cordwood. Beginning with the tree line nearest the stockade, axmen began clearing broad swaths of forest, but once out of sight of the officers these details sometimes degenerated into picnics. Disgruntled guards would require no work of their prisoners, and sometimes all of them would lie down together, chatting and napping until it was time to return. With only one guard to oversee each crew of three, some Federal woodchoppers became dangerously familiar with the only men who stood between them and freedom.[44]

That familiarity threatened the security of the entire prison. Inmates routinely crossed the dead line at night to swap baubles for food; the sentries of the 55th Georgia, especially, finagled for consecutive guard posts to offer this illicit trade better safety and secrecy—thus circumventing the administrative logic that the next guard would enforce the prison rules if the nearest one did not. The dead line offered the only early warning against an assault on the stockade, and with his guard force so weak, fatigued, and discontented, Henry Wirz dared not let the prisoners lose their respect for it. At every guard mounting he repeated his orders to allow no one beyond that flimsy barrier on pain of death, probably growing even more insistent on that point as the crowd inside increased. The failure of the guards to heed Wirz's orders merely encouraged the prisoners to disregard the fatal boundary, leaving a tragedy inevitable, and on April 9 a careless Federal finally encountered a conscientious Confederate.

Caleb Coplan, a young Ohioan captured at Chickamauga, was wandering in the northeast corner of the stockade, apparently in search of material to patch his shelter or his clothing. Something under the dead line caught his eye—a scrap of flannel, some said—and he ducked under the line to retrieve it. The guard brought his cumbersome old smoothbore to his shoulder and let fly with a charge of buck-and-ball. The range was too short to miss, and the .75 caliber ball bored through Coplan's breast near the heart. Onlookers carried him to the hospital tents a few yards away, where he died the next day—the first man killed at the dead line.[45]

So little confidence did Colonel Persons have in the majority of his garrison that he made an urgent appeal for reinforcements, meanwhile calling on nearby towns to supply him with a makeshift force on the excuse that he feared an imminent mass escape. Up in Macon Howell Cobb, recently placed in command of Georgia's Reserves, telegraphed serial appeals for regular troops to meet the crisis, but Joe Johnston could spare no men from the Army of Tennessee and the commander at Savannah would not do so without orders from higher up. Those orders finally came, but not before Sumter County hearts beat a little faster: from Americus alone several dozen men scrambled aboard the train, armed to the teeth. They remained two days; on April 22 the 57th Georgia rolled in from Savannah, more than six hundred strong, and the Florida Light Artillery came up, dragging four guns—three of them captured in the battle of Olustee. From the northern slope of the prison, Aaron Elliott may have glimpsed the bronze muzzle of a Napoleon smoothbore past which his New Hampshire friends had carried him, back when the piece braced the Federal fighting line.[46]

The reinforcement tripled the garrison, easing the strain for a time. The impromptu militia went home with the thanks of Colonel Persons, and now the locals could even laugh about their scare; one observer made fun of both the motley phalanx of minutemen and the women of south-west Georgia, whom he accused of frantically stuffing all their money into their stockings. Confederate scrip might be suffering from wild inflation generally, he noted, but the cash that had known the touch of ladies' limbs was "on the rise."[47]

At the beginning of April Captain Wirz had expanded the system of organization, lumping the squads of prisoners into detachments for the dual purpose of calling the daily roll and distributing rations. Previously the entire population had been segregated into "nineties" alone. In Wirz's new hierarchy, the detachment consisted of three squads of 90 men each; the squads of 90 were further broken down into five equal messes. At seven o'clock every morning Confederate "sergeants" of the 55th Georgia, many of them really only privates with navy revolvers strapped on, would saunter into the prison to call out the names on their lists. The procedure consumed a couple of hours, for the sergeants were frequently assigned as many as six detachments, and the 1,620 men on those rolls would include Frenchmen, Germans, Italians, and Slavs whose names mystified rural Georgians. Some of them merely counted heads, or took the word of the Yankee sergeant in charge of the detachment that everyone was present. Any faces not present had to be accounted for, and since the squads did not necessarily live together this, too, wasted much time. Huts had to be searched all over the camp for those who had slept late, or whose illness had weakened them too much to move; often, especially after midsummer, the truant would be found dead in some solitary den. The absence of one member concerned the whole detachment, for Wirz found that roll call went more smoothly when incomplete attendance cost the prisoners food. If the Confederate sergeants could not account for everyone by the time they left the gate, the short detachments would have no rations issued to them that day. As the prison grew Wirz must have relaxed that rule somewhat, perhaps understanding the difficulties of finding men who had crawled away to die in that multitude, for at least by June he had begun to reinstate the daily issue for any detachment whose missing men turned up by the middle of the afternoon.[48]

Some wily prisoners would flit from one detachment to another, answering to the names of men who had just died or were otherwise absent, hoping to pick up an extra ration. This "flanking," as it was known, could only work for a few, for if the daily return totaled many more than were supposed to be in the stockade, Captain Wirz would question it. On April 1 he found some two thousand additional rations required over the day before and he burst into the stockade to settle it, ranting at the damned Yankees who had played the April Fool's Day trick on him. The joke turned on them in the end, for Wirz instituted his new squadding system in response to the abuse, keeping everyone in ranks until the entire prison had been counted. That revealed the source of the duplication, and he stopped rations that day for everyone on the side of the creek that had supplied the ghost brigade: they found they could suffer from tallying too many men, as well as for producing too few.[49]

The rations of the prisoners were supposed to mirror those of their captors, according to Confederate law. The Congress at Richmond took that statute seriously. James Armstrong was ordered down from Columbus to serve as the post commissary once his department assumed responsibility for the prisoners, and he tried to meet that obligation, which required him to feed each prisoner a pound and a quarter of meal daily, and either a pound of beef or a third of a pound of bacon, with occasional small portions of vinegar, molasses, and salt. When meat or meal fell short, he could supplement them with what Georgians called peas—perhaps black-eyed peas, known to Yankees as beans. To guard against a failure in transportation he loaded his new 2,100-square-foot warehouse with at least two or three days' provisions; in the early months he kept as many as five days' food on hand, presumably issuing the oldest first, but much of the meat came off the cars in decay and the meal often turned moldy before he could distribute it. Captain Armstrong's office saw frequent crises, for neither the government nor his agents in the field could always answer all his wants, even in a summer of bumper crops, and much of the time he had to substitute one staple for another. Though he found he could easily handle the first ten thousand prisoners, he began to feel the pinch as thousands more squeezed into the stockade. The overtaxed railroad system could not keep up with stores sent from the north or west, and he was often forced to appeal to the local agent,

Harrold, for an emergency allocation. Usually Harrold came through, but as the corn crop ripened on the stalk he could not always get meal, either, even by begging for it over a six-county area.[50]

The cornmeal created a problem even when it arrived in abundance. In rural Georgia, and perhaps throughout cornpone country, grinding mills were not equipped with bolting cloth, so the meal was delivered with the cob ground up in it. Southern women sifted the meal in the course of making bread, one pound at a time. Precious few Federal prisoners owned any sifters, and neither the commissary nor the cookhouse staff could practically separate thousands of pounds of meal: when Colonel Persons sent out for bolting cloth, he was told that none could be found in the entire Confederacy. The shredded cob turned hard and sharp as the meal dried, taking a toll on the delicate walls of sick men's intestines, irritating the dysentery and diarrhea that weakened so many of the prisoners. Some of them managed to worry holes through flimsy pieces of tin or brass to make their own sifters, but most of those inside the pen had no access to such materials.[51]

Each day, shortly after Captain Wirz made out his daily return from the roll-call count, he would present a requisition for that many rations to Quartermaster Winder, who passed it along to Captain Armstrong and detailed a couple of wagons to begin hauling the food. In the afternoon one of Winder's clerks would lead the first of those wagons through the north gate, and the long process of distribution began. More than once dark fell with part of the prison unfed; as the increasing population made that more common, the commissary decided to double up on rations one time, and thereafter to dole out food on one day for consumption on the next. One hitch the cumbersome commissary bureaucracy could not foresee, however, was the daily influx of hundreds of hungry new mouths. If a contingent of prisoners arrived after the morning requisition was complete, as usually happened, those men could not be fed that day; even after their names had gone on the roll, they diminished the commissary's reserve to the extent that he had not anticipated their coming, and after successive days of such surprise arrivals a significant shortfall accumulated. The prison passed its ten-thousand-man capacity on the first day of May, but the trains kept coming; in order to assure enough food for everyone, Captain Armstrong would have had to cut the overall portions.

John Whitten, the Iowa color-bearer, made his first complaint about short rations at Andersonville on April 19, a day in which he recorded watching seven hundred more prisoners march in the gate. Ten days later, after remarking upon the 45 percent population increase inside the prison in that same period, he wondered if his captors intended a policy of gradual starvation.[52]

At least partly because of citizen complaints, the Confederate War Department had begun to thin out its prisons elsewhere, sending the surplus to Georgia. Within those ten days in late April nearly twenty-nine hundred prisoners shuffled through the gate from Danville, Virginia, and Cahaba, Alabama. The train that pulled in from Danville on April 21 carried over six hundred, most of whom had been taken at Chickamauga seven months before. Some of them were already quite sick and had to be carried in, like Thomas Genzardi.

Genzardi had been ailing all winter: no sooner had the Richmond surgeons declared him recovered from cholera morbus than they moved him down to Danville, where he promptly came down with pneumonia; three weeks after the doctors discharged him for that affliction he returned with acute bronchitis, and lay another twenty days in the hospital. Barely a week after going back into the prison proper he found himself on a boxcar headed south, and by the time he reached Camp Sumter his bowels began troubling him: not only did he lose control of himself now and then, he was passing blood. After one night in the stockade, and doubtless with the help of friends, Genzardi worked his way to the north side, where the hospital still sat. The surgeon had talked Colonel Persons into handing over the tents Lieutenant Wright had finally found for the 55th Georgia, so the hospital now stretched along much of the north wall, but still it could not meet the demand. A man had to sink pretty low before Surgeon White would admit him, but Genzardi fit the bill. An attendant or two helped ease his withered form into a vacant slot under the rotting canvas.[53]

During the previous winter Robert E. Lee had dispatched some of his army to North Carolina in a bold plan to capture the garrison at New-bern, seize the U.S. gunboats on the Neuse River, and drive the enemy at least temporarily from Washington and Plymouth, where the Federals kept substantial outposts. Lee hoped the raid would free much in the way of supplies and permit the North Carolina troops to recruit their ranks, which it did, but the attack on Newbern fizzled. The Southern divisions nevertheless clung to the fringes of the sounds for three months, looking for an advantage.[54]

They saw that advantage in April. Reinforced by an ironclad ram built on dry land upriver, one strong division moved against Plymouth while a couple of brigades threatened Newbern. Designed on the presumption of Union naval superiority, the Northern defenses in the sounds were emasculated by the surprise appearance of this virtually invulnerable Confederate ironclad, which sank one Yankee gunboat and held the rest at bay while Southern infantry closed in. After three days of pounding, the post commander at Plymouth ran up the white flag. He surrendered four full regiments, parts of three others, and a battery of artillery—upward of three thousand men, altogether.[55]

For more than a year past, Union soldiers had considered the Carolina sounds good duty. No serious threat had arisen since the expulsion of the last Confederate defenders in March of 1862, and the various town garrisons had seen no active campaigns in sixteen months. The mild weather and the comfortable quarters there lulled many a veteran into reenlisting: three of the infantry regiments at Plymouth had just "veteranized" in January. That pleasant occupation came to an end with the surrender, on April 20. Regiments of North and South Carolinians took turns escorting the tenderfoot cavalcade to the railroad at Rocky Mount, five days away, where cattle cars scooped them up for the four-day journey to Andersonville. Commissaries along the way had not anticipated so tidy a catch, and the first group of prisoners went three days without food; their guards dared not even allow them off the cars to sleep at night, so sullen were the eyes that peered from the darkness.[56]

The first lot emerged from the sweltering cars at two-thirty on the last day of April. They formed up six hundred strong while a Southern sergeant began taking their names. Though weary and sore from days on the thumping hardwood floors, they otherwise showed good health; the wounded had all been left behind. Among these enlisted men stood a Massachusetts captain, Ira Sampson, who had been sent here by mistake: he should have been put off at Macon, with the other officers. So, too, should the chaplain of the 16th Connecticut, but late in the afternoon these two followed their comrades into the bull pen. Captain Sampson, one of those who had reenlisted for the comfort of heavy artillery duty, could find no suitable words to describe the sight that met him inside the gate. "'Tis horrible," is all he scribbled in a pocket diary, jotting down his slightly inflated estimate of twelve to fifteen thousand men crowded into what looked like sixteen acres. He found a few square feet of open ground, soggy with recent rains, and at dark he lay down, trying to forget his predicament by staring at the bright fingernail of a waning moon.[57]

The first of May fell on Sunday, and the Connecticut chaplain preached an early service. By eight-thirty the guards called him and Captain Sampson outside to backtrack for Macon, and on their way they hove to a siding to let another train pass that carried several hundred of their comrades from North Carolina, who were greeted at Andersonville by a rainstorm. For four straight days the cars disgorged men whom their fellow prisoners began to call Plymouth Pilgrims; with them came one woman, the wife of Private J. W. Leonard of the 85th New York, who refused to leave her husband and who acted as hospital matron for the wounded; another lady, the wife of a steamboat captain named Herbert Hunt, followed with her husband a couple of weeks later. But for one straggling group of sick and wounded, the last of the subdued bandbox soldiers reached Anderson depot well into the evening on May 2, too late to stand for the ritual of name taking and squad organization. The guards bivouacked them between rows of blazing pine branches. In the morning Captain Wirz roused them early and counted them into squads, stirring the lethargic and depressed crowd into motion with perhaps more profanity than he generally employed—which was usually enough; Wirz may have been a little nervous, for Major General Howell Cobb was scheduled to make an inspection tour of the prison that day.[58]

Cobb's impending appearance may have indirectly provoked the killing of George Albert. This poor Teuton, held prisoner during most of his life in America, had dwelt at Andersonville nearly since it opened. Some said he had gone crazy, though perhaps they judged him only by his inability to comprehend English. With General Cobb coming, and so many new prisoners on hand, Wirz may have given particularly stringent orders again. Those newcomers had strained the camp larder, though, and Albert was suffering from diarrhea, so he would have been hungrier than usual. He ventured from his tattered tent at the hospital, reached for some bread that lay across the dead line, and in so doing he found the land he had emigrated for—in the form of six feet of Georgia clay. His killing stood as a lesson to the three thousand men who had come in over the past few days.[59]

Looking about them, the Plymouth prisoners saw ragged veterans living in pine-bough wigwams or low-slung tents fashioned from a couple of blankets stretched over a fragile ridgepole, barely high enough to slither in on one's belly. Some of the novitiates clubbed together to build little wickiups with blankets or overcoats, but a sufficient set of poles now cost $2.50 in U.S. currency, and those who had no money could not buy the necessary framework. Because of a sudden ban on wood details, neither could they forage any, and despite plenty of money numbers of the new prisoners went weeks without any shelter at all. Exposed to the sun for the entire month of May, one Connecticut Pilgrim recorded attacks of pounding headaches day after day. Those who needed only a handful of saplings to shield themselves from the weather grew increasingly irritated with their captors as they gazed upon the expansive pine forests in the distance.[60]

The reenlisted veterans and the recruits who came from Plymouth represented nearly a million dollars in federal, state, and local bounties, not to mention whatever regular pay they carried, and one money-conscious inmate estimated they brought half a million in cash into the stockade. That may not have been too ambitious an exaggeration, and the introduction of so much currency stimulated trade inside the bull pen for months afterward. A sailor cast into the prison a month later reported the place "flooded with greenbacks," which seemed to help drive up the cost of everything, but the money drew goods into the stockade from outside, via the guards and the sutler's shack, in quantities the wornout barter system could no longer attract.[61]

The Pilgrims would need their cash, accustomed as they were to living on more than cornmeal, rancid bacon, and beans; one of them viewed his reenlistment bankroll as the only thing that saved his life. Even the Confederate guards at Andersonville complained of hunger while hypothetically drawing the same uncooked rations as the men inside the stockade, but the prisoners suffered more—especially those who had been held longest—because so many of them lacked any utensils. A man with no container might be able to collect his cornmeal in a feedbag fashioned from a coat sleeve or a pantleg, but he would have a rare time trying to cook it. With plenty of willing Yankee artisans standing idle, the ever-toiling Richard Winder continued his postal campaign for lumber and nails through April, and by the end of the month his next priority, the cookhouse, neared completion. The big baking pans had arrived at last, and some kettles, and on May 5 Winder sent his chief clerk into the stockade to enlist a few cooks and bakers.[62]

The clerk, James Duncan, was said to be a refugee from occupied New Orleans, and he lived with his family in a cabin between the depot and the prison. Some of the prisoners called him Captain Duncan, while others seemed to think he was a sergeant, and a military tribunal later tried him as a major. In fact he was nothing more than a detailed private: he may have been an efficient taskmaster, but he did not seem particularly honest. It was he who supervised the afternoon distributions of rations.[63]

The inauguration of the cookhouse finally allowed Captain Wirz the opportunity to end the wood details, at least for a time. Too many prisoners had escaped while enjoying a privileged stroll in the forest, in spite of their pledges not to do so: one trio even overpowered their guard, appropriating his clothing and his musket, dragging him along for fifteen miles before letting him go. The increased pressure of so many new prisoners demanded wood details and guards in numbers that once again strained the garrison, reinforcements notwithstanding, so with the theory (if not the fact) of offering cooked food to everyone, Wirz announced that the wood crews would cease to go out. Inside, those who wished to cook anything had to either grub in the ground for tree roots or rely upon the incidental scraps carried in by paroled workmen. Within six weeks a small handful of chips would sell for a quarter.[64]

One means of gathering wood was by carrying out the dead. In the prison's early days there had not been many of these: after Adam Swarner died on February 27, three days passed before anyone else joined him in the cemetery. One man died on each of the first four days in March, then seven perished on March 5, four more March 6, and seven the next day, most of them from pulmonary ailments. From there the daily toll rose steadily until autumn; by May the prisoners were dropping at the rate of nearly twenty a day.[65]

A man in John Whitten's company died of pneumonia the evening of April 16. The following morning Whitten and a few companions carried the body out the south gate and more than half a mile to the north, where the post commander was turning Ben Dykes's land into a graveyard. The luxury of coffins was a thing of the past, and now they laid the bodies shoulder-to-shoulder in trenches, like a recumbent line of battle. The gravediggers could still not bear to throw dirt directly on the lifeless faces, though—not even Yankee faces. To compensate for a lack of lumber, the workmen dug a seven-foot swath three feet deep, then left a six-inch shoulder on either side while going down another foot. Placing the day's dead on the floor of this indented pit, they covered them with puncheons—slabs of rough-split pine—that rested on those shelves, forming a common (if somewhat leaky) casket. Most of the Andersonville prisoners showed enough consideration to remain alive until they had trimmed down to fit the rather snug accommodations in this sylvan golgotha.[66]

Not long after Whitten performed the final service for his friend, during which he picked up some valuable deadwood on the way back to the stockade, Quartermaster Winder found that his little cemetery crew could not keep pace with the spiraling mortality. At Winder's request, about the second week in May Captain Wirz paroled a couple of dozen men, many of them from the 4th Iowa, to help bury their own comrades. James Davidson drove one of the two wagons Winder ultimately assigned to the detail; Charles Tibbles and his brother, George, dug the trenches; John Younker helped carry the dead from the wagons to their graves on an old litter with a great hole torn in it; Wilford Crandall followed behind, filling in the trenches after someone else had laid down the puncheons. While the shovelers filled, another man placed a marker at the head of each body for future identification; at least until April those markers had consisted of full headboards, with name, state, regiment, and company of the deceased carved upon them, but that extravagance soon gave way to mere stakes consecutively numbered, corresponding to entries in the hospital register that gave the bare facts of death and burial. As the number of daily dead climbed, Wirz paroled more men to dig the graves: by August about thirty soldiers labored under a foreman from the 1st Georgia Reserves, W. W. Byram, digging and filling as much as a hundred feet of trench every day.[67]

At first the friends of expired prisoners collected the bodies inside the south gate, and when the gates opened each morning they carried them through the sick-call throng to the roadside, to await the wagons. The sun baked them horribly there, and the need for some sort of shelter for temporary storage was obvious to everyone, but the living kept Richard Winder too busy to trouble himself unduly about the dead. The scorching days of June therefore arrived with no deadhouse, so Henry Wirz directed a few of his own paroled prisoners to throw something together. With little in the way of materials they could only manage to fashion another heterogeneous three-sided lean-to out of poles and rotting pieces of abandoned blankets, with a trimming of the ubiquitous pine brush, but it forestalled decay a little and afforded a token of human dignity. That sentiment was lost on the new prisoners who had to pass that primitive mortuary just before they entered the stockade: for them it served as the grimmest of introductions. Those already inside also disliked the location because it did not offer much opportunity to pick up firewood.[68]

Several times each day the drivers of the two makeshift hearses would pull up in front of the deadhouse and start tossing the bodies aboard with the indifference of a couple of medieval sextons cleaning up after a plague, one of them taking the ankles and the other the shoulders. They piled them several corpses high, with twenty or more to a load. The rough handling burst some of the more bloated carcasses open, so the noxious fluids inside them ran out of abdominal ruptures and gaping mouths, sickening even the sentries standing their posts a hundred feet away. James Duncan supervised these ghastly funeral caravans, too, since the wagons came from the quartermaster's department, and so scarce was transportation that he often required the charnel wagons to perform double duty, swinging by the depot on the way back from the cemetery to pick up part of the day's rations.[69]

Duncan also managed the cookhouse once it opened, but he was swimming against the tide right from the start. For some time already he had been boiling occasional cauldrons of rice or soup, but on May 7 he attempted his first fully cooked meal of boiled beef and cornbread. Either the kitchen or its cooks proved inadequate to the task: they managed to feed prepared rations to only half the camp, and could only reach that proportion by cutting down on the amount of cooked beef they handed out. Those who drew their meat and meal raw searched high and low for some firewood, mostly without success.[70]

Part of the blame for the culinary failure of May 7 might have been credited to the distraction of a large number of citizens, mostly ladies, who flocked to the post that day in hopes of some Saturday amusement. At Andersonville they found all the diversion they desired, wandering about the post virtually at will in spite of the crowded smallpox hospital just beyond the tree line. Susan Malone probably came up from Americus to see her fiancé, Colonel Persons, and she may have stood among those who glanced in the gate at the cloistered Yankees, while the more athletic civilians clambered up the guards' ladders for a panorama. Some who sympathized with the prisoners' foreshortened menu tossed extra loaves of bread over the palisade, prompting one bitter fellow (who caught none) to suppose they did it in play, to watch the Yankees scramble for scraps. In the afternoon the off-duty troops staged a booming sham battle for the benefit of their guests, thrilling the prisoners briefly with the false hope that their cavalry had come for them, and the ladies reciprocated with a potluck dinner spread under the shade of the pines. When their gay afternoon was done the visitors climbed aboard the train or into faded buggies and made their way home—and none too soon, for a captain from the inspector general's office arrived in Americus that very day, taking a weekend room there before his Monday tour of Camp Sumter. His train passed almost within sight of that injudicious levee.[71]

The guards at Andersonville might be throwing mock battles for sheer entertainment, but to the north the armies already grappled in earnest, churning their neat ranks into windrows of corpses and cavalcades of cripples, sloughing off in the process those vast columns of captives who would make their way to southwest Georgia by foot and rail, packing the log stockade so full that three months hence the old prisoners would look nostalgically back upon May as a time of plenty.

Up in northern Alabama, George Shearer had just returned from his reenlistment furlough, and it contented him perfectly to watch most of William Sherman's army strike out for Atlanta while his regiment remained behind. The drafted Knud Hanson rode clumsily along, helping to clear a path for that army with the 1st Wisconsin Cavalry, to which he had been assigned six weeks before. In Virginia, Ira Pettit caught his breath after two days of brutal fighting at close quarters in a tangle known as the Wilderness. Samuel Melvin, a private in the 1st Massachusetts Heavy Artillery, walked a beat in a big fort outside Washington, dreaming of the discharge that awaited him eight weeks away, while secondhand tales of the battles buzzed through the barracks behind him. Hiram Jepperson still stood guard at Point Lookout prison, in Maryland, where the duty was bleak and boring. In just two months that spring, Union guards at Point Lookout had shot four Confederate prisoners for offenses as slight as offering a personal insult. The time seemed right to put that sort of aggressiveness back in the field.[72]

3 ⤙ H Then Spoke the Thunder

owell Cobb returned to his home in Macon in the middle of April, 1864, after six months in Atlanta as commander of a militia organization known as the Georgia State Guard. The term of the State Guard had expired now, and Cobb had been assigned to head the Georgia Reserves, a fresh culling of the state's population that was meant to include boys under eighteen and men from forty-six to fifty. The various State Reserves were creations of the Confederate Congress, but Cobb found the actual recruiting of his new command stymied by his old rival in state politics, Governor Brown. Brown had exempted thousands of Georgia citizens from service because they held state or local offices, though Cobb pointed out that many of those officeholders had sought their positions merely to avoid conscription: districts that had gone without justices of the peace for years were suddenly represented by several, most of them able-bodied men of draft age. Nor, Cobb added, did most counties need the hosts of deputy sheriffs and court clerks who had collected about their county seats, because the war had suspended most court business. No county needed more than a sheriff, a jailor, and a single court clerk, Cobb argued, and those positions could readily be filled by older men or by those physically unfit for service.[1]

Joe Brown largely ignored the protests, so Cobb began fleshing out his command with what farmers and merchants he could find. He should have been able to fill several regiments automatically from the enrollment lists of eligible men, and indeed the 1st and 2nd Georgia Reserves sprang into existence in Atlanta almost instantly, late in April. The 3rd Reserves simultaneously gathered at Macon, and a fourth regiment lagged only a few days behind. Most of the recruits were seventeen-year-old boys and men in their late forties, with a sprinkling of younger teenagers and the occasional thirtyish unfortunate with an expired exemption or some physical defect. They came in their own clothing, which varied from homespun to broadcloth, and their state gave them nothing but more of those old smoothbore muskets with the gaping muzzles. With the exception of an infrequent veteran among the officers, they proved perfectly innocent of drill.[2]

No sooner could General Cobb boast a few complete companies than the war office ordered him to provide a guard for Andersonville so the regular troops could return to the front. That had been the impetus for his visit to the prison on the day the last of the Plymouth Pilgrims passed through the gates. When Cobb returned to Macon he left his chief surgeon behind to make a closer inspection of the post, but he dared not send any of his half-organized Reserves to such important duty just now. President Davis's military advisor prodded Cobb with a telegram on the same day he inspected Andersonville, notifying him that the government required two full regiments of Reserves for Camp Sumter, but still Cobb stalled a few days.[3]

Even as Cobb guided his horse around the dead line inside the prison, industrious Yankees burrowed toward freedom. The general probably rode right over one tunnel, for within thirty-six hours of his departure a number of prisoners slipped away through one. It happened after dark on May 4: the escapees hoped to put as much distance as they could between themselves and the stockade by the next morning's roll call. Someone caught sight of a prisoner as he emerged, though, and spread the alarm. The camp came alive, somnolent troops spilling out of their blankets under arms while sergeants rushed about with burning pine knots. The prisoners inside even grew interested, but for all the excitement no one turned up any of the missing men that night. Captain Wirz fumed, and the guards around the stockade turned especially strict the next day, while a local hunter named Benjamin Harris put his dogs on the scent. All that day and part of the next Harris followed the route of the flight, and on the evening of May 6 the exhausted, dejected fugitives staggered back into the stockade.

A couple of weeks later another squad dug its way to freedom, but Mr. Harris and his dogs eventually tracked all of them down, too. Afterward, survivors of Andersonville would swear the dogs routinely tore unmercifully at the flesh of runaway prisoners; contemporary diaries tell no such tales, and sometimes testify to the opposite. Those whose escape attempts failed did, however, often find themselves fitted with a ball and chain, and by early June New Jersey Sergeant Eugene Forbes counted dozens of men thus hobbled. Another punishment Captain Wirz offered for escape was a set of stocks built near his headquarters, in which the recalcitrant Federal could be uncomfortably pilloried for several hours like a backsliding Puritan. Within a year stories of the ball-and-chain treatment would enrage Union authorities and citizens who deemed it a prisoner's duty to attempt escape, rather than a crime to be punished, but the same treatment was meted out to runaway Confederates in at least one Northern prison.[4]

On May 9 Howell Cobb promised to send Colonel Persons one regiment within a couple of days and another two days after that, and in token of Cobb's good faith it was the colonel of the first regiment who delivered that message to Camp Sumter. The collision of armies in northern Georgia and below Virginia's Rapidan River shook the Confederate War Department out of a relative lethargy, however, and the requests for troops from the prison garrison turned into peremptory orders that would brook no further procrastination. Bypassing the usual chain of command, Adjutant General Samuel Cooper wired Edward O'Neal directly on May 12, ordering him to report to Joe Johnston's Army of Tennessee with his 26th Alabama; apparently he issued similar orders to the commander of the 57th Georgia. Three days later an obviously confused Cooper telegraphed that those regiments (mistaking the 57th Georgia for the 56th) should report directly to Richmond. The second telegram came too late: on May 14 the core of Camp Sumter's garrison boarded cars for Atlanta after a gala send-off by local belles, who served up another picnic to the blaring of a brass band. Their places were taken by James Fannin's 1st Georgia Reserves and most of Robert Maddox's 2nd Reserves, which had come from Atlanta two days before in such haste that they left a good many of their arms and accoutrements behind. Cobb's Atlanta recruiting officer pushed the completion of the other regiments as quickly as he could. The last of the 2nd Reserves started on its way before the veterans left Andersonville, and the third regiment had already begun electing its officers in the camp at Macon.[5]

May 15, 1864, thus proved an anxious and chaotic day at Camp Sumter, for the green Reserves held most of the stockade guard posts for the first time. On this same Whitsunday some industrious prisoners, whose tunnel had been discovered on Friday evening, concluded that they had been betrayed by a fellow prisoner. By late afternoon they thought they knew who he was, and in a body they confronted Thomas Herburt, the one-legged Canadian immigrant known as "Chickamauga" for his endless chattering about that battle: others called him "Poll Parrot," for both his volubility and his aquiline beak, or "Pretty Polly," in sarcastic reference to his wholly unattractive visage. Herburt had been in prison nearly eight months, now. He had nothing left to trade for extra food, and no skill to offer (the bull pen generated little demand for gardeners), but he went frequently to the gate to speak with the guards or to pass out of the prison altogether, and his accusers suspected him of marketing the information he had gleaned in his hobbling jaunts around the camp. Whether it was true or not, a throng of prisoners began threatening him, perhaps roughing him up a bit. To escape them he swung over to the south gate, Long-John-Silver fashion, and called for Captain Wirz, demanding to be let out.[6]

At first the sentry would have nothing to do with him. Herburt raised his voice, insisting on immediate passage, but the guard, a mere boy, refused. Undaunted, Herburt crawled underneath the dead line. The sentry—evidently one of the new Reserves, else he might have known that Herburt was frequently allowed outside—did not know what to do. Captain Wirz had asked Richard Winder to have the prison regulations printed, and the posters had only recently come back from the Americus newspaper office, so the penalty for violating the dead line would have been freshly and conspicuously displayed at the gate; even if the sentry had been illiterate, Wirz had doubtless given these new guards a more emphatic indoctrination than he customarily administered at inspection. Nevertheless, the killing of a man seems a terribly final punishment for crossing an arbitrary line, and especially so to a boy only two weeks off the farm. It did not enhance the young Confederate's resolve that he faced a helpless, harmless cripple, and he simply ordered Herburt to get back into the prison proper. The one-legged Yankee refused, hopping back and forth on his crutch and babbling about the enemies he had in the camp. This went on for several minutes, attracting a crowd of spectators along the dead line. Finally the shouting of the guard drew the attention of those outside the gate, and the commander of the relief carried the news to Ben Dykes's house, where Captain Wirz had retired under the impression that his day's work was over. Wirz climbed awkwardly aboard his horse, an old white mare, and in a few minutes he arrived before the south entrance, dismounted, and went inside through the wicket door in the main gate. He found Herburt just to the left of the gate, still within the dead line. In the gruff tone he usually assumed before large groups of prisoners, he demanded the cripple's business.[7]

Perhaps to win back the respect of his fellows, Herburt turned to Wirz and said he had lost the confidence of his comrades, and so wished to be killed. Wirz responded that he would be happy to accommodate him, and drew his pistol. He could only have meant it as a menace, for both of the Colt navy revolvers Wirz alternately carried were defective, and would not fire: one had a broken spring, while he kept the other unloaded because its chambers flashed over dangerously, discharging more than one round at a time. But the threat seemed sufficient, at least when Wirz uttered it in his prison voice, and Herburt fell momentarily silent. Wirz ordered some of the onlookers to take him back across the dead line; after assurances that the guards would not fire, some of them dragged Chickamauga back under the scantling. With that Wirz holstered his revolver and turned to go, reaffirming the sanctity of the dead line by shouting to the sentry that he should not hesitate, but shoot the cripple—or anyone else—who crossed the forbidden perimeter again. Satisfied that enough Yankees had heard his ultimatum, he departed through the wicket.[8]

The captain had hardly emerged from the gate enclosure when Herburt's fear of his comrades' retribution overcame his dread of the musket. Perhaps supposing Wirz had only been bluffing, or that the guard remained timid, he scooted under the dead line again, poking with his crutch at all who remonstrated with him. The sentry leveled his piece and warned him away yet again, but Herburt sat down and remarked that he would rather be killed by his enemies than by his friends. The youth obliged him. The bullet hit Herburt in the side of the face, near the hinge of the mandible, angling down into the thoracic cavity. Wirz heard the discharge and hurried back to the scene, clambering up the ladder to stand beside the boy. He saw the victim kicking his one leg and thrashing about inside the dead line, and ordered up another guard to take the post.[9]

The bullet silenced Chickamauga instantly, but he writhed in his muted agony for a long time as the sun set behind the gate. At last, in the twilight, someone carried him to the hospital, but the surgeons had all gone home. They found him there in the morning, choking out the last few hours of his obscure life.[10]

The hospital still sat inside the north wall when Herburt died there. Both Captain Wirz and Surgeon White had complained of the location on several counts: Wirz because he had to leave the north gate open for the passage of surgeons and the dead; White because the hospital's poorly located latrines washed right through the improvised wards when it rained. Both Wirz and White objected that neither of them had enough room with so many prisoners coming in from the renewed fighting. White could pitch fewer than three dozen tent flies to shelter several hundred of his worst cases, and he had had to refuse admission to as many more for whom he could only prescribe occasional medicines. Also, when the prisoners could find wood it was invariably pine, and their thousand little fires generated a dense pall that hung inside the palisade, which blocked most of the breezes that might otherwise have blown the smoke away. Incorporated into the prison as it was, the hospital remained vulnerable to the forays of the more unscrupulous prisoners, who entered the tents with increasing frequency to steal the food, bedding, and personal possessions of those too far gone to resist. The patients still lay upon the ground, with a mattress of musty straw or pine needles if they were lucky, and their Federal nurses largely ignored them, or worse. An uncommon percentage of these orderlies did not hesitate to prey upon their sick comrades: the day before "Chickamauga" was shot, a Plymouth prisoner saw the chief hospital steward and his subordinates "feasting upon what I have the strongest reason to believe was designed for the sick." This witness judged the Andersonville hospital attendants "wretched fellows of the worst stamp."

An independent inspector from Richmond corroborated White's evaluation, seconding his call to move the hospital outside the stockade. Even as the sentry sent his bullet through Thomas Herburt's breast, paroled prisoners knocked together a board fence in the grove of trees nearest the prison, on a slope off the southeast corner and in the fork where the branch from the stockade met Sweetwater Creek. Like the main stockade, the hospital was a slightly racked rectangle, 340 feet long and 260 feet wide. Stockade Branch, with its accumulated effluvia from the prison sinks, passed just north of this enclosure and barely a hundred yards from the new hospital's well. A smaller tributary of Sweetwater Creek coursed the southern extremity of the hospital, where the patients or nurses could wash their clothes; the hospital sinks consisted of nothing more than logs placed along the lower end of this stream.[11]

On the evening of May 21—as another Saturday picnic broke up, and the local ladies wended their way homeward—some of the hospital stewards started carrying the hospital equipment down to the north gate, where wagons waited to truck it around to the new site. The next morning they began transporting the patients themselves, on litters, to the spot where the ration wagon usually entered. As quickly as each of the rickety wagons could creak out the gate, over the branch, and around the rise where Captain Wirz's headquarters sat, the surgeon's detail unloaded its feeble passengers and sent it back for another contingent.[12]

The exodus of the sick opened up another couple of acres for the crazy little shebangs of new inmates, but men enough to fill that acreage stood right outside the gate. A Vermont cavalryman watched three wagonloads of patients emerge from the stockade while his covey of prisoners stood for the usual head count and detachment assignments in front of Wirz's headquarters. About five hundred men lined up in that lot, mostly from Grant's first fights in Virginia, and over the next three days nearly three thousand more hungry bellies joined the multitude inside. Within a couple of days the grounds of the old hospital disappeared under a variegated canopy of blankets, tents, and rubber ponchos.[13]

New prisoners who came inside early enough on May 22 enjoyed the spectacle of a camp thief suffering the summary punishment meted out by his intended victims. Caught in the act, a pilferer was set upon by some of the stronger and more honest inmates, who pinned him to the ground while another amateur barber applied shears and a razor to his scalp. As in the case of the shoemakers' recruiter, this treatment was offered to only one hemisphere of the skull, leaving no doubt that it had been administered for some deliberate transgression: complete tonsorial services were generally rendered only for a price—about ten cents.[14]

Thievery became more common as spring turned to summer. Individual brigands gravitated toward one another, forming alliances, and these bold gangs preyed upon the weak and the solitary, taking food almost literally out of their mouths. Surgeon White had complained of them in the open wards of the old hospital, but with the removal of that ready source of plunder they seemed to turn upon the general prison population. Four days after the relocation of the hospital, some more would-be victims pounced upon one who came skulking about their hovel in the night: they bucked and gagged him outside their tent until seven o'clock in the morning, then offered him the same half-domed hair fashion of the previous miscreant before throwing him into Stockade Creek, opposite his growing den of nefarious comrades on the south side. These more organized hoodlums, whom the other prisoners began to refer to as "raiders," decided to deal directly with this aggravating tendency toward vigilante justice; later that intensely hot day—Friday, May 27, 1864—one of the raider gangs descended en masse on a squad of prisoners who had turned out to defend one of their messmates, thrashing them soundly. In the afternoon another wolfpack ambushed a platoon of fresh inmates who had not yet found a place to set up their traps, relieving them of many of their belongings while they still suffered the initial shock that hit everyone thrown into the bull pen. The newcomers put up a good fight once they pitched in, but the raiders had armed themselves with cudgels and slung shot: their weapons, numbers, and the element of surprise carried the day. They retired sullenly, leaving several cracked heads, only after the nearest guard fired his piece. All of this had happened in broad daylight, signaling a new threshold in the raiders' daring.[15]

Perhaps the worst of the raider chieftains was Willie Collins, called "Mosby" by those who feared him. He claimed he had been born in England in 1835. At a hair under six feet he was also the biggest of the leading footpads, and one of the few who seemed not to have been a professional bounty jumper. Like a true patriot, Collins had enlisted at Philadelphia in the first six months of the war, but he started his military career on the wrong foot. During that first boring winter at Washington he struck for home without the formality of a furlough, but he came back in time to fight at Second Bull Run, where he caught a bullet in the leg that prevented him from getting off the field with his comrades. The Confederates swept him up in the wake of the battle, but three days later they paroled him on the field. For the next six months he avoided active duty—first because of his wound, then on the excuse of his parole, and finally with the claim that he was sick. Almost five months after Bull Run the surgeon of a Baltimore hospital pegged Collins for a malingerer and tried to send him back to his regiment, but he escaped into the city. At last, sometime in the spring of 1863, Collins returned to the ranks despite a distinct limp from his old wound, and apparently he fought at Gettysburg. By autumn he had been promoted to corporal, probably because his strapping physique commanded such respect, but during the Bristoe campaign his courage failed him. The very evening that Shepherd Pryor was wounded in a skirmish with other Yankees, Willie Collins slipped past the pickets and gave himself up. Like Captain Pryor, Collins quickly found himself on the road to Richmond, and on the fourth day of March he arrived in Sumter County, Georgia, where Shepherd Pryor now sat as sheriff.[16]

John Sullivan, a substitute from the 76th New York, tented with Collins. They had both served in the First Corps, had deserted within forty-eight hours of one another, and had been delivered to Richmond together. They had also arrived at Andersonville on the same train, and Sullivan had been Collins's foremost henchman ever since: barely sixty-three inches tall, the twenty-seven-year-old Sullivan would have needed an ally the size of Collins to prevail against most of his victims. His name may really have been John Sullivan, or it may not; others identified him as Cary Sullivan, and one prisoner referred to him as "Terry." Sullivan had enlisted from Rochester, where there were Sullivans enough, but bounty jumpers also congregated there routinely, and they seldom operated under their own names.[17]

Another of the strong-arm Irishmen was John Sarsfield. He had enlisted twice within sixteen days in September of 1863, each time as a substitute for a different man but both times under the same name. The second time he could not get away before the provost marshal sent him to the front, but he deserted before reaching his assigned regiment, the 140th New York. It had been a close call, though, for he had only escaped by dashing into the forest and giving himself up to the first Confederates he encountered. The time and location threw him into company with Collins and Sullivan, with whom he remained a prisoner at Belle Isle until Andersonville opened. At twenty-three Sarsfield was the same stocky size as Sullivan, so he, too, would have had to throw in with other brigands to succeed at that occupation.[18]

One prominent hooligan, Charles Curtis, said he hailed from the Canadian Maritimes. Also a substitute, he had deserted early in the spring from the Federal hospital at Morehead City, North Carolina, so he had come directly to Andersonville. Curtis was even younger than Sarsfield, and he stood the nineteenth-century average of five-feet-eight, but some considered him the most dangerous raider of all. Matching him in size was Patrick Delany, an Irish laborer drafted from Reading, Pennsylvania, the previous September. Delany spent thirty-one days in the army before he, too, deserted at Bristoe Station. It had been Delany whose departure from Hospital 21 in Richmond had made room for Thomas

Herburt the winter before. Delany had tried to pass himself off as a shoemaker in order to get out of the stockade (perhaps taking some lessons from Sarsfield, who actually was a cobbler), but Winder's difficulties with the shoe shop had blocked that avenue to the outside.[19]

As May progressed the raiders enjoyed a constant source of fresh booty, and occasionally a reinforcement, for hundreds of captives passed daily through the south gate. By the end of the month more than seventeen thousand men filled the stockade: another thousand lay in the new hospital, and nearly fifteen hundred others had taken their last wagon ride to Mr. Dykes's woods. New companies of Georgia Reserves kept coming in, too, to buttress a garrison that was falling woefully under-strength. Thomas C. Jackson, an Atlanta merchant and now a captain in the 2nd Reserves, made his first visit to the pen the day after his arrival. Reporting the shocking sight to his beloved wife Josie, he wrote that the Yankees appeared to lie on top of one another inside the stockade, like so many hogs. Some of them actually burrowed in the ground. Their dead lay baking in an indiscriminate heap where the prisoners themselves had piled them, and the faces of living and dead alike had all been blackened by the smoke from their pinewood fires—as were those of the guards, for that matter. Captain Jackson fervently hoped he might be sent back to Atlanta, preferring to face Sherman's host.[20]

Many of Georgia's other citizens did find an opportunity to go to Atlanta that May, but they did not appreciate it so well as Captain Jackson might have. In light of Sherman's movements Governor Brown issued a proclamation demanding activation of the militia, including certain civil officers who had heretofore enjoyed exemptions. He continued to protect legislators, judges, sheriffs, county clerks, and employees of the penitentiary and railroad, though he asked these to come forward voluntarily. From Sumter and surrounding counties some fifty petty officials and militia officers departed, among them Major Timothy Furlow. Thanks to the addition of a few militia companies from elsewhere, the major was promoted to lieutenant colonel of a battalion that eventually bore his own name. Furlow had recently written Howell Cobb to express his anxiety over the security of the prison. Partly because of that correspondence with Cobb, partly because he was a very wealthy and influential man, and partly because of an escape attempt by some resolute Federal prisoners, Furlow's battalion was armed with some old muskets—minus the bayonets—and promised an assignment to the garrison at Camp Sumter. That sat very well with Colonel Furlow, who had lived in nearby Americus for fifteen of his fifty years.[21]

The safety of the stockade sparked the concern of other Confederates in May. The Macon newspapers fretted over it, while Major Thomas Turner, an experienced prison keeper from Richmond, shuddered at the prospect of a Yankee raid on Macon and Andersonville, which might free twenty thousand veteran soldiers who had only a few raw regiments to oppose them. Turner reported the danger to General Winder, who simply passed the warning along to the adjutant general. Yet the whistles still blew and the prisoners kept rolling in, hundreds at a time.[22]

In the same report Major Turner also revealed misgivings about the hostility between Colonel Persons and the successive commanders of the troops, who were usually full colonels and outranked the post commander. As the fracas over Mr. Selman had demonstrated, the prison commandant could not function without cooperation from the man in charge of the troops, and in order to assure that cooperation the post commander ought to outrank them both.[23]

It happened that Colonel Persons was absent from Camp Sumter again on the day Turner filed his report. Leaving Colonel Fannin of the 1st Reserves in charge, Persons ventured into Americus on May 25 to marry his Sumter County belle at the Methodist church; he also appears to have afforded himself a brief (and altogether unofficial) honeymoon. Trouble seemed to develop whenever the colonel left his command, and on the day of the wedding Captain Wirz learned of arrangements for a massive escape. Immediately he stiffened the guard and posted an announcement on the prisoners' letter box that he was in full possession of their plans. Employing local slaves, he began the next day to dig a trench around the inside of the prison between the stockade and the dead line, uncovering at least one tunnel. The rumors had spoken of far greater preparations than a single tunnel portended, however: when prisoners approached the officers supervising the digging and inquired about rations, those officers offered to feed the Yankees rations of grape and canister if they tried to escape.[24]

An informer must have given Wirz better information by May 27, for he shifted his digging parties to the western walls, where the shovels bared several parallel tunnels running under the stockade. Ringleaders of a prison coterie known as "the League" had organized clandestine companies and regiments from the various detachments, mostly among the older ones, swearing their members to secrecy with a blood oath. One tentative break on the night of May 24 had been foiled by a driving rainstorm, so another was scheduled for the afternoon of May 25, but that one was postponed when Wirz made his announcement. Half-informed prisoners anticipated that the same plan of May 25 would be carried out the following day, or the next after that: when the gate opened at three o'clock to admit the ration wagon, the impromptu colonels and captains of those battalions would rush for the entrance—hence the previous day's solicitation about rations. Other squads would boil out of the tunnels like ground hornets, attacking the guards from behind and unbarring the outer gates in case the mob inside could not burst them. It was a desperate plot indeed, certain to see hundreds of unarmed inmates killed, but the prisoners numbered ten times their keepers, whose inexperience further encouraged the conspirators.

Hearts pounded as the hour approached; hopes soared. Then, at two o'clock, couriers began galloping back and forth outside. The Reserves came marching out of their camps in a body, forming in an awkward but ominous line of battle on a rise overlooking the stockade. The Florida regulars manned their battery, and finally Captain Wirz appeared on a sentry box. In his thick German accent, and with the best volume he could muster, he announced to the grimy masses once more that he knew their script, and that he would have no choice but to transform it into a tragedy by sweeping the prison with canister at the first hint of an uprising. The working crews kept digging as he spoke, uncovering several more tunnels and filling them all in: one of them reached sixty feet beyond the palisade.[25]

The people of Sumter County learned of the near escape via Saturday's issue of the *Republican*, which praised Captain Wirz for having discovered the plot in time. Citizens perhaps dreaded a mass escape worse than they feared Yankee cavalry, which might at least heed the discipline of its officers. Thousands of vindictive prisoners would know no such control, and the Americus editor predicted "murder and rapine would follow wherever they went."[26]

Inside the stockade, the failure so demoralized those who had been privy to the plan that most of them gave up the notion of escaping in common, assuming with good cause that no joint effort could elude the inevitable eye of a traitor. The blasted expectations tantalized their imaginations, and those prisoners who rose by four o'clock on the morning after the aborted escape thought they heard artillery fire, which they assumed heralded the advance of their own forces, but as though to seal their gloom some twenty-two hundred more captives were thrown into their midst over the next two days. In addition to breaking the conspiratorial spirit, the ill-fated attempt brought Furlow's militia battalion to Andersonville, and during the last four days of May Quartermaster

Winder braced the palisade from further undermining by clamping the tops together with great iron staples and a frieze of pine cleats. The artillerymen stood beside double-shotted guns, and all in all the prison was tighter than ever.[27]

Samuel Melvin left his comfortable fort on the outskirts of Washington at midnight of May 15, on his way to join the Army of the Potomac. The next day he spread his blanket under a tent at the mouth of Potomac Creek and slept, as he put it, "first rate." Perhaps few men so near the battlefront could sleep that well, especially when they had not yet known war up close, but Melvin was a special case: he was a heavy artilleryman, and all his duty had been of the spit-and-polish variety. Even with almost thirty-five months of service behind him he could listen to the cannon grumbling less than twenty miles away and write "Ain't this a gay romantic life?" To him it still was, for in fifty days he expected to climb aboard some steamer or train that would start him home to Lawrence, Massachusetts. What better topping on the sweet dessert of freedom than a few weeks of active campaigning and perhaps a battle to tell the folks about? Melvin was only twenty-one, and like most young soldiers on the verge of discharge he envisioned a blissful life of blue skies and fair weather, beginning with a long-planned voyage to England with his devoted companion, John Dow, who had recently become adjutant of the regiment.

The following day Melvin's enthusiasm waned. After marching all day with knapsacks strapped on over thick frock coats, his regiment reached the front, where Melvin slept cold on the ground in a place he could not name, unaware that he had come to the field known as Spotsylvania. Throughout May 18 he listened to the shelling and musketry ahead of him, watching doctors as they hacked off arms and legs in their mobile butcher shops. Once, when the regiment moved, he saw a dead man in the road. At night the erstwhile artillerymen—infantry, now—actually pitched their tents as though still involved in some practice bivouac. Veterans unrolling from sodden woolen cocoons must have laughed at them when the sun rose, but until noon these well-trained novices kept to their shelters. In the afternoon two Confederate divisions swept toward the Federal right flank, which consisted at the moment of those heavy artillerymen, and, for the first time since the war began, Samuel Melvin hurried himself to a real emergency. With the skirts of their coats flying behind them, the Massachusetts men raced across the farm of a young Virginia widow and leveled a volley at the enemy, who answered with a furious fire. The fight raged hotter than First Bull Run, and generated nearly as many casualties in one-third the time, among one-third the number of participants, but in the annals of this war it registered barely a footnote: the standards had changed by 1864.

For Private Melvin the battle of Harris's Farm carried greater significance, although he never learned the name of the struggle. Here he fired a rifle at live men for the first time; here he saw his companions maimed and killed. One wounded friend appealed to him for help, and Melvin gave him his shoulder in a three-legged race for the rear, but Southerners sprinted around the regimental line and tilted toward them. Melvin had to abandon his comrade to save himself, but in the smoke and confusion he must have turned the wrong way; soon he could see none but grey uniforms, and he threw down his rifle.

At first he registered nothing but praise for his captors. His feet still suffered from the punishing marches of his three days of active campaigning, and the Confederates who took him gave him a horse to ride; some of the guards bought his ration of coffee, albeit with Confederate money. Three days later, when they sent him to Gordonsville, he remarked that his escort proved "everlastingly kind," as combat soldiers tended to be toward prisoners. At Lynchburg he grew hungry, though, and found the local citizens hawking little loaves of bread at one dollar apiece, and a week after his capture he complained that he had been deprived of every possible comfort. The next day he and those taken with him began the slow, jolting journey south, and at noon of June 3 he jumped out of the boxcar at Camp Winder—as he (and some Confederates) called Andersonville—squinting at the bright sunlight after his seven days of virtual darkness. After the ritual assignment of detachment and mess, he passed by Captain Wirz's headquarters and through the south gate. By now the traffic of forty thousand feet had kneaded the banks of Stockade Creek into a great swamp, the morass extending up both slopes of the prison. The quagmire widened as it reached the skeleton framework of the sinks Wirz had just finished building near the eastern stockade wall, where the palisade choked the water's passage and created a nasty reservoir of diluted excrement every time it rained. The guards directed Melvin's detachment toward this reeking bog, and here the established prisoners seemed to wish them to camp, for they warned the newcomers away from the little alleys that survived between some of the shebangs.

This was the worst camp yet, even for the hardiest veterans, but it seemed more than the spirit could bear for brass-button soldiers who had slept in clean, spacious barracks only three weeks before. "And now our Sorrow has fairly begun," wrote a Pennsylvanian who had caught his first glimpse of the interior a few days previously. At last one of Melvin's messmates found someone willing to sell his tent site on higher ground, and for $4.50 the three of them moved up there. With no shelter they fared rather dismally that night, for the rain began early in the evening and came down hard for three hours, relenting only slightly before morning came. At the cost of another $5.00 they procured a rubber blanket for roofing, sitting huddled beneath it all day June 4 as the downpour continued, watching what seemed to be a steady procession of prisoners carrying dead men across the creek to the south gate.[28]

Samuel Melvin despaired almost immediately, though occasionally he tried to bolster his own courage with confident journal entries. That first full day at Andersonville, still hale and strong, he recorded his first doubts that he would survive. Beginning with the shock inflicted by the grisly sight that met them inside the south gate, bandbox soldiers like Private Melvin seemed to suffer worse than those captured fresh from the slaughter of the battlefield. Generally the garrison soldier entered the stockade better equipped than his battlefield counterpart, with more money and in better nutrition, but his morale—his determination to live— more often succumbed to the jarring contrasts in his condition. Neither Melvin nor his two partners would survive the summer, and at least sixty-four others of their regiment would perish at this place.[29]

The bright sunshine that greeted the prisoners of the 1st Massachusetts was a rarity for the month in which they arrived. May had been dry, and very hot, but as if to compensate for the deficiency the skies opened in a driving thundershower late on the morning of June 1, drenching the poorly protected inhabitants of the stockade. The next day remained cloudy but quite hot until another deluge descended late in the afternoon, lasting until nearly midnight. That pattern repeated itself on June 3; it poured all day long June 4, and each of the next seventeen days brought either heavy, soaking thundershowers or steady, round-the-clock rainfall. From the afternoon of June 11 until nearly noon on June 19 the sun never shone, and precipitation fell most of that time: one nonstop torrent lasted from Sunday evening, June 12, until Wednesday night, June 15.[30]

This monsoon turned the surface of the entire stockade into slurry. Those without tents or blankets had to walk about all night, hoping for enough of a respite during the day that they might sleep for a few hours in mud that was not too deep. Some, fortunate enough to own a shelter half, a rubber poncho, or a blanket, could not afford poles enough to support their structures against that volume of water: pockets filled and sagged between the fragile rafters, finally coming down on the occupants in the middle of the tempest. Even those with sounder homes, like the sailors who inhabited a village of blanketed longhouses near the south gate, awoke to a soaking as high winds or the sheer velocity of the rainfall drove moisture through the fabric. Others found themselves washed out of their blankets as runoff came sheeting down the slope from the northern end. At first the better-prepared prisoners—at least those who were not camped where the sinks backed up—viewed the daily afternoon showers as great purifiers because they carried much of the swamp sewage away and washed the constricted streets and paths clear of their scattered filth. The stockade trapped stagnant, fetid air laced with the searing pine smoke; the rain brought easier breathing, and seemed to suppress the smell for a time. But when the storms began to last all day, or for several days, and their every earthly possession turned green with mold, the prisoners grew disgusted. Both exercise and the usual prison commerce virtually ceased, but almost no one escaped a drenching, for endemic diarrhea and dysentery propelled an endless parade to the sinks and back even at the height of the storms, and every shoe collected several times its weight in mud. About the only items anyone tried to save from the ubiquitous water were diaries, and for all the protection a square-foot shred of poncho could offer, it was usually only the penciled entries that survived. To worsen the misery in the pen, the rain made for chilly nights, and one freak cold front dropped the temperature to what one Vermont cavalryman considered average for a winter day in Virginia. As anyone could have guessed, the pneumonia that had nearly disappeared with April began to show up again at Dr. White's hospital.[31]

The unprecedented wet season made hot meals even more vital to general health, but few enjoyed them. Captain Wirz had begun to allow small wood details to go out under guard again at the end of May, largely because the prison population had long ago outstripped the capacity of the cookhouse: as a result of the press of men, and possibly, too, because the shreds of cob baked into the cornbread proved painful to sensitive intestines, the quartermaster resumed issuing raw rations to alternate halves of the prison. Wirz sent out as many prisoners to chop wood as he could arrange to chaperone, on the old ratio of one guard to three men, but because the garrison afforded so few surplus troops the details frequently returned too short of wood to supply the prison: on the last day of May one New Jersey sergeant described two sticks of pine with which thirty men were expected to cook their dinners. Nor could they divide those pieces among themselves very equitably, armed with nothing more than a table knife and a railroad spike for splitting instruments. And even these understrength details could not always go out, for when some of the workmen gave in to the overpowering impulse to run away Captain Wirz would withhold the privilege for the next day. On the 9th of June he permitted no wood details to go outside; the next day he relented somewhat, but required anyone who wished to cut wood to sign a formal parole against any escape attempt. Those who swore to that oath found the guards exceedingly friendly and willing to do whatever they could for the prisoners, echoing the same familiarity and poor discipline that had led Wirz to forbid the wood details at the end of April. At least in one detachment, though, every last man refused to take the oath, so they realized no wood, but Wirz gave them cooked rations instead. Others complained over the next week of drawing no wood on one day or another, although some of them were issued raw rations almost continually.[32]

Not only did the rations come raw again now, but sometimes in noticeably reduced portions. On May 30, in particular, the distribution seems to have been stretched thin, probably to feed the sixty-four hundred men who had entered the prison over the past ten days—amounting to another 55 percent increase in the population. The prisoners complained directly to Colonel Persons when he visited the stockade, and he indignantly ordered an increase in the per capita ration: his orders were heeded instantly, and a Vermonter who had moped over drawing only a half-loaf of bread and about two ounces of meat on May 30 rejoiced the next day, when he got cornmeal instead of bread, remarking "if we can get as mutch meal every day we shall have plenty to eat." Such a sudden surge in demand might have caught the most efficient of commissary officers off guard, however, and nothing survives to indicate any extraordinary talent in the Andersonville Commissary Department. Captain James Armstrong, who had finally arrived from Columbus at the end of May on his assignment as commissary at Camp Sumter, now bore direct responsibility for keeping the storehouse full of enough food. Prison diaries tracked the success of his efforts, from the widespread complaint of short rations on May 30 to the grumbling over a lack of variety through the rainy weeks of June; later that month Armstrong's larder apparently caught up with the burgeoning mob of Yankees, and for several days the prisoners hailed a wonderful improvement in the quantity, if not the quality, of the food they received. On June 25 one of the Plymouth Pilgrims, accustomed to heaping garrison portions, commented "We got a very large ration, much more than we ever got in our own lines."[33]

Sometimes the shortages developed between the ration wagon and the individual soldier as a result of finagling or incompetence on the part of the sergeant in charge of his mess. These sergeants would detail a few men to carry the squad's allocation from the wagon to an area nearer their campsite, where the others gathered round with their cups, plates, or pieces of board or pantleg to collect portions of soggy rice or meal. Despite precautions intended to prevent favoritism, the system offered temptations for the weak-willed sergeant. Six days after his arrival from Plymouth, a Connecticut soldier noted that several prisoners had been caught defrauding their fellows of their food. "They are worse than the rebels," he concluded. On the same May 30 when his comrades noted a shrinkage in their issue, Sergeant Darius Starr supervised the apportionment in his mess, confessing "Drew rations & got a pretty good ration myself." Starr had been appointed to his position only that morning, after a dispute over the previous evening's lopsided dole, which had led to some men going without food altogether.[34]

Another difficulty may have been James Duncan, the man detailed to take charge of the cookhouse. Numerous prisoners suspected him of withholding portions of the rations issued to them, especially salt, which they claimed they had to buy from the guards. Salt represented one of the most prized and negotiable products in the wartime South, and anyone who handled the condiment found it a far more profitable item to embezzle than Confederate scrip; suspiciously enough, one citizen of hardscrabble Anderson Station began offering salt for sale that summer. Duncan ultimately proved to be less than scrupulous in his duties, and there is no reason to suppose that a profiteer would stop at salt. The prisoners detailed in the cookhouse and bakery would have had even greater reason than Duncan to misappropriate food, for, although they received an extra ration for their labor, they also needed vegetables and fruit to sustain good health. Such dainties could be had for a price, especially in early June, but they cost a great deal in the common coin of cornbread, particularly after many of the prisoners' palates began rejecting it.[35]

With June, cornbread and cornmeal became the principal staples of the prison diet. The bread, cooked from dough mixed with hoes in long, open troughs, might have revolted a free man at the outset. Frequently the inexperienced bakers fired their pans at too high a temperature in order to speed the process, turning out loaves that were charred on the outside and raw in the middle, but the most unappetizing feature of Andersonville cornbread was the crisp black morsels that filled it: one visiting Confederate observed that the dough seemed to be leavened with flies. In the suffocating heat of a Georgia summer the only way to ventilate the bakery was to throw open the doors and windows, and the stockade swamp bred clouds of flies that periodically hovered over the camp.

When inmates drew raw meal, they generally mixed it with a little water, put it over a stingy fire, and ate warmed mush. Some built clay ovens to bake their own bread, while the true gourmand rolled moistened meal into little dumplings to boil in the soup he made from bacon, beef, or beans. To avoid scurvy, some soaked their meal and deliberately let it sour, to distill a primitive beer that helped stave off the disease. The monotony of the diet eventually turned even the greedier appetites away from both meal and pone, and more than one prisoner made grim jokes about the "Corn-fed-eracy." Cases of diarrhea and dysentery multiplied and worsened as the coarse, unbolted meal took over the prison menu, while the cooking of it consumed much of the prisoners' time. Those with only a single cup or pan in their mess often detailed one man to keep that receptacle going all day, feeding the men in shifts—if they could find the wood.[36]

Henry Wirz tried early in June to improve both the amount and the palatability of the prison cornmeal. Appealing to Colonel Persons, he pointed out that fully one-sixth of the daily ration consisted of the ground cob, which so aggravated the intestinal diseases that were filling the cemetery. Wirz asked Persons to arrange for the quartermaster to bolt the meal or sift it before doling it out, mentioning that this would require him to add another quarter pound or more to meet the stipulated ration. Additionally, the captain wanted some buckets for the hundreds of messes within the prison that had no containers and could not draw their cooked beans, rice, or liquid rations like molasses and vinegar; he had heard that a supply of buckets at Columbus awaited only a requisition. Persons made another fruitless search for bolting cloth, but he could find neither that nor sifters large enough to satisfy the needs of twenty thousand men (similar requests by the commanders of Confederate troops had gone unanswered), but within five days of Wirz's application Quartermaster Winder did secure 450 buckets from the Columbus manufacturer. Some squads drew as many as four apiece.[37]

The Union prisoners' own homes provided one other source of nourishment. They were allowed to write letters home, and many did—usually as soon as they reached the stockade. These missives were restricted to a single page each, so as not to overburden the officers who had to censor them, and they could not discuss military operations. At least in the prison's early days most correspondents dared not speak ill of their captors, either, lest Confederate officials reject the letter out of spite. One of the Plymouth Pilgrims wrote his wife that his condition was "by no means a desirable one," but as a sop to the censor he added "I suppose it might be a great deal worse." Left unsealed, such letters were dropped in a small wooden mailbox near the south gate, and once they had been approved Captain Wirz would forward them to Richmond for delivery by flag-of-truce boat at City Point. The average soldier's first impulse was to assure his family that he was still alive, and to give them his address, but the new arrivals almost always asked for boxes of food or clothing, too. One terribly optimistic entrant asked his parents for a coat, shoes, stockings, a blanket, an assortment of knives, a bottle of whiskey or rum, and a bucket, besides an impossible list of groceries.[38]

These letters generally reached their destination (though sometimes not for many months), and the relished boxes frequently did come back, though occasionally only after having been lightened of contraband articles like liquor or weapons. Letters sent to the prison also reached the addressees, though somewhat irregularly, and each day clerks posted a list of recipients near the mailbox. Now and then injudicious comments condemned the epistle to the fireplace, but more often the envelope would fall victim to some express handler along the way who could feel the coins included inside for return postage; these same hands also rifled the boxes now and then.[39]

For some captives the stockade mailbox served as a vehicle for escaping the crowded interior, at least temporarily. Anyone who wished to communicate with Captain Wirz left a letter offering some special qualification for service outside, on parole. It might be that the applicant was a baker, or a carpenter, whose trade was useful; perhaps he was a hospital steward who could serve the post surgeon, or an experienced clerk, or a multilingual European capable of untangling the foreign tongues that isolated so many prisoners. As many as a hundred such Yankees wandered about on parole outside the palisade, keeping the prison's books and raising its buildings. The more stubborn Federals viewed them as traitors, especially when some of them seemed to be helping to build a battery commanding the railroad, 150 yards off the northwest corner of the prison: "forging their own chains," Sergeant Forbes called it.[40]

Such labor seemed little like treason to those who thus managed to earn double rations and temporary freedom from the cloud of prisoners. By the end of May crowding within the stockade had reached critical proportions: on the first of the month the Plymouth Pilgrims had taken the population beyond the most liberal estimate of its capacity, and every day brought hundreds more new prisoners. Informal lanes that had shrunk to eight feet in April disappeared altogether by the end of May, leaving only the two main thoroughfares running away from the gates, variously called South Street—or Main—and North Street, better known as Market. Richmond seemed deaf to all warnings that the prison had surpassed its manageable limit. As early as May 9 Howell Cobb had urged the expansion of the prison—it could not be begun too soon, he said. Major Turner had also recognized a few days later that Andersonville needed to be enlarged if it was to serve as a holding pen for the entire Confederacy, and he recommended a new enclosure on Sweetwater Creek, where the greater volume of water might keep the camp cleaner.[41]

Colonel Persons yearned to ease the overcrowding as much as anyone, and he made application for the expansion, but permission was slow in coming; he begged General Cobb for the services of an engineer—any engineer, but Cobb could find none free. Finally Persons began the work on his own initiative, but early into the project he discovered that resources at Camp Sumter prohibited an entirely new stockade. Hardware for two more sets of gates would have been difficult to procure, while a lack of support from the quartermaster general made it unlikely he would be able to hire the services of another practical mechanic like Mr. Heys, who would have been necessary to supervise the more complicated facets of construction. Colonel Persons was a lawyer, not an engineer; left entirely to his own devices, he had to resort to the simplest solution, and the one that would consume the least materials. He therefore chose merely to extend the existing stockade northward, which required him to build only three sides of the new rectangle and obviated thorny details like gates and stream diversions. The broadaxes and adzes that had squared the original stockade logs had departed with the impressed workmen who used them, so the new logs would have to go up with the bark on. General Cobb challenged Colonel Furlow with an offer to send his share of slaves to work on the addition if others would do the same, but the result was disappointing. Without authority to impress more labor, Persons relied upon Henry Wirz to supply him with workmen. A few of those who wished to take the jobs hesitated from either ethical reservations or the fear of their fellows, some of whom muttered about "building a cage for their own occupation," but later they may have regretted missing their chance: since the expansion would redound to their own benefit, and because outside work meant double rations, a sufficient number of prisoners came forward willingly enough. Colonel Persons himself supervised the layout, aiming for two stakes driven parallel to the east and west walls, a little over five hundred feet away. That plateau on Ben Dykes's property offered the most level land near the original prison, and would yield thousands of prime tent sites. Late in May the first few axes began singing, a cappella, the chorus growing fortissimo as June began.[42]

A week after the first yellow pine left its stump to become part of the new stockade, Ira Pettit rejoined his regiment near Bethesda Church, Virginia, not ten miles northeast of downtown Richmond. Ira had been guarding wagons for a couple of days, during which a sack of mail had reached his company. He found four letters held for him, one of them from his sister Lucinda, including a new photograph of her that revealed the same wide face and sleepy eyes of her soldier brother. Ira had read them all, tucked them in his shirt, and had fallen into lazy gossip with his comrades when the popping of musketry foretold trouble on the skirmish line. That yipping Rebel Yell quickly followed, catching the recumbent regulars off guard, and the right flank of the division buckled. Eventually the Federal commander swung reinforcements into line and plugged the gap, but not before the enemy swept up a couple of hundred prisoners—Ira Pettit among them.[43]

Hiram Jepperson had passed Bethesda Church that same morning: finally relieved of guard duty at Point Lookout, his 5th New Hampshire marched that way on the road to Cold Harbor. Charter members of the regiment doubtless pointed out the scenes of their passage there during the Peninsula campaign of 1862, but Hiram had not enlisted until August of that year, and he had had to lie about his age to do that. Now, a little older and a bit taller, he prepared to face his fifth battle. At the first hint of dawn the next morning his brigade trotted silently forward with the rest of Grant's line in an all-out assault on the Confederates' new works. Unlike the rest of the Union troops, the New Hampshiremen reached the enemy line and even bolted over the ramparts, chasing away the defenders. Converging fire from either side soon subdued the jubilant Yankees, though, killing forty-six outright in the 5th New Hampshire alone, and a counterattack drove the regiment back. The last of the

Federals dared not brave that crossfire, and so threw their hands in the air, and Hiram Jepperson was one of them. His comrades would suppose he had been killed, and that seems to have been fine with him.[44]

Both Ira Pettit and Hiram Jepperson left Richmond on June 8, arriving at Andersonville six days later in the midst of a three-day deluge. As they waited to be counted off in front of Captain Wirz's headquarters, on the prominence southwest of the stockade, they may have noticed the charnel wagon as it rounded the corner from the hospital with the day's grisly harvest—which, on June 14, included the emaciated corpse of the musician Thomas Genzardi, né Salvator Ginsardi.[45]

Despite the efficiency Colonel Persons manifested, the War Department wished to find a replacement for him—preferably someone of higher rank, since the commanders of all the Reserve regiments stood a grade above him. Henry Wirz had also requested a promotion as a means of gaining obedience to his orders and results from his requisitions, and John Winder had warmly recommended it, but no stars came for Wirz's collar; nor could the department have reasonably offered any promotion high enough to answer his needs. The garrison now consisted of four regiments of Reserves, Furlow's battalion, the detachment of the 55th Georgia, and Dykes's Florida battery, so a brigadier general would not be too exalted a personage to take over the post. Through May Howell Cobb had corresponded languidly about it with Richmond, making a nomination or two, but on June 2 he telegraphed President Davis directly, asking for an experienced officer.[46]

At Davis's behest, Samuel Cooper named John Winder himself, whom Cooper had recently offered his choice between that assignment and another. Winder had asked for the other, but the president's insistence forced Cooper to go back on his offer. On June 3 he sent Winder a special order putting him in command of Camp Sumter. Three days later, while the disgusted Winder and his son Sidney prepared for the disagreeable journey, Cooper sent him further instructions to make his personal headquarters at Andersonville, putting the name in quotation marks since it was still merely a nickname for the prison. In that message, Cooper also burdened Winder with the "general supervision" of the Macon prison.[47]

Word of Winder's coming raced ahead of him, filtering into the stockade by June 12, courtesy of a voluble Confederate surgeon. The general himself did not arrive until the 16th, passing right through Anderson

Station for Americus, where he hoped to rent a house and board his family. He stepped down in Americus just after another of those drenching downpours, followed by Sidney, one aide, and his inspector, Lieutenant Samuel B. Davis, who lamented drawing an assignment so far from his Richmond sweetheart. Winder took a room in town, waiting until morning to make the inaugural tour of his new bailiwick.[48]

Winder had perhaps anticipated great deficiencies, but when he made his debut at the depot he was stunned to find how few troops stood ready for duty, and how lax was their discipline. While inspecting the guard for more than twenty-three thousand prisoners he scanned rosters totaling only 2,867 men, the vast majority of them Reserves, fewer than 1,500 of whom were present for duty. The Reserves suffered particularly from illness; measles and pertussis had stricken these rural lads, most of whom had never seen anyone with such contagious diseases but who, for the first time, were now thrust into close proximity with men from populated areas. The camps had been located and arranged with little more forethought than a backwoods revival, and their grounds lay filthy and unkempt. The Reserves looked as raw as any men Winder had ever seen under arms, and the sentries' carelessness alarmed him. On June 13 two more prisoners had escaped from the resurrected wood details; that night, when seven sentry posts along the stockade failed to call the hour, Captain Wirz discovered that more than a dozen prisoners had tunneled out, and the missing guards had absconded with them. The very day that General Winder announced his assumption of the command, some of the woodcutters turned on their guards again and escaped. Winder thus introduced himself to his new subordinates to the distant echo of Ben Harris's baying hounds.[49]

In his first communication with Richmond, Winder advised Braxton Bragg that his force ought to be doubled if they were to avoid trouble, and the next day he rode up to Macon on the train, partly to inspect the prison there but primarily to ask Howell Cobb for more Reserves. It turned out that Cobb could not spare another man, yet on the day Winder visited Macon more than eight hundred Union prisoners passed him, bound for Andersonville from the west, where Bedford Forrest had captured them. Henceforth, Confederate victories would bring Winder nothing but grief.[50]

For all the labor expended on the prisoners' new hospital, that department remained entirely inadequate. With some twelve hundred patients, the enclosure already exceeded its maximum comfortable capacity by one-half, and the doctors had had to turn away at least that many less serious cases that might otherwise have merited admission. On June 19 alone the seven sick-call surgeons treated 2,665 "outpatients" in the little enclosures built for that purpose outside the south gate of the main stockade, and between sunrise of that day and the next dawn 40 men died in the hospital itself: at that rate, every one of the 1,222 men on the hospital register could expect to meet his Maker within a month. Chief Surgeon White counted more than two hundred tents within the board fence, but most of them were little shelter tents or flies in poor condition, and White needed walled hospital tents to the same number. He also needed better drugs, and more of them. In order to receive any medicines, he first had to send his requisitions to the medical director in Atlanta for approval, after which the purveyor in Macon would supply him with whatever proportions he had on hand—never anywhere near the prison's needs. The delay incurred by such triangular correspondence often left the Andersonville doctors without the antidote for certain illnesses until the outbreak had surged dangerously, or even subsided. Sometimes the hospital ran out of pharmaceutical supplies altogether: for three days in mid-June prisoners complained the doctors had nothing to prescribe at all. Often they would substitute herbs or folk remedies, handing out sumac berries by the spoonful to combat scurvy, or tiny pills of rolled pine pitch to curb diarrhea. Some days the surgeons simply held no sick call except to dress wounds, having nothing to offer for internal ailments.[51]

In the middle of June Surgeon White took another clerk into the hospital headquarters with him, to keep up with the growing list of patients. Dorence Atwater, a teenaged cavalryman captured during the Gettysburg campaign, started his duties by recording the names of deceased prisoners on June 15. Appalled at the number of entries he had to copy each day, he began surreptitiously transcribing the entire death register on loose sheets of paper. He consulted the earlier register to gather the names of everyone who had died since the beginning of the prison—commencing, ironically enough, with Adam Swarner, of Atwater's own 2nd New York Cavalry: within six weeks of taking the job, he would add the name of Swarner's brother Jacob, of the same regiment. The volume of deaths and the need for secrecy required him to work quickly, and when he could not decipher the previous clerk's orthography he made his best guess at the name, so his covert list contained many errors, but in a year's time it would serve as the basic source for identifying the graves of the dead. In June Atwater almost invariably scribbled a diagnosis of chronic diarrhea alongside a new entry, but amoebic dysentery had begun to make its appearance as the foul-smelling swamp filled with the infected cysts that carried the disease. The last victim of smallpox expired on the Fourth of July. The soaking rains of June brought several men to their graves with respiratory afflictions, an outbreak of typhoid claimed a few, and the near-total lack of vegetables was beginning to take its toll: among the myriad lists of intestinal ailments, Atwater recorded a few ominous cases of scurvy and dropsy; boys in their teens blamed rheumatism or sprains for the gradual stiffening in their legs, unconsciously recording the first symptoms of a disease that would kill them.[52]

In a tone that belied the urgency of the situation at Andersonville, General Winder recommended that his force be doubled and that a new prison ought to be instantly begun, to distribute the Yankees into more manageable camps. The concentration of prisoners—he now had more than twenty-four thousand—created an opportunity for the same dangerous shortfalls in provisions that had inspired the construction of Andersonville in the first place. When General Cooper responded to Winder's letter he said nothing about reinforcing the guard, merely demanding an accounting of the large number of absent Georgia Reserves—many of whom, it turned out, were detailed in their respective trades. Cooper did, however, authorize Winder to investigate new prison sites in Alabama. Perhaps thinking of the threatening situations that had developed during Colonel Persons's excursions away from the post, Cooper denied Winder's request to board in Americus: as unpleasant as Andersonville might be, that is where he must quarter himself. Winder considered the unanswered issue of reinforcements important enough to send his inspector, Lieutenant Davis, with a personal plea to Richmond; the lovesick lieutenant departed immediately.[53]

General Winder's energy, seniority, and his relative influence in Richmond do seem to have sparked a few rapid changes at the prison. Perhaps because Winder had better success demanding quartermaster and commissary funds, local purchasing agents began advertising for unlimited quantities of corn and bacon right after the general took command, and the prisoners noticed an immediate improvement in their rations. Work resumed soon afterward on the prison sinks and Stockade Creek, with a view toward reclaiming the offensive swamp and realizing Henry Wirz's double-dam notion, and carpenters began building a new cookhouse on the plateau beyond the stockade extension, to avoid contaminating the prison water supply. These and other ameliorations all began upon the appearance of a man posthumously charged with conspiracy to destroy the health of Federal prisoners.[54]

While he made provisions for the prisoners' health, Winder took simultaneous steps to prevent their getting away. He installed a young Georgia veteran as drillmaster, and he opened his first general order with an admonition to the sentries, whom he promised to hold responsible for any escapes. Those chasing the latest runaway woodchoppers showed none of their former restraint: they returned a few of them the next day, one of whom had been shot in the leg while another had been grazed on the head by a bullet. On June 19, one of the rare clear nights that month, a prisoner gained the sentry's permission to cross the dead line and kill a snake; another guard farther down the stockade saw him by the light of the full moon and, knowing nothing of the special arrangement, emptied his musket at the trespasser, wounding instead two innocent occupants of a nearby tent. Winder's stern official order to the guards went up on the gates and at the regimental headquarters on June 21, and discipline momentarily turned so strict that some prisoners suspected Union cavalry might be on its way. Testing his troops in the manner of new commanders in any era, Winder called out the entire garrison and kept it in line of battle all day, thus augmenting the rumors of a raid. Late that evening an unfortunate Pennsylvanian lost his balance as he tried to avoid one of the ubiquitous mudholes on his way to or from the sinks, and he crashed against the dead line. It was another clear night, and the moon had just begun to wane, so the Pennsylvanian also fell victim to a blast of buck-and-ball that struck him, some said, in the bowels: the officer of the guard climbed up to the pigeon roost and commended the young sentry even though the screaming prisoner lay on the proper side of the dead line. Security considerations kept the gates closed after dark, so the wounded man could not be taken to the hospital until the morning; his cries tormented the rest of the prisoners all night, but despite such inattention, despite the inevitability of peritonitis, and despite the next day's rumor that he had died, he appears to have recovered.[55]

General Winder's stringency seemed to convince the guards, at least the young ones, that it might be better to err on the side of the trigger. One greying private of the Reserves misinterpreted the sudden frequency of shootings as the product of adolescent longing to kill a Yankee and thereby establish manhood, and he forwarded his observations directly to the top. James Anderson sharpened a pencil and filled both sides of a small sheet with accounts of the shootings of June 19 and 21, directing the note to Jefferson Davis himself. Denying that he harbored any sympathy for Union soldiers, Anderson nonetheless asked the president if this were not un-Christian treatment of fellow humans, especially since there had been no real violation of prison discipline. Anderson hinted that he expected the president to conceal the source of the complaint from officers who might retaliate against him, but to no avail: Davis passed the letter on to the secretary of war, who in turn mailed it right back to Andersonville for General Winder's comment. By then Private Anderson had been detailed as passport agent on the Southwestern Railroad, but Winder appears not to have exacted any revenge upon him, allowing him to retain that more pleasant assignment and even authorizing a furlough for him.[56]

In order to back up his demanding discipline, General Winder installed a provost marshal and built him a strong log guardhouse with a miniature stockade, just across the tracks from the village, in which he might confine negligent or insubordinate guards. The provost marshal, Captain W. Shelby Reed, had come to Andersonville with the general on a thirty-day assignment; by the end of June Winder asked the adjutant general to leave Reed on the post permanently, since the consolidation of two regiments had left the captain without a company. Confederate soldiers at Camp Sumter soon came to call the guardhouse Castle Reed, in honor of both the captain and Richmond's infamous Castle Thunder.[57]

In spite of Winder's tightening of discipline, or perhaps in reaction to it, the prisoners continued to escape. The old general severely curtailed the wood details, later prohibiting them altogether and closing that path to freedom. Some of the other paroled workmen broke their word and bolted, like Sidney Moore of the 154th New York, who was one of the few to get away clean. Moore slipped off from his job as a carpenter at the new bakery on the evening of July 8, traveling at night with infrequent meals begged from slave cabins. Twenty days later he encountered roving Federal cavalry south of Atlanta, and within another week he had shouldered a new rifle and rejoined his regiment.[58]

Moore enjoyed rare luck, though, and most of those who craved liberty were forced to fall back on their tunnels, which multiplied in late June and early July. Nearly all these desperate burrows began north of Stockade Creek, where a higher concentration of clay offered more tenacious earth: most of the sandier soil south of the swamp would cave in at a touch. Confederate officers learned—or were told—of three tunnels in the two days after the last dead-line shooting, one of them stretching an unbelievable 130 feet beyond the stockade wall; one lay beneath the treacherous topsoil of the south side. The discoveries seemed to come with the help of informers, for prison officials often marched straight to the mouth of a shaft; sometimes they detected the masterminds of the various efforts, forcing them to dig up their own tunnels and bury them again.[59]

For all the odds against them, determined and clever Yankees kept digging. Armed with tin plates, an occasional shovel, or even oyster shells, they frequently started their holes from a well. Prisoners had been digging such wells for fresh water ever since the creek became tainted with runoff from the cookhouse refuse and the internal sinks. The water that came straight out of the ground may have been a little gritty, but it was purer and delightfully cooler. One of the Plymouth Pilgrims sank his well less than three weeks after he arrived, hitting plenty of water twelve feet down. The groundwater table did not rise so high farther up the slope, so other wells went much deeper. Several soldiers fell into them in the darkness, and on the night of June 19 three tentmates tumbled into their well when its soggy sides gave way: one of them suffocated before his friends could dig him out. Captain Wirz asked James Duncan to deliver his empty commissary barrels to the prison for use as curbs around the wells, both to prevent such cave-ins and to keep men from falling headlong down the holes.[60]

Some of these excavations provided good water, while many merely served to disguise tunnel entrances for diggers who had no intention of finding water. At night they would fill up the bottom of the hole with dirt from the tunnel, which began halfway up the shaft, and by day they would pretend to continue the well, removing the refuse material without exciting suspicion. Wells that seemed to remain forever under construction chanced drawing the attention of would-be informants, but that was the only reasonable means of tunneling. The method of secretly disposing of hundreds of cubic feet of dirt in makeshift bags—described by some Andersonville memoirists—not only carried greater risk of discovery but wore out the prisoners' supply of such bags; once well-digging began, the former practice ended.

The sergeant major of the 16th Connecticut undertook three tunnels in just ten days. He abandoned the first on May 21, when he broke into the side of the old hospital latrine; the second caved in after he and his cohorts had bored ninety feet through the clay; the third actually led five men to temporary freedom on the morning of June 10, but the sergeant major did not join them.[61]

Those who succeeded in opening their tunnels seldom ran far before they were caught. Their absence could not go undetected long beyond the morning roll call, and usually a freshly opened tunnel would continue belching bodies until a sentry sounded the alarm, bringing out the rest of the troops and the dogs. General Winder dispensed with the contracted services of Benjamin Harris, instead detailing a corporal of the 1st Georgia Reserves to keep his own dogs near the prison. Edward C. Turner brought his hounds from White County and tied them near his quarters, between the stockade and the railroad tracks. A fellow Confederate said the forty-seven-year-old Turner "looked as if he had seen pretty hard times," but now the erstwhile farmer began to prosper. The quartermaster offered a reward of thirty dollars for each escaped prisoner returned to the prison—the same amount then paid for the capture of deserters; with the help of a young private from the 3rd Reserves named Driskill, Turner began collaring hundreds of dollars' worth of Yankees.[62]

While some prisoners did their digging below the surface, others continued to shovel dirt above ground. Those laboring on the new stockade did so because they believed it would ease their overcrowding, which had reached unbearable proportions. The procession of new prisoners seemed never to end, though. Nearly 1,200 entered the stockade on June 15, only somewhat fewer the next day, and over 400 more two days later. Another 877 entered the day after that, and 813 between June 21 and 24. "There is hardly room for them to lie down," wrote one prisoner, echoing similar observations in other diaries. Those who swung the axes and shovels apparently began to think along the lines of the New Jersey sergeant who had accused them of "forging their own chains": rather than working for their own comfort, it appeared they were just helping their captors to accommodate more prisoners. On June 25, with the addition nearly finished, the working crews struck. It also happened that the prisoners were told on June 25 that no more letters would be accepted for forwarding, but any connection between those two events is difficult to trace: perhaps the workmen threw down their tools in protest of the withheld privilege, but it seems more likely that the work stoppage was related to the accelerating influx of prisoners. In fact, the threat to cut off postal service may have come in response to the laborers' action, for both mail circulation and the stockade project resumed simultaneously.[63]

The overcrowding, the monotony, the bland and unvaried diet, and the endless cavalcade of death started wearing upon the prisoners, creating a completely new disease. A gradual decline in hygiene seemed to be the first symptom. As early as the first of May the personal cleanliness of the prisoners became the subject of public comment when the Americus newspaper editor remarked on the abundance of water in the stream and the failure of the Yankees to avail themselves of it. One of the Plymouth

Pilgrims who went into the stockade on May 3 also found plenty of water, but stood dumbfounded at the filthy inmates, whom he likened several times to "rotten sheep," blaming them for their own condition. Late arrivals might have raised the excuse that they had no soap (though that did not stop others from bathing), but the quartermaster was still issuing soap at least as late as May 20. Most of those who initially resolved to keep clean later lost that determination, and diary entries of daily trips to the stream often began to lapse after the first couple of weeks' confinement. By summer's end nearly everyone seemed content to wallow in filth.[64]

Next, the unwashed prisoner despaired of ever gaining his freedom. Exchange rumors filled the camp almost every day, promising release in "a week," or as soon as the summer campaign was over, or on some specific date. So persistent was the story of a July 7 date for parole, which appeared to be corroborated by the compilation of descriptive lists on July 4, that even the most skeptical dared to hope; the camp therefore sank into universal gloom when that day passed. Some of the rumors originated with Confederate officers or newspapers, or even New York papers, as a byproduct of the confusing exchange negotiations; others sprang spontaneously from wishful thinking.[65]

Whatever the source, the serial disappointments withered the will of hundreds of men who, saddened by the death of so many comrades and by the ubiquitous misery, simply gave up the struggle for life while still in perfect health. Some expressed an unshakable apathy, not even caring for news from home; some stopped eating. By the second half of June the prison doctors began treating patients for something they called "nostalgia": between June 18 and 20 eleven prisoners were carried to the gate with this vague malaise. It might even have been contagious, considering that the first six admissions came from only three squads, and it appeared to strike the youngest especially hard, with drummer boys, civilian newsboys, and navy powder monkeys among the first few victims diagnosed. The chief surgeon gave it the label of "mental depression," stumbling upon the term psychologists later adopted for it, and he deduced that it robbed the sufferers of their resistance to the diseases around them. Indeed, three of those first eleven died, and inside the stockade other seemingly robust young men began to lay themselves down and perish from what amounted to terminal homesickness.[66]

4 ❧ T A Deep and Muddy River

he four-gun Federal steamer *Water Witch* lay at anchor behind Ossabaw Island, south of Savannah, on the evening of June 2, 1864, the anniversary eve of her last commissioning at New York. Theoretically the crew's one-year enlistment would end that day, but American sailors of that century were not traditionally released until the cruise formally ended with the ship's return to its home port. This habit sometimes created hard feelings among those who did not care to ship over, and antagonism of that sort may have contributed to the careless atmosphere on the deck of the *Water Witch* that night. The previous afternoon the officers had held the customary inspection, and the crew had practiced clearing the decks for action and loading the guns, but dismal rain and pitch dark had prompted the skipper to drop anchor with landfall dangerously close on either side of the sound. Nor did he cast out picket boats, judging that his crew of sixty-five was too small to afford piecemeal distribution, even for that precaution.

In fact, the crew of the *Water Witch* was too small to neglect such a precaution. The vessel's greatest threat lay in any boarding party that might be allowed to venture too close, and sometime after midnight that hypothetical boarding party cast off: 117 Confederate sailors and 15 officers in seven cutters, guided by a slave pilot in the lead boat, slithered toward the somnolent prey like so many crocodiles. In the glow from a bolt of lightning, the inexperienced deck officer of the *Witch* glimpsed one of the boats, hailed it, and was answered with "Who the hell are you hailing?" The Southern lieutenant leading the expedition bounded aboard the steamer as his men opened a volley, completely surprising the four-man watch, but the supine Yankees fought valiantly once aroused. They killed the Confederate lieutenant, his pilot, and several of his men, but the boarders swarmed over the bulwarks too quickly to be stopped by a few cutlasses and revolvers. The Federal officer, a mere acting master's mate, forgot to sound the usual signal to repel boarders, so his assailants easily gained control of the hatches.[1]

Belowdecks, British-born Andrew Muir awakened to the racket of shooting and shouting, and with the rest of his mates he tried to reach the fracas, but within ten minutes it was all over. Two of the crew lay dead, thirteen were wounded, and the rest were all either unarmed or disarmed, so there was nothing to do but surrender. One crewman, an escaped slave, slipped over the side and swam to the island, where a U.S. bark picked him up in the morning. The rest, including the short, brawny Muir, remained aboard the *Water Witch* until her pilotless captors ran her aground the next day, whereupon they transferred the prisoners to shore and started them for the interior. Young Muir must have lapsed nearly into shock: having completed his year's contract by more than a week, he had every right to look forward to his discharge and a berth in the profitable wartime merchant service. Perhaps an impulsive yen for adventure had spurred him to enlist, or a thirst for prize money, but his ship had taken no prizes and at this very moment he enjoyed the bitter fruits of his only naval adventure. His entire life had seemed to stretch before him like a gilt gift just the night before, but instead of tasting the exhilarating freedom of mustering out he was forced to endure a journey inside baggage cars ending, on June 7, with the rotting smell that greeted nostrils new to Anderson Station.

The twenty-two-year-old sailor lined up with hundreds of Yankee soldiers, his own crewmen, and some bluejackets from Richmond prisons while pencil-toting Confederates counted them. With his reddish hair, ruddy complexion, and stocky stature, the guards might readily have guessed his Irish bloodline, but that meant nothing to them: all they wanted to know was his name, which they credited to the second squad of the twenty-seventh detachment. That done, they pulled the creaking south gates open and waved in more than a thousand fresh prisoners, taking them inside in whatever increments they could crowd within the gate enclosure at one time. In the middle of the afternoon Seaman Muir marched into the stench of the stockade, came to a halt, and fell out of line to look for a place where he might lay down that evening. Just south of him stood the raiders' promiscuous complex, and if he glanced back toward the gate he might have seen the other sailors' lodges, but he was probably delayed in his decision by the crush of people who would have kept him milling along South Street. At some point in this preliminary perambulation he may well have lingered an instant over the exact spot where he would die, thirty-four days later.[2]

In their substantial shanties near the south gate, the chief raiders may have noted the rugged little sailor and offered him a haven, or a taste of food. However it came about, within a few days he had aligned himself with one of the gangs, each of which needed regular recruits not only to prey upon more victims but to fend off the raids of other bands that coveted their accumulated wealth. One faction that stood distinct was a syndicate of gamblers who congregated near Mr. Selman's sutler hut, by the north gate, whose cash attracted interest from all the raiders; their very affluence behooved them to unite for their own protection.[3]

The same afternoon that Seaman Muir entered the gate, one shocked Yankee scribbled an observation that unscrupulous prisoners did not wait for a dead man to cool before rifling his pockets, and at night they grew even bolder, robbing sleeping denizens in their shebangs by either cutting out their pockets or putting knives to their throats, sometimes running away with even the blankets that covered them. The stouter and better-prepared inmates managed to fight off their assailants, and lone raiders still frequently suffered beatings, head-shaving, bucking and gagging, or summary immersion in the more disgusting end of the creek, but by the middle of June the raiders had so well augmented their ranks that most attempts at resistance failed.[4]

Organized daylight robberies, such as that of May 27, became more frequent. On June 13 one man was relieved of his cap and canteen at midday, while he suffered a seizure. Just before noon on June 18 a Pennsylvanian named Erwin was knocked to the ground and robbed of his watch and nearly a hundred dollars. Three Jerseymen tenting together found themselves set upon by a platoon of burly thugs who took everything they had, down to their boots and blankets. An orderly sergeant, either too new or too naive to fear the thieves, was lured into one of their tents on June 27 and robbed of fifty dollars, and that same afternoon raiders roamed all over the camp, pillaging virtually at will. Estimates of their total number ran as high as 400 or 500; one who was in a way to know thought them only 150 or 200 strong, but that constituted a sufficient force to terrorize the milling masses: some of the more brazen of them swore they would seize every cent in the prison by the Fourth of July, if they had to kill everyone who resisted them.[5]

A lanky Illinois cavalryman wondered whether he could not do something about the raiders. Sergeant Leroy Key, a Mississippian by birth, had turned twenty-four years old that summer: at six-foot-two he was one of the bigger men in the prison. For a brief spell early in life he had hoped to became a wagonmaker, but he had spent most of his days as a farmer near Bloomington, and the work had made him strong. Measles had put him on his back eighteen months before, and a surgeon's suspicion of incipient tuberculosis had led to Key's discharge from the infantry, but Key doubted the diagnosis enough to reenlist in the 16th Illinois Cavalry. He was indeed sick, and his lungs would kill him by the time he was forty, but he felt fit enough for a scrap now, even after four months in this hellhole.[6]

Sergeant Key conspired with other prisoners to found a prison defense force. Secretly, lest the raiders attack them before they were ready, they began forming into companies of thirty men, each headed by a dependable "captain." By June 28 they had wholly or partly organized thirteen such companies, and Key judged he was nearly ready to initiate his attack. Word had leaked out, though, and that afternoon Key was strolling near the north end of the prison when he recognized Charles Curtis standing before him, suspiciously far from his customary range. Hearing the pounding of feet behind him, Key turned to find five of Curtis's henchmen bearing down on him with knives in their hands. Curtis approached to whispering distance and reached up (he was fully half a foot shorter than Key) to put his hand on the vigilante chief's shoulder, pulling the taller man back around to face him; Curtis, too, held a knife now. He told Key he had heard the cavalryman was recruiting a band to "clear out the Irish." Key denied it.

"Well," Curtis said, "you are getting up a band for some purpose; what is it for, if not to clean out the Irish?" Key responded rather boldly that he aimed to rid the camp of raiders, not Irish, advising Curtis that he had nothing to fear unless he considered himself a raider. Perhaps thinking that Key was just another competitor, and thus a potential ally, Curtis put away his knife and shook hands with him, gesturing that he was free to go. At least that was the way Key told it five months later, and he went on to say that that night of June 28 the camp was filled with cries for help, punctuated by an occasional shout that someone was being murdered. Such sounds had become commonplace, though, and Key dared not risk his half-organized and unarmed police force in the dead of night.[7]

The next afternoon a prisoner named Dowd, said by some to be a newcomer, was confronted in his tent by a squad of ruffians who demanded the money they knew he owned. The men not only outnumbered him, they were armed with an assortment of Bowery-style weapons, but Dowd courageously refused to yield anything up, even after they began beating him. He fought them, alone, until they had pounded his face bloody and pinned him to the ground. They cut nearly two hundred dollars out of the waistband of his trousers, where one of their snitches had seen him sew it, and they pulled his watch out of his pocket. So battered was Dowd's face, and so still did he lay, that the news spread around the stockade of a murder committed in daylight, but Dowd regained his feet not long after they left him. He staggered over to the gate, asking the sentry to call the officer of the guard.[8]

Dowd's bludgeoned face and bleeding shins testified to the brutality of the attack, and the officer called for the sentry to let him out of the wicket. Dowd remained at headquarters about an hour, after which he returned with a detail of Confederate guards led by a lieutenant. They strode directly down Market Street while Dowd pointed out the men who had attacked him, incidentally fingering the more notorious of the other raiders. One of those whom Dowd accused, John Sarsfield, promised he would "cut Dowd's heart out and throw it in his face" as the guards marched him away. The first few arrests came easily enough, but as the chilling news spread through the brigands' hovels they started looking for places to hide, eluding the guard detail very effectively for a time.[9]

Dowd's success with the officer of the guard probably stemmed from the efforts of Sergeant Key, who—either personally or through an envoy—had asked for Wirz's assistance that morning as the captain walked the dead line. Key promised not only to help ferret out the raiders, but to institute an internal police force. At first Wirz shrugged off their pleas about the lawless element, snorting that it was shameful for twenty-five thousand men to let a few dozen thugs intimidate them, but the appearance of the battered Dowd helped change Wirz's mind, and he reconsidered Key's offer. In light of his own limited manpower, Wirz asked the quartermaster to supply these vigilantes with clubs. During the course of their discussion with the commandant the prisoners asked if they might not punish the raiders, and Wirz promised they could, provided they adhered to the rules of courts-martial and if their sentences were approved by higher authority: he consulted General Winder on that point, and the general sustained him.[10]

Encouraged by Wirz's cooperation, Key and his "regulators," as they came to be known, christened their cudgels in the hunt for fugitive raiders on June 29. They chased them to every corner of the prison, and savage brawls erupted as the more stubborn rascals resisted lopsided odds. Once cornered, most of the miscreants went down before a tight crescent of flailing clubs, though a few of the more determined endured a dreadful pounding before they would yield. As each of the ruffians surrendered he was thrown out the gate to the Confederates, who put him under guard. The prison cadre appear to have manacled some of them with ball and chain, and put others in the stocks, but they confined the majority of them in the gate enclosure, and by late afternoon several dozen bandits stood within that smaller stockade. Concerned at the crowding of so many dangerous men inside that little pen, Wirz insisted that a portion of them would have to be released. Against the protest of the new regulators, some of those suspects who had no serious accusations levied against them were thrust back into the general prison population. When the other prisoners heard they were coming, they rushed to the gate to meet them, falling quickly into opposing ranks as though for a stag version of the Virginia reel, but this proved a more deadly cotillion, for as the freed raiders reentered the prison the twin receiving line bristled with a motley array of clubs: the villains-turned-victims dared not turn right or left, lest they invite a charge of buckshot from the sentries, so they had to run the gantlet. They put their arms over their heads and sprang forward, but those who staggered or fell met no mercy. That evening the story drifted through the rest of the prison, and out to the Confederates, that one of the culprits had been beaten to death.[11]

The hunt for more of the principal raiders continued into the twilight. Tasting certain victory and augmented by volunteers, the relentless posses prowled and probed in every hovel, spinning the entire prison into such a frenzy that Wirz thought it imprudent to open the north gate to let the ration wagon through: besides, the quartermaster's men were all occupied in the chase, and calling the detachments for distribution would interrupt the manhunt. A ration of meat had been issued that morning, leaving at least some of the recipients commenting on the generous quantity, so the captain announced that no more food would enter the stockade until all the suspects had been rounded up. Even with their bellies growling, some of the Yankees silently praised the prison keeper for taking such an interest in their welfare, one of them confiding to his diary that "Capt. Wurtz deserves great credit for his prompt action in the matter."[12]

Pursuit resumed in the morning, with Confederate soldiers and regulators again poking and snooping indiscriminately. The tide had obviously turned, and most of the fugitives relied more on concealment than resistance; some of them even buried themselves in the burrows dug by tentless prisoners on the steep slope north of the creek, closing up all but a fraction of the entrance. The more peaceable inmates were occasionally surprised to hear of messmates or members of their old companies who had been arrested as raiders, and it appears that at least a few perfectly innocent men landed in the impromptu jail merely on the word of malicious companions bent on settling a personal grudge.[13]

At nine o'clock that morning, when he would ordinarily have been holding roll call, Wirz called the detachment sergeants to his headquarters. They gathered more than a hundred strong in front of his office door, where he apprised them that General Winder had approved their request for a trial of the raiders by their true peers. The sudden and enthusiastic applause of the sergeants startled the colonel of the 1st Georgia Reserves, who stood nearby, and the colonel ambled up to see what was going on. Wirz told the sergeants he must have a pool of two dozen competent jurors from their ranks—preferably from among the most recent arrivals, to avoid undue bias—and he tossed some slips of paper into one of their tall Hardee hats. The sergeants began drawing, and, when the required twenty-four had drawn marked ballots, Wirz signaled a clerk to take down the jurors' names. With that he nodded to the guards, who faced the sergeants about and marched them back into the prison; they were undoubtedly the only Yankees ever to pass into that stockade cheering.[14]

The trials opened immediately. A member of the 8th Missouri assumed the role of judge advocate, appointing counsel for the defendants, and together they empaneled a twelve-man jury from the twenty-four. Edward Wellington Boate, a fortyish newspaper reporter skilled in shorthand, served as court clerk. The court sat inside the south gate enclosure, and the raiders were brought in singly to face their accusers. Witnesses one after another recounted tales of robbery, beatings, and murder, most of them no doubt exaggerated, although many a prisoner had probably died as a result of the drubbing these men gave him, or from the lack of clothing, shelter, food, or money they had taken from him. Even as the court heard testimony, regulators ransacked the raiders' dens, turning up thousands of dollars in buried cash in addition to watches, jewelry, weapons, and—as rampant rumor had it—the mortal remains of at least one of their victims. No one seemed willing to say he had actually seen a corpse himself, but as the story circled the camp it grew, with two bodies found and, finally, "several."[15]

During the course of the day the wicket door opened to release numerous minor malefactors back into the stockade, where they had to run a gantlet that now stretched 150 yards into the prison, but in spite of the expansion of that punishment no more fatalities resulted. Others among the accused drew lighter sentences in the way of corporal punishment, or were even set free, but six had been condemned to hang. Most of their names probably surprised no one: big Willie Collins, the notorious "Mosby" whom prisoners recognized as the foremost of them all; Charles Curtis; John Sullivan (Collins's principal cohort); Patrick Delany; John Sarsfield (who would not be cutting out anyone's heart); and auburn-haired Andrew Muir, the desperate young sailor who, but for the negligence of his commanding officer, might have been safe at home or aboard some sleek merchantman. Muir had been in the stockade for twenty-three days now.[16]

John Winder declined to execute these sentences until they had been approved at Richmond, and he sent Edward Boate's transcripts to the capital by special messenger; meanwhile, the half-dozen condemned men went into the stocks, wondering whether their fellow prisoners would ever find either the authority or the nerve to hang them. Dowd, his face still swollen and bruised, gathered up his belongings that evening and set up camp outside, on parole of honor to stay within a mile of the stockade, Captain Wirz having offered him that chance to elude the vengeful friends of the criminals he had undone.[17]

While the raiders had been essentially eliminated, and the regulators instituted a police court to adjudicate future differences between inmates, Andersonville's other miseries had not abated. The worst problem facing the prisoners on June 30—once rations were finally issued—was the sheer lack of space. The 16 stray captives who arrived that day carried the stockade population over 25,000, exclusive of another 1,400 in the hospital, and these men shared the habitable portion of the original sixteen acres. After deducting the swamp and the dead line, about eleven acres remained in which those 25,000 might perform all the functions of life. That worked out to barely twenty square feet of ground per man: almost precisely the surface area of a common grave.[18]

The mere difficulty of moving around convinced Captain Wirz to suspend the daily roll calls after June 20, and the last day of that month saw the worst overcrowding in the prison's history. The next morning, while excited witnesses wrapped up their testimony at the raiders' trials, some axes began to echo from the northern wall of the stockade, and before long some of the logs there fell, revealing a second palisade on the other side: the addition begun by Colonel Persons had been finished. The woodchoppers—detailed Yankee prisoners—opened a ten-foot gap in the wall, and Confederate officers pronounced the extension ready for occupation. Every detachment numbered above forty-eight, they said, would have to move into the new area.[19]

Despite the filth in the old stockade, many prisoners preferred to remain. Their little shebangs provided relative comfort, and many of those structures' fragile frameworks might not bear dismantling and reassembly. Some had paid considerable money to former tenants for their sites, while others had improved their locations with wells, which provided them with not only water but income: temporary "water privileges" sold for twenty cents. So many displayed a reluctance to move that orders came for everyone in the subject detachments to file into the new enclosure on penalty of having their shelters and property confiscated. Some prisoners heard this directive announced in conjunction with a two-hour deadline, which precipitated a minor panic around ten o'clock as more than twelve thousand men, some of them quite feeble, lumbered toward the north wall under the burden of all their earthly belongings. There were those who welcomed the change, though, like one Pennsylvanian who had been forced into a plot near the swamp, where the stench hung thickest. Some who wanted to stay where they were avoided the migration by exchanging squads with men in lower-numbered detachments who occupied more undesirable portions of the old stockade. At least one sailor whose shebang sat close to the north wall remained within earshot of his 69th detachment without budging at all.[20]

The imagined two-hour limit notwithstanding, the pitiful little hegira lasted more than six hours. As the bedraggled wayfarers trundled through the aperture, Confederates promised (in good faith) that they would soon see some actual barracks: even as they spoke, the quartermaster was looking for lumber and tools, that they might construct their own buildings. The shuffling prisoners seemed to believe that pledge no more than they credited the occasional assurance of an imminent exchange agreement, but the clean ground and fresher air brightened their spirits. Their departure from the old stockade also sweetened the air noticeably there, some thought, by spreading out their collective respiration.[21]

The street system in the original enclosure had evolved haphazardly, with the two principal avenues extending from the gates and a number of smaller, perpendicular paths running over at least the northern end of the prison; another track, called Water Street, connected the two main boulevards via the narrow end of Stockade Creek. These passageways had grown increasingly crowded with the prison's homeless, especially in the closing nights of June, when they could find nowhere else to sleep. A regular pattern of streets in the new section was therefore one of the prison keepers' first considerations, and Confederate sergeants did reserve the lanes, but the bustle of moving made them difficult to navigate for days.[22]

Water posed the first and greatest problem on the new ground. Those who had owned wells on the other side had been forced to abandon them, so the only source was the common trough at the stream, which turned a tad greasy when runoff washed over the cookhouse refuse that lay just upstream from the stockade. The cleanest portion of the available stream, at the western dead line, lay some four hundred yards away from the most distant corner of the new stockade. The actual passage of that route covered a much greater distance, all of it through the mud churned by a teeming multitude with fifty thousand feet and just as many elbows, which offered the constant threat of a spill. Tents had therefore hardly sprung up in the new section before the more industrious began boring for water. Within two days the fresh plain was pockmarked with the mouths of new shafts, but the lower water table here turned these projects into major undertakings, in which whole detachments collaborated. More than a week after the addition opened, a Connecticut sergeant major from the south side wandered up on the plateau to visit, finding one well that he probably overestimated at sixty-five feet deep—and still dry. A Vermont cavalryman who ought to have been accustomed to deep wells in his own rockbound hills seemed surprised when his messmates did not strike water until they had dug what they, too, may have overreckoned at fifty-eight feet.[23]

If there was initially no water, there was at least an abundance of fuel.

The working crews had left great heaps of slash and limbwood, and by their first evening the residents of the new stockade began to flail at the remnant of the partition between themselves and the old prison. Axes came out of hiding places and sang away all night, and on the morning of July 2 only a fragment of the intervening wall stood upright at either end, where the woodchoppers dared not trespass upon the dead line. Whole messes laid in a substantial store of wood, and one cavalryman supposed that he and his tentmates had amassed enough to last all summer. Richard Winder had had plans for those timbers, though: Wirz wanted him to build a good bridge over Stockade Creek. In the morning Winder sent a detail inside to confiscate what axes he could find and whatever logs still remained intact; to assist him, Wirz withheld rations on that end of the prison until Winder collected enough material for his bridge.[24]

It was well the prisoners stockpiled what fuel they could put their hands on. The extension of the walls added numerous sentry posts to the stockade, bringing the total to fifty-two, which increased Captain Wirz's daily guard detail and strained the understrength garrison anew. The escapes of June had sparked Wirz to consider prohibiting any more details from passing out to the forests, especially after the embarrassing episode on the first day of General Winder's tenure, but with the combination of plentiful wood inside the prison and additional pressure on the guards outside, Wirz—or more likely General Winder—finally resolved to withhold the privilege. For the next six weeks, the only men who would carry firewood into the stockade would be those who had already sworn to paroles for work outside.[25]

The sergeant major of the 16th Connecticut, Robert Kellogg, was among the last that June to enjoy the outside air, which prisoners thought so sweet and visitors found so putrid. Just before the crusade against the raiders opened, he spent two consecutive days cutting wood, and as the guards led his detail back to the stockade one afternoon he spied some "redroot," a prized tuber on the Andersonville menu. He dug at it hastily, alternately whittling at it with his pocket knife and pulling on it with both hands. Finally the sergeant of the guard, whose relief was nearly up, forced him to abandon the effort and fall in with the rest of the detail. In his disappointment Kellogg forgot his knife in the dirt, and failed to notice the loss until they had reached the shadow of the gate. He pleaded with the sergeant, who refused to let him return for it, perhaps suspecting another Yankee trick. A knife was too vital a possession for any prisoner to let go without a struggle, though. As they neared the stockade gate Kellogg saw Captain Wirz sauntering by on his old white mare, and he made bold enough to hail him. Wirz listened patiently to the prisoner's story, then told Kellogg to lead him to the spot. While the sergeant major trotted back toward the wood line, the captain rode along behind; a happy Kellogg found his knife, and the prison commander personally escorted him back to the south gate.[26]

Fifteen months later Sergeant Major Kellogg would return this favor by doing his best to see that Henry Wirz was hanged. While admitting he had never seen Wirz inflict any cruelty upon a single prisoner, Kellogg nevertheless maintained that the commandant must have done so. In the presence of the man who had taken time from his endless duties to help an anonymous prisoner retrieve his knife, Kellogg told the eager officers of the military commission, "We all understood him to be a cruel, over-bearing, heartless man."[27]

The vacation from roll calls ended amid drum taps at nine o'clock on the morning of July 3. Those drums—beaten by Federal prisoners, who provided their captors with the only musical talent at Andersonville—brought the camp to its feet. The Georgian roll-call sergeants, their pockets bulging with onions and eggs to sell to the prisoners on the sly, called their various squads into formation. The two-week lapse in the daily routine had taken a toll, however, and a task that usually required no more than two hours collapsed in confusion after several. Better than three thousand prisoners had come in since June 20, had never attended a roll call at the prison, and had no idea where to line up; half the camp had moved into the new stockade, leaving no one certain where the detachments should assemble; hordes of men had furtively changed squads, either to avoid or to take part in the resettlement, and to further confound matters many of them decided they had made bad bargains and tried to cancel those exchanges with unwilling parties. July 3 saw the customary quota of flankers, too, who flitted from squad to squad collecting dead men's rations.[28]

Death and hospital admissions had whittled most detachments well below their complement of 270 men by now, so Captain Wirz decided to rectify that problem and sort out the jumbled roll call at the same time. For the second time since he came to Camp Sumter, he ordered the sergeants to resquad the entire prison.

While the normal roll call might have posed a nuisance, especially for those impunctual enough to be caught cooking priceless food with scarce fuel, it was not particularly strenuous. Confederate sergeants generally kept one squad on its feet only long enough to count heads or take names, letting those prisoners sit down while they went on to the next squad; they usually excused the sick and lame from attending, too. Resquadding, on the other hand, proved a severe trial for everyone. The only Yankees excused from this formation were the regularly paroled workmen and the "Negro Squad," under a white "sergeant" named Otis Knight, who occupied themselves by building the earthen approaches to Richard Winder's new double bridge over the creek, on Water Street. Otherwise, every prisoner had to walk, crawl, or be carried into ranks, and had to remain in place however long it took to enumerate all twenty-five thousand men.

As hours passed, men stricken with intestinal attacks wandered away, and that encouraged others to fall out for water, for July 3 turned terribly hot. Inevitably such truants interrupted the count, and the detachments would have to realign all over again amid a flurry of shouting and swearing. The procedure dragged on throughout the day, and finally Wirz authorized his sergeants to say that no more rations would be distributed until the new rolls were complete and accurate. By nightfall all the squads had been equalized and the total population was tabulated, but the prisoners' names and descriptions still had to be entered on the rolls to render those documents more trustworthy; the ration wagon therefore did not pull in that day. Few suffered any great deprivation as a result, for many had collected rations twice on July 2, some of them remarking again on the generous quantity. Others kept a little reserve of cornbread or meal, and so staved off starvation, but a second day without food might have left everyone hungry.[29]

It may have been hunger, or perhaps a loss of reason or a desire to explore his new surroundings, that led the man who called himself James Babb to commit a mortal indiscretion in the early hours of July 4. Babb (an unlikely name for a man who claimed to have been born in Naples) had enlisted nine months before as a substitute for Alonzo Bickford of Meredith, New Hampshire—a man he never met; Farmer Bickford was one of fifty-four Meredith citizens drafted in the early autumn of 1863, forty-seven of whom quickly secured either substitutes or exemptions and went on with their lives. Babb had been a prisoner now for about half of his total service, since Olustee: he had been one of those untrained recruits who fled that battlefield with the 7th New Hampshire. By this point he must have been destitute, and some said he had gone crazy, though it seems suspicious that the men deemed crazy always happened to speak foreign tongues. Sometime after one o'clock that morning Babb wandered past the dead line in the northwestern corner of the new end. It was pitch black—the very moment of the new moon—but the sentinel on post sixteen fired into the murky darkness at the sound, hitting Babb in the knee. Sympathetic hands dragged the victim away as other musket flashes punctuated the darkness, and when the sentry on that perch tried to call out the hour at two o'clock, a voice from the prison drowned him out with "you son of a bitch." Babb whimpered till morning, when the doctors admitted him to the hospital; he lingered just over a month.[30]

The next morning, shortly after the wounded Neapolitan went out the south gate forever, the drums beat for roll call again, regardless of the holiday. Every man in the prison belonged to a new detachment now, with a new location for forming up, and when the restless squads fell in they were confronted with a ream of blank descriptive rolls. Each detachment sergeant took half a dozen of them from his Confederate counterpart and began recording the names, ages, and occupations of the men under them, adding their height, hair and eye color, and an assessment of their individual complexions. These rough vital characteristics served as the only means of identifying the Civil War soldier, and the prison authorities could use them for everything from advertising escapees to exchanging prisoners with the enemy. Those captives who had dared to believe in the rumor of a July 7 exchange brightened at this seeming confirmation as their sergeants began filling out the rolls, and the camp buzzed with parole gossip all day.[31]

Independence Day began with the leftover heat of the day before, and it intensified as the morning progressed. At noon the blazing sun hid behind black clouds that rolled into position like stage props and stopped, and those prisoners who owned shelter fled to it; those who did not huddled for four hours under the wind and rain of what several witnesses judged to be the most violent thunderstorm they had yet seen. Detachment sergeants protected their squad rolls as well as they could, lest a soaking blur their delible ink, for those few sheets of paper might represent another day's sustenance for the entire prison. As soon as the sky cleared the sergeants finished their lists and turned them in, and by dusk the north gate opened for the commissary wagon. Nearly forty-eight hours had passed since any food had come into the prison.[32]

Those who made their diary notations before evening thought they would see no rations this day, either, which prompted some pretty bitter entries. One unlettered Sooner wished "deth to the g d rebs[.] i hope they will all die." Even the more articulate suspected the "cursed Rebs" of having used the reorganization as an excuse for withholding rations on the Fourth of July. Because of the late start, some few prisoners did not receive their July 4 rations until the next morning. Regular distribution resumed on the afternoon of July 5, so the only provisions that were actually lost were those of July 3. This was the only day in the fourteen months of Andersonville's existence—including August 9, when a meteorological calamity prevented most of the prisoners from being fed—that the whole prison was denied food. That did not preclude future allegations that it was a regular practice, however, and by September of 1865 former prisoners seemed to compete with each other to recall the greatest number of consecutive days the entire stockade was denied food; some who may have compared notes testified that no rations entered the prison July 3, 4, or 5, while one said he received none for four days—stretching it to five days with another telling.[33]

Henry Wirz ultimately paid with his life for policies such as withholding rations, but the Fourth of July famine may not have been his fault, or that of any Camp Sumter Confederate. On July 2 a new Massachusetts prisoner noted that there "were no rations issued being out of the same." That was the day on which some rations were ostensibly withheld until enough of the old stockade timbers came out the gate. Sergeant Major Kellogg, who sometimes spoke with or eavesdropped on the quartermaster when he entered the prison, heard that officer let it slip on July 3 that he had no rations to give out, even if the descriptive rolls had been completed in time. The vast number of mouths at Andersonville made it immensely difficult to collect and store enough food, particularly perishables, and Commissary Armstrong was no longer able to maintain his preferred three-day reserve; a ten-day cushion, such as General Winder is thought to have desired, was wholly impractical. Mr. Harrold, the Americus purchasing agent, had recently advertised an offer to trade sugar mills and boilers for corn and bacon: Confederate quartermaster and commissary funds had obviously proved too uncertain and inflated to attract sufficient supplies, and in desperation those departments seem to have fallen back on the barter of surplus equipment. Rather than risk a panic by admitting that they had no food to give out, Wirz and Winder may have tried to turn the crisis to their advantage by using the threat of withholding rations to gain both the bridge logs and the prisoners' cooperation in the reorganization; that ploy would also have helped to divert the inmates' inevitable resentment from Confederate authorities to those Federals who were disrupting the process.[34]

An unusual number of prisoners complained of the foul meat that came their way the evening of July 4—another indication the commissary was taking anything he could get. Subtle hints of a precarious food supply did not disappear with the resumption of regular rations on July 5, either. Mr. Harrold had to appoint an assistant merely to secure local provisions for the Confederate guards' hospital at Camp Sumter (which consisted of two rough board barracks near the railroad tracks), and the Sumter County Ladies Soldiers Relief Society established a committee to look into the suffering of the Andersonville guards. Three weeks after the resquadding, General Winder scratched a frantic note to Samuel Cooper, explaining that he had nearly 30,000 prisoners, more than 2,500 guards, 500 laborers, "and not a ration at the post."[35] Given Winder's earlier paranoia about an escape by 12,000 hungry Yankees in Richmond, when at least his guards were adequately fed, his situation at this prison must have driven the old man to the verge of apoplexy.

Prisoners who still had money could buy almost anything imaginable to eat. James Selman's sutler shanty, just inside the north gate, periodically offered cucumbers, watermelons, muskmelons, onions, and potatoes, as well as wheat, flour, coffee, sugar, salt, fowl, and some real delicacies like seafood. Selman's prices were among the highest in the prison, but he paid fairly exorbitant premiums to the farmers and women who brought their produce and baked goods to the station: those suppliers gouged everyone at Camp Sumter, needy Confederate guards included, and General Winder had to post a price scale to limit that sort of profiteering, threatening to confiscate the inventory of anyone he found in violation.[36]

Selman's sutlery, with its big lean-to, was only the most obvious of several grocery alternatives. North Street (or Market Street, as the ten-foot-wide avenue from the north gate was more often called) teemed with part- and full-time peddlers hawking rough corn meal, pones, and an assortment of edibles. Those prisoners with more capital gave Mr. Selman some real competition, setting up their own stores. The most prosperous of these prison entrepreneurs were two men known to their fellow inmates as George Fechnor and Charles Ellis. Fechnor sometimes used the alias of Charles W. Ross, and he told a fantastic story of having been commissioned in the 1st Kentucky Mounted Rifles (a unit that did not exist), claiming to have been captured in an 1862 skirmish at New Castle, Kentucky (an action that did not occur) before he was formally mustered in as an officer. One Delaware prisoner judged Fechnor a niggardly, heartless man, and accused him of running the principal Andersonville gambling syndicate; a Pennsylvanian described Ellis as "the gambler sutler and general swindler."[37]

Fechnor swore that he came into the prison on the first of June without a penny, and started selling his cornbread ration at ten cents per day, buying eggs and vegetables from paroled workmen and selling those in turn, building up such a cache of goods that he was soon obliged to build a little shed to house it. His rags-to-riches tale seems highly implausible, but it fit Fechnor's fiction of long confinement, which he probably invented to cover some transgression like desertion or bounty jumping. The trial testimony, including his own, casts him as a natural wheeler-dealer, and like most such men he probably carried a grubstake in reserve wherever he went. Sometime before the arrest of the raiders, he and Ellis bought a six-by-six lot and set up shop on Market Street, near Selman's sutlery: there is reason to suppose that they even acted as Selman's agents. Immediately after the raiders' demise the two expanded, locating a new store a few rods to the north, on the corner of Market and the principal street leading to the new stockade. They dug a deep cellar in which to store their vegetables out of the killing heat, later adding stockpiles of staples and canned goods. Boarding this cellar over with planks, they topped it off with a shanty, dealing their wares from behind an impromptu counter. They bought their stock from desperate inmates, paroled clerks and laborers returning from outside, or even from Selman himself, who sold them their bulk items: they went through a sack of onions and three bags of potatoes every day, and on two occasions the grocers paid Selman $324 for a barrel of sorghum molasses. At night they closed up their window and slept on the floor.[38]

So well did the two partners prosper that they adorned their establishment with a painted sign, hired three employees, and ultimately built a second shack on another lot. Their reputations for gambling implied that at least one of them must have had some connection with that activity, if not both of them, though perhaps they merely staked card sharps or rented a building for gaming space. Fechnor himself admitted that Andersonville hosted numerous professional gamblers who dealt faro, "honest john," euchre, and poker, and he seemed familiar with both the games and the gamblers. Some of them operated independently, he said, while others pooled their talents and employed runners to lure plump pocketbooks. Freelance gamblers, often mere innocents yearning for a little income, marked up boards and bought or carved dice to furnish their own chuck-a-luck concessions: in fair weather hundreds of ragged prisoners huddled all day around these desperate enterprises along Market Street. Friendlier card games saw token stakes like cigars, while poker players regularly bet ten U.S. dollars on a single hand. Thousands of dollars changed hands every day. Hungry men who watched relative fortunes won could not restrain themselves, and some felt the need to make formal personal resolutions never to partake of the gambling. One middle-aged Massachusetts private said the gaming never let up, even on Sunday. "Things are carried on very curious in this place," he reflected; "it must be cursed of God and man."[39]

The croupier's calls mixed with the cacophony of itinerant traders who, having no storefront to draw customers, roamed about, constantly chattering of the merchandise they offered. The cornpone and meal merchants were the most common, for nearly all the bankrupt Yankees gave it an occasional attempt. So great was the supply of those commodities, though, that they sold slowly, and for only a dime or fifteen cents per day's ration. Stomachs turned by the thousands against the monotonous diet of prison bread, driving its value even lower, and the only buyers were generally the most pitiful cases. Proud men scorned the haggling necessary to realize even a few cents in profit, but most of them tried it once or twice, hoping to buy some lifesaving vegetables.[40]

Eugene Forbes, the New Jersey sergeant, found the whole north side of the prison alive with trade. It reminded him of Chatham Street, in New York City.

"Who wants the wood?" one man cried, while another bellowed "Where's the lucky man who will buy the tobacco?" "Here goes a bully dress coat, only $4," another chanted, as someone else offered sarsaparilla beer at ten cents a glass. Hordes of other vendors simultaneously hawked eggs at twenty-five cents apiece, mustard and soda, or an endless array of garden vegetables. Speculators dealt in sugar and salt. Money-changers abounded, and at least one civilian New Yorker—John Morris, a government wood contractor captured with the Plymouth Pilgrims—bought up all the state currency, savings bank checks, and bounty certificates he could find, at a fraction of their face value.[41]

"Andersonville," said George Fechnor, "was a city—a market place. All it lacked of being a bazaar was the women." Commerce seemed to flourish even more after the raiders had been rounded up, but as the cash began to flow more freely so, too, did it begin to drain out of the prison. As a sutler, James Selman was the only Confederate at Camp Sumter authorized to deal in greenbacks. He collected a substantial amount directly from the prisoners, and eventually Fechnor's fat bankroll came his way, also. When a U.S. dollar left the stockade in Selman's pocket it never returned, and the increased volume of business from the first of July merely abbreviated the life-span of that economy. At that rate it would not be many weeks before the prison had been completely cleaned out of currency.[42]

Like most cities (and Andersonville would become the fifth largest in the Confederacy), this one included a host of tradesmen as well as merchants. Hardly an occupation could not boast at least one representative inside the palisade. Barbers could be found in any quadrant; at least one dentist practiced, and one doctor. Two well-supplied watchmakers found more than enough employment, and one of them took on a journeyman. Bakers built clay ovens at ground level, some of them several feet wide; half a dozen tailors plied their needles, and as many cobblers repaired rotting footgear. Wherever land becomes precious, of course, the real estate speculator also appears, and Andersonville brokers began peddling tent-sized lots on the authority of the most ludicrous titles.[43]

Though but one grand slum itself, the prison also boasted various neighborhoods, some of them less desirable than others. There was the south side, where Sergeant Major Kellogg, the sailors, the Negro Squad, and—until recently—the raiders all camped, and where the shebangs drifted down a fairly gentle slope to within fifty feet of the sinks and swamp. By far the majority of prisoners lived on the north side, though, with its great expanse of flat plain; the north side was further divided into the "new" and the "old" stockades. Because the plateau dropped off so precipitously, residences here did not approach so close to Stockade Creek—with the exception of one colony of several dozen tents on a slight elevation just uphill from the sinks. Surrounded on three flanks by the soggy swamp and on the dead-line side by virtually constant runoff from the hillside, this island provided a haven for a hundred men or more. Some wag who had served in the Missouri bootheel in 1862 named the place Island Number 10.[44]

Andersonville had its ethnic ghettos, too. As early as April 1 the editor of the *Sumter Republican* remarked on the proportion of foreigners inside the stockade. Germans rivaled the Irish in numbers—though even many of those who preferred their parents' tongue were native-born Pennsylvanians and Midwesterners—while French, Swiss, and Italian immigrants conversed in what seemed, to Scotch-Irish Georgians, a perfect Babel of fluid gutturalism. Russians and other Slavs mystified the Yankee prisoners themselves, as did the occasional flurry of Spanish or Portuguese, and a few Great Lakes Indians added the whispering tones of their Algonquian dialect. A Catholic priest from Macon exaggerated only slightly when he said the stockade housed every nationality in the world. Captain Wirz, who was trilingual himself, employed a number of nonnative prisoners in and around his office to translate for those who could not speak English, including the Italian, Guscetti, who spoke seven European languages, and whom Wirz assigned to the hospital as an interpreter for the surgeons. Noticing his habit of interviewing German-speaking prisoners in his office (or foreigners they supposed to be Germans), some Yankees suspected Wirz of a vague, evil conspiracy.[45]

The stockade had long since collected a representative of every branch of the Federal service, too. Prisoners wore trousers trimmed with infantry blue, cavalry yellow, and the scarlet of artillery, as well as sleeves decorated with the green-and-gold caduceus of the hospital steward, and one commissioned Union surgeon tended to patients of his own army, having come voluntarily with the Plymouth prisoners. Several other officers camped inside with their men, notably Major Bogle, and the assistant secretary of the Confederate War Department authorized the commander of the Macon officers' prison to send a lieutenant of the 35th U.S. Colored Infantry to Andersonville to keep Bogle company. Most of the other officers who found themselves behind the palisade still wore sergeants' stripes, either because their commissions had arrived at regimental headquarters after they were captured or because they had not yet been mustered in; the suspicion that numerous officers voluntarily disguised their rank in order to share the fortunes of their men had little substance, if any. Black soldiers maintained their own squad, congregating near the south gate, and unlucky sutlers tried to pursue their mercantile inclinations on Market Street. Civilians milled about in once-white shirts or plain coats, among them Quartermaster Department teamsters, employees of the Topographical Engineers, telegraphers, contractors like John Morris, and simple suspects like David Cable, the would-be Ohio diplomat, whose emaciated frame would last but a few days longer. There were even those two women prisoners at Andersonville, captured with their husbands at Plymouth. One, Mrs. Leonard, insisted on accompanying her man into the stockade, but Wirz installed the other in a tent near headquarters, giving her husband a job in the hospital.[46]

Dysentery and diarrhea had reduced many within the prison to skeletons, and the clothing of those with much tenure had begun to fall apart. Chickamauga captives and other Belle Isle inmates had arrived at Camp Sumter ill-clad, and even in the spring "fresh fish" had taken particular notice of numerous filthy old-timers who owned but a few ragged rem-

Brigadier General John H. Winder (White, Wellford, Taliaferro, and Marshall Family Papers, Southern Historical Collection, University of North Carolina, Chapel Hill, N.C.).

Captain William Sidney Winder,
in a sitting from about 1870
(Mrs. John Henry Winder III,
Winston-Salem, N.C.).

Captain Richard B. Winder, about
1880 (Mrs. John Henry Winder III,
Winston-Salem, N.C.).

Captain Henry Wirz, in a photo purportedly taken during his 1863
journey to Europe (Library of Congress).

A. J. Riddle portrait of John H.
Winder, probably taken at
Andersonville on August 16, 1864
(Dave Mark Collection,
Linthicum Heights, Md.).

Heavily retouched Riddle photo
of a Confederate captain, believed
to be Henry Wirz, also probably
taken on August 16, 1864
(Dave Mark Collection,
Linthicum Heights, Md.).

Riddle stockade photo #1, looking southwest from a guard post just north of Stockade Creek, on the east wall of the prison. The trees at right center shade the star fort and Henry Wirz's headquarters (National Archives).

Composite of Riddle photos #2 (left half), looking northwest toward the north gate and Selman's sutlery, and #3 (right half), looking up the east wall of the prison (Massachusetts MOLLUS Collection, U.S. Army Military History Institute, Carlisle Barracks, Pa.).

Riddle photo #4, looking south-southeast from the same vantage point as photos 1, 2, and 3 (National Archives).

Riddle photo #5, showing the sinks and the unchanneled end of Stockade
Creek in a view taken from the first guard post south of the creek on the
east wall (National Archives).

Riddle photo #6, from the northeast corner of the stockade, showing one of the lanes that survived in the "new" stockade nearly seven weeks after it was first occupied (Massachusetts MOLLUS Collection, U.S. Army Military History Institute, Carlisle Barracks, Pa.).

Riddle photo #7, showing the central and upper section of Stockade Creek and, indistinctly at the lower right, the approach to the double bridge. Taken from one of the "pigeon roosts" just south of the north gate (Massachusetts MOLLUS Collection, U.S. Army Military History Institute, Carlisle Barracks, Pa.).

Riddle photo #8, showing the ration wagon inside the north gate; James Selman's sutler shanty sits in the center background (National Archives).

Riddle photo #9, looking across the earliest graves in the prison cemetery; this is probably the southwestern section of Section K of the modern cemetery (Massachusetts MOLLUS Collection, U.S. Army Military History Institute, Carlisle Barracks, Pa.).

Riddle photo #10, picturing the burial detail on the afternoon of August 16, 1864, as the body of Leander Farnham, Company A, 1st Vermont Heavy Artillery, is placed in the trench. Note the dilapidated stretcher (National Archives).

First Sergeant Lawson Carley, 5th Iowa Cavalry, who kept a diary at Andersonville (Carley Family, Albuquerque, N.M.).

Another Andersonville diarist: Charles E. Whitney, 154th New York (U.S. Army Military History Institute, Carlisle Barracks, Pa.).

Dr. Joseph Jones, who inspected Andersonville for the Confederate surgeon general in September of 1864 (Joseph Jones Collection, Tulane University, New Orleans).

Turn-of-the-century view of Andersonville village. Left to right, the three buildings are alleged to be John Winder's office, Ben Dykes's store, and Henry Wirz's winter office. In 1909 a monument to Wirz was raised in the immediate foreground (Peggy Sheppard, Andersonville Welcome Center, Andersonville, Ga.).

Colonel Norton P. Chipman—the judge advocate who railroaded Henry Wirz (Roger D. Hunt, Rockville, Md.).

Colonel William Henry Noble, 17th Connecticut, who was the highest-ranking Yankee ever held at Andersonville (Roger D. Hunt, Rockville, Md.).

The hanging of Henry Wirz in the courtyard of the Old Capitol prison, opposite the U.S. Capitol and on the site of the present Supreme Court building. Wirz has just dropped through the trap (Library of Congress).

Postwar Andersonville: The depot, about 1868 (National Archives).

Postwar Andersonville: The road from the station to the stockade, about 1868;
the stockade is barely visible in the distance (National Archives).

Postwar Andersonville: View from the large earthwork on the northwest corner of the prison, looking southwesterly down the stockade perimeter. The main stockade is visible at the upper right, and through the gaps in the second palisade (National Archives).

Postwar Andersonville: View of the ditch outside the earthwork on the northwest corner of the stockade, about 1868; the photographer has spun his camera about 150 degrees to the right from the preceding photo (National Archives).

The Andersonville cemetery shortly after the 1865 improvements
(National Archives).

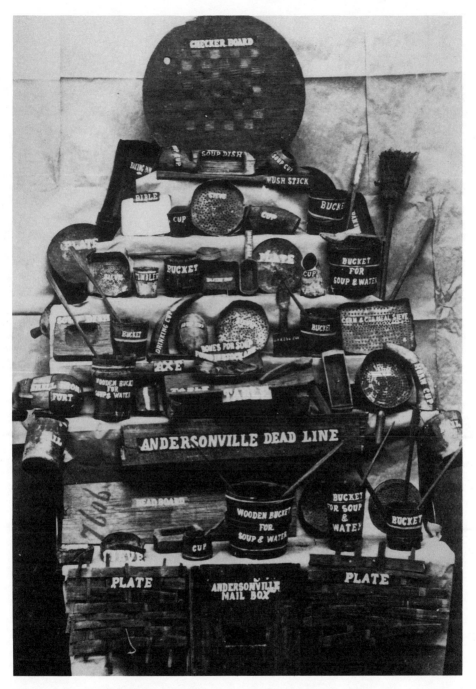

Relics retrieved from Andersonville by the 1865 Quartermaster Department detail
(National Archives).

Andersonville today: The stockade site as seen from a reconstructed portion of the palisade in the southeast corner. The Providence Spring monument is at far left, and Stockade Creek occupies the swale. The stakes at right mark the location of the dead line and the stockade wall, respectively (photo by the author, 1991).

Andersonville station on a misty December morning (photo by the author, 1991).

Section E, Andersonville National Cemetery, in a view taken from the approximate location of A. J. Riddle's camera in his photo #10 (photo by the author, 1991).

Section H of Andersonville National Cemetery: the last interments were in the left distance (photo by the author, 1991).

nants of uniform that frequently failed to cover them decently. With the battles of May and June the prison saw its share of amputees, who walked about with the stumps of their arms exposed, unable to find a place in the hospital until those stumps flamed with infection. Blind, deaf, and lame men stumbled about, prevented from following their traditional urban calling—begging—because the most sympathetic prisoners had nothing to give them. By August the most helpless of the sick had developed the earthen equivalent of bedsores from lying motionless on the ground, and maggots filled the open wounds. Often a new prisoner would circumnavigate the whole prison within a few days of his arrival, and, like William Farrand Keys, most of them returned from these exploratory expeditions profoundly depressed by the squalor and suffering. To make the actual misery seem even worse, everyone in the stockade wore the soot-stained face of a refugee from a minstrel show: pine smoke painted them "like so many Sweeps or nigers," wrote one cavalryman. The pungent smudge from the most common variety of firewood had likewise tarred their guards' complexions, but the palisade trapped the abundant smoke of the pitiful little fires inside, lending the camp an unreal air—as though it were a picture of "The Bottomless Pit," mused one Pennsylvanian.[47]

Those weakened by illness or too poorly clothed to avoid sunburn could do little but lie in their shelters all day, where they dwelt upon their plight sometimes to the point of insanity. Often they would not, or could not, partake of the time-consuming preparation of food, nor did they engage in the traditional daily "skirmishing" after the lice that infested their remaining garments. For some like these, monotony proved a deadlier enemy than hunger or disease. Despair tainted even their dreams. In July one of the Plymouth Pilgrims described a recurring dream in which he was a passenger on a steamboat upon "a deep and *muddy* river" with a wild current. The boat seemed to be sinking, so he made a heroic leap to the hurricane deck of another, which also appeared to be going down. At last he sprang to the flotsam of a third wreck and kicked his way toward shore while the faces of his comrades sank beneath the water; the nightmare continued to plague him for at least another fortnight. An Ohioan experienced "terrible dreams of home" one cold, wet night. Others dreamt more happily of visiting with wives and children, or of having been paroled to the company of dear friends, but the shock of waking proved all the more devastating. One was "troubled by obsessions of home and Mother almost every night." A grey-haired Massachusetts private who lamented having left his wife and six children for the lure of bounty money tried to effect spiritual communication with them from the confines of the stockade. On June 7 William Peabody wrote his wife that he had heard from her via a strange, ethereal creature who told him he would "come home all right." On the third Sunday thereafter he consulted a pair of prison charlatans, "Doc Bromfield" of Philadelphia and Oliver Fairbanks, "medium," of Paterson, New Jersey. Poor Peabody begged his wife for "the test" of this seance, but it never came, and his weary bones filled a slot in the prison cemetery by the first of September.[48]

The rampant gambling dens reflected an attempt to break the tedium, but reading served as the most common diversion. Bibles predominated, as might have been expected anywhere in the Christian world in 1864, but newspapers like *Harper's Weekly* circulated until they were thumbed to shreds, bringing as much as six bits on the secondhand market. As befit the cultural descendants of Benjamin Franklin, Pennsylvanians in the prison seem to have established an informal lending library: one of them devoured the first volume of John Headley's *Great Rebellion* while another condescended to read a cheap novel called *The Three Spaniards*; a month after finishing *The Great Rebellion*, the first man borrowed a biography of William Penn.[49]

Others whiled away the endless hours carving pipes, rings, or buttonhooks, frequently with astonishing detail, and some whittled chess pieces for double-duty entertainment. Checkers—or draughts, as the Civil War soldier knew the game—offered some fun, and others played cards without the ruinous stakes of the Market Street establishments. Determined to profit from the passing time, certain prisoners amused themselves with the study of algebra or one of the strange languages that clicked and hissed about them: Sergeant Major Kellogg spent a few days trying to learn German.[50] When those pastimes grew tiresome, anyone who could walk might go visiting, especially if a gaggle of new prisoners came in with news from home or the regiment; in this way did Samuel Melvin learn, on July 10, that his brother had been killed twenty-five days before. Old hands inevitably pumped newcomers for anything they might know about paroles or the progress of exchange negotiations, and that topic monopolized most discussions every day. The myth of the July 7 exchange sent morale plummeting when it proved false, but it interfered only briefly with the volume of rumors in that vein.[51]

The noise of thirty thousand men never really subsided. The stockade echoed all day with a clatter and clamor that rose sometimes to a muffled roar; at nightfall it tapered to a sibilant hum, ceasing altogether only for those whose last sun had already set. Prison society continued into the night, especially after the criminal element had been subdued, and corners of the camp resounded with sailors' yarns or patriotic songs bellowed for the aggravation of the guards; here and there the murmur of a prayer vigil rose from before the tents of dying men. By ten o'clock these chorales usually broke up for lack of firelight or warmth, and gradually the low moans of the sick swelled to fill the darkness with a mournful lullaby. Even those sufferers sometimes drifted off to another form of sleep in the wee hours, though: one delirious boy kept his neighbors awake all night, but he fell silent at last and they found him at sunrise, dead. Only in the grey predawn of three or four o'clock did the stockade approach anything that could have been called quiet—and that was the hour when some hopeful insomniacs thought they heard artillery in the unlikely distance. With the worst of the night's chill, which always precedes first light, the unhappy tenants would begin to stir. Bathers and laundrymen sought a place along the creek, while others thought longingly of coffee. The early risers might awaken to the cheery sounds of birds singing their morning challenges, as though nothing at all had changed in Mr. Turner's woods: until the Fourth of July one Vermont cavalryman reveled in the soothing song of a mockingbird that habitually perched in a pinetop just outside the stockade, but axes brought the tree down on July 5 and the serenade ended.

"Makes it seem lonesome," the Vermonter remarked, waking to a silent dawn. All that remained to his morning was the redolence of the swamp and the compressed humanity, which told the nose that another day had begun at Andersonville.[52]

The failure of the July 7 parole rumor coincided with a little religious revival within the stockade, as though some prisoners concluded they could put no faith in governments and so determined to put some in God. Perhaps the two events had no relation to one another; revivals sprang up with some frequency in those days—one had gripped nearby Americus for most of April, swelling the congregation and weakening the front steps of the Methodist church there—but on the very night following their great disappointment an unusual number of Federal captives held a prayer meeting, which they vowed to make a prison institution. They came together again on Sunday, July 10, a few of them offering sermons to accompany their collective supplications. Word of their gathering spread, drawing men from all over the prison a week later. One of the bigger and more regular confraternities met in the southeast corner of the stockade, beneath two of the three tall pines that represented the last vestige of William Turner's forest inside the stockade.[53]

For a few, Andersonville forged uncertain notions into firm belief. The conversions did not come like that of Paul, in a bolt from the blue, but very gradually. Those who would believe had to wrestle with the inescapable sight of immense suffering against the notion of a merciful God. After finishing his morning chores on August 19 Corporal Charles Lee, of the 16th Connecticut, "sat down and got deeply interested in reading about Paul's preaching and suffering." The sergeant major of Lee's regiment, Robert Kellogg, had been pious enough when fate threw him in the stockade, but he, too, spent four months there before he could reconcile that apparent contradiction. The men who had come in with him were dying daily by the last week of August: Lee noted on August 15 that their regiment had lost at least one man every day for nearly two weeks, and Kellogg's last healthy messmate had fallen lame with scurvy on the final Sunday of that month, when the young sergeant major spent the entire day pacing back and forth in front of his tent, enduring what he called a "precious time" considering "God's promises." Three days later, as the only sergeant no longer sick, he took charge of his squad, but still his conversion was not complete. Not until the first day of 1865, long after he had been delivered from the horrors of Andersonville, could he find the conviction to profess his faith and join the Congregational Church.[54]

Swarms of Irishmen and continental Europeans offered plenty of occupation for a Catholic priest, as Father William Hamilton had discovered when he visited the stockade in May. When he returned to his Macon pastorate, Hamilton wrote of the unattended faithful to his bishop, in Savannah, and the prelate responded by directing three Georgia priests to minister to them. From Atlanta came John Kirby, and from Savannah Peter Whelan (an Irishman, like Kirby) and a French priest named Clavreul. Father Hosannah, a multilingual Jesuit, volunteered to come from Mobile. Clavreul remained at Camp Sumter from July 15 until August 20, when he started vomiting so violently that his colleagues put him back aboard the train for Savannah. Father Kirby stayed a few weeks, too, but Peter Whelan did not leave the stockade from his arrival on June 16 until the first of October, when most of the inmates had been transferred elsewhere; Father Hosannah departed only a few days before that.[55]

Despite the three other priests, and several Protestant clergymen who toured the throng in June and August, it was Peter Whelan whom many prison annalists incorrectly recorded as the only cleric to venture inside the stockade. Though most of the Yankees were at least nominal Protestants, and still harbored the lingering mistrust of Catholics that had helped to fuel the Know-Nothing party a few years before, Whelan's devotion to his faith and its adherents earned their admiration. Even the profane Captain Wirz watched his tongue in front of him, and granted him nearly anything he asked. Whelan lived on the post, eating the government rations Wirz allowed him, and he spent every day either inside the palisade or in the hospital, passing from man to dying man beneath an umbrella that shaded him from the blazing Georgia sun, often abbreviating the sacraments when several souls lay simultaneously on the brink of release. Whelan was sixty-two; the pace wore out two of his younger comrades, and he suffered poor health himself, but still he and the battered umbrella came through the wicket every morning of that long, lethal summer.[56]

Father Whelan had to interrupt his routine on Sunday evening, July 10. General Winder's application for execution of the condemned raiders had come back from Richmond with approval to proceed, and Winder had decided to turn the doomed men over to the Union prisoners on Monday afternoon. Since June 29 the six had lain manacled in the stocks night and day, for nowhere else could they be held so securely. Perhaps their doubts of their fellow prisoners' resolve had begun to wither by now, or they may have hoped the eleven-day ordeal might be deemed sufficient punishment, but they sensed enough real peril in their situation to accept the priest's attention when he came to console them. Only big Willie Collins claimed not to be a Catholic; the rest availed themselves of the last rites while thunder echoed ominously in the distance.[57]

The next morning turned off a little cooler, with some cloud cover, but by ten o'clock the sun had broken through as hot and humid as ever. About noontime the south gate opened to admit a wagonload of tools, timbers, and green lumber, courtesy of General Winder; a crew of Federal carpenters descended upon the wagon while a cordon of club-wielding regulators kept the crowd from the coveted materials. There, just inside the gate on the edge of South Street, they began throwing together a rough platform under Leroy Key's direction. The deck included a long trap held up by props; when they began adding steps and a pair of upright four-by-four posts to support a doubled-up overhanging beam, dame rumor had all the evidence she needed: news of the raiders' imminent hanging hissed across the creek and up the slope.[58]

The raiders' shebangs lay tumbled nearby, but many of their friends survived in the prison. The regulators held tight to their clubs, which they had improved with wrist loops, anticipating a preemptive sally by some of the hoodlums' former allies. The raiders' cohorts did not strike, perhaps because they shared their chieftains' hope (and the suspicion of many other prisoners) that there would be no hanging—that the gibbet stood for no more than a theatrical symbol of the regulators' determination.[59]

The scaffold went up very near John Whitten's tent. Corporal Whitten had been a vigorous, rugged man when the flag passed out of his hands at Missionary Ridge, but he had thinned considerably in the intervening thirty-one weeks. His ankles had already begun to swell with scurvy, and his sturdy young frame ached as though with arthritis. He had known most of the raiders since Belle Isle, but as his strength left him he came to fear them. He applauded the notion of a little hanging, as did most of those from around the stockade who craned their necks to see what was going on down by the gate.[60]

Seven hundred fresh captives from the Army of the Potomac were thrust into the prison that afternoon. Some had only recently donned their uniforms: in barely two months they had left home, seen six or seven weeks of brutal campaigning, and now they found themselves cast into incredible crowding and filth; within another hour they could add the vivid memory of a mass execution to their list of adventures. Unable to find immediate space, many of these neophytes probably lingered along South Street, wondering at the portentous construction before them.[61]

Around four o'clock, while regulators tied six nooses close together upon the crossbeam, the skies burst once more, soaking the newcomers and cooling the stagnant air. At half past four the grim notes of the "Dead March" drifted over the walls in muted tones, and the gates opened to reveal the paroled Union musicians who comprised the Camp Sumter band. Behind them strode a guard detail, and between those guards slunk the six surly raiders, glancing nervously in all directions. Captain Wirz rode in on his old white mare, with Father Whelan walking beside him. Whelan busied himself with prayer, his latest appeals for clemency having gone unanswered.[62]

Wirz reined up before Sergeant Key and the serried regulators, announcing rather formally the delivery of the six condemned men according to his promise to abide by the decision of the prisoners' court. Turning to the six, he invoked divine mercy on their souls, whereupon he marched his guards away and turned his back upon them, Pilate-like. Key's men

surrounded the rascals and began binding their hands. Now reality struck
the bullies face-first, and they started to quaver. The first of them had
already begun to mount the steps when Charles Curtis wrenched himself
away from the groping hands, muttering "This cannot be." From somewhere beneath his clothing he produced a dirk and stabbed at his executioners, wounding some of them and opening a gap in their ranks. In an
instant he was loose, crashing through the nearby shelters toward the
creek. Regulators surged after him while spectators stampeded, fearing
the raiders' friends had risen to free them. The throng knocked one man
into a shallow well, from which he called in vain for help. Thick mud
slowed Curtis, but he wallowed deeper, crossing the stream and staggering up the far slope. His pursuers raced around by the bridge to close his
escape, falling on him in such numbers that the exhausted fugitive could
not resist.[63]

While they dragged the gasping Curtis back over the bridge, other
regulators shouldered his five companions together on the scaffold and
fitted the ropes around their necks. Once Curtis had joined them, Key
offered them time for whatever last words they might have. In a voice
broken by fear and exertion, Curtis blurted that he had never killed
anyone, and if there was a man present whom he had robbed he wished
that man would come forward so he could ask forgiveness. No one answered. Andrew Muir made a sad little speech about himself—"a poor
Irish Chap," one prisoner remembered him saying—and he swore he had
never dreamt such an end awaited him when he entered the stockade
barely a month before; in response a fellow gunboat sailor in the crowd
yelled that they were all guilty and deserved death. Curtis bequeathed his
watch to Father Whelan, who mumbled Latin prayers at the foot of the
gallows, and then a half-dozen meal sacks went over their heads in lieu of
hoods. From beneath the burlap Pat Delany wished his friends farewell:
"Boys, God be with you all, and me." Hulking Collins and the compact
roughnecks Sullivan and Sarsfield apparently had nothing to say. At
eight minutes past five, with a hollow square of regulators all around and
more clouds hovering overhead, the appointed executioners knocked out
the props at either end and the trap swung from beneath twelve muddy
shoes.[64]

So rotten was big Collins's rope that it snapped. Some read the tumble
as a sign of his innocence, and called for the regulators to release him, but
his longtime reputation as "Mosby" lent the notion little credence.
Thomas Goodman, a civilian prisoner whom Collins had once assaulted,
bundled him back up the stairs with the help of Leroy Key and a few

others. Collins wailed piteously for mercy this time, but they quickly reknotted the rope, balancing their burly charge on the remaining gallows planks. Barely a minute after he first hit the ground they pushed him off again, and he dangled awkwardly on the shortened cord until he and the others were, as one onlooker pronounced it, "*dead, dead, dead.*"[65]

The prison assumed a rare silence, punctuated only by an occasional curse from the forgotten man at the bottom of the well. By one man's watch the six twirled for twenty-seven minutes while more than twenty-six thousand prisoners looked on. Even those who called loudest for these executions could not put the gruesome image out of their minds for days. On July 12 several Yankee diarists noted lingering preoccupation with the incident, and one of them seemed most upset that the prisoners had had to perform the execution themselves, as though they had begun to feed upon one another. Still, Father Whelan felt the vast majority of the prison population approved of the hangings, and the available evidence bears him out.[66]

By six o'clock the raiders' bodies lay in the deadhouse. Leroy Key and his principal lieutenants followed the corpses through the gate, carrying all their possessions, and after giving their parole of honor they joined the exiled Dowd outside, beyond the reach of promised vengeance.[67]

The regulators elected a new leader who acted not only as chief of police but also as the magistrate for the camp, holding daily court in a communal shelter they styled the "temple of justice" over such petty disputes as the ownership of a tin cup. Like the city police they emulated, however, the regulators attracted the corrupt and self-interested who smelled opportunity in the exercise of such consolidated authority. According to one witness, some of the regulators had, themselves, taken to thieving within a couple of weeks of the hanging. George Fechnor, whom some prisoners saw as nothing but an opportunist and cheat, held sway briefly as chief of police; by then one German soldier, who particularly resented the sumptuous rations they drew, considered the regulators wholly as bad as the raiders had been. As early as August 9 an Indiana prisoner agreed, observing that the Westerners who had founded the organization had been largely replaced by "the rounders of New York and Brooklyn" whom the regulators had been intended to eradicate. A year later Sergeant Major Kellogg also remembered that the raiders and the regulators were cut from the same cloth.[68]

Even with this temporary improvement in prison discipline, the horrors of the stockade still drove men to escape. The disappointment that followed the foiled conspiracy of May lay six long weeks in the past.

Reinforced with the unbowed spirit of more recent arrivals, many in the stockade responded to the shattered hopes of July 7 by plotting another break. Like the plan of late May, this one included a number of tunnels under the stockade—part of which had been undermined for toppling— and another desperate rush on the guards. To enhance the effectiveness of their sheer numbers, the ringleaders again assigned captains to companies and regiments of their most earnest men.[69]

A day or two after the hanging, Captain Wirz got wind of the plot. Uncertain of the details, he kept his own counsel for at least twenty-four hours, but he did apparently charge the stockade sentries with greater vigilance, which seems to have cost one Yankee deserter his life. Just after dawn on July 13 Francis Devendorf, a New Yorker who showed the white feather in the Wilderness, ventured down to the creek for a cup of water. The stream ran clearest as it entered the stockade, and most prisoners tried to stretch as far upstream as their arms and the dead line allowed. Most of the guards winked at the frequent violation of that fatal boundary there, but after Captain Wirz's sharp admonishment today's sentry would permit no one to encroach upon the scantling. Devendorf or someone near him reached too far, and the deep boom of a big smoothbore echoed across the camp. Devendorf caught the musket ball and fell, dying, while one of the buckshot winged a bystander.[70]

The next day, at noon, "Sergeant" Otis Knight, chief of the Negro Squad, was culling the forest floor for firewood with his black followers when a runner came calling his name: once again Captain Wirz had hailed all the detachment sergeants into line in front of his office, on the rise overlooking the southwest corner of the stockade. In his thick Zurich accent Wirz told them what he knew of the plot: that six thousand men planned to tunnel out, storm the batteries, overpower the guards, and release the rest of the prisoners. Solemnly he begged them to warn their various detachments against such an undertaking, for once it began he promised to spray the stockade with canister "so long as there was a man kicking." Changing the subject and softening his tone somewhat, he admitted that the exchange talks had stalled, claiming the Union negotiators hesitated to trade Confederate soldiers for their own because of "the Negro question," and because so many of the Federal prisoners had nearly, or already, completed their enlistments. Someone asked Wirz if he would assist them in presenting a petition to their government asking for an immediate exchange, and Wirz naturally agreed, offering whatever stationery they needed. Another detachment sergeant raised the issue of firewood, the stockpiles of which had dwindled with surprising speed; Wirz expressed sympathy, noting that he had already assigned Knight's squad to the wood detail. With a final warning not to gather in large groups before the gates on penalty of having a shell dropped among them, he sent them back inside.[71]

A few hours later, while mess sergeants divided their squads' daily rations in the gloaming, the prison commandant decided to stage an escape drill. Two of the Florida gunners stationed near Wirz's headquarters yanked the lanyards on blank cartridges to bring out the garrison, but the signal sparked pandemonium inside the stockade. Those who had heard of Wirz's threat suspected the escape had begun, with all its attendant slaughter. Terrified Yankees dove into the little excavations in which they slept, or behind the slightest irregularities in the raw earth, screaming at their dazed comrades to take cover. Some who dared to remain standing saw similar panic strike outside the prison, too: from nearby camps and scattered dwellings women fled into the forest, some of them carrying children; one lady fainted dead away on a road leading to the prison. A few Confederate soldiers also took to their heels, but the greater part of the troops emptied onto their stump-strewn parade fields and trotted toward the stockade. A regiment flew to each corner of the prison, where their short-range smoothbores might generate a deadly crossfire without much danger of reaching their friends at the other extremity. Each battalion fired off an uneven volley of blanks, then marched back to quarters while the officers grumbled over their performance. A visitor from Savannah felt certain the Reserves would have no trouble quelling an escape, or at least so he tried to convince his local newspaper editor, but one of the prisoners observed with some satisfaction that his keepers could not muster more than twenty-five hundred men.[72]

One platoon of plotters intended to put their tunnel to use despite the demise of yet another escape scheme. Before dawn on the second morning after the drill, a sergeant named English crawled out to finish the opening. While he gouged at the clay the passageway collapsed behind him, and as his air supply diminished he clawed desperately for the surface. In his frenzy he attracted the attention of the sentries when he broke through, about five feet outside the stockade. The guards helped dig him out, then threw him in the stocks for a twelve-hour stint. Meanwhile, inside the walls, Wirz kept his human terriers at work all day long, uncovering other shafts in various stages of completion, including the one meant to weaken the palisade. He found some of them with the assistance of an informant, and one frustrated squad cast about for someone to blame, settling on a suspected traitor whom they treated to the customary barbering, adding the more permanent touch of a tattoo, in the shape of a "T," etched across his forehead and down the bridge of his nose. Their artistry complete, the outraged tunnelers began flailing at his ribs with sticks; only the intercession of the officer of the day and a file of guards saved him. Wirz demanded the men who had beaten his spy, withholding rations from that part of the camp until they delivered themselves up for punishment, but the captain's wrath had subsided by the time they surrendered and he simply turned them back into the prison.[73]

Wirz kept his word about the firewood, sending the black prisoners back into the pines each morning to cut a few wagonloads. The yield amounted to barely ten loads daily, but without more guards he could manage nothing greater.[74]

It seemed as though Wirz had also spoken true about the Lincoln administration's refusal to exchange prisoners. Thousands of the Yankees at Andersonville had passed beyond their time, and Washington might not have the benefit of any more service from them, but more of the prisoners credited their government's stated objection to further exchanges: the Southern reluctance to count all black troops equal to white soldiers. That appeared to infuriate the captives all the more. Irritation with Lincoln, which had begun to germinate in the spring, came to full bloom after Wirz spoke to the detachment sergeants.

"The Everlasting *Nigger* must be protected," one of the Plymouth Pilgrims complained, "and the soldier may take care of himself." In his diary, a sergeant of the 4th Vermont raged over his country's willingness to let her soldiers languish and die over a matter of strained principle, lamenting "we must stay here because they can't agree on some nigger question." The government could not think very much of its defenders, he concluded. "I have no desire to be immolated upon the altar of the 'irrepressible nigger,'" complained a New Yorker. William Farrand Keys, a highly articulate former schoolteacher taken prisoner in the Wilderness, grew increasingly bitter toward the president as the summer progressed. "Father Abraham," he wrote in August, "I wish you had my ration of wood to boil coffee for your family, I think you would soon bring on an exchange." A week later, commenting on the exaggerated rumor that 125 men had already died that day, Keys asked "What do you think of that, father Abraham? Could you enlist that many in a day?"[75]

"If the government don't get us out they may go to the Devil with Abraham Lincoln," scribbled one bitter private, "I will not vote for him again." Even John Whitten, who carried the flag into all the fights of the

5th Iowa, boiled over at his country's apathy as the last day of his three-year enlistment passed and scurvy bent his legs from beneath him. By September a visiting Confederate surgeon found the Union prisoners damning their own government up and down for abandoning them in the name of racial equality, and Keys confirmed both the sentiment and its widespread expression. When rumors surfaced on the first of that month that the negotiators had agreed to overlook the matter of runaway slaves captured under arms, Keys and his cronies doubted it. "When we consider that it leaves Lincoln's pets the confiscated contrabands out in the cold we can easily judge what reception it will meet with in Washington," he wrote; when that pessimistic prediction proved sound, the embittered Keys remarked "it appears that the federal government thinks more of a few hundred niggers than of the thirty thousand whites here in bondage."[76]

Nor was that attitude restricted to the lower echelons. A few weeks later Lincoln's secretary of the navy, Gideon Welles, would chastise both Edwin Stanton and the president on the subject of prisoner exchanges. Like many, Welles supposed that the issue of black prisoners served merely as an excuse for holding up the cartel ("behind the subject of exchange there were matters undisclosed to me," he wrote), but he found the pretense repugnant in its own right. An old-line Democrat, Welles readily comprehended the slave owners' perspective even if he no longer supported it, and he reprimanded Stanton for his intransigence. He confided to his diary that "to absolutely stop exchanges because owners held on to their slaves when they got them was an atrocious wrong, one that I would not be a party to."[77]

The accumulating resentment crystallized on July 15, when a few sergeants began circulating the exchange petition on Wirz's foolscap. One of the early drafts of that document seems to have carried the implied or explicit threat that the Andersonville prisoners would swear allegiance to the Confederacy if their own government did not deliver them from their present misery. Even with that controversial caveat the paper drew support, but tempers flared as the copies made their way around the prison, and many refused to sign. Those who originated the article lobbied vigorously for it, in stump speeches and private arguments, but finally the authors yielded to their comrades' demands and submitted their petition for review by the detachment sergeants, en masse.[78]

The sergeants met at noon on July 19 to rework their memorial, with Edward Wellington Boate recording the proceedings in shorthand. By the time they finished they had stripped the document of much of its rancor and fulmination, but a good measure of pathos remained as the body of the petition described the horrible conditions within the prison. Each detachment sergeant carried the final draft to his men for approval, and on July 20 they gathered again to select a committee of six to carry it through the lines to the government, naming Boate chairman of the committee.[79]

The petition represented a final gasp of indignation for many bitter wraiths who went to their crowded graves in contempt of the nation they had sworn to serve. A few others found posthumous but long-lasting expression of their outrage through their survivors, however: in Saint Albans, Vermont, near the Canadian border, the parents of a stockade victim raised a marble slab to their boy, Joseph P. Brainerd of Company L, 1st Vermont Cavalry, who died at Andersonville "on the 11th day of Sept. 1864, entirely and wholly neglected by President Lincoln . . ."[80]

5 ◆ M But Yet the Will Roll'd Onward

Most of July had been oppressively hot, and because of the heat southwest Georgia's corn crop looked good, at least on the high ground that had escaped the June soaking. The wheat, too, seemed to have recovered from the drenching that had threatened to destroy it. True to the rest of the month, the afternoon of Tuesday, July 19, turned abominably muggy despite hovering clouds that would bring a shower after the sun set. At the Methodist church in Americus stood a wedding party, sweating discreetly while Reverend Juriah Harris plodded through the ceremony.

The bride, Miss Carrie Meriwether, hailed from the vicinity of Augusta. Beside her stood Charles Furlow, stifling in the full uniform of a Confederate first lieutenant. It had already been a long war for the groom: he had seen his older brother killed while leading a company in the Shenandoah Valley, under Stonewall Jackson, and Charles himself had carried a rifle through not only that campaign but the Seven Days, Second Manassas, South Mountain, and into the cornfield at Antietam. After Fredericksburg he began to earn regular notice as a mounted courier and aide on the staff of his former colonel, George Doles, and, when General Doles was killed at Cold Harbor, it was Lieutenant Furlow who brought the body home. The death of his chief left him unemployed, but his father commanded the local militia at Camp Sumter, and Colonel Furlow spent a few days finagling a place for his boy as adjutant of his battalion. After three bloody years at the front Charles felt willing enough to accept this inglorious duty, and his presence at the altar reflected his faith in a future that he might now survive to enjoy. With Lieutenant Colonel Furlow looking on, Charles and Miss Meriwether pledged themselves to each other. The guests fled gratefully out to the open air of the church's front platform, which had suffered such heavy traffic during the April revival, and the newlyweds slipped bashfully away to the first night of their half-century together.[1]

While Lieutenant Furlow and Miss Meriwether exchanged their vows, five regiments of Yankee cavalry were just finishing up a day and a half of railroad wrecking only ninety miles to the west. They had swooped down from northern Alabama under Lovell Rousseau, tearing up thirty miles of track on the West Point & Montgomery and the Columbus railroad lines near Opelika, temporarily cutting off any supplies from Alabama. In the course of burning four depots they destroyed twenty thousand pounds of bacon—two days' rations for the entire prison at Andersonville—and hundreds of barrels of sugar and flour. Also consigned to the flames were six boxcars of leather, nail kegs, and shovels, all of it probably bound for Richard Winder's shoe shop and his sanitation efforts at Andersonville.[2]

Rousseau's raid threw southwest Georgia into a panic. He had brought with him as many veteran troops as John Winder could have mustered from all his Reserves and militia, and until Rousseau veered toward Marietta late on July 19 his course seemed set for Sumter County. General Winder asked Richmond again for permission to distribute his prisoners, and Samuel Cooper finally gave him that latitude. Richard Winder commandeered a locomotive for the project, but then General Winder postponed the removal: instead he opted for defense, and the locomotive went into service collecting the field hands for which he appealed. General John

Bell Hood, who had recently replaced Joe Johnston at the head of the Army of Tennessee, offered as much as a brigade of infantry reinforcements if the Yankees should turn toward the prison. The secretary of war gave Howell Cobb authority to call up the exempted men and even the detailed Reserves for temporary service in the militia, but Governor Brown had already sent those same men to Atlanta to face Sherman's host. Hood's brigade did not come, and Cobb, Joe Brown, and the Davis administration fell into a perilous debate over prerogatives. For the moment, John Winder was on his own.[3]

The old man moved with surprising speed. By the afternoon of July 19 he had already put several slaves to work with shovels, throwing up artillery lunettes at one corner of the stockade. Officers and men rushed nervously about, hurrying the laborers, while inside the pale the daily routine of distributing the rations continued as usual, except for a noticeable decline in the overall quantity. James Duncan (or one of his assistants) let it slip that the Yankee horsemen in eastern Alabama had interrupted the supply of cornmeal and meat, and the rumor of an impending raid burned its way through the camp like a prairie fire. Those reckless masterminds of the aborted grand escapes again readied their covert battalions for a rush at the gate, and even a few men with scurvy-shortened hamstrings planned to join them.[4]

Slaveholders sent their field hands by the score, and in many cases they came themselves, armed with a motley arrangement of weapons. A carload of women arrived, too, some of them carrying infants, fresh from the districts that lay in the Yankees' path. By morning the giddy prisoners congregated on the hillside north of the creek to gawk at the refugees and to watch some two hundred black backs bent over shovels, flailing at the red clay.[5]

The biggest earthwork—which nearly everyone came to call the star fort, though it was cut in the shape of a sawtoothed oblong—went up in front of Captain Wirz's headquarters, off the southwest corner of the stockade. From there the Florida guns could sweep not only the stockade but everything around it, and the officer supervising its construction ordered a dozen embrasures cut in it, that Captain Dyke might cover whatever quadrant the raiders struck. The acting engineer officer staked out six more batteries around the rest of the prison, leaving the smallest of them on the eastern side, facing the forest and Sweetwater Creek: no attack seemed either likely or feasible there.[6]

While the slaves shoveled, the prisoners prayed for deliverance. Insane gossip continued to smolder, fanned by frightened sentries: Union cavalry was coming, with Kilpatrick at its head; he was only sixty miles away—fifteen miles away.

"Only hope the Raiders would come," longed a Massachusetts man. "We could help them."

"God hurry them through," scrawled a first sergeant of the 9th Ohio Cavalry: his own regiment rode with Rousseau. By now his former comrades were halfway back to Sherman's army, yet the rumors ran so strong that one prisoner was told the suicide squads would storm the walls that evening.[7]

Some could not wait for their cavalry to come for them, but decided instead to take advantage of the hysteria among the guards and open a new tunnel. Early on July 20 a hundred or more men gathered around the opening, crowding each other into the shaft, arousing the guards' suspicions. Winder had recently begun posting a string of pickets outside the stockade, and in the full moonlight they had no trouble pinpointing the exit. That afternoon the preponderance of those who had made it out came back through the gates, crestfallen; three of them did elude the pickets that night, and three more slipped away the next evening, but by July 23 most of them had been recaptured, too.[8]

The night of July 20 also brought the sounds of steam whistles and cheering, signaling the arrival of still more militia reinforcements, and dawn rose on an additional three hundred laborers who dug all day long in heat one onlooker described as "scorching." The prisoners' hopes began to fade. The guards refused to tell them anything now, but camp gossips revised the rumor with accurate reports that the raiders were nowhere near Andersonville: they had come no closer than Columbus. And they had never had any intention of freeing Federal prisoners, but rather were satisfied to burn a few flour mills. From the delirium of near rescue, the camp sank to the dismal reflection that such destruction could only diminish their own supplies of food, which were already dangerously low. As early as July 17 the commissary started running out of meat, and the next day the prisoners had to wait until late in the evening for their daily ration, which had arrived by train only that afternoon.[9]

Confederate authorities worried about food, too, but not only for their prisoners and not just during such acute shortages. Quartermaster General Alexander Lawton appealed to Howell Cobb to intervene with Governor Brown on the subject of freeing Georgia's overseers from militia duty. Heretofore Cobb had had trouble finding recruits for his Reserves because of Brown's copious exemptions, but the governor was less generous about releasing potential militiamen, who constituted his own personal army. Overseers comprised a significant pool of men, because many plantation owners had saved theirs from conscription by paying what amounted to a commutation fee for them; others who owned fifteen hands or more had been able to retain overseers by simply posting bonds to assure they would remain in that capacity, for without white men at the whip productivity was certain to decline and the specter of slave insurrection loomed large. Production, however, was the issue with General Lawton, who pointed out to Cobb that two Confederate armies depended upon corn from southwestern Georgia. "Our condition as to grain is becoming critical," he concluded.

Nearly thirty-three thousand men at Andersonville also depended on provisions from southwest Georgia, now that the road to Alabama had been cut. Two days before Lawton sent his telegram to Howell Cobb, Captain James Armstrong watched the quartermaster's detail load the last ration from his echoing commissary building at Anderson depot. He suffered a few anxious hours before the next trainload of supplies rolled in, and he was forced to hand out short rations the next day. Armstrong shuddered to hear that the damage to the railroad would require more than a month's work to repair.[10]

The commissary's responsibilities extended now not only to the prisoners and the guards, but to five hundred ravenous black laborers, who worked feverishly through the night by eerie torchlight, and to scores of Yankee prisoners who earned double rations because of their work outside. If Richard Winder could have had his way, though, a lot more Yankees would have started drawing double rations: besides the regulators, the graveyard crew, the office clerks, the hospital nurses, the quartermaster's fatigue details, the musicians, and the cooks and bakers, Winder wished to employ hundreds of other paroled Yankees in the improvement of their own condition within the stockade, but until now he had lacked the materials.[11]

Recently, despite the handicap of a spending limit of fifty dollars per thousand board feet, Captain Winder had secured the lumber he wanted for barracks—and to complete the new cookhouse he had begun just north of the prison, where food waste could not pollute Stockade Creek. Thanks to Rousseau's horsemen he still needed nails, but he remained hopeful they would come; for the moment he concerned himself with unloading nearly seventy-five thousand board feet of yellow pine.[12]

That job fell to the Negro Squad, as prison documents invariably labeled it. At that time somewhat fewer than seventy black prisoners lived at Andersonville, huddling in their own enclave near the south gate. Most of them had been captured at Olustee, and belonged either to the 54th Massachusetts or to the 8th or 35th U.S. Colored Infantry regiments, the former of which was raised in Pennsylvania and the latter in North Carolina. Some who had been slaves had to worry periodically about going back under the lash (as did those, probably, who had always been free but were coveted by slave owners), but Captain Wirz resisted turning over any such alleged contrabands. Individual guards committed some petty cruelties against them, but for the most part the prison authorities treated their black prisoners little differently than they did the whites ones: they seemed to reserve their greatest animosity for the white officers who served with the Colored Troops.

Black prisoners did complain that they were sometimes forced to work, and whipped if they refused. At least one sergeant of the 54th Massachusetts who staged a one-man strike was turned back into the prison in tears from a severe whipping, but the blacks seem to have suffered no official punishment when they declined to join the slaves who were working on the fortifications on July 20. Instead, they were put to work on the lumber piles. The opportunity for exercise and extra rations probably contributed to their impressive survival rate: despite a longer average incarceration than most prisoners, only a dozen black soldiers died at Andersonville out of about a hundred who eventually landed there. White mortality exceeded 30 percent overall—more than twice that of blacks—and it ranged much higher for those who entered the prison so early. However involuntary their labor may have been, it seemed to redound to the blacks' benefit.[13]

For nearly three weeks now a white prisoner, a private, had had charge of the Negro Squad as its "sergeant." Otis Knight, a carpenter from Worcester, Massachusetts, had been captured in the initial assault on Petersburg, and had entered the stockade on June 19. He may have been chosen for his civilian calling, with the intention of making him foreman of a regular construction gang, but for most of his tenure he was occupied with making his charges clean up their campsite, or with complaining about rations that seemed to come up short. One of the guards had confiscated a collection of eggs, potatoes, and onions from Knight's black wards just a couple of days before, perhaps out of personal spite for their refusal to help with the earthworks; Knight had already spoken with Captain Wirz about that sort of thing.

On the morning of July 22 Knight led some of his men down to the south gate, where dozens of prisoners champed to get outside for work or medical attention. A lingering agitation over the recent raid still infected the guards, and the rumors of a planned outbreak had not yet subsided. That break was supposed to come at some point when the gates opened, so the sentries who stood by to let the paroled men leave held their muskets in nervous readiness. The officer counting off the details found the prisoners pressing more anxiously than usual that morning, and he grew alarmed; so did the guard, who leveled his weapon. Perhaps he meant only to threaten the insistent Yankees, but the muzzle of his smoothbore pointed directly at Otis Knight's belly, and at least one witness said Knight grabbed at the barrel to turn it away. That was all the guard needed: the hollow report of his musket reverberated inside the gate enclosure, which filled with smoke. The crush of prisoners naturally recoiled, leaving Knight and two other victims on the ground, but in a few moments some of their comrades returned to carry the wounded men to the hospital. The two others survived, but the gutshot Knight died the next day, and his name was entered on the hospital register beside the abbreviation "Nig. Sgt."

Even Knight's friends from his old regiment did not show much sympathy for him, judging his death to be his own fault. In a week or two his anxious wife would open a letter from him, never guessing that he was already dead.[14]

The slaves working on the entrenchments had brought their owners' own tools, which Richard Winder could not touch, but somewhere he found more than a hundred shovels to replace the shipment lost to Rousseau's cavalry. On the unseasonably cold morning of July 25 the 95th detachment of prisoners formed at the gate, having agreed to clean up the swamp, and marched out for their implements. Wirz's endeavors of May had consisted of building simple dikes on either side of the creek, but the passage of so many bathers and clothes washers had broken them down, and the banks had turned to muck again with alluvial overflow and the filth of those too lazy or sick to make their way to the sinks on the other side. While the earth-burnished blades of shovels twinkled in the sunlight around the fort that was still growing before Wirz's headquarters, Yankees inside chopped away at the slope north of the creek, dragging dry clay down to fill the stinking bog. Others hammered at the decrepit sink structure, salvaging what boards and frame they could to build a new set. Robert Kellogg, who scorned those of his comrades who worked outside for double rations, saw no patriotic lapse in working for extra food inside. He flailed at the clay with the rest, keeping one eye open for any roots he might be able to use for firewood.[15]

So objectionable had the swamp become that the internal improvements drew widespread applause, but for more observant inmates the work served notice that the Confederates had every reason to believe the prisoners would be staying here indefinitely, and that the rumors of exchange and parole were just that—rumors. With all the forts springing up around the palisade it seemed unlikely that any roving cavalry could release the prisoners, and even if they tried to do so they would have to shell the batteries, in which case they could not avoid drawing a great deal of blood inside the stockade. A Macon newspaper predicted an exchange on August 6, but some who had hung their hopes on such sparks before could not bring themselves to believe it now. Despair had gripped many by late July, but, unlike the clinically depressed patients diagnosed with "nostalgia," these men suffered from a more active hopelessness: one cavalryman tried to cut his throat with a knife too dull to do the job; another rigged his suspenders into a noose, draped them over the flimsy rafter of his shebang, and tried to hang himself; one scorbutic Vermonter expressed an intention to do away with himself, but the disease killed him first; a fourth prisoner stepped under the dead line and asked the guard to shoot him, only to fail when the sentry refused.[16]

Not all the guards were so sympathetic, especially when the post and prison commanders fretted over an approaching raid. News of another one came by telegraph on July 27, just after a few hundred fresh prisoners stumbled through the south gate. Most of these had come from the Shenandoah Valley, where they were swept up by Jubal Early. Among them were large numbers of hundred-day men, principally from the 135th Ohio National Guard. These poor devils had arrived in Maryland to guard railroads and bridges the previous May, expecting to go home by the end of August, but fate had thrown them in front of Jubal Early's raid on Washington. In five weeks their regiment would return to Ohio, where the survivors would tell and retell the tale of their summer's campaign into the age of the airplane, embellishing the story a mite with every retelling, but for at least thirty-three of them Andersonville wrote the final chapter. As an introduction to the prison, these fair-weather warriors saw the book slammed shut on another man's story within two hours after they entered the gate. An emaciated Pennsylvania cavalryman—a German-born blacksmith named William Unversagt—shouldered his way to the watering hole with them, and one of the uninitiated new men reached too far beyond the dead line to find clear water. The sentry just above them decided that this would be a good time to reiterate the lesson of the line, but instead of punishing the unwitting culprit he put his bullet through Unversagt's brain. The German dropped dead in the creek; strangers dragged him out of the freshly diked ditch (hastily, so he would not bloody the drinking water) and laid him with the day's dead. The next morning the creaking charnel wagon carried him to his grave, which confused Federal groundskeepers later marked "Unknown."[17]

Prisoners who watched Unversagt fall cursed the guards for murderers. They supposed that each sentry who killed a prisoner was awarded a thirty-day furlough—a myth that won widespread acceptance as the result of a misunderstanding in Furlow's militia battalion. Perhaps it began with a pun on the militia commander's name and worked its way through the rest of the garrison as a joke, finally entering the prison as some pigeon-roost sentry's retort to a taunting prisoner. Whatever its genesis, many of the prisoners believed it, and Wirz's habit of relieving guards who had shot men seemed to corroborate the notion, as did the guards' newfound readiness to shoot. Perhaps a few simpleminded Georgia Reserves believed it, too. It seemed not to harm the credibility of so preposterous a rumor that Confederate sergeants occasionally reprimanded trigger-happy sentinels within earshot of the Yankees, and of course the captives could not know that Wirz filed charges against such excessive zeal. Nor did it seem to occur to those who credited the furlough fable that, had it been true, the understrength prison garrison would have melted away behind a blaze of gunfire.[18]

Private Unversagt had come to his death at least indirectly as a result of the news that Federal cavalry had bolted forward again from Sherman's army, sweeping around Hood's right flank toward Macon. General Hood's cavalry commander, Joe Wheeler, detected the departure of more than two thousand Union horsemen on July 27; the telegraph wires started singing abruptly, and Howell Cobb and John Winder immediately resumed their worrying that the Yankees had designs on the prisons at Macon and Camp Sumter. It happened that the raiders, under Major General George Stoneman, had been ordered to cut the Macon & Western Railroad below Atlanta, but this time Cobb and Winder did have genuine cause for alarm: just as he left army headquarters General Stoneman had asked William Sherman's permission to free the Macon and Andersonville captives, and Sherman had granted him license to do so—after he tore up the railroad.[19]

That same day General Winder issued an appeal to the citizens of nine counties surrounding Andersonville, calling for fifty wagons and two thousand slaves properly armed with axes, picks, and shovels. He promised to return that work force in time for the not-too-distant harvest season, whether the fortifications were completed or not, buttressing his plea with an unsubtle threat to impress the labor and transportation if the people did not respond. One prisoner thought he saw an additional 250 blacks working on the trenches by July 31, but that appears to have been the extent of the slave owners' response.[20]

On July 28 Joe Wheeler heard of another three thousand Yankee cavalry arcing toward the Macon & Western out of the west, under Edward McCook, and from Stoneman's stragglers he learned that that general had determined to advance directly on Macon—and the Union officers' bastille. This news spurred the respective prison commandants to even greater efforts. Fearful of yet another mass escape attempt, Wirz reminded the prisoners not to gather in large groups near the two gates. Should any such throngs accumulate there, he again threatened to open his guns on them. To punctuate his decree, he elevated one piece slightly and loaded it with a solid shot: as he probably suspected, the arrival of several hundred new prisoners that afternoon attracted the usual horde of gawkers, hawkers, and newsmongers, whereupon a Florida cannoneer yanked his lanyard and sent the twelve-pound ball sailing over the prisoners' heads. Those coming through the gate flinched in anxious confusion, but the stockade veterans recovered quickly; remembering the false alarm of a fortnight before, they even summoned enough courage to jeer at their keepers.[21]

Twice that night the guards found cause to send another round across the prison. The next morning Captain Wirz defined the prohibited area with a few scraps of white linen suspended from poles, east of the gates. Many still seemed not to understand the significance of those flags, for when Wirz added more of them a week later one sergeant feared they might be range markers, but no more crowds collected in the forbidden zone and the lanyards fell slack.[22]

Joe Wheeler had split his cavalry to simultaneously check McCook and chase Stoneman, but Stoneman outdistanced Wheeler's smaller wing. Governor Brown, who had joined Howell Cobb in Macon, appealed for every man who could find a musket to report for duty, and Cobb collected all the militia he could find, adding them to his incomplete new companies of Reserves. Governor Brown had recently ordered Furlow's militia battalion to the defense of Atlanta, but he canceled those orders in light of Stoneman's foray; that battalion, at least, would remain at the prison.[23]

Stoneman approached Macon from the east on July 30, only to be turned back at the Ocmulgee River by a ragtag agglomeration of Georgia

Reserves, militia, and impromptu citizen companies. Having failed either to destroy the railroad as Sherman had ordered or to accomplish his own pet projects, Stoneman raced wildly back into the waiting arms of Wheeler's detached brigades, which welcomed the general and hundreds of his men to the very prisons they had hoped to liberate. Wheeler himself confronted McCook the same day, near Newnan, and sent him packing.[24]

Unaware they had been reprieved, General Winder and Henry Wirz girded for the last ditch. They enhanced their numbers with boys who had just turned sixteen—youths drained from the piney woods by the last two frantic proclamations. Some of the lads could barely see over the stockade from their guard posts. While these boys climbed the ladders the construction gangs worked in shifts all night, and Winder put his diminutive garrison under arms in the new trenches as each length of them was completed.[25]

Neither did the prisoners understand that their liberators had been undone: it was not until the day of Stoneman's repulse, July 30 (just as laborers put the finishing touches on the star fort), that they even learned the particulars of their captors' obvious uneasiness. The word came via the Negro Squad, which filed back into the stockade that afternoon. Some of them had stolen fleeting moments with slaves at work on the trenches, and during those seconds at a water cask or a latrine their legendary underground information system had done its work. The black prisoners brought their white comrades the accurate report that Federal cavalry had shelled Macon that very day. The tale set tongues to wagging, involuntarily lifting the spirits of men who hardly dared to hope again.[26]

The following morning the slave gangs began dropping the remaining trees on the northwest corner and the north side of the stockade, working their way around the eastern wall while others moved in with shovels to build the bastions laid out by the engineers. The pines fell in windrows with their tops tangled, and men with hatchets went among them, sharpening the ends of their branches to form the defensive obstructions known as abatis. The landscape beyond the palisade grew almost as bare and desolate as that within. The work on the sinks and the creek continued, and Richard Winder's agents finally signed up a few cobblers, all of which hinted that the commandant anticipated no difficulty in repelling any attack on the prison, but indications of desperation seemed to belie that complacency. Southern sergeants roved the prison, looking for artillerists who might be willing to take the Confederate oath and serve as instructors (or as actual gunners) for the crews of twelve surplus cannon they had found to fill the new forts—overtures one Connecticut Yankee called "the cheekiest thing yet." The night of July 31 portended immediate action, for the work continued through a pounding thunderstorm; in the flashes of lightning the prisoners could see miserable Confederates lying under arms in the fresh mud of their parapets.[27]

Though it was clear any assault on the works would cause considerable bloodshed among the prisoners, the euphoria of impending release blossomed for two solid days. No trains came from Macon during those forty-eight hours, further encouraging the Yankees even though that failure in transportation meant scanty rations again on August 1. Not until late that afternoon did three trains roll into Anderson depot in quick succession, bringing wounded Federals and Confederates and, at last, some rations. Still hopeful, at least one prisoner misinterpreted the cars as the ride home for paroled hospital patients. Others brightened that evening at the unmistakable sound of cannonading from the direction of Macon.[28]

The last lingering illusions about imminent freedom crumbled on August 2. Just after another terrific thunderstorm sent lightning crashing into some of the surviving trees right outside the stockade, four hundred Union cavalrymen trudged into the palisade. The drenched new prisoners brought discouraging news: they, General Stoneman, and many more of his men had been captured. Numbers of McCook's men had also been gobbled up at the Newnan fight, among them a towering Iowan named Lawson Carley and that reluctant cavalryman from the fjords of Norway, Knud Hanson. The remaining raiders had fled back to Sherman's army in confusion, and the desperate affair was over.[29]

Whole troops of horse soldiers entered the gate without blankets, tents, or any of their cooking apparatus, and in some cases without even their coats or caps. So freely had they plundered homes in the path of their raid that the Confederates took everything from them during the registration process in front of Wirz's headquarters. Prodding guards tossed watches, jewelry, silverware, and at least one painting into piles and boxes for future identification by their rightful owners. Georgia Confederates had begun to turn particularly vindictive toward Union cavalrymen since the July raids began, and with these troopers the guards took their greatest revenge, relieving them of everything useful or negotiable. For four days yellowleg prisoners drifted in from Stoneman's and McCook's columns, dousing the final spark of hope among the thousands they joined.[30]

Lest other Yankee cavalrymen try their luck, the borrowed slaves shoveled around the clock, closing the last gap in the fortifications. At night, inside the stockade, discouraged prisoners who tried to sleep could hear the slave gangs' mournful work songs carrying word of their bondage heavenward.[31]

During the frantic fortnight from July 18 to August 1, while the administrators of Andersonville fretted over cavalry raids, the armies facing each other around Atlanta had grappled three separate times. On the 18th John Bell Hood took over for Joe Johnston, whose defensive tactics had irritated Jefferson Davis. Two days later Hood struck one of Sherman's armies at Peachtree Creek, north of the city, and two days after that he pounded another one east of town, killing the commander of that wing. On July 28 one of Hood's corps fought one of Sherman's at Ezra Church. These and smaller actions generated thousands of unwilling guests for the Confederacy.

One of those was James Bradd. On July 22 the colonel of the 13th Iowa dispatched Bradd's company to support another regiment a mile and a half south of the Georgia Railroad. They filed into powerful entrenchments, but in the afternoon a double line of Arkansas infantry and dismounted Texas cavalry threw themselves against those works. Yelling like banshees, the Confederates swept over one end of the trenches and circled behind the isolated Iowans, forcing them to throw down their weapons and march to the rear.[32]

The prisoners did see Atlanta after all, marching through it between tandem ranks of bayonets. They made their first camp at East Point, where the railroads forked to Alabama and Macon, but their hosts could offer them no transportation: so many wounded needed the cars that Bradd and his comrades had to walk. With a single piece of hardtack and a slab of rancid pork apiece, they started south alongside the railroad tracks. Two days later the bedraggled blue column arrived in the streets of Jonesborough, where the citizens sneered and swore at the first Yankees they had ever seen. Two more days brought them to Griffin, where they found cornbread and bacon plentiful, if not tasty. That afternoon one train collected part of the column, but Bradd's contingent had to wait through a rainy night for a second one, which picked them up late the next forenoon. Despite a painfully slow pace their cars ran off the track twenty miles above Macon, injuring some of the prisoners badly and leaving the rest to stand under guard until late that night, when another train backed up from Macon to take them aboard. They slept in the cars until the locomotive lurched forward early in the morning, covering the eighty miles to Andersonville in seven or eight hours. Captain Wirz spent two hours counting and recording them while they stood beneath the broiling sun, and Bradd entered the gates at four o'clock on the afternoon of July 29, nine days before his twentieth birthday.[33]

The sight of the suffering multitude stunned Bradd, but he consulted his Bible for solace and bathed daily at the creek to ward off disease. He arrived just as Stoneman's raid abbreviated the supplies from Macon, and the Alabama connection had not yet been repaired, so prison rations fell dreadfully short, but even after his portions increased he complained of rotten bacon. After ten days inside the stockade he developed diarrhea, which quickly worsened, and soon his daily ablutions began to lapse. Two weeks after the diarrhea appeared he recorded that he was very weak, and at the end of his first month at Andersonville he started passing blood—flux, he called it, which the doctors would have diagnosed as dysentery. By then he could hardly walk, and he only left his shelter at the insistence of his bowels.

"It is only a question of time in here," he wrote. "Some will hold out longer than others but all are a going down."[34]

While James Bradd had found the people of Jonesborough contemptuous of him, not all Southerners felt so harshly toward the prisoners. Reverend E. B. Duncan, a Methodist minister who followed evangelical circuits in the tradition of Francis Asbury, came up from Florida to preach to Captain Dyke's artillerymen. His sermon caught them on Sunday morning, July 31, as they stood to their guns awaiting Stoneman's Yankee horde. He intended to speak to the prisoners inside the stockade that afternoon, but when he walked over to General Winder's office in the village he was told Captain Wirz would have to issue that pass. Back he came to prison headquarters, behind the so-called star fort, but Wirz had gone home for the day. The clerks told Duncan that Wirz lived about two miles away (since June he had boarded his family with the post butcher, a fellow named Bass), so the parson opted to stay overnight.[35]

The next morning Reverend Duncan returned to Wirz's headquarters. Wirz, who had begun to feel vaguely ill, greeted the minister rather courteously; he offered him a permanent pass to enter the stockade, but warned him of the seven o'clock roll call and the nine o'clock sick call that might interfere with his intentions. Duncan waited until ten to go in, but he still had to pick his way around hundreds of sick men whom the overburdened doctors had not yet examined.[36]

Duncan carried a recent Macon newspaper with him that contained an article about an upcoming prisoner exchange. As he worked his way up Water Street and across the double bridge, a crowd gathered around him and barred his path, dozens of voices pleading with him to read the piece. He wished to save his lungs for his sermon, so he handed the paper over to a spokesman for each of the successive throngs; every few paces the way would close again as a new rush of ragamuffins called for an encore. Finally Duncan reached Selman's sutlery, just inside the north gate, where someone overturned a box for him. With the chanting of hucksters and gamblers echoing in the background, he climbed atop the box and waved the men closer to him, so he would not have to shout. The sun had burned away a cool morning mist and began to beat unmercifully, but Duncan spoke for hours while hundreds and perhaps thousands of prisoners crowded around him. His throat dried out, but the smell of the place reminded him that the water might be tainted, so he asked for none. An afternoon shower cooled him somewhat, but his congregation remained and he continued until his voice gave out. Some of Andersonville's more affluent residents invited him into the shade of their shanty, offering to fetch water for him, and in a very short time one of them returned with a bucket and a dipper; the bucket and the brief absence of the man who brought it suggested that he had stopped at a nearby well. The water looked so clear, and Duncan's mouth had gone so dry, that he overcame his reservations and drained the dipper, finding the contents equal to the best he had encountered in Georgia.[37]

The exchange story in Reverend Duncan's newspaper contained an element of truth, for a special exchange had been in the works for a long time. Since June letters had been passing between Sam Jones, the Confederate commander at Charleston, and John Foster, the Union general who kept that city under his guns. On July 22 Adjutant General Cooper gave John Winder the freedom to move the Federal officers at Macon to Charleston, and to transfer a like number of Andersonville prisoners to Macon to take their places. Winder did transport some six hundred officers, but Stoneman's raid seems to have discouraged him from shipping any enlisted men within reach of Yankee cavalry. The negotiations for a special exchange and the departure of the six hundred officers lent credibility to rumors of an August 6 exchange, but when the flags of truce met in Charleston harbor only a hundred men crossed to their respective lines—generals and field officers to a man.[38]

The only Camp Sumter prisoners who would see exchange in the next fortnight were Edward Wellington Boate and the five other members of the petition committee, plus a supplementary delegation of fifteen men. The two July cavalry raids had apparently postponed their departure, but on August 9 they marched over to Anderson Station with their well-thumbed petition. Of more than thirty-eight thousand Federal enlisted men whom the cars had thus far delivered at the depot, these were the only ones who had yet boarded the return train.[39]

The first day of August brought other visitors besides Reverend Duncan. From the adjutant and inspector general's office in Richmond came Lieutenant Colonel Daniel T. Chandler, whose mission included a formal inspection of the prison. To assist his endeavors Colonel Chandler brought with him Major W. Carvel Hall, and to season his report he carried a generous infusion of righteous indignation.

Chandler appears to have been one of the least devoted of that small company of men who held field commissions in both the United States and Confederate armies during the Civil War. Hostilities had caught him in San Antonio as major of the 3rd U.S. Infantry, with a brevet as lieutenant colonel. He surrendered with the rest of the post, and for the next ten months he remained in the North on parole, awaiting exchange. Though he was only forty-two, Chandler asked to be put on the retired list as soon as he was exchanged. He was a native of the District of Columbia, which is to say that he was a Southerner, and during his antebellum army service he had acquired property in Louisiana that he wished to look after; in December of 1862 he resigned his U.S. Army commission altogether. Early the next February Federal pickets on the lower Potomac caught him trying to sneak a rowboat into Virginia from Saint Mary's County, Maryland. He sat in a jail cell at Washington's Old Capitol Prison until late October, 1863, when Union authorities permitted him to cross the lines under a flag of truce to arrange his exchange for the son of Governor Andrew Johnson, of Tennessee, whom the Confederates held. But for the influence of Johnson's esteemed father, Chandler might have spent the rest of the war in prison, or if the Federal commissioner of exchange had had his way he might have swung as a spy; as it turned out he secured the exchange, and in February of 1864 he took an appointment as lieutenant colonel in Samuel Cooper's adjutant general's department—to avoid Confederate conscription, or so he later claimed.[40]

Like many in the Confederacy, Colonel Chandler probably foresaw the demise of that nation by the final summer of the war, and at Andersonville he witnessed the misery that might stir a conquering Union to retribution. If he did not compose his observations with an eye toward appeasing the vengeful victor, he at least proved ready enough to cite his critical reports of Andersonville and other prisons as a means of currying favor with the conquerors after the Confederate government had collapsed.[41]

Chandler and Major Hall perambulated the prison in company with Captain Wirz, whom Chandler found genuinely concerned about conditions there. As testimony to that, the 95th detachment of prisoners continued shoveling dry clay on top of the swamp from the north slope, cutting little channels for drainage, and reconstructing the sinks with a sluice to clean them out. The colonel reserved high praise for Wirz, whose energy he considered worthy the assignment of several commissioned subordinates, but nothing else about the prison earned his commendation. He found the overall enclosure too small, and the stream polluted by cookhouse waste; the absence of a regular street system inhibited all attempts to police the camp of filth, and the prisoners had no barracks; rations included nothing to prevent scurvy, and often had to be issued raw to men who owned no cooking utensils; most of the doctors showed incompetence, and the hospital proved wholly inadequate. He judged the garrison particularly inefficient. Of nearly four thousand names on the combined rolls of the 55th Georgia, Furlow's battalion, Dyke's battery, and the four Reserve regiments, 45 percent were sick, absent without leave, under arrest, or detailed on other duty; many of the infantrymen carried no bayonets, while 452 lacked any weapons at all. Except for the 55th Georgia and Dyke's artillerymen the garrison desperately needed training under competent drillmasters—the efforts of Winder's Georgia lieutenant notwithstanding—and the fragment of the 55th Georgia constantly teetered on the verge of mutiny. Post supplies fell pitifully short in every category. The doctors could dole out no medicine because they could not find any; the quartermaster could not supply enough transportation because he had no power to impress it. The post commissary, Captain Armstrong, avoided an inspection of his books by locking them up and departing on sick leave as soon as Chandler arrived, but from the prisoners themselves Chandler learned of their insufficient rations—which should not have been so surprising, in light of the recent raids.[42]

In an addendum to his report, Chandler mixed praise and rebuke in his assessment of the various officers at Camp Sumter. Wirz, Richard Winder, and Colonel Henry Forno—a veteran Louisiana officer recently assigned to command the troops—all met with his hearty approval, but three surgeons, one staff officer, and General Winder drew Chandler's criticism for inefficiency and incompetence. John Winder suffered particular censure. The manner in which Chandler offered his condemnation of the general suggests that the two of them held a conversation on the state of affairs in the stockade: Chandler appears to have found great fault, while the mercurial Winder must have responded sarcastically, or with at least theatrical insensitivity, as though he were deliberately ruining the health of his prisoners. Although Winder's own actions contradicted any such notion, Chandler took that response to heart, recommending that Winder be removed to another assignment.[43]

Chandler also forwarded a plan for permanently reclaiming the swamp alongside Stockade Creek. That plan came from the pen of Cyrus B. Harkie, a civil engineer who also happened to be the colonel of the 55th Georgia. Chandler's submission of the document implies that Harkie was a far better engineer than he was a soldier, for even Chandler commented on his utter incompetence as colonel of his regiment. Harkie's performance during the 1862 Kentucky invasion had featured what some considered a habitual neglect of duty, with such particular transgressions as selling captured mules for his own profit and handing out unauthorized furloughs as personal favors. In December of 1862 his subordinate officers banded together at Cumberland Gap to demand his resignation, and apparently the men stood Harkie on a stump and forced him to perform certain indignities with a tentpole. After this humiliating episode he signed the desired resignation, but once free of his tormentors he asked the secretary of war to withhold it, only to be dismissed later by a court-martial when his regimental officers brought charges against him. The capture of most of the regiment the next September removed many of the witnesses against him, however, and by late April of 1864 he had secured reinstatement. Had the War Department assigned him to the command of the remains of his regiment he would have superseded the very efficient lieutenant colonel, Alexander Persons, so Harkie did not see orders to resume that office until June 20, after John Winder had replaced Persons as commander of the post. Even then he acted as a staff officer, declining to take command of the depleted, contemptuous regiment.[44]

Chandler learned a garbled version of the Cumberland Gap mutiny that dated it more recently, and located it at Camp Sumter, but this negative observation did not prejudice his opinion of Harkie's drainage report, which he endorsed. A month later the War Department assigned its chief engineer to implement Harkie's plan, but by then either the removal of most of the prisoners had obviated the project, or Wirz's August efforts had proved satisfactory, for the work seems never to have been undertaken.[45]

Harkie remained on post for a few more weeks before submitting another resignation, which he also seems to have retrieved. He spent the rest of the war in southwest Georgia—he called Randolph County home, now—and he retained his commission until the surrender. A month before Appomattox he entered a Macon hospital, suffering from gonorrhea; he returned to duty March 20, disappearing at war's end into the same obscurity whence he had come.[46]

Judging by Chandler's introductory comments, General Winder suspected even before it was submitted that Chandler's report would be entirely unfavorable, as indeed it proved to be. The colonel did not complete his evaluation until four days after he first entered the gates, and no one saw it for several days after that, although he may have dropped some hints about the faults he found. The palliative measures Winder had already initiated therefore had nothing to do with Chandler's complaints.

Winder had generated his own assessment of the prisoners' condition before Chandler ever showed up, and his inspector had arrived at many of the same conclusions. For a week prior to Chandler's visit Winder had occupied police crews on the swamp and sinks, laying the foundation for the first of Henry Wirz's dams, and paroled masons and carpenters had nearly finished relocating the cookhouse. Winder had already arranged to build barracks presently, as well, but first he must make some room: on August 2 more than a thousand Federal soldiers filled railroad cars bound for Andersonville, threatening to crowd the stockade beyond the greatest number of men it ever held.[47]

During the Stoneman scare an Ohio cavalry sergeant remarked upon the growing proportion of sick men within the prison proper. Each mess seemed to have at least one man ailing. "Every tent is a hospital," wrote the Buckeye. The stockade addition had not been open a full month yet, but, because of the limitations of Dr. White's infirmary, the prison's streets had been refilled by sick men who had not so much as a blanket to their names. That same August a surgeon, probably Dr. White, examined the interior of the prison in the company of another officer—no doubt Colonel Chandler—whom some prisoners mistook for Captain Wirz's replacement. Inside, the doctor found five thousand men he considered sick, hundreds of whom still gathered at the south gate each day to seek treatment at the makeshift dispensary. It helped both to appease Chandler and to open some space in the prison when White issued an order, perhaps through Wirz's office, for all the sick to report to the doctors. The response swamped the surgeons in the little medical enclosures just outside the gate, and they simply began choosing men for outright admission to the hospital. Wounded prisoners from Macon and the Atlanta battlefields began to arrive that evening, and ersatz ambulances shuttled them from the station to the hospital, spurring the more sanguine and imaginative prisoners to suppose the traffic rode in the opposite direction: from that misinterpretation arose the speculation that ghost battalions of sick were on their way to Hilton Head, via Savannah, and that seemed to confirm the new tales of an August 3 or August 6 exchange.[48]

Hospitalization of the infirm continued throughout the next day, until more than nine hundred men had been removed, but a sea of sick remained, waiting all day in the hot sun only to be turned back and told to try again the next day. August 4 proved hotter still. The surgeons began calling names before sunrise, ignoring the regular sick call, and Wirz waived the daily roll call, but the procession had so jammed the hospital wards that it finally had to be halted; harried attendants herded the anxious applicants back to their quarters so the day's rations could be handed out. Referrals resumed under another blazing sun on August 5, but the hospital had begun to burst by then and doctors could choose only a fraction of the hopeful mass. Hundreds of those sent to the hospital in the past few days lay, uncovered by either tent or blanket, in the hospital streets, and the ward surgeons quickly ran out of medicine altogether. Now the doctors at the south-gate dispensary could tag a man for admission only when the Grim Reaper opened a vacancy, which was fairly often: a Plymouth Pilgrim named Asa Root entered the hospital late on August 3 and noted the deaths of two men from his own regiment within four days, then a strange hand recorded the final entry in Root's own diary. Similar mortality plagued the stockade, too. Three days without shade had taken their toll: deaths jumped from an average of 74 per day on the first four days of August to 90 on August 5 and 103 on August 6—the first time more than 100 men died within a single twenty-four-hour period. To reduce unnecessary exposure, the surgeons began calling out the sick by individual detachments.[49]

As Daniel Chandler noted, scurvy had begun to assail thousands at Camp Sumter. Samuel Melvin feared he had come down with it, and made an unsuccessful attempt to fight his way through the throng of sick on August 3; Samuel Gibson, one of the Plymouth Pilgrims, tried that day and the next to escort his failing messmate to the doctors, and in a few days he, too, began to suffer symptoms. On August 4, John Whitten's birthday, he recorded that he felt like an old man, hardly able to get about even with a cane; two days later his hamstrings began to contract, drawing his legs up short, and within two weeks he could not walk at all. Edwin Forbes complained of a sore mouth and throat on August 5. All these rheumatic aches and tender gums served as sure signs of the vitamin deficiency known as scorbutus. Only those fortunate enough to obtain fresh fruits and vegetables could avoid it after many months of incarceration, and even they described tokens of the disease in most of those who lay around them. By mid-August any prisoner could point to an afflicted tentmate whose legs and feet had begun to swell, and a former schoolteacher remarked upon numerous comrades who were "rotting alive" with advanced scorbutic ulcers.[50]

Despite the obvious prevalence of scurvy, some did not realize they had contracted it. Henry Adams, another Plymouth prisoner, passed a week of vague illness and weakness before observing that his leg had turned lame; a few days later, when he found he could not walk, he treated the problem with liniment. He never stood upright again, and perished after two months of suffering from an ailment that might have been cured with a few onions. Adams was one of the poorer prisoners, but even his more affluent comrade, Sergeant Major Kellogg, could not avoid a brush with that deadly scourge.[51]

In the report he compiled for Colonel Chandler, Isaiah White advised issuing antiscorbutics like rice, beans, vinegar, and molasses. Presumably at General Winder's behest the post commissary requisitioned extra quantities of those items, and barely a week later beans began to appear in such noticeable volume that at least a few prisoners carped about the monotony; the quartermaster gave these grumblers the welcome reply that he would soon feed them sweet potatoes until they complained of them, as well. Apparently the commissary suppliers failed to obtain as many of those as they expected, but by August 22 the oldest detachments of Yankees started to draw enough molasses to soak their cornbread in it: Kellogg, who customarily waxed critical of anything Confederate, judged it far superior to the Northern variety. These preventive rations saved Kellogg, Forbes, and Gibson from the worst of scurvy's effects, and brought a few like John Whitten back from the jaws of death, but for Melvin and Adams they came too late.[52]

The surge of hospital admissions that first week in August did little to relieve the crowding, for more new prisoners arrived than the doctors could accommodate in their wards, and the number of Yankees within the stockade stood well over thirty thousand on the evening of August 5. The next morning regular sick calls resumed, with the surgeons sending no one to the hospital unless death had opened a "place" for him there: the doctors at Andersonville did not often lapse into the common medical tabulation of "beds," so ludicrous was the term in the face of such want; instead they referred merely to the space a withered body might occupy on the earth beneath one of those rotten tent flies.[53]

The normal sick call at Andersonville convened at the south gate each morning at eight. All the worst cases clustered together in the custody of their respective detachment sergeants, who led them individually out the wicket to one of the partitioned stands erected against the exterior of the stockade. In each of those cubicles waited a surgeon (or a civilian contract physician) with a paroled prisoner, who acted as his clerk. So long as his medicines lasted, the doctor prescribed for the ailments he diagnosed, and when pharmaceuticals ran out he resorted to folk cures, or suggested vegetable products that could probably not be obtained anyway. Some of the attending physicians adhered to prescriptive formulas concocted by the regular surgeons, who apparently doubted the competence of their colleagues. The ambulatory patients took their turns first, then returned to the bull pen with whatever medications they had been offered, shouldering their way back through an insistent wall of other sick who often jostled them enough to dash those curative powders and liquids on the verminous earth. The crippled and decrepit waited in the broiling sun or driving rain until as late as two o'clock before they saw a doctor, and some who had crawled as far as the gate, or had been carried there, lay dead when the hospital steward sounded his final call. Friends of the victims— or even strangers, greedy for a few sticks of wood—carried those silent patients directly to the deadhouse, while clerks granted them posthumous admission to the hospital and made their best guesses at the maladies that had killed them.[54]

As the rising sun bathed Andersonville's eastern palisade in scorching scarlet on August 4, 1864, a Connecticut private named Henry Burke stirred in his blanket near the dead line. Perhaps some of the sick disturbed him as they crowded toward the gate in the stifling dawn heat, hoping to get out of the stockade: they may have interrupted a pleasant dream of his rural home along the eastern fringe of the Taconic Mountains. Burke thrashed a little, and in the trancelike moments just prior to waking he rolled under the dead line. Still inspired by the strictures of the Stoneman scare, the closest sentry called out only once, then fired on the startled sleeper before he could scramble back to safety. Burke caught the slug, a New York cavalryman lying nearby stopped some of the buckshot, and after some initial howling both of them fell into line with those clamoring for the attention of the surgeons.[55]

These two would survive their wounds only to die of scurvy and typhoid fever, respectively, but two days later another prisoner experienced a more abrupt encounter. At about two o'clock on Saturday afternoon, August 6, a new prisoner waited amid a knot of men seeking water at the bridge, but someone ahead of him stretched too far upstream for the comfort of the sentinel on the first post south of the creek. That guard emptied his smoothbore at the trespasser, hitting the innocent newcomer instead. Shot through the head, he fell like a stone.[56]

Yankee diarists commented angrily on the flurry of gunfire that first week in August. All of a sudden the guards were enforcing the dead line in earnest, at first because their officers had demanded greater vigilance of them, but after August 4 their stringency may have arisen from outrage over the excesses of Stoneman's raiders. At any rate, the rash of shootings appears to have been out of the ordinary. In the fourteen months of Andersonville's occupation 149 prisoners died of wounds: both Norton Chipman, the judge advocate who prosecuted Henry Wirz, and John McElroy, the poet laureate of the prison, tried to imply that all 149 perished at the hands of the guards. Both also charged that far more than 149 men had been shot to death inside the stockade: Judge Advocate Chipman put the figure at 300.

Original diaries and official post documents tell a much different tale. Only 11 prisoners seem to have been killed by sentries, while even fewer were wounded by them: the high ratio of fatalities would reflect the deadly effects of .75 and .69 caliber buck-and-ball loads at such short ranges. At least 6 of all the shootings also seem to have been accidental, and 2 were deliberately provoked, while Otis Knight was responsible not only for his own death but for the injuries to the men who were wounded by the blast that killed him. In fact, most of the 149 who died of gunshot wounds had arrived at Camp Sumter with injuries suffered on the battlefield. The frequency of shots—particularly at night—convinced a great many prisoners that random shootings were an everyday occurrence, but the majority of those reports came from guards who injudiciously discharged their weapons into the air as they ventured to or from their posts. Black powder charges had to be replaced periodically, especially in damp weather, but manually unloading a muzzle-loading musket with a ramrod and worm was hard work; post regulations prohibited the firing of weapons except in the line of duty, so the lazier troops escaped detection by doing it in the dark—mostly. One lounging Illinois infantryman, James Dennison, watched the slug from such a shot land within six feet of him in broad daylight.[57]

The majority of the eleven men killed at Andersonville died for a violation of the dead line, which Colonel Chipman tried to characterize as a diabolical invention created to legitimize the systematic murder of Union prisoners. In so doing he overlooked similar dead lines in Northern prisons, though surely he knew about them. In his self-righteous fury he also neglected to consider that scores of Confederate prisoners were shot or bayoneted by their Federal guards—at least thirty-one of them fatally—for such minor misconduct as failing to extinguish a light, urinating away from the sinks, approaching too close to a sentinel's post, or "insulting" a guard. Northern sentinels frequently fired indiscriminately into prison quarters, and from time to time Southern prisoners appealed for relief from such vindictiveness. A Federal surgeon in a Saint Louis prison hospital made formal complaint about the reckless sentries there, one of whom shot into a ward and shattered a Confederate patient's leg, narrowly missing the Union attendant who leaned over him. Colonel William Hoffman, the U.S. commissary general of prisoners, also chastised the commander of Camp Chase, Ohio, for his trigger-happy garrison. In none of these cases, however, was a Union soldier found culpable for killing a prisoner.[58]

Compared with the smaller Northern prisons like Camp Chase, Camp Douglas, and Point Lookout, each of which enjoyed a substantial garrison, Andersonville did not see a disproportionate number of prisoners fall to the sentries' guns. One Federal prison established at Newport News in April of 1865 never held more than thirty-six hundred prisoners from first to last, but within seventeen days guards shot two of them and bayoneted another to death—all after the war had essentially ended. For all their lack of discipline and their alleged savagery, the Georgia Reserves did not shoot their captives at half that rate.[59]

Henry Wirz would hang to atone for the dead-line killings and other imagined or exaggerated cruelties, and even his associates found him harsh, but he did not lack sensitivity entirely. Clerics and ladies who met him found the captain courteous and accommodating (two adjectives seldom attributed to his prison persona), and he displayed a covert sympathy with some of the prisoners under him. Of the two women who sojourned at Andersonville with their husbands, he provided Mrs. Hunt with a private tent outside his headquarters and lodged Mrs. Leonard at his own home after her husband died, at least until she began insulting Elizabeth and the girls. In order to free several dozen drummer boys from the misery of the bull pen, Wirz paroled them for make-work projects at the hospital or around camp, assigning one as a messenger at headquarters and taking another home to stay with his family.[60]

Most prisoners stood ready to abuse the slightest privilege. When wild blackberries came ripe, Captain Wirz sent the boys out to pick them for the sick, hoping to offer the fruit both as an antidiarrhetic and an antiscorbutic, but few blackberries ever reached the mouths of those who most needed them. The drummers returned laden with berries, some of which found their way into Andersonville's open-air market while the bulk of them went to the nurses—paroled Union prisoners—who transformed them into pies and alcohol for their own bellies. So riotously drunk did the blackberry wine make the hospital stewards that Surgeon White dismissed several of them and turned them back into the stockade.[61]

In the days after Colonel Chandler's inspection, Captain Wirz began to show visible signs of illness. His arm always troubled him, and it must have sustained a persistent temperature with its perennial infections, but that first week in August he grew feeble from something more acute. Numbers of prisoners died that month from what the doctors called intermittent fever, which was probably spread by the swarms of mosquitoes that began tormenting the prison and the hospital about that time, replacing the troublesome flies of early summer; Wirz's August malady yielded symptoms similar to that.[62]

For a few more days the captain continued to come to work, sick, but in the evenings he needed help mounting his old white mare: even when he felt well Wirz could use only his left hand to pull himself up, and that arm was weakened by a massive old injury to the deltoid muscle, so when his legs began to fail him the clerks would drag a chair out and he would climb into the saddle from that, swaying precariously the whole two miles homeward. By August 8 he weakened sufficiently to request a furlough, retiring to the three rooms his family shared at the Bass home. Nine days later the rumor leaked out that he had died, and indeed he sank so low at one point that he submitted to the long, painful rail journey to Augusta in search of treatment.[63]

General Winder acted immediately to fill Wirz's place. With so few dependable officers available he lacked much choice, and he selected one of the junior members of his own staff, twenty-year-old Samuel Boyer Davis. Born in Delaware and raised in Baltimore, Davis had gone South at eighteen as a private in Latimer's Virginia battery. Later he joined Isaac Trimble's staff as an aide, and was shot through the lung and captured with General Trimble at Gettysburg. Six weeks later he escaped from a Pennsylvania hospital, made his way back to the Confederacy through his native state, and since his recovery he had served with General Winder. It had been he who carried Winder's urgent recommendations back to Richmond in June, and the young lieutenant rose directly from the role of a glorified messenger to the responsibility of caring for more than thirty-two thousand Federal prisoners.[64]

In his last few days on duty Wirz had begun to take advantage of the forest refuse left by the great slave gangs, using it for the benefit of the prisoners. Since the June escapes, and perhaps at Winder's insistence, Wirz had allowed no one to enter the forest for wood but the black prisoners, obviously because they were a lesser risk: not only were Georgians less apt to fall into negligent fraternity with black woodcutters, Georgia's strict slave code gave them far less chance than the whites of gaining ultimate freedom if they did slip away. Unfortunately, the Negro Squad was too small to supply the whole prison, and firewood consequently grew quite scarce again. The extensive clearing for fortifications produced massive piles of limbwood within sight of the prison, so Wirz felt more comfortable about doubling his wood squads: limited now only by the paucity of transportation, he also quickly doubled the daily ration of wood. On the final day before his sick leave he transferred the Negro Squad and one white detachment to the job of dragging in the lumber for the long-awaited barracks.[65]

In light of Wirz's nervous nature, it is probably just as well that he fell ill when he did. The three most terrifying days any Andersonville commandant ever experienced began on what was probably the first full day of Wirz's absence.

The morning of August 9 began with the promise of the same heat that had marked August thus far. One of the Plymouth Pilgrims had been coughing up blood for some time, and his tentmates awoke at dawn to find him dead. They trussed him up in the usual funereal fashion—toes tied together, hands folded across his breast—and carried him down to the south gate. Some Vermont heavy artillerymen brought down one of their comrades, as well, and with scores of other ragged pallbearers they awaited the opening of the great portals. No roll call interfered, for none had been held since August 4, and when the straining hinges creaked open they all shuffled out to deposit their spiritless burdens in the dead-house, scurrying among the fresh pine stumps for an armload of sticks and chips before turning back toward the stockade.[66]

While the day's dead piled up under the rude shelter, fresh candidates for Southern graves marched in from prison headquarters, where Lieutenant Davis had just subjected them to a much more thorough search than Wirz usually conducted. Like most who saw the stockade for the first time, these newcomers gaped in horror and disbelief at the milling mass of humanity, wrinkling their faces at an odor that seemed to penetrate their very skin. The thirty thousand captives already there consumed every square foot of dry ground not taken up by the streets and dead line, and a couple of hundred had gravitated by now to that tiny, swampbound island north of the sinks. Thousands still lacked any shelter at all. Those who wandered up to the plateau could see the timber frame of the first barracks building rising in the northwest corner, long and narrow, but at present that empty rectangle did nothing for the prisoners but rob them of that much more space.[67]

Some detachments had already begun queuing up for rations at noon when the sky suddenly began to turn grey, then black. The storm started with one deafening peal, the rain cascading as it never had before. Thunder crashed right overhead as lightning danced all around the stockade, and the accumulated filth of a month washed down the slopes to Stockade Creek, which started swelling fast. Wells filled and overflowed; sheeting runoff swept through the tents, breasting little clay dikes that surrounded most of the hillside shebangs. The tightest roof in the prison could not withstand this torrent, and no one inside the stockade avoided a soaking.[68]

The deluge continued in full force for two hours or more. As water pooled in the tamped trough on either side of the palisade, it sought downhill escape, and on the first leg of its journey to the Gulf of Mexico it began to eat away at the hard-packed red dirt with which whip-driven blacks had backfilled the upright logs. The downstream wall dammed the branch, forcing diluted sewage to creep up both banks, threatening to inundate the island and the lower fringe of huts on the south side. Just as scurvy had loosened the sockets of a quarter million teeth inside the pen, the daily ebb and flow of Stockade Creek had weakened the grip of clay on log. The weight of water pressing at thirty or forty times its normal volume told against the east wall from the inside, and the pressure increased as the runoff cut deeper into the furrows. At last a log or two on either side of the creek's exit splashed into the water downstream, each prying up great gobs of clay as its base lifted out of the earth. Through these apertures rushed the restrained reservoir, battering at the surviving logs and bringing them down like straws. Thus freed, the flood drained out of the prison with enough velocity to suck the brand-new drinking and bathing flumes with it, taking a good part of the sinks, too. Boards, dead line, and stockade posts all snarled in a logjam just above the hospital.[69]

All sixteen of Camp Sumter's guns stood mounted now in the various forts around the prison, and two of them burped a sodden blank cartridge apiece. Muffled as they were, the twin reports brought Georgians running with muskets in their hands. First came Furlow's militia, loping around to the gap, expecting perhaps to see Yankees pouring out by the thousands. Two months before—even one month—a hardy corps of defiant leaders might have propelled their fellow captives through that God-given door: they had planned even more desperate escapes on at least two previous occasions. Now, though, most of the masterminds of the May and July plots had passed beyond any practical hope of escape. John Whitten had been eager on May 27, but he could no longer walk and his teeth were falling out. A cavalryman who had arrived only a few days before observed that the majority of prisoners were too weak to make the round-trip to the sinks unaided, let alone to fight their way to freedom and begin the long trek north. Many of those who owned the grit or vigor did not even know of the opportunity until it had passed: a rainstorm usually brought out a multitude of bathers—a Pennsylvanian said the prison looked white with naked men in the downpour of August 2—but this storm pelted so violently that anyone with a shelter to his name crawled into it and stayed there. The word naturally spread more slowly under such circumstances, rippling up the opposing slopes with little bellows of surprise instead of flashing the length of the prison in one ascending cheer; before anyone could have organized a spearhead, the militia muskets waited to greet it. The mere terror of the dead line checked most individual efforts, too. Only four men disappeared that day, but as many as three of them may have been invalids who lay in the path of the flood, too far gone to crawl or swim away; their bodies could easily have washed into the Sweetwater and floated down to alligator country. A New York cavalry sergeant noted that some of the more helpless prisoners drowned during the storm, right where they lay.[70]

Rain continued to carve at the foundation of the prison even as the variegated companies of Reserves quickstepped through the mud. Rushing water gouged arroyos a yard or two deep, loosening the stockade logs at the creek's entrance. A hundred feet of the palisade yawned open beyond the sinks when, suddenly, logs began toppling at the upper end, rafting down toward the other opening. Yankees on the south side waded into the roaring creek, soaked to the skin anyway, to trap these precious lengths of potential firewood and guide them to shore. Several hundred more Confederates arrived to block this second rift, putting up a bold front despite the apparent disintegration of the prison walls.[71]

Within three hours of the first clap of thunder the worst was over. The storm abated, though it did not stop, and black faces appeared around the enclosure as overseers turned their gangs away from the earthworks and set them to saving the stockade; had it not been for the presence of those slaves, General Winder judged, a mass escape could not have been averted. Amber muck flew in clots as the laborers plied their shovels, and any white man who lacked either a commission or a weapon joined them. Menacing guards stood two abreast on the pigeon roosts, warning those who had claimed the logs not to damage them (on pain of the entire camp losing rations for five days, one Yankee heard). Apparently the phalanx of militia crowded close enough to the ruptured east wall to banter with those inside, for one of the prisoners heard an older local man profess he had seen no such rainfall in that region in all his days. The guards remained under arms in front of those vulnerable gaps all that night and into the next, when they and their blue-clad charges were equally drenched by another cloudburst nearly as heavy as the first.

"Well, Johney," wrote a Pennsylvanian, "it does me some good to see you get wet."[72]

Dawn of August 10 revealed a pitiful sight. The storm had punished many a failing soldier beyond recovery; the sickest of those who slept in the streets could not raise themselves to make way for the day's traffic, and numbers of them had died under the driving rain. Hardly a man did not complain of some degree of rheumatic affliction after the torrent, but life resumed around them. Most of the breaks in the palisade had been repaired by then, and Lieutenant Davis finally dared open the gate for the ration wagon. Paroled carpenters began roofing the first barracks building while framers mortised the timbers for another, but the construction and ration distribution both ceased when the skies opened up again. Some detachments therefore lost the evening half of their victuals, and even those who beat the rain to the ration wagon and obtained enough wood could not boil their raw beans because of this latest drenching. During the night part of the lumber for the repaired sink flume disappeared (sacrificed to cook some late-night supper, no doubt) so when the south side of the prison drew no rations on August 11 it was perceived as punishment for this theft. Even if it was—and it is far more likely that distribution had simply fallen behind—Lieutenant Davis must have forgiven the transgressors by the next morning, when he issued double rations on that side.[73]

General Winder had relaxed enough by August 12 to let the garrison stand down after more than forty-eight hours under arms. This awful fright had taught him a lesson about auxiliary lines of defense, however, and that very day he commenced a second concentric stockade around the prison, on a perimeter midway between the original prison wall and the forts that frowned down upon it. Not only would the new wall offer insurance against another collapse, or an organized break, it would also discourage tunneling and protect the flanks of the forts in case of an enemy raid. The work gangs began three sides of the second enclosure simultaneously.[74]

The storm that had offered the hesitant prisoners their freedom also gave them drink. About midway up the north slope on the western side, where the rain had cut great ruts in the denuded dead line, a stream of clear water still bubbled forth when the last of the flood had drained away. So precious was fresh water inside the prison that this liberated spring brought men from every quarter. Emanating from an aquifer too deep to have suffered yet from the veneer of sewage on the surface, the water tasted better than any in the stockade. No one could claim ownership in that no-man's-land beyond the dead line, so thousands who owned neither the means nor the strength for well digging lined up with cups and buckets tied to poles, reaching over that mortal barrier to quaff their thirst. Ultimately the prison police squad undertook a little public works project, obtaining permission to enter the dead line long enough to divert the watercourse to the inside. Safely beyond the sentry's purview they dug a reservoir at the end of their little canal that served thenceforth as a community fountain. The crowds that formerly milled so dangerously at the stream migrated to the line before this pool, taking their draughts under the supervision of a police constable: the last prisoner had been killed jostling for a drink at Stockade Creek.[75]

The pious among the Andersonville unfortunates viewed the water as a divine gift, and dubbed it Providence Spring. Years later, prisoners who felt that the hand of God had spared them from the services of Mr. Byram's burial detail came back to build a great stone memorial to that infinite mercy, and they chose to place it over the spring. Former Confederates and local people who heard the story scoffed, pointing out that this was only the best of several springs at Andersonville and that it had existed long before the prison; it had merely been disturbed and driven underground during the construction of the stockade, they insisted. Federal prisoners helped corroborate the existence of other springs, but the reveries of their more romantic brethren prevailed.[76]

Whatever the source of the spring, it appeared at the height of the prison's occupation. When the exhausted garrison finally stacked its arms on August 12, more Yankees lived at Andersonville than ever would occupy it again—just under 33,000. During that week 682 men died, and General Winder begged Richmond to stop sending any more prisoners his way. Either by accident or design the prison influx diminished to a trickle on the same day Winder made his plea, and a climbing death rate helped ease the crush of living bodies.[77]

6 ❧ J Each in His Narrow Cell Forever Laid

ohn Winder's own inspector had recommended removing at least fifteen thousand prisoners from the stockade even as Daniel Chandler started through the gate. As the new commander of all prisons in Georgia and Alabama, Winder had already been authorized to distribute his captives anywhere he could, but the interior of those states offered no prefabricated security for such numbers of Yankees. A new stockade would have to go up somewhere, and Winder had been casting about for a site since the beginning of July. His early choices had not pleased the adjutant general, who preferred expanding the prison at Cahaba or building a new one in southern Alabama, so Winder had suggested isolated inland locations between Wilmington and Charlotte,

North Carolina, between Charleston and Florence, South Carolina, or between Augusta and Millen, Georgia. At last Winder's chief aide, his son Sid, found a spot five miles north of Millen on the Augusta & Savannah Railroad. General Winder notified Samuel Cooper, who approved the location and sought authorization for the impressment of labor and materials if it proved necessary. The repulse of Stoneman's and McCook's raids seemed to dull the urgency of the situation, at least for Richmond officials, and General Cooper waited four days before passing along the secretary of war's authorization.[1]

It was during those four days that the stockade washed down, and nightmares of lean, hungry Yankees kept Georgians awake for miles around as the garrison lay out in the rain for two days and nights. One of those citizens whose dreams were disturbed, a Macon photographer, thought the prison offered a worthy subject for his camera; he may have wished to record it before Winder moved the mass of inmates away, and, once the danger had ebbed, he—and perhaps one assistant—loaded his equipment for the sixty-mile journey to Camp Sumter.[2]

Like General Winder, Andrew Jackson Riddle hailed from Maryland. An early daguerreotypist, he had come to Georgia a decade before to photograph the gentry. In the first months of the war he opened a gallery in Richmond, but somehow he secured a position as a semiofficial military cameraman. That was perhaps his means of avoiding conscription, for he was not yet forty, but it must have been a foolproof exemption if he dared to enter a post garrisoned mostly by men ten years his senior: old men forced into the Reserves might just call the enrolling officers' attention to a conspicuously healthy and younger civilian.[3]

Riddle probably arrived at Anderson Station by Tuesday morning, August 16. Doubtless he had written ahead for permission before transporting all his cumbersome equipment so far. General Winder therefore expected him, and he buttoned on a fresh collar to sit for a private portrait, wearing an old uniform coat in the stifling August heat. Captain Wirz also appears to have crawled out of his sickbed for a picture, but his pained expression betrayed his condition. The ride to the village from his quarters proved too strenuous for the frail captain, and before the day was out he collapsed entirely, prompting prison gossip that he had died.[4]

Riddle's first stop at the stockade would have been the prison headquarters behind the star fort, where Lieutenant Davis would acknowledge his permission to climb the guards' ladders and choose his scenes. The most logical place to start would have been the nearby south gate, but on the morning of August 16 some twenty-five hundred sick men crowded about that entrance. Riddle continued around the palisade counterclockwise, looking for the most marketable views. Photographers in the North had already learned how readily the public embraced war's more shocking aspects, and few scenes would have shocked Victorian sensibilities more than the sinks. Probably gagging from the smell, Riddle and his helper stopped under the east wall and the photographer carried the device up to the first pigeon roost north of the creek, stationing himself on a length of the stockade that had washed away one week previously.[5]

Riddle began with his camera facing the southwest corner, where little knots of prisoners circled around their detachment sergeants, defining the outer limits of the day's massive surgeon's call. A couple of gamblers or vendors sat behind shaded tables with customers gathered round, and one prisoner lay in a fetal curl, dead or dying unnoticed on the dirt beside them, but the real subjects of the artist's composition were the men squatting along the twin rails of the camp latrine. Those facing him glanced up at the commotion on the guard's platform; some of those with their backs toward him looked at the camera over their left shoulders. As he operated the shutter (Riddle photo #1) the right half of his frame caught the missing lengths of post headers, stolen five nights before. Behind all this the south slope of Andersonville rose to reveal the thin pines that remained around the star fort and the headquarters building.[6]

Like the day before, August 16 was a bright, blazing day, and the sun rather bleached this first study. Judging by the lapse of time between this photograph and the next, Riddle himself must have raced down to treat the plate, and when he returned he probably spun his tripod due west, up Stockade Creek to the bridge. If so, this photo would not survive; perhaps it did not develop well. From that same post he turned still farther to his right, aiming across the "island" toward Selman's sutlery building and the north gate in his third shot and almost due north in the fourth, capturing the dead line, the top of the stockade wall, the next sentry post, and a man diking his tent against the constant drainage from hillside springs (photos #2 and #3). Most of the inhabitants remained inside their shebangs, out of the merciless sun. It was, said one prisoner, too hot that day even to nap, for all that a man sweat.[7]

Before leaving this post Riddle swung back to his left to complete the panorama. Focusing on the center of the south wall, he caught a few more Yankees in embarrassing poses at the sinks (photo #4); some of the hillside burrows appear above the latrines. Possibly he recorded a sixth image of the southeastern corner of the stockade that included the three imposing pines standing like a bridal couple and a rejected suitor on the south slope. If he did so, however, this plate also failed.

Still fascinated with the sinks, Riddle dragged his equipment over to the first post south of the creek. At high noon he centered his lens on the island (photo #5), picking up the end of the sinks, the sluggish stream that had been diverted to flush them, and, in the upper left, the excavations prisoners had made to fill the swamp. The myriad tents on the north slope disappeared into apparent infinity atop the plateau.

Gathering up his camera, plates, and solutions, Riddle proceeded to the northeast corner of the stockade. Climbing to the final platform on the north wall, he looked back the way he had come, framing one of the new stockade's irregular avenues where it skirted the dead line. Two dozen men turned to pose for him, their arms folded or their hands on their hips, while a couple of curious heads protruded from tents (photo #6).[8]

The shadows in this last image indicate that the sun had passed its zenith some time before. Riddle stopped for lunch, probably parking his entourage beneath the tuft of trees near the new bakery; perhaps he begged some food from the cooks. After a leisurely meal he set up temporary shop again around the northwest corner of the stockade, to record the swamp from another direction.

By midafternoon Riddle ascended the guard post just south of the north gate. Training his camera on the southeast corner of the prison, he picked up Stockade Creek in the middle foreground (photo #7). Portions of the substantial levees of early August remained, but most had been washed down in the torrent one week before. Still, the stream had since been wrestled back into an eight-foot-wide bed, and primitive drainage ditches funneled water into it from the boggier floodplain on either side. A few prisoners perched along the banks, rinsing their clothes, while at least one naked man stood scrubbing himself (and thus blurring his torso) in the upper end of the knee-deep creek, just below the indistinct bridge. Earlier that same day prison carpenters had been working on the great sluice that contained the entire upstream reach of the creek, repairing the damage from the flood of August 9; this time they had boarded not only the sides of the stream but the bottom as well, to eliminate as much sediment and excrement as possible from the camp's principal bathing and laundering facility. A dozen yards behind the washermen crouched other prisoners, too feeble or careless to traipse across the bridge and down to the sinks, squatting shamelessly with their white buttocks bared for the photographer. The three surviving pines stood tall and straight near the southeastern corner of the camp, mutely signaling the faithful like the spires of a Gothic cathedral, and in the distance a dense forest clouded the horizon—the last fragment of the late Sheriff Turner's woods. Some of these trees shaded the hospital, and some would fall in a few days, sacrificed to General Winder's second stockade perimeter; little earthen batteries would sit among their stumps.[9]

Perhaps Riddle wished to compose another panorama from this side. He may have snapped other views from the northwest corner or from this same guard post that never saw print (that would explain the lapse of nearly three hours between this image and the one before), but for whatever reason the south gate, the deadly watering hole above the Water Street bridge, and the sea of shebangs above and below the north gate were not preserved for posterity. It was getting late now, though, and Riddle had to concentrate on noteworthy events in prison life. At four o'clock the ration wagon creaked in, and the Macon artist turned his attention to that pitiful sight. Half the wagonload had been handed out by the time he set up and focused, but the process stopped and the men stood still long enough for the shutter to open and close upon them (photo #8). All but three men in the immediate foreground faced the camera or stood in self-conscious profile, including one who sat alone, his legs too weak or drawn with scurvy to support him. Even the wagon driver posed self-consciously. Some incongruously well-dressed individuals in front of the sutler's shack (perchance James Selman and his clerks) mounted themselves on elevated spots for their nameless places in history. At the tailgate of the wagon stood a man with a long chinstrap beard who wore a checkered civilian shirt. He seemed to be the doler of rations, who had momentarily interrupted the ladling of beans and the distribution of the dark, burned, squad-sized squares of cornbread that looked like folded blankets. Perhaps this was the quartermaster's assistant known as Humes, or the detailed Irishman whom other Federals would trounce nine days hence, after he savagely clubbed a prisoner who complained of favoritism; possibly it was James Duncan himself.[10]

After this last mass portrait Mr. Riddle carried his tripod and box down the ladder and turned his little procession north, toward the cemetery. The sun sank lower now, and Riddle hurried to capture Andersonville's more tragic side. The burial detail—including Wilford Crandall, the Tibbles brothers, and John Younker—would receive 107 bodies from the quartermaster's wagons that day. They had buried 45 of them in the second half of a trench begun the day before, and when the photographer arrived they were busily squaring off the sides of a new excavation right behind it. The little shelf that supported the puncheons was no longer a part of the process: the prisoners died much too fast for such luxurious civilities now.[11]

While the workmen sweat out the last few feet of the new trench, Riddle aimed his camera across the road, to the graves of spring and early summer. Apparently a man—it may have been the cemetery boss, W. W. Byram—stood among the rows of rough headboards with his arms folded as the photographer opened the shutter (photo #9).

Then Riddle propped his tripod at the end of the fresh trench while Younker and another man lugged in the first few bodies on the decrepit stretcher. The first man buried in that row, C. F. Barber, had been a member of the 112th Illinois Infantry in life. The second, William Jones of the 19th Maine, had been laid low by enteritis, and dysentery had killed the next, R. A. Johnston of the 19th Massachusetts. Riddle signaled that he was ready to shoot just as the litter bearers carried in Leander B. Farnham, aged forty-five, of Company A, 1st Vermont Heavy Artillery. Farnham had enlisted only eight months before, joining the same company in which his younger brother served as a sergeant; both had been captured below Petersburg near the end of June, and the brother lay dying back in the stockade. Looking at Farnham's wasted form, the surgeon had diagnosed marasmus as the cause of his death, and the dead man's bony ribs protruded through a gap in his blouse. The litter crew started to lift the body off the canvas when Riddle asked them to wait, and to stand as though dropping the corpse into line. Younker's comrade responded halfheartedly, perfunctorily lifting a corner of Farnham's shirt while balancing the corpse on the end of the stretcher. The lankier Younker lifted one of Farnham's wasted knees by the trouser leg as the rest of the crew gathered around, leaning on their shovels (photo #10). Behind them stood three idlers with their sleeves rolled down and their hands in their suspender loops or pockets: one well-fed young man in a white jacket and jauntily tilted hat was probably Riddle's Macon assistant; the other two rangier youths were perhaps a couple of off-duty Georgia Reserves whom Riddle had employed for the day. Beyond them all, others readied another body from the wagon—the mortal remains of a Michigan cavalryman named Palmer. Riddle worked his shutter, Leander Farnham dropped forever into place between Johnston and Palmer, and the day's session ended. As the sun settled beyond the railroad the sweating graveyard detail bent back to its work, and A. J. Riddle headed for the depot with ten glass plates that would serve as his principal claim to lasting fame on this earth.[12]

Mr. Riddle had cause to hurry. Rumor had already reached Andersonville that the Yankees were stirring around Atlanta—some even said that the city had already fallen. Judson Kilpatrick had made a reconnaissance west of the city, tearing up three miles of railroad track and burning some buildings at Fairburn, after which he pulled back, but the news coming south by telegraph initially indicated that the threat was much worse. The wires still stopped at Fort Valley, leaving Andersonville several hours behind on information, so, by the time Riddle and his protégé had packed his camera equipment for the northward journey, the Confederate camps had just begun to come alive.[13]

Requests for troops fluttered in from Atlanta. General Hood asked John Winder if he would be able to spare Furlow's militia battalion, and now that his fortifications were nearly complete Winder guessed he could afford those five hundred men, but either Colonel Furlow or his men balked. Whether it was because they preferred to defend their own homes or because they feared to face the Yankee horde around Atlanta, Furlow's men would not budge. The 3rd Georgia Reserves seemed willing, though—perhaps because so many of them hailed from the imperiled territory north of Macon—and Winder sent them in place of the militia. In the growing darkness excited Reserves prepared to leave for the front, forming in noisy companies around blazing pyres of pine slash, shouting and firing off an occasional gun until a special train came to pick them up. Gleefully they boarded the cars for Macon, where some of them drifted away to their homes, never to be seen under arms again.[14]

Howell Cobb shook his head in disbelief when he learned that this Reserve regiment had disembarked in the city. He had warned Winder less than a week before that the militia served under the authority of a short-term state mobilization and could remain at Andersonville only at the pleasure of the whimsical Governor Brown: the Reserves, Cobb implied, were consequently the only guards Winder could depend upon, and Cobb instantly proposed sending the 3rd Reserves back to Camp Sumter in return for Furlow's battalion. Although the regiment was allowed to linger a few days in Macon, General Hood ultimately concurred. Perhaps Hood preferred the relatively healthy militia to the boys, old men, and cripples of the Reserves, and he insisted on the substitution.[15]

The next day Andersonville learned what Hood had discovered the day before: Kilpatrick's Fairburn raid was over. The telegraph keys fell silent momentarily; even as the Confederates started to relax, though, Kilpatrick gathered himself for an even greater effort well below Atlanta. This time his target would be the Macon & Western Railroad.[16]

The 3rd Reserves was the biggest regiment at Andersonville; it constituted more than a quarter of Winder's effective force. Without it he could not field seventeen hundred men, and the prisoners outnumbered his garrison nearly twenty to one. On the morning of August 17, near the mailbox at the south gate, a Confederate officer posted a clipping from the *New York Herald* that featured a headline promising another upcoming exchange or parole, but well-trained cynics doubted it, accurately gauging the notice as an effort to placate the prisoners during the emergency: camp gossip still maintained that the evacuation of Atlanta was then under way. Even outside the prison, rumor put Andersonville in imminent danger, with Kilpatrick's legions bearing directly down upon the place.[17]

Federal forces pinched Andersonville from above and below in mid-August. While Kilpatrick siphoned off the prison garrison, Yankees in Florida whittled away at the supply of provisions. Bolting forward from their seaside camps, several Union regiments descended on the Florida Railroad, which trailed down to the Gulf Coast through the state's best ranchland. For several days they disrupted the movement of beef and salt, but on August 17 their raid fell apart when Florida cavalry surprised a small garrison at Gainesville and captured two-thirds of it: a few chagrined Florida Tories joined nearly two hundred Ohioans and New Englanders in the long trek to Andersonville by rail and steamboat, stopping at Tallahassee and Quincy for the loyal citizens to gloat over them. The rest of the expedition retreated to the Saint Johns River, having accomplished nothing more than causing another brief but acute food shortage inside the bull pen: beginning with the day of the Gainesville fight, prisoners complained for several days of slim meat and salt rations.[18]

By August 22, when the first of this latest crop of Florida prisoners arrived, the resected supply lines began providing better portions of food again, but the six-day lapse had seriously impaired the health of men already forced to live on the nutritional edge. Amos Stearns, a Massachusetts man who had fared better than most during his three-month incarceration, missed his first roll call on August 23. A weakened older private, also from Massachusetts, made his final diary entry that same day, stopping in midsentence. To supplement four days of scanty rations yet another Massachusetts native, Seaman Frederic James, cooked some bean-and-rice soup on August 20, stirring in one raw egg and hard-boiling another. The repast disturbed his fragile intestines, but he bought one more boiled egg the next day. He deteriorated steadily from there, probably stricken with salmonella, and on September 15 strange hands carried him to the graveyard. A fourth Bay State man, a sharpshooter, complained on August 22 that he was so feeble he could hardly walk, despite much better rations that day. "Hope I am not going to break down," he wrote, eleven days before his death. A Vermont cavalryman who would die of scurvy began recording his symptoms on August 24, and by August 30 he could not walk without a cane. Another Ver-monter—a friend of the Farnham brothers, both of whom were dead now—began to feel ill for the first time in two months in the days after the little famine. "I don't know how I shall make out," he confessed, "but I am going to try."[19]

Camp Sumter had suffered all along from a shortage in fruits and vegetables, much of the local crops having rotted on the tree and vine in the July heat, and even the agent for the Confederate hospital at Ander-son depot could not find enough to keep Georgia's own sons hale. The prisoners had suffered a lack of green truck for weeks on end, and the famine of late August aggravated dormant scurvy in men who had not tasted a tomato, an onion, or a plate of peas since spring. Henry Stone noticed that his gums seemed abnormally sensitive for several days, finally shuddering to think that he had come down with scurvy. Amos Stearns complained of sore, stiff legs, missing the symptom, but Sergeant Major Kellogg immediately recognized the ailment and put himself in line for the surgeon's booths. John Whitten had felt poorly for a month, but by the time his rations resumed their earlier volume he could no longer walk. Without rescue he expected the scurvy would kill him, and all his tentmates lay in a similar condition, perfectly hopeless.[20]

Hopelessness may have been the most common emotion as the final week of August opened. On a trip to the sinks, an Indiana soldier could not ignore the poor souls who had preceded him there on legs too wobbly to carry them back to their lairs. Bereft of strength and will, some of them had lain down—even days before—to wait for death; so filthy were they that prisoners nearby would not help them. A relatively new Iowa pris-oner found himself nearly that far gone less than four weeks after he first entered the stockade: weakened by diarrhea and the light menu of the past few days, James Bradd doubted on August 22 whether he could last much longer, and five days later he closed his diary entry with "Good by Father & Mother." Another man, who had apparently lost all his friends as well as his faith in ultimate liberation, walked deliberately into the forbidden barrens beyond the dead line the night of August 25, challenging the sentry to shoot. Twice the guard missed, whereupon the suicide called for him to do his duty and be done with it; the third charge struck him in the head and killed him instantly.[21]

Clouds of mosquitoes hatched in the surrounding wetlands about this time, adding another element to the misery inside the walls. With heat, hunger, and discomfort even the more congenial prisoners had turned sullen, snappish, and surly, and the buzzing horde of tormenting insects evoked worse still. After mentioning a night of particular torture during which he must have spent every hour swatting and scratching, one of the Plymouth Pilgrims remarked that "Privation and abuse have made me Selfish and more like a Devil than a man." Perhaps repenting some offense to a comrade, he observed that he was ready to fight with anyone. His cynicism persisted despite the confession, though, and as he mourned the death of a close friend the next day he compiled an invoice for the dead man's heirs: "I have his due bill for $19 borrowed money & I expended on his account during his last illness $5.00 total $24.00."[22]

On the morning after complaining of pain in his knee and ankle joints, Pilgrim Ira Forbes scolded himself for quarreling over a wash pail. Those suffering from scurvy and rheumatic pain snarled even at friends who bent every effort to their comfort. Amos Stearns ministered diligently to Preston Champney, an old comrade who had invited him into his tent when Stearns first arrived, but in his final days Champney whimpered that his nurse treated him unkindly. Stearns tried often to help him outside where the doctors could see him, but the painful jaunts to the south gate all proved futile. Champney died six days after the first complaints of insensitivity, and perhaps Stearns did grow a little callous; his greatest regret on the day of his friend's death seemed to be that his mess sergeant would not give him Champney's rations.[23]

John Whitten noted a particularly saintly friend who tended him and his ailing tentmates "as if we were his brothers," and such charity seemed an abundant virtue, at least among prisoners from the same state or regiment. One Pennsylvanian walked the length of the prison three or four times a day to visit a failing friend, bringing him water and occasionally bathing him. Once he washed his friend's hair in a solution of tobacco juice to kill the lice that infested it, and finally he helped him out to the hospital, where the sufferer died within days. The same Samaritan then turned his attention to another member of his own company, whom diarrhea had so weakened that he could not control himself. For three days the volunteer nurse laundered the incontinent skeleton's threadbare wardrobe and rinsed his body until that companion died, too.[24]

As the situation inside reached its nadir the prisoners grew even more resourceful in their attempts to escape. Charles Ellis and George Fechnor—or whatever their real names were—found one of the most novel methods: they let the Confederates open the gates for them, and simply walked out. In order to supply the balance of officers exchanged earlier in the month, prison authorities demanded a certain number of sergeants who had either been on the verge of mustering in as lieutenants before they were captured or whose commissions had arrived at regimental headquarters after they were taken prisoner. The prison police scoured the stockade for anyone who fit that description, and that appears to have been the source of Fechnor's Kentucky romance, in which he imagined having been captured with a fresh commission in his pocket nearly two years before. Eleven men ambled out of the stockade the morning of August 24, and thanks to Fechnor's quick thinking he and Ellis walked among them. The next day they started for Macon, doubtless leaving behind two genuine but hapless would-be officers.[25]

The release of these men triggered another spasm of exhilaration for a few inmates, but the enthusiasm was mostly limited to the newest residents. "I can't see the point," wrote a cavalryman who had arrived in May. Another trooper wrote "Can't put much confidence in it," while a veteran of only two weeks in the bull pen gave the rumors no credence at all. Even one of those who found his hopes raised by the omen simply fell all the more despondent when it proved a fluke. By now, most of the prisoners at Andersonville had seen their faith drained beyond regeneration.[26]

A recent series of messages between Ben Butler and Ulysses Grant gave these men good reason for despair. Butler was preparing a ship for a few special exchanges, and for some further talk with Colonel Ould about prisoners and exchange in general. Grant learned of the mission and challenged it, telling Butler he wanted no exchanges made at all for the present. While recognizing how cruel it was to Union prisoners to refuse exchanges, he considered it kindness to those Federal troops who remained in the ranks because the paroled Confederates always returned to the front so quickly. Universal exchange would simply require the annihilation of all Confederate soldiers before victory could be won, he argued.

"If we hold those caught they amount to no more than dead men," he concluded. Given the galloping effects of vitamin deficiencies, the same held true for much of the malnourished multitude behind the pine palisade.[27]

Kilpatrick's cavalry swung as far south as Lovejoy's Station, nearly meeting the same fate as Stoneman's division before fighting its way out of a trap and galloping back to safety. For all the anxiety the raid caused around Camp Sumter little harm resulted, and—thanks to the hesitation of Furlow's battalion—the Yankee raiders managed to escape without interference from any of the Andersonville garrison.[28]

With yet another narrow escape from roaming enemy cavalry, General Winder pressed the construction of a third stockade around his prison. This one would run only sixteen feet beyond the second, and would stand several feet shorter than the other two, serving more as a covered way for troops who might have to shift from one fortified battery to another under fire. Slave gangs began tipping those logs into place in the final week of August, and when news of the third perimeter carried into the stockade it further dampened the denizens' hopes for imminent release.[29]

The most important construction project during the last days of the month was the continued work on the low, narrow, two-story barracks buildings along the northern wall. The first one was completed and two more were going up by August 18. A week later the third and fourth buildings stood ready for roofing, and by the end of the month space had been cleared for a fifth. Though topped with boards, the barracks had no walls, probably less because of the shortage of lumber than from a lack of nails: Richard Winder appealed for more from the Columbus quartermaster, but in a region that still subsisted on hand-wrought nails they came at a premium. The news barracks looked much like two-story livestock sheds, and each accommodated an entire detachment of 270 men, who spooned together for mutual warmth as the nights grew cool. Seniority apparently played no part in gaining a place under the new roofs, and one lanky, ailing cavalryman moved into the first building only eight days after he first reached Andersonville: lacking any other shelter, Lawson Carley slept in the unfinished sheds for a week, probably dodging workmen during the day to catch the only shade available to him.[30]

On the last Monday in August a thin, frail figure in a white shirt and white trousers appeared in the commandant's office to claim his desk again. Henry Wirz had come closer to his final breath than he would for another fourteen months, as his wan face testified. Post doctors had given up on him a fortnight before, and word had spread through the stockade that he was dead, but if a desperate trip to Augusta had not cured him at least it had not killed him, and though he could barely summon the strength to sit upright he wanted to go back to work. The quartermaster sent an ambulance to carry him from the Bass home, and Wirz directed someone to arrange a cot in his headquarters, where he frequently lay down as fatigue overcame him. From the day he resumed his duties the captain found them no less a strain than before, for some of Sherman's army was reportedly on the move again and Wirz suspected Andersonville would be its next target. Impending disaster did not deter him from his work, but at least for a few days he kept to his office, allowing Lieutenant Davis to serve as his legs. When paroled clerks announced the return of "the Dutch Captain" to those inside the stockade, it hardly raised a murmur: one might have expected a livelier reaction from prisoners who later claimed to hold him in such dread.[31]

A number of Sumter County citizens began, about this time, to gather up a collection of clothing and provisions to alleviate the suffering of the prisoners inside the stockade. Bedford Head, a local doctor who had briefly tended prison patients rather than serve in the militia, later said his wife had already sent a couple of packages up to the post by one of his slaves when, sometime around the end of August or the first of September, she solicited a substantial contribution from ladies of her acquaintance, with whom she boarded the train for Andersonville with a platoon of servants to carry the food and clothing. Led by Dr. Head and a couple of ministers, the benevolent procession stepped down at Anderson depot and began filling up a wagon sent over by surgeons at the hospital. Certain officers—principally Shelby Reed—inquired why these civilians seemed to be using army transportation, and when Reed learned of their destination he kicked up a profane fuss.

Dr. Head thought this had all been arranged with General Winder, so he stepped over to Winder's office in the village and asked for a pass. Winder had already heard of Captain Reed's objections, which seemed to revolve around the argument that suffering Confederates deserved first refusal of the goods, and Winder decided to sustain his provost marshal. Head subsequently claimed that he criticized this change of heart, whereupon General Winder flew into a tirade against Yankee sympathizers and swore the provisions would never go to the Federal prisoners. Captain Reed had followed Dr. Head into the office by now, and he asked Winder to confiscate everything for the Confederate hospital, but Winder would not go that far. Ultimately the good doctor returned to his fellow philanthropists and broke the bad news. They retrieved their donations, giving them instead to some destitute Confederate troops who arrived on the down train—perhaps harbingers of the 3rd Reserves, who would have been coming back from Macon about then to replace Furlow's militia.[32]

The disappointed pilgrims may have been the victims of a misunderstanding. No more than a few days before their arrival at the prison the Americus paper had published another appeal for vegetables, vinegar, soft soap, and bedding straw for the hospital at Andersonville, but the agent who made that request acted on behalf of the Confederate facility called Sumter Hospital and the few score of guards who composed its patients, not the teeming wards of the Union prisoners. Post officials might understandably have waxed indignant upon learning that local citizens intended their benevolence for the enemy before their own men: that might explain the vehemence of Reed's and Winder's reactions.[33]

A more practical element may have entered into those officers' resistance, however. The prison hospital was much more vast than the post infirmary, and the supplies brought by the Americus altruists could hardly have stretched to serve a significant number of patients. Not only would that have fatally diminished the nutritional effectiveness of their offering, it would probably have created unrest among the majority who tasted none of it. Anxiety over getting a fair share of available food had just ignited a vicious melee at the ration wagon on August 25, when the Irishman in charge bashed a remonstrating prisoner's head in with a club; the mob behind the victim fell upon the Irishman, giving him a fearful drubbing, and open riot erupted for a few minutes until the guards rushed in. Concern over the potential for a similar incident had struck Lieutenant Davis a few days before, when fewer than a hundred suits of Federal uniforms arrived for the prisoners from their own government: recognizing that the clothing would not make a dent among the thirty-two thousand ragamuffins inside the stockade and hospital, and that the distribution of such a limited stock might create a stampede, Davis simply turned the new uniforms over to the paroled prisoners on the outside.[34]

Dr. Head remains the chief witness to this rebuff of Christian charity, but his story was corroborated by a Georgia lieutenant and by Ambrose Spencer, who claimed to have come out of his political isolation to take up the case with Confederate authorities. Spencer had already proved himself a liar with his false claims of Mexican War service and his tale of having recruited an entire artillery battalion for Confederate service, and later he would similarly perjure himself before the Wirz tribunal—during which he testified that he confronted General Winder over the donated provisions. Each of Spencer's successive statements to the court seemed to contradict the one before. First he implied there were two conversations, one of which included himself, Reed, Wirz, and Richard Winder, and took place at the depot the day after the incident; the other discussion purportedly involved Spencer, his wife, several other ladies, and General Winder, and ostensibly occurred three days subsequent to the foiled mission. Spencer specifically said Captain Wirz was not present at the second meeting, but finally he lumped the two separate gatherings into one, maintaining that Wirz was, indeed, present during his talk with General Winder that September day. Contorting the story one final time, he said he knew nothing about the September effort to provide for the prisoners, and that he, his wife, and the other ladies did not become involved until February of 1865. Just to tie the noose a little tighter around Wirz's neck, though, Spencer dredged up a recollection that the captain had muttered something about installing all those kindhearted ladies in a whorehouse on the post.[35]

General Winder left Andersonville on September 17, 1864, and Richard Winder followed him by the end of that month, so no dialogue including either of them could have occurred there in February of 1865. According to those close to him, neither was Henry Wirz in any condition to be lounging around the depot during the first half of September: he barely had the strength to sit, and for a few days in the middle of the month he retired to his bed again. Spencer's involvement was obviously imaginary, and the best evidence for the infamous vegetable confrontation therefore originates with a single reluctant prison contract physician.[36]

In September Ambrose Spencer would have been too busy with other business to attend to petty disputes at Andersonville. That summer he had applied for a post under War Department jurisdiction as a claims agent for Georgia's third congressional district. The appointment required the recommendation of someone the Confederate government could trust, and Spencer solicited the approval of the second auditor in the Treasury Department, who had known both Spencer's father and his grandfather. So impressed was the bureaucrat by those forebears that he vouched for the applicant without ever having met him. Ultimately Spencer's appointment drew criticism from Mark Blandford, a Georgia congressman who characterized Spencer as "a man of notorious bad character and disloyal sentiments," but the deed was already done by then. For two months beginning in early September, Spencer ranged the country between the Flint and Chattahoochee rivers, stopping over in each of a dozen county seats from one to six days as citizens brought him their bills for chattel, goods, crops, and equipment the army had required of them.[37]

Spencer would find plenty of work as a claims agent, for Hood's army and Andersonville had taken a great deal from people who would rather not have given it up, at least at stingy government rates. Impressment had also become increasingly necessary because, even at the low prices it fixed, Richmond paid its bills very slowly. Richard Winder waited more than a month for $75,000 to settle accounts that were supposed to have been paid by August 1, and another $50,000 debt had accumulated against the ill-fated shoe shop at Oglethorpe. Winder had been crying for money since the middle of July; his credit among the local suppliers had run out completely, and he needed a quarter of a million dollars just to pay for August purchases and immediate needs.[38]

As Richard Winder cast desperately about for cash to pay for supplies already consumed, the prison hospital demanded more and more. Randolph Stevenson took charge of the hospital in place of Isaiah White, who had become the chief post surgeon, and Stevenson presented the surgeon general with a plan for a new hospital at Andersonville. The current one sat along swampy ground too near the effluvia seeping out of the stockade sinks, and he proposed relocating it on higher ground with forty long, low sheds for the shelter of two thousand patients. The project would be cheaper in the midst of that timber-rich country than it might elsewhere, he reasoned, but, while he observed what poor luck the quartermaster had had meeting previous hospital requisitions, he offered no suggestions about paying for the materials.[39]

Even as Dr. Stevenson composed his plan, a battle raged a hundred miles to the north that would deliver most of the men in the stockade from Andersonville—if not from captivity. As Captain Wirz had revealed to his clerk, most of the Yankees besieging Atlanta had been in motion since August 25: disappointed at Kilpatrick's failure to cut the city's last lifeline with his cavalry, William Sherman decided to do it with his whole army. Abandoning most of his trenches, he swung around Atlanta for Jonesborough, twenty miles below the city. At first John Bell Hood could not imagine where the Federals had gone, for he had sent most of his own cavalry raiding deep along enemy supply lines; unlike the pessimistic Captain Wirz, Hood seemed to hope for an instant that the foe had retreated. He learned differently on August 31, when a strong Union force struck at Jonesborough. William Hardee rushed there to meet it with his own corps and one other, and for a time the Confederates blunted the onslaught with desperate counterattacks, but that night Hood called the additional corps back to Atlanta. Obviously still confused about the enemy's intent, he left Hardee to fight the bulk of Sherman's army alone on September 1. That spelled the end of Confederate hopes for Atlanta: Hardee was cut off, and had to satisfy himself with defending the road to Macon, while Hood turned the remains of the Army of Tennessee toward the roads leading west, out of the city. Atlanta had fallen.[40]

Had the Federal behemoth rolled on another sixty miles to Macon, the railroad that kept Camp Sumter alive would have been amputated from most sources of supply. Only Hardee's fragment of Hood's army lay in the way of such a disaster, but Jefferson Davis apparently did not know how precariously matters stood until September 5, when he read Hardee's latest telegram.

Meanwhile, John Winder seems to have been left nearly in the dark; perhaps in an effort to avoid panic, or possibly because he bent all his energies toward raising and forwarding anyone who could hold a rifle, even Howell Cobb appears not to have communicated with Andersonville. Surely the commander of the largest military prison on the continent ought to have been warned through channels that his post lay within five days' march of an overwhelming and virtually unimpeded foe. The arrival of 107 sick and wounded Federal prisoners from the Macon hospitals implied some sort of trouble, though, and Macon papers confirmed it when they drifted into the stockade with news of the disaster on the raw, drizzly afternoon of September 3. Still, General Winder spent the first days of that month in blissful attention to administrative detail and bureaucratic haggling, making out returns and evaluating yet another report of a new prison site in Alabama. Even the adjutant general's office did not appear overly troubled: office functionaries copied routine responses to Daniel Chandler's inspection report and ordered the army's chief engineer to oversee the implementation of Colonel Harkie's plan for reclamation of the Andersonville swamp, knowing all the while that Sherman's various corps sprawled unmolested in front of Hardee's exhausted remnant.[41]

Despite the outward calm, one sign that Winder knew of the crisis was his insistence that cooks work all night to stockpile prepared rations, as though for a projected movement; a sudden tightening of prison discipline served as another hint. Thanks largely to the neglect or ignorance of the Georgia Reserves, prisoners had been sneaking out of or away from the stockade regularly since Kilpatrick's last raid, walking off by ones and twos from outside details or bribing guards to let them slip away: two dozen had escaped since August 24, and John Winder had already asked the adjutant general to arrange some courts-martial for some of the more negligent sentries. On the last day of August a prisoner strolled nonchalantly up to the south gate with a bucket, asking to go out for water: the closest water was inside the stockade, and except for the routine details no prisoners were allowed to go out at all, but the gullible sentinel let this man through, and that was the last anyone saw of him for a while. Then, on the overcast, moonless night of September 3, another pair tunneled out and ran for it, but a more conscientious sentry sounded the alarm and Ed Turner put his dogs on the trail. In light of the rampant reports of Sherman's success circulating inside the pen, it behooved the commandant to clamp down, lest a general break erupt, and when the guard on post thirty-two thought he saw a prisoner cross the dead line in the darkness the next night he blasted a round into the shadows. Unfortunately, this sentinel was not an especially good shot: the offender escaped, while the tentmates of some poor sleeping innocent awoke with his brains splattered all over them. In testimony to the guards' greater vigilance, though, only one other prisoner escaped over the next four days.[42]

John Winder's first official inkling of Hood's defeat (or at least the earliest surviving evidence thereof) came down from Richmond by wire the day after the shooting. In three freestanding sentences Samuel Cooper ordered Winder to get his prisoners out of Andersonville as quickly as possible. Rush completion of the stockade at Millen, Cooper said, but above all get them away: Charleston or Savannah would do for the present.[43]

The order came none too soon, for the disaster had so disrupted the rail lines that rations were growing scarce again at the north gate. Given the distance of Winder's headquarters from the Fort Valley telegraph office, the general probably did not receive that wire until very late on September 5 or early the next morning, and he spent September 6 holding mandatory prison roll calls and arranging transportation. During the day two messages reached Howell Cobb from Hood's headquarters, ordering him to send Winder all the Reserves at Macon to aid in the relocation, and Cobb offered to lend the 5th Reserves for that purpose. Winder optimistically judged that he could run five thousand men a day out of the prison, but as a precaution against their escape he decided to announce to them that they were on the way to a general exchange.[44]

Confederate roll-call sergeants entered the gates at dusk on September 6 to spread their edited version of the news. At the first telling the tale must have met only skepticism, for serial exchange rumors had disappointed everyone too often, and had transformed the pen into a city of cynics. The methodical manner in which they notified the various detachment sergeants gave this information the flavor of real business, though, and it appeared consistent with the story of Sherman's victory. Muffled spirits dared to climb again. When leaders of prison squads told their men to be ready to leave for Charleston at a moment's notice, the stockade erupted with a rippling cheer that floated like a flock of starlings, lighting here and there as the word carried on the wind. Faint voices piped little hoots of joy, and reeling skeletons tried to dance, driven by the tandem delirium of exhaustion and exhilaration. For hours the camp crackled with the chatter of a sleepless multitude, as happy talk of home burned like a campfire at every little lodging. Outside, locomotives from Macon whistled as they brought the 5th Reserves in cars that would carry the first lucky lot of Yankees away. Almost everyone had been taken in by the cruel exchange ruse, but some doubts remained: one Vermonter predicted it was "only a change of prisons to avoid a recapture."[45]

The first eighteen detachments packed their belongings for the voyage. Lawson Carley, the rangy Iowa cavalry sergeant whose health had failed quickly in his single month of confinement, found himself among those designated for the initial evacuation. The instructions indicated a midnight departure, but the long, cool night passed without the creak of another gate. Not until dawn did ten detachments march gaily out of Andersonville, serenaded by wild cheering; they stopped in front of Captain Wirz's office, where the pale commandant sat in a chair in front of his headquarters, too weak to do more than count the giddy prisoners as they formed before him. At seven o'clock the first three detachments climbed into cattle cars with a fresh dole of ample rations. The engineer loosed a shrill note or two from his whistle, and those left at the depot sat down in flea-rich sand to wait for another train. After seven hours in the broiling sunshine they saw a locomotive come wheezing in with fewer cars than the first; even with more than five dozen men packed in a compartment the train could only accommodate two detachments, and Confederate officers waved the rest back to the stockade. It was a despondent thousand who returned to the pungent palisade that afternoon, but their dejection evaporated that night, when Confederate sergeants called them out again. At midnight Sergeant Carley piled his aching bones on the floor of a boxcar in which he would remain confined for the next thirty-two hours.[46]

Counted by a hand that may or may not have been Wirz's, a few more detachments plodded out in the morning twilight of September 8 and headed toward Macon with their fists full of cornbread and bacon. From Macon they turned sharply to the right, down the Savannah road, creeping along in rickety cars on wornout railbeds. Pining to follow, their former neighbors watched the black smoke of their passage disappear into the north, but the railroad could not meet General Winder's schedule: several more detachments had to be turned back in when night fell, marching back to the prison from within sniffing distance of a dinner the Americus Ladies' Relief Society had spread for outward-bound guards of the 5th Georgia Reserves. Transportation returned later that night, the Reserves took leave of their hostesses, and the detachments that had been disappointed earlier were called out again. Taking advantage of the darkness, scores of brazen impostors from high-numbered detachments fell into line, answering to the names of men who failed to respond, but the flankers often found themselves turned out when the missing parties returned from the sinks or some other last-minute errand. Despite the uncertainty and suspicion about where their captors might be taking them, every man seemed bound to get away: could any place be worse?[47]

Before each detachment struck out for the depot its invalids had to be carried over to the barracks, displacing the healthier inhabitants. General Winder may have decided against transporting the weakest of the prisoners partly from humanitarian concern over their ability to survive the trip, but the evacuation proceeded so much more slowly than he anticipated that he probably doubted he could complete it before the enemy arrived—in which case it would be better to let them recapture those of their troops least able to bear arms. That consideration began to occur to the inmates themselves as they said goodbye to their ailing, pleading comrades: if there were really going to be an exchange at the end of their train ride, they supposed the Confederates would unload the sickest prisoners first, shifting the greatest possible burden to Union hands. To counter these logical deductions and keep the transient prisoners happy, Southern sergeants manufactured vivid tales of the jubilation exhibited by those in the earlier detachments at sight of imaginary Federal transports.[48]

Dawn of September 9 revealed that the slope north of Stockade Creek stood almost bare, and most of the shebangs on the south side had been emptied, as well. On September 10 the Plymouth Pilgrims started moving out—what was left of them—and railroad logistics improved sufficiently that numerous trains rattled north during the day. Sergeant Major Kellogg led his squad out, leaving behind ten out of the ninety who were too far gone to travel. Henry Adams limped along with him, helped by some friends, elated to be leaving in spite of the scurvy that wracked his bones and would kill him in forty days. Henry Wirz sat in front of his headquarters, watching the procession with his bad wrist resting on the arm of his chair and his chin cradled in the palm of his left hand; one prisoner who passed the captain that day thought he seemed reflective, even sympathetic.[49]

The next morning a locomotive named the Emerson Foote took away sixteen more carloads of Yankees, many of the Plymouth crowd among them, and Samuel Gibson followed them that evening in a train twenty-three cars long that hauled twelve hundred prisoners at once. With all these southside detachments gone, the original bounds of Sidney Winder's prison lay virtually deserted.[50]

At least three trains left Andersonville that September 12: one departed early in the morning, another at midday, and a third as the sun set. They all traveled with excruciating caution, averaging a dozen miles per hour, with doors thrown open against the heat. Miles of corn and wheat swept by, baked and ruined on the stalk for lack of hands to harvest them, and destitute refugees crowded every depot. Desperate passengers who doubted the exchange lie took advantage of the lumbering pace to burst past their guards and bolt through the open doors. It was a dangerous game—one unfortunate Yankee died when he jumped or fell just a few miles above Andersonville. Thomas Horan, an Indiana infantryman who had lain in the stockade for six months, leapt for freedom and landed on his forehead, readily trading a faceful of dirt for the few days of liberty it bought him. Those without the will, stamina, or opportunity to follow these reckless few begged news from Confederate sentries at each railroad station, but those guards fed them conflicting gossip, some holding to the exchange story while others—more honest, or cruel—told of another Georgia bull pen.

Henry Stone opened up his diary when his car stopped at one depot on the way to the new pen at Millen. "We are fooled this time, I guess," he wrote. "Going to another prison."[51]

The cars from Camp Sumter divided their optimistic cargo between the ports of Charleston and Savannah, as though in token of impending repatriation. Even as the first detachments had left Andersonville, Ben Butler had proposed an exchange of those who were too sick for duty, and his War Department authorized it, unexchanged black prisoners notwithstanding. Some actually would see the old flag before Christmas: Leroy Key and Lawson Carley reentered Union lines by Thanksgiving Day. Paul Renno, a German immigrant serving as a substitute for a Massachusetts man, would not only see Thanksgiving under the U.S. flag, but would return to the front lines in time to worry about being captured again.[52]

For most of the hopeful Federals, these cities merely served as way stations on the road to stockades some of them would find far worse than Andersonville. After a brief improvement in at least the matter of overcrowding, rations, and water, the new pens at Millen and at Florence, South Carolina, quickly deteriorated below the summer standards at Camp Sumter, and guards grew increasingly testy, killing men just for coming too close to the dead line or for the crime of asking a question. Not a few of the still-healthy lads who climbed aboard trains at the Anderson depot yet gave their bones as manure for Southern soil.[53]

By the morning of September 13 fewer than sixteen thousand men remained in the Camp Sumter stockade, but General Winder itched to empty the place. He called for trains enough to carry away another five thousand that day. More diarists left the stockade that Tuesday than on any other occasion, passing before the headquarters building where, on this day, unfamiliar lieutenants counted heads—for Captain Wirz had collapsed again.[54]

Samuel Melvin tottered out that evening, fresh from recording the agonizing death of the last of his close comrades; written reveries of that long-planned jaunt through Europe no longer colored his journal. As the cars filled, the engineers pulled their throttles a little farther back to oblige General Winder, but it was more than wornout Southwestern rails and rolling stock could bear. The last locomotive to pull away that night derailed only a couple of miles above Anderson, toppling and smashing a few cars: cleanup crews found several prisoners and a number of guards crushed beneath the wreckage. The shaken survivors collected on the banks of the railroad cut, not far from Henry Wirz's sickbed, where sentries contained them under lowered muzzles until dawn.

The next morning's walk back to the stockade tried the limits of men on the brink of exhaustion. Private Melvin could not take another step beyond the depot; an ambulance bore him to the prison hospital, where he lay down on his rubber poncho, never to rise again. The following day he scribbled a grim entry in his journal, ending with the plea "I want to go home." Those were the last words he ever wrote.[55]

The massive exodus that second week of September threw the entire post into confusion, and that confusion offered frequent opportunities for escape. In six days sixty-six prisoners slipped away, and most of them either gained their own lines or found a quiet end in some Georgia swamp or forest.[56]

Among the first to flee were a dozen members of the burial detail. Wilford Crandall ran away with one squad and the Tibbles brothers with another, all on September 8, while James Davidson and most of the rest bolted away over the next three days, leaving the frail Captain Wirz no choice but to turn the remainder of the untrustworthy detail back into the stockade. As when escapes had presented a problem before, Wirz (or General Winder) decided once again to replace the white crew with a black one, impressing both slave hands and imprisoned U.S. Colored Troops to the number of several dozen. Foreman W. W. Byram of the 1st Georgia Reserves fell ill about then and withdrew from his duties as supervising sexton, leaving the interment of nearly five thousand more Union soldiers to the predominantly illiterate blacks. Briefly the reinforced detail found enough time to split puncheons again, protecting the rows of hollow, staring eyes with those primitive sepulchers, but records keeping instantly disintegrated. Over the next six weeks the proportion of unidentified graves climbed from barely 1 percent to more than 13 percent. In their first week on the job the blacks lost nearly twice as many names as the white gravediggers had in more than six months: thirty-eight soldiers found anonymous graves on September 17 alone.[57]

Illiteracy and inefficiency were not the only causes of all the unidentified burials that autumn. The open-air barracks along the northern wall of the stockade housed hundreds of mosquito-, fly-, and lice-tormented men, most of whom had been carried there during the past week's evacuation, and now they lay among strangers. The four men who bore John Whitten to the sheds inadvertently separated him from his two other remaining tentmates, but scurvy had robbed all three of the use of their legs and Whitten could only beg his porters to seek out his friends: too busy lugging in other invalids, they could not oblige him. Whitten never saw the lost comrades again, and within a few weeks he gave them up for dead. Like Whitten, many of those crowded around him in the barracks were the sole survivors of messes broken up by death, hospitalization, or transfer; delirium and language barriers kept the surgeons from learning who they all were, so no one knew what names to pin on their ragged blouses when the daily details of pallbearers carried their withered carcasses out to the deadhouse.[58]

They died, too, with uncommon speed once their messmates left them, for not only did they represent the unhealthiest element of the prison's heyday, most had also lost the only hands that would have nursed them. Nor was there anyone to defend them against raiderlike depredations, and the barracks drew a collection of lupine loungers who plucked food from the mouths of the sick as remorselessly as Willie Collins ever had. The hospital outside still held two thousand cases as bad or worse than these, and overburdened surgeons could not begin to offer adequate treatment. They swept through the inside barracks once or twice a day, tapping a forehead here and there as a signal to the litter bearers, but they passed the hopeless by. Inattention thus stepped in to more than double the overall mortality. During the first half of September the daily toll averaged 102, but in the second half of the month, when the stockade population had been reduced by nearly two-thirds, the charnel wagon still carried an average of 82 bodies to the cemetery every day.[59]

The writhing mass of sick beneath the shed roofs defied any effort to keep track of their individual condition, and at least one patient lay dead among them so long that his flesh putrefied and no one would carry him to the deadhouse. At last his aroma demanded attention even from that callous throng, and someone scooped out an oblong pit and rolled him into it.[60]

No more trains sounded at Anderson Station until September 15, when the wreckage of three nights before had been cleared up and the track had been repaired. The next day nearly six hundred more of those in the stockade made their way to the depot for the journey to Camp Lawton, as Confederates styled the new stockade at Millen, and for the first time since May 21 fewer than thirteen thousand Yankees occupied Andersonville, including those in the hospital.[61]

By then a new face hovered above the prostrate patients in the post hospital: that of Dr. Joseph Jones, one of the most respected of the South's younger medical men. Just past his thirty-first birthday, Jones had graduated from what would become Princeton University and the medical college of the University of Pennsylvania. The slim Georgia native looked most gentle and unassuming with the silky tuft of goatee on his chin. At the age of twenty-four he had taken a professorship at Georgia's medical college in Augusta, and research seemed to be his first love. Now he was a major in the medical department, and the surgeon general had sent him down to Camp Sumter to study the effects of the late smallpox epidemic and the progress of malarial fevers on unacclimated Northerners.[62]

All of one day Dr. Jones and his clerk, Louis Manigault, toured the tented wards of what Manigault characterized as a "so-called Hospital." The place appalled them both. A board fence penned more than two thousand patients and all their attendants inside a grove of pine and oak divided by a languid rill that had swollen into an open cesspool. The fetid end of Stockade Creek passed just outside, and the combined stench overpowered the visitors. Tents erected during the spring and summer no longer shed the rain, and patients lay shoulder-to-shoulder in them, usually with no kind of bedding except a blanket and sometimes without that. Even the floors of the tents showed signs of human excrement, and Dr. Jones witnessed perfectly ambulatory patients squatting promiscuously around the hospital, indolently responding to the urgings of loose bowels. Too few surgeons worked the wards to offer effective treatment, and the paroled prisoners who served as nurses seemed wholly unsympathetic to their comrades' plight; the patients reciprocated, Jones felt, with justifiable mistrust of the nurses. On September 16 he decided he had seen all he needed of the hospital, and that afternoon he approached Captain Wirz about going inside the stockade.[63]

Wirz had been back in his office a day or two, but so tightly did the fever still grip him that he might have served as a test case himself. As politely as possible he refused Jones a pass into the stockade—why, he did not say, but perhaps General Winder had warned him against unnecessary traffic there in response to the rash of recent escapes, or in reaction to the critical reports of other visitors, like Colonel Chandler. Jones appealed to Winder himself and obtained permission, but the day was too far gone by then for any effective observations. Followed by his clerk and his family servant, Titus, Jones retired to the cool comfort of a wall tent that some black prisoners had raised for him in a stand of pine southwest of the depot.[64]

Jones conscripted other workmen to erect a little morgue out of loose boards and canvas some fifty feet from the prison hospital pale. Early the next morning, September 17, he selected a couple of corpses from the assortment arrayed in the ramshackle hospital deadhouse and opened them up to examine the effects of their illnesses. After dissecting bowels, brains, and hearts, Jones piled everything back into the appropriate cavities and sewed the bodies back together as handily as he might have sutured a living patient. Then, rinsing off the blood, he returned to the stockade gate with his pass. Captain Wirz had taken another day in bed, but his substitute ordered the wicket opened for Dr. Jones. Inside, the doctor encountered a sight surpassing the hospital for pathos: "one of the most heart rending scenes imaginable," his clerk called it. The healthiest prisoners had all migrated to Millen; fewer than eleven thousand of them remained within the walls, but Jones judged that at least three thousand of those were sick. Here even the healthy used their tent doors for latrines, shamelessly hunching or standing, urinating, alongside the fires where their breakfasts boiled. Trash littered every yard of ground: remnants of uniforms or blankets, bones, and great chunks of the despised cornbread lay everywhere. Two thousand of the most indisposed prisoners jammed together under the four open sheds, with only one surgeon to attend them all. The smell from the feces-saturated banks of Stockade Creek impressed even these two, who had spent the previous day in the noisome hospital.[65]

Jones and his clerk wandered all over the post, sauntering from the stockade to the cemetery and back to the hospital. Mr. Manigault found it worse than anything he had ever seen, though he had witnessed a cholera epidemic in northern China and the squalor of a prison in Shanghai; somehow it horrified him more to find such sights on American soil. Revulsion, however, did not translate into pity for the Yankees who had "clad every one of our families in mourning," even when he found a young prisoner laid out on the dirt in the glaring, fist-clenched frustration of recent and needless death. The Federals themselves seemed oblivious to their own misery, apparently satisfied to lie in their filth. Manigault saw one malefactor locked in the stocks behind Wirz's headquarters—probably one of the recaptured gravediggers, whose escape had violated his parole—but the pilloried miscreant whiled away his punishment by flipping contentedly through the pages of a novel; a year later a U.S. government prosecutor would paint those stocks as instruments of diabolical torture.[66]

Dr. Jones observed that scurvy and intestinal diseases were still carrying off the most men. He blamed combinations of these ailments for the majority of the mortality attributed to marasmus and other indefinite diagnoses, and for the deceptive impression left by the emaciated corpses in the deadhouse that the prisoners were starving. Jones found intestinal complaints endemic, while more than a quarter of the surviving Yankees—much more, he noted—showed symptoms of scurvy. He even discovered that one of the ward surgeons was suffering from it, as did many Confederate soldiers in the field, so its prevalence in the prison did not especially surprise him. The problem lay not so much in the quantity of the food issued as in its monotony, he thought: if prisoners did not draw full rations it was only because of fraud on the part of the post commissary or because the Federal mess sergeants cheated their own men, and Jones heard enough complaints of the latter variety that he gave it more credence. Even so, he pointed out, Confederate troops often campaigned on less food than the Andersonville inmates. Though he suggested antiscorbutic vegetables and their derivatives, he acknowledged the logistical difficulties posed by such massive quantities of perishables. He supposed that soft bread, chicken soup, and fresh milk might ease the rampant diarrhea and dysentery, but he must have doubted the probability of obtaining those items, too. When he dissected eight more bodies on September 19, Jones found that the intestines of many patients had developed ulcers and begun to mortify from some cause ominously similar to hospital gangrene, and he concluded that a substantial portion of these sufferers could not have been saved by any treatment whatsoever.[67]

Apparently too few subjects remained to support a pathological study of smallpox: only 128 victims had been diagnosed with anything like variola or varioloid, and more than half of them had died, while most of the rest had disappeared in the recent hegira. Jones did, however, investigate the various fevers that had killed more than 300 prisoners and nearly 40 guards. Typhoid proved to be the principal villain, bringing down the native Georgians at almost three times the rate that it felled the Federals. No one had determined yet that typhoid spreads through bacteria in fecally contaminated water, so Jones expressed surprise to learn the ailment had subsided among the Confederate troops in June, after they moved their camps away from the slopes of Stockade Creek. That same June had marked a similarly dramatic decline in the cases of typhoid among prisoners, as well—thereby suggesting that the guards' latrines had fouled the creek for all of them. Unadulterated springs at their new camps interrupted the epidemic for guards and prisoners alike, at least until August, when flash floods washed the bacilli-laden sewage up both slopes of the creek and flooded shallow wells. Jones did strike near the mark when he attributed the unusual Confederate susceptibility to the extremes of youth and age among the Georgia Reserves, but their rural origins probably played an even greater role: more of the Federals hailed from crowded, filthy cities, many of them in Europe, where they may have developed a certain resistance.[68]

The disease that especially captured Jones's interest was gangrene. Andersonville surgeons had first seen it early in the third month of the prison's occupation, among some Belle Isle prisoners who had frozen their feet the previous winter. Next it showed up in the vaccination scars of prisoners inoculated during the spring, and thereafter in the sores that erupted on the limbs of those who came down with scurvy. Ultimately the slightest wound invited infection: a scratch, a shaving nick, or even a mosquito bite. Like its cousin, which produces tetanus, the anaerobic bacteria *Clostridium welchii* thrives in soil contaminated by feces, so gangrene spread rapidly inside the stockade, diving deep into wounded tissues where no oxygen lived. Eating away at the dead meat inside, it left behind a layer of pus that attracted maggots, and the uneducated provincials who watched its progress thought the maggots, themselves, were devouring the flesh.[69]

Gangrene did terrible execution at Andersonville, yet for all its virulence hospital records do not often credit it with killing its victims. Local treatment with iodine, nitric acid, and patent medicines yielded only pain, and the traditional extreme of amputation succeeded in a slight majority of cases, but usually some other complaint won the honor of having extinguished life. The plurality of recorded infections settled in men who arrived wounded from the battlefield, and so carelessly did prison nurses switch washbowls and bandages from gangrenous patients to the gangrene-free that few escaped the bacterium: many of the names listed as its victims belonged to wounded men, and a large proportion of those said to have died of wounds probably succumbed to the secondary infection. Still more who died under other diagnoses also perished from gangrene.[70]

Simon Bolivar Hulbert was such a one. Fighting below Richmond with a regiment from western New York, Hulbert suffered a slight flesh wound in the right arm on May 16. With a couple of stitches and a clean bandage he might have been back on duty the next morning, but Confederates stepped in the way of his retreat and a fortnight later he landed in Andersonville. Three weeks after that the wound, which ought to have healed by then, began to throb. It grew steadily worse until the middle of July, when he thought it looked so "evil" that he lined up at the morning sick call. A hospital steward in one of the outside stalls poured caustic soda on it, wrapped it up, and for two more weeks Hulbert came back daily for the same treatment—convincing himself, through his diary, that the arm felt better.

By the first of August, however, Hulbert conceded that the wound was still infected. The steward scoffed when he returned to sick call, refusing him another dressing and insisting that he would be fine. Frightened, Hulbert turned his day's ration of cornmeal into a poultice and wrapped it around the distended member, to no avail: the pain and swelling worsened. For the next eight days he tried to see the surgeons, but that was the week of the wholesale hospital admissions, and each day he was turned away. So desperate was he by August 8 that he swathed the gaping sore in a searing tobacco concoction. The next evening, after the stockade washed down, he found he could no longer write, so he asked a friend to make his daily diary entry for him. In the wake of the torrent his amanuensis wrote, rather ironically, that the arm was not quite so bad. Hulbert must have lapsed into delirium that night or the next day, for the tentmate carried the diary back to New York without further entries. Hulbert died on the afternoon of August 11: a comrade recalled later that he sat up as though from a nap, groaned, and fell back stone dead. Because of the backlog of bodies, he did not go into his grave until August 13, nominally undone by scurvy.[71]

Surgeons followed the case of John Mahler, of New Jersey, more closely. His vaccination scab began to swell and ooze during the summer, and, when gangrene had eaten his arm away in a three-inch radius around the inoculation, the sick-call surgeon granted him admission to the hospital: Mahler was one of the lucky ones who fought his way to the gate on the morning of August 5, but that was his last instance of good fortune. He begged for amputation, but with the infection already advanced to within a couple of inches of the shoulder joint the ward doctors feared it would do no good, so they fed him quinine and whiskey for his chills and fever while they washed the green and yellow eruption with straight nitric acid. If this treatment accomplished anything, it only accelerated the infection, but that may have been the kindest course of all. Within three days the gangrene crawled into Mahler's shoulder and halfway down his forearm. His pulse soared to 157 and he came down with dysentery: often the gangrene attacked the irritated interior of the colon, as Dr. Jones learned during his autopsies. The arm swelled to bursting and stank unmercifully, but the surgeons could only add a daily dose of turpentine. The patient died August 14, and the beleaguered clerk entered dysentery as the cause of death.[72]

Nor were prisoners the only victims. Sixteen-year-old Thomas J. Cole joined the 3rd Georgia Reserves during Rousseau's cavalry raid, in July. He had never wandered far from his father's farm in Butts County, midway between Macon and Atlanta, and shoes had never served as part of his daily wardrobe. He arrived at Andersonville with a pair of brogans on, however, and they irritated an insignificant scratch on his left foot, just below the ankle. The nearest he ever came to the stockade was the sentry box, and he did not approach the prisoners' hospital at all, but, just before the evacuation of prisoners began, his foot turned so sore that he had to be relieved from duty. A week later his comrades carried him from his tent over to Sumter Hospital—the parallel pair of two-story barracks buildings alongside the railroad. In seven weeks the wound had grown to look like a carbuncle, but ten days in the hospital transformed it into a gaping, putrid lesion four inches in diameter. The flesh dropped away to reveal his ankle joint, his lower leg started to swell and ulcerate, and he wailed piteously whenever the doctors tried to touch it.[73]

Cole would survive, however. He would live into the twentieth century and raise five children, but he would have to sacrifice the leg in order to save the rest of his hide.[74]

Youth sustained Cole—unlike one of the other Confederate patients at the opposite extreme of the military age limits, whose gangrenous leg came off above the knee only to attract a second infection. Painful quantities of quinine, turpentine, and nitric acid seemed to arrest the spread of the gangrene, but Dr. Jones did not like the looks of this patient the last time he saw him: he lay alone in a small tent, feeble and feverish, his face the color of an old bullet except for the burning cheeks, and he refused to partake of either food or hope. Shortly after his final examination of this patient, Dr. Jones departed with Titus and Mr. Manigault for a more pleasant sojourn near a female college in Macon, where Jones began sorting his ream of notes and outlining his report.[75]

Jones concluded that the size of the guard, the stockade, and the medical staff all ought to be increased despite the recent reduction in prisoners. Shelter, raiment, and a more varied diet should be provided, he wrote, and with the final addition of strict hygienic regulations he felt the South would have met its moral obligations to its vanquished guests. No one in the Richmond government ever saw that detailed report, though: Jones worked on it through the winter and spring, completing it just at the collapse of the Confederacy.[76]

Dr. Jones and his entourage left a post rippling with nervous anticipation. The evacuation had left Camp Sumter embarrassed for guards because many of the Georgia Reserves who had escorted trainloads of prisoners to Savannah and Charleston had not been allowed to return: Sam Jones retained the entire 5th Reserve regiment at the latter city, for instance. At Andersonville the remaining garrison reverted to double duty again, and sentries who were dismissed from guard duty one morning found themselves climbing back up to the pigeon roosts that evening. Nor could General Winder spare any more troops to transport prisoners; from the day after the train wreck until September 28 he sent fewer than six hundred more prisoners to Savannah, and then only men too sick to require more than token security.[77]

The paucity of troops at the post caused but a fraction of the anxiety, though. The greater fear came from John Bell Hood's efforts to distract Sherman's army. Hood concluded that his only hope of drawing the overpowering foe back from Atlanta was to sever enemy supply lines in Tennessee, so he planned to sidestep his entire army around Sherman's right flank and lunge up into Tennessee's underbelly through Alabama. That would lay Andersonville wide open, so Hood was obligated to forewarn Winder. With the dawn of September 18 the Army of Tennessee began its shift from the Macon railroad to the West Point line, and Hood advised Winder to get the rest of his prisoners out as fast as he could.[78]

General Winder was already gone from Camp Sumter. Shortly after writing the pass for Dr. Jones on September 17 he departed for Millen, to press completion of the stockade there.[79]

Hood's warning telegram also made reference to a couple of thousand men at Camp Sumter whom he intended to exchange. Despite the breakdown of the cartel, battlefield commanders still occasionally traded prisoners they had lost to each other, and before Hood began his last quixotic campaign he wished to reinforce his depleted legions with as many men as he could barter with the proceeds of Andersonville. On September 17 seven hundred lucky captives from the Atlanta campaign left the stockade for Sherman's lines, followed two days later by eleven hundred more. An additional three hundred prison patients died during those same three days, leaving fewer than nine thousand prisoners inside the palisade and just under two thousand in the hospital.[80]

The prisoners who departed Andersonville in September carried with them the last of the U.S. currency that had fueled the summer market there. Few of those who remained had heard the clink of coins in their pockets in many weeks, and most could no longer even boast the pocket. Either they had spent their little fortunes over a long imprisonment or they had fallen ill and been robbed. The incidence of scurvy among them testified to their poverty, else they could have bought a few onions to save their lives: scarcity of cash depressed the inflated prices of July, and one Vermonter managed to trade his pen for half a dozen yams and three peppers, though at his stage of destitution he called even that a bad trade. Nowadays the most common medium of exchange was brass buttons, and sutler James Selman saw little sense in fishing a dry pond. Late that month Selman closed up his shop, told Captain Wirz he did not feel well, and headed for greener pastures.[81]

Richard Winder left Andersonville for Millen a few days after Selman decamped, and Lieutenant James H. Wright of the 55th Georgia took over as quartermaster. Wright's department bore the responsibility for trucking the daily provisions from the commissary building to the stockade, and then issuing them; the inmates apparently assumed he still had charge of all aspects of prison provender, for when he first ventured into their enclosure they asked him about their grub. He made some remark—probably mere speculation on the autumn livestock slaughter—that the querulous prisoners interpreted as a promise of more pork and beef. The very next day a great many prisoners complained that their portions had been drastically cut rather than increased, which may have reflected a deliberate shrinking of commissary stockpiles: expecting to abandon the prison momentarily, officials may have allowed provisions to run low rather than leave them for the enemy. The shortages that began on September 27 continued sporadically thereafter, though, with no such ready excuse—suggesting instead that quartermaster clerk James Duncan found his new boss easier to hoodwink (or to corrupt) than Richard Winder.[82]

7 ❦ A April Is the Cruelest Month

utumn's nightly chill bore down on a barren, depressing landscape as September of 1864 closed. On all sides of the prison now the forest had been whittled back, both by the log-hungry slave gangs working on the outer stockades and by firewood details: with the coming of cold weather the troop commanders had resumed the daily assignment of guards for that purpose. Camp Sumter now encompassed a mile-wide halo of stump-pimpled swamp and swales. The lower half of the stockade lay empty as the remaining tenants shrank from the redolent sinks; prisoners short on apparel and nutrition huddled together above a Market Street that stood more silent these days. The dead line was gone, or nearly so—stolen to feed campfires when the mass migration interrupted the chopping crews—and, in the absence of most of the summer's great muttering horde, Captain Wirz seemed in no hurry to rebuild it.

Even the Confederate side of Andersonville wore an air of desolation. Eleven of the post's sixteen cannon had disappeared to fill lunettes at Millen, leaving all the fortifications except the star fort yawning with the impotence of toothless pit bulls, while the Floridians who stood to those guns and the Georgians on the pigeon roosts looked more mendicant than military: Richard Winder had sought new uniforms for Captain Dyke's artillerymen and the 55th Georgia since the middle of July, with no success, while the Reserves remained clad in the remnants of whatever they had brought from home or bought from the prisoners.[1]

With the imminent completion of the stockade at Millen, General Winder dared shuttle still more Yankees from Camp Sumter to Savannah. At dusk of September 27 more than eight hundred of them shuffled out the gate, leaving hundreds of helpless comrades behind; in the last stages of scurvy, Ira Pettit told his departing friends that all was well with him. The next day nearly a thousand others took the cars. Trapped in their shebang, Samuel Foust and his three scurvy-hobbled tentmates cast doleful eyes on the backs of their disappearing detachment: only one of the four would ever leave Andersonville. Foust began to complain of long, lonesome days. Aside from his three sick companions, just one of the men who still lived within the stockade walls knew him, and that fellow stopped every day to chat and try to cheer the tentful of failing Pennsylvanians.[2]

The first day of October brought John Winder back from Camp Lawton. His construction schedule there lagged several days behind—he had expected to have the stockade finished already—but he sent Cousin Richard on to push the project while he closed up affairs at Sumter. He remained a week, during which he answered the Richmond bureaucrats' delayed reactions to Daniel Chandler's August report. Because of the evacuation, most of Chandler's criticisms no longer applied, but an old soldier like Winder could not ignore such official criticism. Even as he composed his reply, however, he shipped off another 1,859 of the healthiest Federals, and the stockade population at Andersonville dropped below 4,000 on the day he signed the cover letter on the sheaf of correspondence. Two thousand more prisoners still strained the hospital's resources, but Winder intended to leave no able-bodied captives behind and he had already begun to transform the post into one great medical facility. On the broad ridge south of the stockade, behind Captain Wirz's headquarters, paroled Yankee carpenters offered up the remaining boards from Dick Winder's lumber yard for more sheds to house the sick, as Dr. Stevenson had advised.[3]

Perhaps, in his last days at Andersonville, General Winder donned his dress uniform for another Americus wedding. On October 5 Colonel Timothy Furlow, who had married off his son in July, gave his daughter away to a captain of the Georgia Reserves at the same Methodist church. This was one of those bright social affairs Southerners needed to lift their spirits, and the aisles filled with the local gentry. It proved to be a heavier burden than the weathered church could stand, though, especially after the spring revival, and when the wedding party gathered in front of the vestibule the platform collapsed, throwing everyone into the dust. The groom brushed off his wife's dress and his own uniform and returned— presumably after a kiss—to Camp Sumter, to join General Winder on his journey to Millen.[4]

When the general left, on October 9, he seated a new man at his old desk. Colonel George C. Gibbs, a Floridian whom Winder had known since the beginning of the war, had worked for him before: as a staff captain in 1861, Gibbs had recommended a promotion for one of his clerks, Henry Wirz. Gibbs took command of the 42nd North Carolina in 1862, but intermittent fever sent him home the next year. He asked for, but was denied, an assignment to a "Southern" climate, preferably in his home state of Florida; he therefore tendered his resignation early in 1864, but that summer the War Department reactivated him and put him in charge of the Macon prison. Now that prison lay abandoned, and Gibbs— who had just returned from a month's convalescent leave—moved a little closer to the coveted Florida state line. His orders evidently did not bring him close enough to home, though, for only eighteen days after he arrived at Andersonville he sought another medical furlough, this time for a facial ulcer that three post doctors feared had already attracted the rampant gangrene.[5]

Sidney Winder accompanied his father to Millen, and Colonel Gibbs had no staff of his own, so General Winder left him the services of Lieutenant James Ormand, 2nd Georgia Reserves, who had already demonstrated some administrative talent. The forty-seven-year-old At- lanta merchant acted thenceforward as post adjutant. Ormand, who looked so paternal and benign with his grey hair, struck not a few Yan- kees as a sharp businessman with a ready eye for any extra dollar that might be made. That may not have seemed an unusual observation for nineteenth-century Americans to make about a native of Scotland, but they suspected Adjutant Ormand of making his extra dollars at their expense.[6]

After he arrived at Camp Lawton, General Winder sent for the better part of the Andersonville garrison. Prisoners started coming into the new stockade from Savannah before any troops arrived to guard them, so Winder begged Howell Cobb to intercede with railroad authorities to transport the garrison: he wanted the 1st and 3rd Georgia Reserves and Captain Dyke's Florida artillery right away. By design or misunderstanding the 3rd Reserves, the largest of those regiments, did not come. Instead, Winder saw the gunners and the 1st and 2nd Reserves disembark at Millen. He cared little for the Reserves, and always seemed to be trying to get rid of them; he would have preferred local militiamen, who might serve more conscientiously in the protection of their home territory, but he appears to have especially not wanted the 2nd Reserves. Perhaps they showed even less discipline than the other regiments, for, after complaining of their plundering of the countryside around Millen, Winder sent much of the 2nd Reserves packing. Apparently he replaced them, eventually, with the 3rd and 4th Reserves.[7]

When the men of the 2nd Reserves returned to Andersonville they took over the camps abandoned by the departing 3rd regiment and immediately set about preparing winter quarters. The captain of Company D, Thomas C. Jackson, laid claim to a little cabin with a plank floor, the walls of which he planned to chink and daub, and he hired someone to build a separate kitchen for him nearby. One of Andersonville's more affluent officers, Captain Jackson had shopped unsuccessfully for grey government cloth during the regiment's layover in Macon, but he still hoped to secure enough to tailor a new winter uniform.[8]

Inside the stockade the prisoners also prepared for winter. Captain Wirz had resumed his normal duties now, and to accommodate the sick he had separated them from the healthier men, who still frequently preyed upon them. The barrack sheds became an interior hospital, and Wirz used the site of the proposed fifth barracks to throw up a dispensary, marching the remainder of the inmates south of Stockade Creek, where the sandier soil rendered tunneling less practical. There he reorganized them into detachments of five hundred, with squads of one hundred and messes of twenty-five, and he directed them to build their shanties in regular streets. After a series of cold days and nights that left poorly clad prisoners shivering and sleepless, Wirz warned them that they would probably be there through the winter, and he advised them to dig in. Some took him literally, gouging two-foot cellars beneath their tents, and an abundance of refuse building material allowed most of the three thousand inhabitants to at least protect themselves from the wind and rain. A few even slapped together mud-and-stick chimneys.[9]

From outside, the echo of hammers ricocheted off the plank walls of the new hospital wards, but patients who applied for admission at the south gate still had to be carried around to the drafty tent hospital nearer the swamp. Attendants who had neglected their ailing comrades in the stockade infirmary ignored them all the more in the formal hospital: almost as soon as they entered, new patients there began complaining of a starvation diet; unless the surgeon in charge actually conspired to skim a profit from his ward's rations, it must have been the Federal nurses themselves who appropriated the missing food.[10]

Men carried to the hospital that fall seldom came back. Samuel Melvin perished there September 25, and Ira Pettit on October 18. Samuel Foust was admitted October 23, after the second of his last three friends died, and there he lingered for three weeks. One of the few who survived was John Whitten. Doses of vinegar drove off the scurvy that nearly did him in, stiffening his loose teeth and loosening his stiff legs, and his dismissal opened a spot in the hospital for the dying Foust. Still limping but under his own power, Whitten returned to the stockade, where he began a painful, fruitless, week-long search for his lost comrades.[11]

The faces Whitten encountered included some 370 new ones, representing the first prisoners of General Hood's latest campaign. Among them was Chester Hart, a reenlisted veteran from Illinois, whose company had been guarding the railroad depot at Big Shanty, between Atlanta and Chattanooga. Big Shanty had been the scene of an audacious locomotive hijacking early in the war, but in the wake of Atlanta's fall it had seemed a pleasant backwater garrison to a man who had endured the Vicksburg campaign. An entire Confederate corps swept along the railroad on October 4, though, and Hart retreated with his comrades to the slotted blockhouse near the depot. After a few futile shots the garrison surrendered its arms and plodded south, on the roundabout voyage to Andersonville. Hart arrived there October 11, finding three thousand lice-infested, demoralized indigents, many of them without blankets, some of them even bare-chested, and every one of them as black as an African from huddling over pine-fed fires. Two days later the same Confederates who took Hart gobbled up the station-house guard at Tilton, Georgia, capturing another second-term soldier named George Shearer.[12]

Andersonville may still have shocked someone like Hart, fresh from the relative ease of a post in the rear, but without the summer's crowding it began to look a lot better to the longtime residents. Those with enough stamina found it easier to get a pass for the outside now, where the air was much fresher, because so many hands were needed to carry out the dead and bring in wood. With no more slaves available for fatigue duty, and too few troops, Wirz had to rely heavily on prison labor. Each day he assigned a hefty detail to carry out the dead, few of whom had any friends left to offer that final service for them; even after the total population of Federals fell below six thousand, in the second half of October, they continued to drop at the rate of forty-five a day. About six dozen men went out each day on the wood detail, with twenty-five guards around them. The quantity and variety of food also improved in late October, for some. John Whitten alternately drew cornbread and beans, or rice and molasses, while others enjoyed all of them at once, with some bacon to top it off. Dying of scurvy, Samuel Foust savored some soft wheat bread thanks to the efforts of Father Whelan, who drummed up some money for that purpose when he returned to Savannah. Another scurvy victim who had champed and fretted to leave all through September decided, as October ended, that Andersonville was the best place to await an exchange. Nor was he alone: at least one old Belle Isle prisoner judged Andersonville better by far, especially for rations.[13]

Not everyone saw such improved fare, however, and Whitten only realized his own varied menu by flitting from one detachment to another. Bitter comments about deliberate starvation flavored numerous diaries during the middle of the month, when no Union raids or strategic maneuvers seemed responsible. The culprit may have been a single individual this time, for it was early in October that Captain Wirz appointed James Duncan, who was already chief of the ration wagon, as a temporary sutler in place of James Selman. Few who mentioned Duncan seemed to trust him, and the image they left of him suggests a scoundrel who would diminish ration portions to improve the demand for his retail stores of costly flour and sweet potatoes: he would have found a particularly good market among the new captives from northern Georgia, who had encountered a paymaster within recent memory. Colonel Gibbs quickly suspended Duncan's appointment, though, either out of jealous regard for his own prerogatives or because he saw the conflict of interest, and the discontent among hungry prisoners subsided slightly.[14]

The end of October turned bitterly cold, sending still more men from the motley village south of the creek to the barracks infirmary at the north end. These open sheds bulged with sick now, and the weather beat them unmercifully, so the surgeons sent several hundred more to the hospital outside. Dr. Stevenson could accommodate no more—earlier he had warned General Winder against overcrowding, himself—and in the last days of the month he dispatched doctors through the barracks to separate the invalids from the ambulatory, sending the weakest to the prison hospital and the ablest to their regular detachments. Three of those detachments, fifteen hundred strong, made their way to the cars between October 28 and November 3, including scores of flankers who slipped into gaps in the ranks and gave another name. Amos Yeakle assumed the identity of another Pennsylvanian, one B. Bisel, who had died nine days before. With these hardier souls traveled five hundred of the sick, to thin out the hospital, all of them rattling off for Millen under the muskets of leftover detachments from the 1st, 3rd, and 4th Georgia Reserves.[15]

Left only with part of the 2nd Reserves and the fragment of the 55th Georgia, Henry Wirz found himself dreadfully shorthanded. The two units may have mustered as many as three hundred men, which gave them a one-to-ten ratio against the remaining prisoners. Those were the best odds Andersonville guards had ever faced, especially considering that the better half of the prisoners were too sick to flee, but a thousand Yankees still inhabited the stockade while the rest lay in the separate hospital. That meant Wirz still had to post sentinels around the stockade and hospital alike, particularly at night, and the pigeon roosts on the stockade would consume half his force with the three daily reliefs. That responsibility, plus hospital sentries, the wood guard, and assorted post details, would have kept nearly every man on duty constantly.[16]

Georgia Reserves were not the type to stand such stress for long. Many of them, like Captain Jackson, endured the strain of domestic worries that would have driven most other men to desert. Every man from northern Georgia feared for his family (even Howell Cobb had bought a house in Americus for his own wife and children, in case the enemy approached), and Jackson's wife had fled their home in Atlanta to board with her father-in-law in Upson County, about fifty miles north of Andersonville. Something had gone wrong—a family squabble, or a general clash of personalities—but Jackson's first inkling of trouble was a letter from his Josie, who had taken refuge with a friend in a place called Rice Hill. The merchant-turned-soldier had no idea where Rice Hill was, and his wife failed to tell him where to direct return mail, so he fell into a black mood for several days. Similar family difficulties among those in the ranks tended to thin out any regiment hailing from occupied territory. One teenaged private feared his father would be drafted, leaving the family without an adult male, and he counseled the patriarch to falsify his age. The same boy's illiterate uncle, who shared a beat with him at Andersonville, seemed more concerned about his wife's fidelity.[17]

Other evidence of demoralization in the garrison appeared in the form of general and special orders. The Reserves had to be admonished about the filthy condition of their camps, surgeons had to be cautioned against the propensity of sick or malingering Confederates to wander away from the post, and on November 5 a corporal's guard was established at the rail depot, to inspect each train for deserters before it left Anderson Station. One evening two Georgia Reserves so far forgot their duties that they sold enough whiskey to some of the paroled Yankees to get them roaring drunk.[18]

Rather than exhaust the demoralized garrison, Wirz diminished his daily levy for guard mount, spreading his pigeon-roost sentries thin. The nights turned surprisingly cold in Sumter County at this season (colder than Pennsylvania, opined a dying son of that state), and sentries frequently climbed down their ladders to warm themselves around picket fires. Such lapses along the perimeter invited escape, and eleven men scurried away in the cloudy, moonless nights that first week in November. All were recaptured, most of them within twenty-four hours, but the frequency alarmed Wirz. In Colonel Gibbs's absence Wirz called on the new post adjutant, Ormand, to requisition a special train to empty the stockade. The evening after he submitted that request two more Yankees made off, only to be brought back the next day.[19]

The special train steamed into Anderson Station on the morning of November 11, and at noon the last 841 prisoners inside the stockade formed in column and marched out the south gate, escorted by straggling squads of the 2nd Georgia Reserves. Invigorated by three weeks of a sound diet (which he had supplemented by flanking through three messes), John Whitten turned his back to the prison with no thought of ever seeing it again. The next afternoon the former standard-bearer of the 5th Iowa walked into the new bull pen at Millen—"a nice looking place," he thought, of some forty acres.[20]

With the passage of these last Yankees through the south gate, Henry Wirz exchanged his star fort headquarters for an office in the village. The peculiar administrative structure at Camp Sumter left him in charge of the post during Colonel Gibbs's furlough, in order that he could exercise authority over the troop commanders in a prison emergency. That hierarchy was based on the assumption of a crowded prison, but aside from the patients in the hospital barely two hundred Federals remained at Andersonville, and four of them promptly walked away. These two hundred apparently consisted of detailed clerks, carpenters, nurses, and blacks. Wirz retained the black prisoners as long as he could, using them for the graveyard crew and keeping them, per order of the secretary of war, for identification by professed owners of runaway slaves. The major of the 1st North Carolina Colored Infantry, Archibald Bogle, still remained with his men.[21]

Bogle's days at Andersonville were numbered, however. Sherman's blue behemoth had begun to stir in Atlanta, burning most of the city and threatening a movement, and Camp Sumter authorities hurried to rid themselves of still more Federals.

Howell Cobb warned of heavy infantry columns headed for Macon on Tuesday, November 15, and that day the prison hospital at Andersonville disgorged more than five hundred of its sick. Before these five hundred boarded the train, Confederate officers paroled them: Union authorities might honor those paroles or they might not, but, in case Sherman came into position to capture them, the Confederates might try simply turning them over and demanding equivalents in exchange. The paroles also served to discourage escape, standing for the implied promise of imminent exchange in place of the armed guards Wirz could not spare. Sherman did not move quickly enough to intercept the train, though, and the invalid caravan turned south at Macon without interference. Some of the sick carried mail from friends left behind at Andersonville, expecting to deposit it with Federal officers on the morrow, but these informal postmen would have to hold those letters a while longer: although the clerk at Camp Sumter had counted those five hundred off for exchange at Savannah, the next day they staggered into the stockade at Millen instead.[22]

Three days after the trainload of sick departed, Henry Wirz forwarded eight more Yankees to Millen under special escort. Seven of them were enlisted men, including three prisoners shaved from Sherman's vanguard and four paroled workmen who now refused to do their jobs: with the stockade perfectly empty, Wirz could hardly turn these men back into it without posting guards there again. The eighth Federal was Major Bogle, whom Wirz sent ahead for a personal interview with General Winder; after eight months at Andersonville, Bogle hoped Southern animosity toward Colored Troops officers had abated. Wirz obliged him with a letter of introduction to Winder, explaining in it that the prisoner wished to be recognized and exchanged as an officer. He put all eight

Yankees aboard the regular train with a couple of guards and a Confederate officer who, presumably, also had other business at Millen, but neither the letter nor the special escort brought the major his freedom.
Wirz's counterpart at Camp Lawton simply threw Bogle into a larger
and somewhat-less-defiled stockade.[23]

Not long after Bogle's train left the depot at Andersonville, another
rolled in from the west bearing the most exalted Confederate ever to visit
there. On his way from Selma under orders to take command of all troops
in Georgia, Lieutenant General Richard Taylor—son of the twelfth president of the United States—stopped briefly while his train took on water.
The new depot guard detail notified Wirz of their illustrious guest, and the
captain bustled aboard Taylor's car with a fistful of duplicate requisitions
he had long ago submitted for blankets for the prisoners, wagons for
hauling firewood, and troops to guard his remaining Yankees. The general gladly endorsed the requests, but as his train started toward Macon
again both he and Wirz probably knew it would do no good.[24]

Sherman cut a swath more than thirty miles wide across central Georgia, with Kilpatrick's cavalry ranging beyond even that. The enemy
swung just north of Macon, and two days after Major Bogle passed
through there Kilpatrick's horsemen threatened the city. Like Stoneman,
though, Kilpatrick never crossed the Ocmulgee. Part of Sherman's Fif-
teenth Corps pounded a feisty hodgepodge of Georgia militia northeast
of Macon on November 22, after which the invaders pressed on toward
Millen.[25]

Sherman clearly meant to strike either Savannah or Augusta. The first
destination would bring him directly past Millen, while the second would
land him dangerously close. More than half the former Andersonville
captives had traveled on to Charleston, and General Winder retained
only about ten thousand of them in the stockade at Camp Lawton, but he
and the War Department grew anxious over their fate. At General Hardee's insistence, Winder emptied Millen in the course of three days—
abandoning what he had supposed, only six weeks before, would be the
largest prison in the world. Swinging below Savannah with his peripa-
tetic prisoners, he dropped thousands of sick off for exchange at that
port. The remainder he sent into southeast Georgia under Colonel
Forno, who located a camp for them near Blackshear, north of Okeefe-
nokee Swamp and perilously close to a settlement called Yankee Town.
The new site also lay uncomfortably near several potential routes for
waterborne raids, a favorite pastime for Union generals along the coast.[26]

Not all the Millen prisoners followed this southern route. More than two hundred had already slipped back through Macon just ahead of Sherman's march, wearing Confederate uniforms. These were the first of the turncoats known as Galvanized Yankees.[27]

As early as September, Confederate officials had authorized certain Southern officers to recruit from among the more discontented prisoners at Andersonville, Millen, and in South Carolina. These officers actually seemed to believe in the sincerity of their proselytes, and one South Carolina lieutenant petitioned Henry Wirz to return $110 in U.S. currency that Wirz was holding for a Federal prisoner who had taken the oath. With great logic Wirz wondered what a loyal new Confederate citizen would want with greenbacks, since Southerners were forbidden them by statute; did it did not seem obvious, he asked, that the man intended to desert back to Union lines? The South Carolina recruiter ignored that argument, insisting on the money, and finally Wirz relented.[28]

Lieutenant Colonel J. G. O'Neil of the 10th Tennessee Infantry had realized about 250 converts from Millen, and with these he started back for the Army of Tennessee to reinforce his regiment. Sherman's presence forced him to dip down toward Fort Valley from Macon, so before continuing to Columbus he decided to stop in at Andersonville and see how the fishing was there. He arrived on November 15, the day the trainload of sick started for Millen. With so few healthy prisoners on the post, he might as well not have interrupted his journey, but that afternoon 4 men offered to join him. O'Neil stayed over a night at Camp Sumter, and in the morning 4 more prisoners approached him before he boarded the northbound train. With these 8 and the others at Fort Valley, he turned toward Hood's army.[29]

Among the eight who took the train out of Sumter County with O'Neil sat Hiram Jepperson. With nothing to go home to and no other apparent means of escape, he chose the technicality of treachery. Misled by Hiram's Connecticut River valley twang (or perhaps a speech impediment), a Southern scrivener put him down as Hyson Gypperson, and under that corrupted cognomen he assumed the brief Confederate citizenship he would come to regret. Six months later, never having reached the fragment of the regiment to which he belonged, Jepperson and his fellow defectors fought a fainthearted skirmish at Egypt Station, Mississippi, before surrendering to New Jersey cavalrymen. Then, with exquisite self-righteousness, the government that had resisted all efforts to release these men from their loathsome captivity turned to a discussion of hanging them for their treason.[30]

August Lohmaer had enlisted to fight as a private in the ranks, but his colonel had found him more valuable as a teamster. Thus, during the frantic retreat at Chickamauga, Lohmaer had been caught among the jammed wagons and had lain in Confederate prisons ever since. At Belle Isle he contracted smallpox, breaking out with symptoms after his detachment moved to Danville, but the surgeons sent him down to Georgia after he recovered. Scurvy had prevented him from leaving with the luckier inmates that fall, but hospital doses of vinegar put him back on his feet by late November.

On the morning of November 30, some twenty-five days after his enlistment officially expired, Lohmaer tried to warm himself by wandering around the hospital grounds. A dead line protected the hospital fence, but unlike the line inside the stockade it had not been staked out, and was simply an understood, indefinite boundary: anyone who approached too close would be shot. Eleven more men had recently escaped—two of them the previous night—and Captain Wirz had probably reprimanded the guards again; perhaps Lohmaer even entertained a notion of following the fugitives. Whatever his motives, Lohmaer sauntered nearer the fence than one Georgian cared for, and the sentry put an ounce of lead through his heart. He flopped and gasped for a minute or so before he died.[31]

Exactly 12,200 men had been laid to rest in the Federal sections of the Andersonville cemetery when calloused black hands swung August Lohmaer's corpse from the quartermaster's wagon. The gravediggers had long since opened up a third series of trenches a hundred yards north of the ones filled that summer, extending them ever eastward, and the riven glade threatened to consume all of Benjamin Dykes's woods. Though Dykes had shown himself an ardent proponent of the Confederate government (which his age and infirmity exempted him from actually defending), he had probably begun to sense defeat in the raw November air. If the Yankees came to liberate Andersonville, as may have seemed quite likely in mid-November, the land containing the remains of so many Union dead would probably be forfeit, and the owner of that land might suffer worse consequences, as well. Dykes may have sought to disassociate himself with the prison, therefore, when he objected to all the interments and tried to enjoin post officials from burying any more bodies on his property. Or perhaps he merely wished to wring more money from the quartermaster, as he seemed wont to do: late in October, after Richard Winder left for Millen, Dykes complained to Colonel Gibbs that no one had ever paid him stumpage fees for the timber cut from his land, but when Gibbs forwarded the letter to Captain Winder he discovered that Dykes had already received payment for the trees, which had been measured in cordwood.[32]

Dykes looked for judicial relief about the time August Lohmaer was shot. The backwater baron knew few lawyers, so he approached the former post commander, Alexander Persons, who had taken command of the depot at Fort Valley since General Winder replaced him. Persons filed a petition for injunction on behalf of Dykes, asking that Confederate authorities be restrained from cutting any more of his timber or lodging any more deceased Yankees under his soil. The new quartermaster ignored the proceedings, but Colonel Gibbs and Captain Wirz beseeched a Macon attorney to answer the petition on behalf of the government. The lawyer won them a postponement, but meanwhile Howell Cobb struck Dykes a fatal blow, ordering Colonel Persons to desist from an endeavor inconsistent with his duty to the government. Persons dropped the case, and with the loss of his services Ben Dykes gave up the struggle. Perhaps it satisfied him to have established a formal objection to the use made of his land.[33]

Most of November passed quietly at Andersonville. A couple of dozen patients eluded the hospital guards, but eventually all of them surrendered to the baying of the hounds except three who escaped the night after Lohmaer was killed. Of the 1,359 men in the hospital wards or the paroled prisoner camp on the first of December, 116 had died by December 22, the day Sherman's army rolled into Savannah.[34]

As General Winder had predicted it would, Sherman's progress had all but hamstrung the officers in charge of the latest temporary prison depot at Blackshear. Winder, recently named commissary general of all prisoners east of the Mississippi, had removed his headquarters to another new prison at Florence, South Carolina, leaving Colonel Forno to command Blackshear. When Sherman encircled Savannah he not only prevented Forno from evacuating his prisoners to Florence, he cut off most of Forno's available rolling stock. What few cars remained on the railroad had to be devoted almost entirely to troop and supply movements, leaving Forno all but stranded.[35]

The Blackshear cantonment amounted to nothing more than a camp

in the piney woods where some four thousand Yankees sat surrounded
by a cordon of about five hundred guards. All Forno's troops consisted of
Georgia Reserves brought down from Millen—four companies of the 1st
Reserves, all of the 2nd, and some of the 4th. The rest of those regiments
had stayed behind to defend Savannah. On December 5 Winder sent
Forno instructions to transport his prisoners southwest, to Thomasville,
near the Florida line, so when a stray train rumbled by Forno commandeered it, ordering off a battalion of the 4th Georgia Reserves who occupied it. With the four companies of the 1st Reserves as guards, he
shipped four hundred prisoners down the line, along with an engineer
officer who carried authority to build yet another enclosure. The next
day Forno ran another twelve hundred Yankees down to Thomasville,
but that was all the rail transportation he could muster for a while. Not
until the cold, drizzly, dismal morning of December 10 did the rest of the
prisoners and the garrison start for Thomasville.[36]

The first prisoners climbed out of the cars there amid a torrential
rainstorm and marched a mile to their swampy campsite. In the darkness
and confusion ragged Federals trickled away between negligent guards: a
rejuvenated John Whitten worked his way to an unguarded arc of the
perimeter and was about to run for it when a solicitous comrade shouted
to warn him that he had nearly crossed the invisible, forbidden line between the nearest sentries; this brought the notice of the guards, and a
disgusted Whitten turned ferociously on his well-meaning friend.[37]

On December 11, after most of the Blackshear prisoners had reached
Thomasville, conscripted gangs of slaves started shoveling out the ditch-
line for another stockade. For five days they bent their backs to the work,
but they had not even begun to raise the walls when the imminent fall of
Savannah convinced Confederate authorities to give up this cantonment,
too.[38]

Early on December 19 guards roused the entire camp and put the
prisoners in column. Shortly after dawn everyone started north on foot,
Georgia Reserves stringing along on both sides while the weakened Yankees staggered ten miles through flat pine country. The next day they
pushed on another fifteen miles or more, wading up to their waists
through swamps for as much as a mile at a time; what dry land they
crossed seemed perfectly barren, yet women, little girls, and dogs gathered as though from nowhere to witness their pathetic pilgrimage. The
rain soaked Confederate and Yankee alike that night, brewing mud and
deepening the swamps for the next day's march. The rations came thin
and seldom: those who drew any food at all received three pieces of

welcome Union hardtack and a little beef. John Whitten thought his legs would give out altogether, and on the fourth day out he dropped by the roadside, only to be prodded forward by a bayonet. The crafty and the desperate ducked into forests along the road, but in this desolate waste cold and hunger brought some of them back. At last, three nights before Christmas, the vanguard of the starveling column camped on the banks of the Flint River, just below the railhead at Albany. Women from nearby plantations took pity on them, bringing them some root vegetables with buckets of milk and clabber; their charity did not stretch far, but those touched by it would remember it all their lives.[39]

Before dawn the Albany provost marshal began moving detachments into town and herding them into cattle cars. Then, slowly, the first tired train lurched out of the depot, struggling northward at no more than ten miles an hour. Prisoners huddled shoulder to shoulder in the few cars Confederate officials could find, cramped but at least a little warmer, making their best guess at what time of day it might be when the brakes squealed to a final halt and the doors flew open. Noon had not yet come when they stepped beneath the cold grey sky again, and most of them finally recognized the location, for there stood Henry Wirz: their circular voyage had brought them right back to Andersonville.

John Whitten stumbled the quarter mile from the station, passing through the outer stockade and into the south gate, where lay the horrid pen of bitter memory. Cold and lack of recent use may have quelled the stench of the sinks, but of other comforts Whitten found none. Not a stick of fuel remained in camp; "the rebels have taken everything in the Shape of wood," Whitten concluded, and doubtless the remaining guards had consumed much of it, but the prison hospital attendants had probably scavenged the stockade, too, for their own comfort and that of the patients. Cold, ragged, and exhausted, Whitten prepared himself for a terrible night.[40]

Nearly a thousand dismal Yankees poured into the echoing stockade that day. Another thousand arrived on Christmas Eve, after Whitten's detachment had gone out under guard for firewood, but the newcomers shared none of Whitten's relative bounty: without fire, blankets, or tents, they were already shivering when a cold rain started falling on their bare heads. It continued into the gloomiest Christmas any of them ever knew, and on that day another train delivered two more detachments of five hundred at the depot. To escape the rain some of the more destitute appropriated the abandoned burrows along the slopes of the creek, where earthen overhangs defied precipitation, if not the creeping cold;

one of them sought refuge in an old, shallow well, presumably after clawing out a shelf to keep himself out of the water. In such rude shelters—or without them—three thousand despondent captives embraced and spooned for warmth. By the drizzly dawn of the next day at least one of the burrows had collapsed, suffocating two who had spooned together for warmth like a conjugal couple. There would their bones lie until the eve of the next century.[41]

The last of the Thomasville prisoners straggled in on December 26, and with them came the remainder of the guard. Once again the Federal population approached five thousand, with more than a thousand of them in the twenty-two new hospital sheds on the rise south of the stockade. Back from his latest furlough, Colonel Gibbs enjoyed the comparative security of a garrison nearly fourteen hundred strong—between the Florida artillerymen and the 1st, 2nd, and 4th Reserves—and despite a hefty Confederate sick list only two of the Yankees found their way to freedom in the four weeks after Christmas. If Gibbs could fill the stockade's sentry boxes, though, he experienced more trouble filling the mess tins: until commissary logistics had replenished the warehouse a little, the prisoners complained bitterly of short rations—often barely enough for a single meal in a day. George Shearer's Christmas dinner consisted of cornbread, rice, and molasses. The next afternoon Iowan Amos Ames drew only a pint of cooked peas, a three-inch square of cornbread, and two ounces of cooked beef. Asberry Stephen also tasted beans, beef, and pone that day, grousing that it came late but grateful to find it cooked. There was nothing left on the ration wagon but bread when Chester Hart reached it.[42]

Once Captain Wirz's guard detail could be increased enough to watch more than the south side of Stockade Creek, he allowed as many prisoners to lodge themselves in the old shed barracks as the buildings could accommodate. The rest dug in where they were, some with tents but most without. In the final days of the month Wirz requisitioned some lumber—first strapping, to rebuild the dead line, then planks for more shelter—and indigent prisoners cast covetous eyes upon the little stack that accumulated just inside the south gate. December 31 turned brutally cold after dark, and a few unfortunates who lacked a shred of bedding crept toward the pile to pilfer either boards to lay upon or sticks to burn. The dead line had been reconstructed here, but the sentry frequently climbed down to stand over his campfire on the ground. Each time he did, a few tattered wraiths scuttled past the scantling like rodents, stealing whatever they could carry. An hour or two before 1864 ended, a

German named Christian Konold made his move against the lumber, but he snatched at a board that proved longer than he thought: the far end hit the ground with a resounding slap. Too weak to lift his prize, Konold refused to give it up and started dragging it toward his lair, but he had not yet cleared the dead line when the suspicious guard crept back up to his post and dropped the frail immigrant with a bullet through the head.[43]

A few nights later the new dead line itself came down, covertly sacrificed for a little heat. Day after day the bored, hungry, raggedly clad Federals hovered over snapping, fist-sized fires, toasting their bellies while their backs rippled with goose bumps.[44]

In those first days of 1865 Captain Wirz greeted the highest-ranking Yankee he would see at Andersonville. Finding both Columbus and Macon unsuitable, Confederate authorities forwarded Colonel William H. Noble to Camp Sumter. A couple of scouts had captured him on Christmas Eve, as he made his way back from a Jacksonville court-martial appearance to the post of Saint Augustine, which he commanded; traveling with a staff lieutenant but without either escort or arms, he had been an easy target. The grey-bearded Noble not only ranked all his fellow prisoners there, at fifty-one he was probably older than any of them, and Wirz lodged him in Shelby Reed's guardhouse, which offered not only the shelter of a log hut but the security of a stockade. Once devoted to that use, Castle Reed quickly filled with Union officers captured south of Savannah.[45]

Colonel Noble could not have found a better place to spend his incarceration, as he freely admitted. Captain Wirz allowed the officers to buy extra provisions, just as he did the enlisted men, but that seemed to surprise Noble. More significantly for the Connecticut Yankee, though, Colonel Gibbs befriended him: he did so because, as commander of Saint Augustine, Noble had been uniformly kind to Confederate Floridians—especially to a woman Gibbs identified only as "poor Buddy's mother." Gibbs loaned Noble money, and when no more cash could be found at Andersonville he sent word to Florida friends to raise some.[46]

Following the latest influx of prisoners came an entourage of ladies asking to visit them. Mary Rawson, from the Plains of Dura, somehow gained the acquaintance of Peter Kean of the 16th Iowa. Learning that he had fallen ill, she traveled to Camp Sumter to see him, bringing a basket of food. At the depot she met Captain Wirz, who escorted her to his old office near the stockade and seated her on a bench. When a guard brought Kean into the room, Wirz gave up his own chair for the prisoner.

The meeting between the two was brief, but about every other week thereafter Miss Rawson returned with another basketful of edibles. Ultimately Wirz greeted her casually, asking in a routine, friendly manner if she had come to speak with "her prisoner" again.[47]

Wirz may have been equally courteous, albeit much less trusting, when a "Mrs. Spaulding" came up from Americus to see another Iowan. The captain's eyebrows first rose when the woman admitted that she had learned of the prisoner's presence through a letter he had bribed a guard to send by regular post, rather than filtering it through the censored prison mail, and one of the first things she asked Wirz was how she could obtain some greenbacks to send to relatives in prison up North. She said she planned to travel there and deliver it herself; Wirz told her she would have to ask General Winder for authority to buy greenbacks. Already alert, the prison commandant heard her mention to the prisoner, who was ostensibly a family friend, that she had just returned from the North. After her departure, Wirz inquired into her background and discovered that her husband figured prominently in the organization of what Wirz referred to as a "Union meeting" scheduled in Americus a few days later. Wirz made no effort to arrest Mrs. Spaulding, but he warned the commander of the military district about her.[48]

The most unusual female visitor that winter gave her name as Ann Williams and said she was a refugee from Savannah. She stepped off the train January 15 and immediately commenced mingling with those paroled prisoners who wandered the camp. Wirz ordered her brought to his office when he learned she had been offering her favors to them indiscriminately, sharing beds and lice with at least seven of them in barely twenty-four hours. Miss Williams denied she was a prostitute, claiming she took no money for her little trysts, but she carried a bundle of cash that may have hinted otherwise. Wirz seemed less concerned with her morals than with her politics, though, bridling most at her remark that the Yankees "are as good as we." He dropped a hint of espionage when he reported how she whispered conspiratorily with inquisitive prisoners, and he sent her down to the commander of the nearest military force, in Florida.[49]

The prison hospital had been moved up to the new sheds on the shelf south of the stockade now, and the carpenters surrounded it with a six-foot fence—apparently the same boards that had once encircled the tent hospital down by the mouth of Stockade Creek, for nothing remained to mark that lethal enclosure now but a veneer of excrement and a few small mountains of offal. Wirz blamed the inadequate fence for a rash of near escapes in the second half of January, and he wanted to use the leftover logs from the unfinished third perimeter to build a complete stockade around the hospital. It appears he never managed to begin that project, but once he replaced the lumber stolen by the prisoners he did start some more barracks inside the main stockade. The weather forced him to act, for rain fell constantly between January 18 and 22.

"We have never seen so much water in our streets," read the January 21 edition of the Americus paper, and that same day a girl visiting from northeast Georgia noted in her journal "I never in my life knew such furious rains as we had last night." Rain and severe cold continued into the last week of January; when the weather finally broke, the paroled carpenters went to work on the first of five sheds that would eventually grace the southwestern extremity of the stockade.[50]

Those January rains washed the patriotic devotion out of some more Federals: when Colonel O'Neil came back from Mississippi, looking for more Galvanized Yankees to refill his luckless 10th Tennessee, they walked out of the stockade by the score. A hundred fifty signed up in the first two days after O'Neil arrived, and forty-two more enlisted two days later. Prisoners inside could see them drilling on the surrounding slopes, but they did not judge the traitors half so harshly now as they might have in May. Some of them went out nearly naked, and John Whitten—who had carried the state flag of Iowa at Missionary Ridge—virtually admitted that he would have gone with them if he thought his life still hung in the balance.[51]

February opened with misplaced hopes on the far side of the palisade. Georgia's own Alexander Stephens led a Confederate delegation to a meeting with Northern leaders early that month, seeking grounds on which the war might be ended with Southern independence intact. News of the upcoming conference cheered some of the garrison, who hoped Abe Lincoln would see the wisdom in welcoming the South as a sovereign ally against French machinations in Mexico. That optimism crumbled when the discussion stalled on Lincoln's demand for unconditional reunion, and those who had looked for peace girded for even more desperate resistance. By now the tale of Hood's Nashville disaster had drifted back from Tennessee; everyone knew that Sherman had carried his campaign into South Carolina, and that Lee's army lay trapped at Petersburg and Richmond, but Captain Thomas Jackson still wrote to his wife of keeping up the fight. The rebuff of the delegates even drove Ambrose Spencer to another outburst of his own capricious nationalism, with which he implemented his latest plan for a commission by advertising for a company of overage soldiers to be known as the Sumter Silver Greys, to "go to work in earnest."[52]

If many in the South could not sense the impending end of their revolution, some of those inside the prison could, even after several hundred more captured Yankees came in from Mississippi, Alabama, and Florida. The most reliable evidence of Southern collapse came with a sudden surge of inflation, as Confederate money plummeted to record worthlessness. Within the walls the guards readily parted with their scrip at ten dollars for one greenback now, where days before the rate had been seven or eight to one, and only five to one the summer before; soon the exchange rate would rise to twenty dollars. George Shearer put his hands on some local newspapers that might have told him a great deal had he noted the cost of produce and condiments, and the subscription rate on the masthead bore the same tale. Charles Hancock raised the price of his Americus paper to four dollars a year on the day of Pickett's Charge, demanding five dollars—in advance—by the day John Whitten fell a prisoner, and he had doubled that by the time the stockade began to empty; as the war's last spring approached he doubled it again, to twenty dollars a year, even though a shortage of newsprint had forced him to cut the paper from four pages to a two-page half-sheet months before.[53]

Faced with increasing requests for U.S. funds to send to Confederate prisoners in the North, Captain Wirz found that his stockade sutler could get none from the prisoners at the government exchange rate, and Wirz asked if the sutler could not pay the black-market prices. That sutler was Mr. Selman, who had returned to build another shack for himself as the new series of barracks started going up; he threw this one together on the south side, where most of the prisoners had congregated, and it looked as though he might be in for more booming business. Frustrated in his attempt to take over Selman's lucrative enterprise, James Duncan had shifted to more direct larceny, stealing food and assorted supplies from the hospital warehouse behind Wirz's old headquarters. Wirz had suspected him before, asking the same Macon lawyer who handled the Dykes injunction to prosecute the thief, but the case sat unheard in a country where the civil law lay virtually suspended. So Duncan, still the chief quartermaster's clerk, continued to dole out rations inside the stockade.[54]

Henry Wirz's tenure at Andersonville had begun with greater trouble from the Confederate staff than from the prisoners, and that paradoxical phenomenon seemed to mar the denouement of his career there, as well. With General Winder's sudden death, during the first week in February,

Wirz lost his best ally at the top; thereafter he had to report his problems to the office of General Beauregard, who had never met him. Early in March he encountered a difficulty much like the one he experienced with Edward O'Neal and the 26th Alabama eleven months before, but this time there appears to have been no means of resolving the issue. Lucius Gartrell, erstwhile Confederate congressman from Georgia, had taken command of the first (and ultimately the only) brigade of Georgia Reserves when Sherman marched on Savannah in November. Wounded in the fighting before that city in December, Gartrell received an assignment to Andersonville when the bulk of his brigade returned there as guards. Like Colonel O'Neal the previous spring, Gartrell served as commander of the troops; George Gibbs still commanded the post, but his temporary appointment as colonel led to another question of seniority with Gartrell—who was a brigadier general, if only by virtue of a state commission.[55]

At nine o'clock on the evening of March 4, as Abraham Lincoln relaxed from the hectic celebration of his second inauguration a thousand rail miles away, Captain Wirz heard the tooting of a brass band at a house near his family's quarters. He threw on his coat and went out to investigate, for the only musicians at Camp Sumter were paroled Federal prisoners. The horns serenading his neighbors indeed turned out to be those Yankees, and Wirz shuddered to think what might be said if they were found so far from the prison at night. He learned that a captain of the 2nd Reserves had brought them here, and the captain said he intended to take them another five miles into the country as entertainment for a party in honor of the colonel's wife, who had presented the regiment with a flag. Wirz objected that he had not given permission for the prisoners' musicale, but the captain merely responded that it was all right—he had obtained General Gartrell's blessing. Wirz protested that he alone bore responsibility for (and authority over) the prisoners, but to no avail, nor could Colonel Gibbs have helped Wirz had he been so inclined. Once again the men who commanded the muskets laughed at "the Dutch captain," leading the Yankee musicians off into the night with their pinging, bonking instruments.[56]

Exchange rumors accelerated as spring neared, encouraged this time by sincere Confederate sources. As early as February 4 the Americus paper predicted a general exchange, and the officers of the Georgia Reserves believed it. The rumor flourished through another spell of miserably cold and wet weather at the end of the month, but Captain Wirz sent in a notice early in March that the gossip was entirely unfounded. In fact it proved to be very well founded. On January 24 Colonel Ould had made one last offer to exchange man for man, making no reference to color, and the Washington government—which held over 65,000 Confederate prisoners—seemed willing now to ask no questions: nine days later Ulysses Grant said he would endeavor to exchange 3,000 men a week. Wirz's denial of the exchange seems to have been motivated by the arrival of more recruiters for Colonel O'Neil, who lured out another 138 desperate prisoners. Two days later, after this latest crop of turncoats departed, Wirz reversed himself and posted a notice that the entire prison population would be exchanged within two weeks. Colonel Gibbs ventured inside the pen long enough to corroborate the news, but a trainload of paroled Confederate prisoners that passed through the depot on March 6 spoke even more eloquently of the prospects.[57]

Wirz chose that occasion to admit some barrels into the stockade for the brewing of some molasses-and-cornmeal beer, to allay the effects of scurvy. Perhaps the doctors who had suggested the remedy had waited only for warmer weather, to enhance the fermentation process, but some of the prisoners suspected the Confederates merely planned to bloat them up to a healthier bulk before sending them back to Union lines.[58]

The cartel was in full swing by early February, accelerating the rumors. At last, on March 18, those rumors crystallized into reality for the Andersonville prisoners when more than nine hundred Westerners boarded the westbound train for Vicksburg. Several dozen officers from Castle Reed went along with them, with Colonel Noble in charge, but most of the nine hundred were patients from the hospital: each side tried now to unburden itself of its disabled prisoners first.

It proved an exhausting, tortuous journey by rail and steamboat through Montgomery, Selma, Demopolis, Meridian, and Jackson. Something had gone sour with the deal by the time these ragged wanderers reached the exchange rendezvous, and for a few terrible moments it seemed Union authorities would reject them, but the generals smoothed it over. On March 27, 1865, Thomas W. Horan of the 65th Indiana ended fourteen months as a prisoner when he staggered into Federal lines just west of Mississippi's Big Black River. The surgeons who examined his dysentery-weakened frame weighed him at 106 pounds. He had lost nearly 70 pounds since that first East Tennessee Confederate leveled a rifle at him.[59]

Fifteen hundred more Midwestern Yankees left Andersonville for Vicksburg a week later. Some came from within the prison hospital again—the surgeons released all but the three hundred frailest, who would surely perish on the journey—but this time most of them emerged from the stockade. For sutler Selman and James Duncan these giddy departures spelled the end of their profitable trade, but they played for one final windfall, offering the earliest exchanges to the highest bidders. For fifty dollars (or twenty-five, then ten, and finally for one good blanket) they promised to move names up to the vacancies in those detachments that would leave first. Those in the stockade who had been held the longest did not own so much as a button with which to buy such an indulgence, so it was mostly the newest and strongest who took advantage of it. Captain Wirz learned of these deals, however—perhaps through his landlord, Mr. Bass, who participated in them. Wirz promised that any prisoner he found trying to bribe his way out would be held for the very last train.[60]

The second Vicksburg contingent may have included a smaller proportion of sick men than the first, but the condition of those who were ailing was generally worse. They died by the dozens along the way, and even after crossing into Union lines. In both this lot of prisoners and the last, most walked the final leg of the journey from Jackson to the Big Black—some twenty-five miles—but Confederates in Mississippi suffered from an acute shortage of wagons, so Federal ambulances ranged into Jackson under flags of truce to fetch back those who were too far gone to make it on foot; at the Big Black they transferred these men to passenger cars. Writing on the day of Lee's surrender, an Ohio soldier at the impromptu feeding station on the river's edge said he saw a great many corpses unloaded from the ambulances: one of those boneshaking conveyances, which were built to accommodate two men, carried four prisoners to the river, and all of them were dead when it arrived. Those who survived were "nothing but walking skelitons," he told a lady friend, and some of them perished even after partaking of the soup, milk, tea, and assorted other nourishment provided at the feeding station. Meanwhile, in Savannah, a Confederate doctor suppressed his outrage as he examined hundreds of repatriated Southerners in similar condition.[61]

Even as the first of those fifteen hundred boarded the cars for Vicksburg, Gideon Pillow, the aging and somewhat disreputable brigadier who had taken John Winder's place as commissary general of prisoners, made an effort to rid himself of all the rest of Andersonville's survivors. The Federal commander at Jacksonville, Florida, happened to be General Eliakim Scammon, a Mexican War acquaintance of Pillow's, and the Confederate asked him if he would accept the Yankees from Camp Sumter. Scammon had doubtless heard by now of the privation at that place, and on his own responsibility he agreed to take them. With news of another big Yankee raid coming out of Alabama under James Wilson, it was a relieved Henry Wirz who told his prisoners they were on their way home, and he set about looking for a train for them. Accidents and the heavy traffic had reduced the number of available cars, and it was not until April 4 that Wirz found transportation for the first thousand.[62]

John Whitten's detachment marched out at ten o'clock that morning. With those men went a couple of dozen black soldiers and another forty officers, just brought down from Macon. The weather had turned summer-warm, and with the prospects of going home no one seemed inclined to escape—if any had even had the strength—so the guards rolled the cargo doors wide open and let the more daring passengers hang their feet over the sides. At Smithfield depot the cars crept past a cluster of young women on a day trip, who stood waiting for their train with lunch baskets in their hands. Teenage Confederate guards, jubilant with the dual elixir of springtime and impending peace, fired a buckshot salute over the heads of this comely flock. Little older and no less happy, ragged-but-saucy prisoners blew kisses to the bevy, whose sympathies their "half-naked, . . . starved-looking" appearance aroused. Though stung by such Yankee impudence, the girls emptied their baskets, flinging sandwiches, fried chicken, and sundry desserts into the passing cars.[63]

Wirz forwarded 3,425 men to Albany over the next three days; on the night of April 6 only 15 Yankees remained at Andersonville, all of them in the hospital. From Albany the first lot set out for Thomasville again, on foot, making four miles the first day and eighteen the next, though hundreds of them marched barefoot. Along the road they met paroled Confederates finding their own way home (apparently in spite of orders to return to their units), and the Georgia Reserves virtually ignored the prisoners, several of whom slipped away or fell behind; one disgusted farmer with a double-barreled shotgun brought in some of those tattered stragglers.[64]

Late on April 7 the wornout column halted on the outskirts of Thomasville. Officers from the Reserves rode ahead to town and arranged for rations to meet the wayfarers in the morning, after which they foraged a few bottles of whiskey for themselves while two weary, wiry battalions of ecstatic Yankees flopped in the pine needles amid the patter of evening rain.[65]

The prisoners' glee dissolved the next day. The Federal department commander, Quincy Gillmore, had overruled General Scammon, advising him on April 3 that the prisoners probably ought to be delivered to

Savannah instead: General Grant would decide the matter, Gillmore had written, and Scammon would have his answer by April 19. Scammon could not relay the word to his Confederate counterpart in time, and the news only reached Thomasville at noon of April 8, when the commander of the guard detachment told his disappointed charges their general would not receive them. The prisoners blamed it all on the well-meaning Scammon, muttering of some future lynching, and after a few more hours' rest they turned back for Andersonville in a surly mood. This time the Reserves kept their muskets primed and ready.[66]

At the very moment of U. S. Grant's conversation with Robert E. Lee in a quiet crossroads parlor, these downcast thousand breasted Georgia swamps in their shreds of ancient uniforms. They reached Albany again three days later, just as the Army of Northern Virginia stacked its flags and weapons on that distant shire common. All of those to whom Wirz had said a hopeful farewell came back to Andersonville—all save a score whose strength had failed them in the swamps—and the few remaining surgeons quickly diverted three hundred of them back into the hospital. Among the feeblest whom they turned into the wards was Knud Hanson, the reluctant Norwegian cavalryman who had been drafted on the day of Camp Sumter's bureaucratic birth, and Aaron Elliott, the nineteen-year-old veteran of more than three and a half years of war.[67]

With such short notice of their return, George Gibbs could offer the sullen captives little in the way of nourishment, but he spread himself to raise their spirits, promising them on his personal honor that, for all their disappointment, they would all go free within a fortnight. Though many believed him, the bitter experience had hit them hard. For once conversation lagged behind the palisade, hardly inspired by the repeated news of serial Union victories as Confederate sentries confirmed the fall of their nation's successive capitals: a dangerous apathy seemed to grip the entire prison.[68]

For most of the men in the stockade, though, Gibbs had spoken the truth. The vast majority of them would see Old Glory inside of two weeks. The final exodus began April 17, the day after James Wilson's cavalry column crashed into Georgia from Alabama. Three special trains hauled more than three thousand prisoners north to Macon for the switch to Savannah, but Wilson's Yankees veered toward Macon, so by dawn the locomotives turned around to head south again. Glum faces stared from the car doors when each train stopped for water at Anderson. The dark and ominous outline of the stockade sat on the misty horizon like an evil apparition they would never shed, but faint cheers echoed when replenished boilers emitted a shrill screech and the cars lunged into motion once again; except for fourteen paroled men taken off during the stop, none of them would ever see Andersonville again. Though one more painful trek to Thomasville lay ahead of them, John Whitten, Amos Ames, and George Shearer had at last begun their journey home to Iowa.[69]

Surgeon Stevenson culled another 290 patients from the hospital on April 20 and sent them down to Florida, and the next day he found 20 more who were hale enough to stand the trip. That left him only 32 sick men in a single ward, but one of them did not last the day. Emaciated by bowel complaints and the rigors of the futile march to Thomasville, Aaron Elliott closed his sunken eyes one last time on April 21. His was the only death that day, so the gravediggers carried him straight to the open, waiting trench—the most distant row of that grim crop of standing stakes. His parents, who had begun the month of April by burying Aaron's sister in a muddy New Hampshire cemetery, would not learn of his fate for months.[70]

Seven men died under the surgeon's care over the next week. The post lay almost deserted by then, with only forty prisoners and a few conscientious Confederate officers and men holding on: the fourteen Federals taken off the last passing train on April 18 had apparently been kept behind to perform the daily drudgery of issuing rations in addition to caring for the sick, keeping the books, and burying the dead, for most of the detailed Georgia Reserves had disappeared. On April 28 the drafted Norwegian, Knud Hanson, heaved one final, labored breath and joined the greatest remaining enclave of Camp Sumter Yankees, filling the last marked grave. Hanson's war had begun with the existence of the place called Andersonville, and now it ended with it.[71]

While these few lingered, others continued their happy trip homeward. John Whitten reached Iowa by way of Annapolis on June 1, followed by Amos Ames and George Shearer. James Dennison trailed them by a few days, coming out of the stockade at Florence, South Carolina. Robert Kellogg returned to Connecticut from that same South Carolina prison, where he left the bodies of many of his fellow Plymouth Pilgrims and the withered remains of Sergeant Eugene Forbes, of New Jersey. Nearly 13,000 of the 41,000 who walked into the south gate at Andersonville lay in graves there, and hundreds of the others had perished at Millen, Blackshear, Savannah, or Florence. Some died in the swamps between Albany and Thomasville during those four terrible marches, or on the road to Vicksburg, and many of those who made it to Florida died in the final hours of captivity at Lake City, or just after passing between the flags at Baldwin, or Jacksonville. The ultimate mortality among Andersonville prisoners hovered around 35 percent.[72]

Perhaps the saddest fate awaited those like Thomas Horan, the Hoosier captured as a mounted courier in East Tennessee. After recuperating for four weeks near Vicksburg, where he fretted paranoically over enemy raids, Horan boarded a transport for Indiana on April 24. Still suffering from dysentery and scurvy, he could not eat half the plentiful food, but he notified his brother that he was coming "if God spares me to return home." God did not. For two days the steamer *Sultana* struggled up the flood-swollen Mississippi with a load of passengers nearly six times her designed capacity, and two hours after midnight on April 27 the overworked boilers exploded, casting hundreds of feeble ex-prisoners into the chilly water. Some died of the scalding; some burned in the wreckage; most of them drowned. Of the two thousand men and more aboard, nearly three-quarters were lost, including Thomas Horan. Most of those who died had come from Andersonville.[73]

The last day of April brought the final five Yankee cobblers back from the disappointing enterprise at Oglethorpe. On the afternoon of May 2 a train rolled into Anderson Station bearing Captain Henry Noyes, of General Wilson's staff. Wilson had made his headquarters at Macon in the wake of his devastating raid, and all enemy resistance had effectively ceased. On his way to Eufaula with dispatches for another cavalry commander, Captain Noyes ambled curiously around the depot while his engine crew stocked wood and water. To his surprise, he spied a few lingering prisoners and Confederate officers. Some fifteen Yankees (probably including the shoemakers) stood before one Southern captain, several of them leaning upon the shoulders of their stronger comrades while the officer waved some papers before them. Noyes climbed back aboard his car when he saw the water trough swing away, and just before the whistle blew he heard the Confederate captain—whom he later recognized as Henry Wirz—tell the hesitant prisoners that if they did not sign their paroles they would die at Andersonville after all. The train started to pull away before Noyes could interfere, and later that day the fifteen Yankees departed for Florida.[74]

The next morning, May 3, Wirz chose six more hospital patients whom he thought might stand the trip to Florida for exchange. That evening the few remaining soldiers at the post joined the local inhabitants in a raid on the commissary and quartermaster buildings. By the light of flaming pine knots they carried off the last stores of cornmeal, beef, pork, and blankets without the intervention of a single person, while others broke into the corrals and led away a few lean mules.[75]

The dawn of May 4, 1865, illuminated a bedroom in the Sandymount district of Dublin where lay the daughter of a Sligo merchant, great with child. Forty days hence she and her husband, a talented painter named James Butler Yeats, would greet a son whose artistry would outshine that of his father, though he would choose the medium of language. In sultry Bombay, Alice Macdonald Kipling did not yet know on May 4 that she had already conceived her first child, a boy who would also find his destiny at the tip of a pen. Rising on the open Pacific, the same sun had reddened the yards of the Confederate ship *Shenandoah*, which followed a westerly tack for the southern tip of Japan, her captain scanning the horizon with a glass in search of flags belonging to his enemy in a war that he did not know had ended. Several thousand miles to the east, in San Francisco, a sometime prospector, newspaper correspondent, and Mississippi riverboat pilot worked on some funny stories about the city on the bay. From his headquarters in Santa Fe, New Mexico, a California general wrote Kit Carson to suggest a visit to some chiefs of the Cheyenne, Comanche, and Kiowa tribes. Meanwhile, at Fort Leavenworth, Kansas, the 5th U.S. Volunteers prepared to march for Fort Kearny, where young Hiram Jepperson would spend the next sixteen months of his life. At that moment, in Springfield, Illinois, a somber procession followed the casket of Abraham Lincoln to the tomb. In Pittsburgh, Pennsylvania, a stocky Scotsman not yet thirty years old opened the books on a fledgling corporation and looked forward to the first of his many millions of dollars.[76]

Andersonville prison effectively ceased to exist that same morning of May 4, 1865, when Colonel George Gibbs abandoned the post for his home in Florida. On that day someone, perhaps Captain Wirz himself, noted the final pair of deaths in the remaining hospital ward. Apparently the last of the medical staff had fled; the dead left no friends to identify them, and paroled prisoners gave them shallow graves, scratching a few inches of the red Georgia clay over their faces and planting no stake or stone to mark the spot.[77]

Of the Confederate staff, Henry Wirz alone remained: he noted the next morning that five Yankees still lay in the hospital and seventeen in the stockade, though almost certainly those seventeen enjoyed the freedom of the camp. Why they stayed, and whether their tenancy lasted the rest of that day, are mysteries that must go unsolved, for no hand completed the evening entry. Captain Wirz repaired to his home—the last man to leave his post. Obviously the war was over, and Wirz had carried out his duties to the bitter end. Now he owned no means of supporting his family, let alone of transporting them back to the lost Louisiana land or to relatives in Kentucky. His Confederate pay and commutations of $185 a month would come no more, and any of that money he might have saved was worthless. Perhaps he considered setting himself up as a physician again, right where he was, for certainly he could market no heavy labor with his throbbing arm.[78]

The economics of his plight did not trouble him for long. When Henry Noyes returned to Macon he mentioned his Andersonville observations, and General Wilson sent him back with an escort. After spending the night of May 6 in Americus, Noyes went straight to the Bass house and arrested Wirz in front of his wife and the two younger girls. Elizabeth and Cora started to keen at his removal, but Noyes comforted them with white lies. Wirz dressed in his best uniform. While he and Noyes waited for the train, Wirz wrote General Wilson a letter explaining his limited authority at the prison and asking for protection according to the surrender terms that seemed to apply to everyone else. That letter remained unanswered, and after thirteen days under guard in Macon Wirz started for Washington, still in the company of Captain Noyes.[79]

With the departure of this last Confederate soldier the prison reverted momentarily to the forces of nature, modified as they were by the interference of former slaves who squatted in the vicinity, many of whom took up lodging in the hospital barracks, Wirz's office, and William Turner's abandoned home. General Wilson appointed a paroled Confederate cavalryman, Colonel Joel Griffin, to care for the sprawling cemetery. Griffin frustrated Ben Dykes's plans to build a vineyard on that well-manured soil, and after establishing his authority over the graveyard Griffin tried his hand at beautifying it. He filled in a few shallow graves where cattle or hogs had torn up the earth and exposed bodies, but when he bent himself to fencing the perimeter of the cemetery he quickly saw that it was more than he could manage. Late in June he appealed to General Wilson for help, and just after lunch on July 25 a clattering entourage arrived at the station to assist the caretaker. Out of the cars strode a company each of black foot soldiers and white cavalrymen under Captain James Moore of the U.S. Army Quartermaster Department. With the troops came Dorence Atwater (the former prisoner who had smuggled his list of dead men to freedom inside his shirt), a volunteer nurse named Clara Barton, and a couple of hundred thousand board feet of pine lumber.[80]

Captain Moore pitched his tent between the tracks and the stockade, and, although he and Miss Barton were not getting on well, she moved into another one near him. While the detailed soldiers worked the lumber up into grave tablets and fence pickets, Atwater and Miss Barton compared his list with the hospital register in an attempt to identify every grave. They failed by several hundred, and Captain Moore's men inadvertently sank a few more "unknown" markers at the heads of graves whose occupants Atwater could have named.[81]

The workmen shoveled still more clay over the burial trenches, for the rain had settled Colonel Griffin's fill and Captain Moore found some of the dead men's long hair floating up out of the shallower graves. Moore disinterred no one, either from the stockade or the cemetery, although he later implied that Griffin had moved at least one body, and perhaps two, from the interior of the prison.[82]

Miss Barton spent most of her time answering letters from anxious relatives and dictating corrections to the painted headboards, which she ordered pulled up and relettered by the cartload when she found dates or names wrong. In her scant leisure she toured the empty pen and the hospital, finding them "horrible beyond description." A former surgeon there (Dr. Head, perhaps), gossiped with her about Dr. Stevenson, whom he accused of having married a Southern girl while he still had a wife in Illinois; he added that Henry Wirz bore no responsibility for the cruelties at that place. Miss Barton also met an army medical inspector from Maine who had come down with a view to writing a book about Andersonville.[83]

Captain Moore's detail remained more than three weeks. Miss Barton and Atwater worked into every evening, and toward the end of their mission she sallied into the cemetery one night to find him broken down from exhaustion and emotion—"alone in Gethsemane," she wrote. She helped him back to her tent and put him to bed in her own cot, sitting up all night to watch him, and they returned to the cemetery together again the next morning. Three days later they packed up their belongings and a crate of relics from the stockade, including the prison mailbox and some makeshift utensils. Meanwhile Captain Moore superintended the erection of a flagpole in the cemetery, and at sunrise of August 17 the entire contingent gathered around the pole while Miss Barton and a soldier lifted the first flag to fly over Andersonville's dead.

At first it drooped, "as if in grief and sadness," Miss Barton thought, until the rising sun caught the colors and an errant breeze filled the folds. Behind her a hundred men broke out with "The Star Spangled Banner" while the lady covered her eyes and wept. Then, with a last look at the prison—"at once sad and terrible"—they all started for the station.[84]

Alexander Persons, late lieutenant colonel of the 55th Georgia, returned to Americus with his bride in that summer of 1865. While Captain Moore and Miss Barton attended to the sprawling cemetery that he had begun with the grave of Adam Swarner only eighteen months before, Persons advertised that he would be traveling to Washington City, where he would gladly pursue special pardons for any client "at fees so moderate that none can complain." Like George Gibbs, Ben Dykes, Joel Griffin, and numerous other people associated with Andersonville, Persons had been subpoenaed to attend the trial of Henry Wirz. The man who delivered their subpoenas was that waffling loyalist and perennial office-seeker, Ambrose Spencer, who worked now for the U.S. government prosecutor.[85]

The Northern public had been primed for the case for months. Ex-prisoners had been spinning exaggerated tales of torture and deliberate attrition since the Thanksgiving exchanges at Savannah—since the previous August, for that matter, when a couple of the exchanged emissaries from the detachment sergeants' delegation began telling their stories—and the attenuated victims of dysentery and scurvy who returned in the spring lent their distortions the flavor of truth. That summer *Harper's Weekly* carried engravings cut from photographs of the worst cases of gangrene and emaciation, and newspapers in various cities listed their states' contributions to the death register. A deserter who spent time at Andersonville published a great broadside of the prison early in 1865, bordering it with inventive vignettes depicting unspeakably cruel acts, and the public ate them up.[86]

The trial finally began before a military tribunal in a small, stuffy room in the bowels of the U.S. Capitol, and Wirz was a dead man from the start. Irritated by his assignment to the case at a time when he wished to strike off on a filibustering expedition in Mexico, General Lew Wallace had not taken his seat as president of the court before he convicted the defendant in his own mind. As the proceedings began, Wallace described Wirz's countenance in the most diabolical metaphor, concluding the captain had been a good choice for such "awful duty." A spectator in the gallery also recorded the prisoner in sinister syllables, remarking that everything about him—hair, beard, complexion, and clothing—was black, "a la Byron."[87]

Judge Advocate Norton P. Chipman read his charges on Wednesday, August 23, and examined a few witnesses to confirm Wirz's position at the prison. Then he called a procession of former prisoners who seemed determined to outdo one another in their recollections of Wirz's barbarity. Robert Kellogg took the stand early in the trial, and testified again later, describing the squalor and crowding. Perhaps his newfound religious convictions prevented him from lying outright, and he admitted he had never seen any of Wirz's supposed cruelties, but he could not refrain from insisting "on the other hand, it was true." After Kellogg there came an Ohioan who offered the most wonderfully self-contradictory testimony, swearing that Wirz robbed him of $150 in gold and that he saw the Swiss shoot down another prisoner in "February or June or along in there." Already famous as the killer of John Wilkes Booth, Boston Corbett followed this Buckeye, presenting a couple of pages of hearsay evidence over the futile objections of the defense counsel. Men swore they saw Wirz shoot prisoners at point-blank range, citing names that never appeared on the death register. It was said he committed these murders with a ten-shot revolver, though some of Wirz's paroled clerks testified that he always carried one or the other of two broken navy revolvers, and other government witnesses told of brutal beatings personally administered by this man with a withered left shoulder and a useless right arm.[88]

One of the more imaginative prosecution witnesses identified himself as Felix DeLabaume of the 39th New York. He probably did arrive at Camp Sumter under that name, but the *New York Tribune* later exposed him as Felix Oeser, a deserter from the 7th New York, and indeed the prosecutor obtained the witness from the custody of the provost marshal, to whom he was never remanded. Later, Ben Dykes took the stand and implied there were vegetables around the prison that might have been fed to the Federals, and when Dykes left the courtroom he proceeded to the War Department for his reward—a full pardon for his Confederate activities. Without referring to his services for the prosecution, Ambrose Spencer ingratiated the court with tales of aiding escaped prisoners, going on to exaggerate the cruelty of prison authorities—including Wirz—in a lengthy deposition most remarkable for its inconsistency. Spencer's testimony appears to have been the impetus for a Macon editor's observation that the government's prosecution pitted witnesses against one another in a competition "to develop the most astounding tale of crime and horror."[89]

A young man named Oliver Fairbanks, the "medium" who bilked at least one dying prisoner, provided an interesting instance of manufactured testimony. Captured at Culpeper in 1863, Fairbanks belonged to a New York cavalry regiment. His stepfather, Richard Fair*clough*, was an acting hospital steward with the 2nd New Jersey Infantry when he was taken prisoner later that same autumn. Both wound up at Andersonville, and Fairbanks said his "father" was crippled with scurvy by August. According to Fairbanks, Wirz came into the prison personally to kick the disabled Fairclough into roll-call formation, cursing mightily and threatening to withhold the invalid's food for a week if he did not move. Fairbanks said his stepfather died a month later, and that ten minutes before he perished he asked Oliver to write an affidavit to the effect that his death was due to sheer starvation. Fairbanks did so, he said, and Fairclough signed it with a hand so weak it had to be placed upon the paper. The alleged affidavit survives, bearing a date of August 27, 1864, thirty-four days before Fairclough's death, and it is signed in a perfectly steady hand. Hospital records demonstrate that Fairclough was a patient there during the alleged kicking incident in the stockade—which is supposed to have occurred, besides, on a day when Wirz lay deathly ill at home. Actually, Fairclough remained in the hospital until his death. The stepson was confined separately in the stockade, and his account could only have been pure invention. Prosecutor Chipman not only offered the patent forgery as evidence, but later doctored the names of the principals, changing "Fairbanks" to "Fairclough," lest anyone question the apparent inconsistency in the surnames.[90]

Wirz's two unpaid lawyers did their best, but to no avail. The government had taken months to prepare its case, stinting neither funds nor efforts to procure witnesses, many of whom realized rewards such as those that came to Ambrose Spencer, Ben Dykes, and Felix "DeLabaume," who was never court-martialed for his desertion. Wirz enjoyed no such resources or time, and the judge advocate actively impeded the defense as well as he could, threatening and subverting Wirz's witnesses. When Robert Ould appeared in Washington to testify on the defendant's behalf, Colonel Chipman went straight to Ould's quarters to demand his subpoena; under the parole regulations, that would have required the ex-Confederate to return to his home in Richmond. Ould refused to hand over the document, however, so Chipman simply had the subpoena revoked, forcing the witness to quit Washington and thus depriving Wirz of potentially helpful testimony. It mattered little, though, for the court revealed an insurmountable bias in the motions it sustained: anything tending to implicate the defendant was allowed, however irrelevant or unreliable, on the premise that the court wished to "get at the truth"; any testimony lending human attributes to Wirz's character or impugning the benevolence of Union authorities was disallowed on whatever pretext General Wallace could apply. When defense counsel tried to impeach the fictions of government witnesses, Chipman waved the flag, denouncing them for daring to insult the veracity of United States soldiers, but he suffered no qualms about suggesting that Wirz's Federal witnesses were all deserters, bounty jumpers, or downright "disloyal." The defense tried to show that Wirz helped the detachment sergeants petition President Lincoln for their release, and subpoenaed Edward Boate of the prisoner delegation for that purpose, but Chipman objected—solely on the emotional grounds that the testimony implied a slander on the dead president, whom it left looking rather unsympathetic to the misery of Union prisoners. Incredibly, the court sustained his objection.[91]

The shameless charade continued through September and October, though the tribunal quickly moved to larger and airier chambers in the Court of Claims, beneath the library and near the Senate gallery. Each day Wirz crossed First Street from the Old Capitol Prison to the vaulted chambers of the claims court, where visitors filled every alcove and hovered outside. Sentencing was scheduled for October 24, and that morning Wirz rose early in his cell to answer a six-week-old letter just delivered from Lieutenant Charles Furlow's wife, Carrie. Anticipating the court's will, he warned her that he might be dead by the time she read his words. He protested his innocence, complaining of Confederate officials who remained unmolested despite their failure to aid or supply him, and he lamented all the letters people wrote seeking mercy for Jefferson Davis, wondering "where is the one who ever raised his voice in my behalf." Though resigned to his fate, he refused to forgive the witnesses "who have sworn to these enormous falsehoods."

"I have cursed them often," he told Mrs. Furlow, "& my curse will I leave them as my legacy." He thanked her for an offer to care for his daughter Cora, and he bid her farewell from "the poor despised Prison keeper of Andersonville." He gave the letter to a guard, who passed it on to an officer who kept it for a souvenir. A couple of hours later, only moments after listening to expert testimony that Wirz's physical condition would have prevented him from beating or slapping anyone, the court found him guilty on all counts and sentenced him to hang.[92]

On the chilly morning of November 10 Wirz rose in his cell at the Old Capitol and wrote a last letter to his wife, whom he had apparently not been allowed to see although she had boarded in the city during the trial. Later that forenoon, after giving a few final strokes to a stray cat that had wandered in to share his confinement, he emerged from his cell with a black cambric robe draped over his shoulders. He shook hands with one of his lawyers and followed the guards into an enclosed courtyard, where chanting soldiers and other spectators hung like vultures in the treetops. There was his life offered up to appease the public hysteria; the officers in charge even denied Mrs. Wirz the final comfort of taking his body.[93]

Some who had served prominently at Andersonville fled the country if they could: with Edwin Stanton in ultimate control of prosecutions, they had cause to fear that they, too, would be sacrificed. Southerners remained convinced that Wirz's trial was deliberately orchestrated to distract attention from the Union role in suspension of the exchange cartel, which in turn had led to the lengthy imprisonments that allowed diseases like scurvy and dysentery to take such a toll. Three years after the war Jefferson Davis almost hoped for a trial on the lingering allegations of attrition, telling a friend "if the field of inquiry be freely opened, it will not be difficult I think to prove that the accusing is the offending party." Both Davis and Richard Winder spent long months in prison awaiting just such a trial, but in the end the wretched Wirz's life satisfied Northern indignation. Even James Duncan, the one real villain of Andersonville, earned only a fifteen-year sentence, and he escaped after serving barely a year at Fort Pulaski, Georgia.[94]

One unlikely victim of the War Department's self-protective wrath was Dorence Atwater, the very prisoner whose secret list had identified so many of the dead. Secretary of War Edwin Stanton wanted the list for his department's own purposes, and paid Atwater three hundred dollars for it. Atwater wished to publish the names for the benefit of survivors, but for some reason Stanton objected, though he allowed the quartermaster general to publish Captain Moore's version. When Atwater retained the copy that he had used to assist Moore, Stanton had him arrested. Court-martialed for theft, Atwater endured a couple of months in a New York penitentiary before the secretary relented. Ultimately Atwater did put his list in print, but for the rest of his life he burned with resentment at his government's treachery.[95]

Meanwhile, back in Georgia, emancipated blacks drifted onto the abandoned prison site and took up lodging in the empty Confederate buildings. Two women came down from the North to teach the freedmen's children, fashioning a school out of one of the wards in the old Sumter Hospital and transforming the other one into their own dormitory. The missionaries' only contact with the outside world was the occasional visitor who had been driven to endure the punishing railroad journey by the sheer enormity of the suffering that had been Andersonville. While the youngsters frolicked between the buildings where dozens of drafted Georgians had died, the pilgrims would sneak between the yawning gates into the old stockade, where weeds, ferns, and bushes throve in the fertile, fatal soil. Within a year or two the palisade had begun to tilt here and there, but shoes and rags and scraps of once-precious wood and leather still littered the reclaimed earth. The roofs of the guards' perches frowned down on the intruder, throwing a cold shadow across his path, but the banished mockingbird had returned.[96]

Armed with the pardon he had won for testifying against Wirz, Ben Dykes repaired to Sumter County to demand the return of his land. Colonel Griffin, the caretaker of the cemetery, drove him off the prison grounds and told him to keep out of the buildings there. Dykes launched a ten-year campaign to win back the property, offering to sell the cemetery acreage to the United States if President Johnson was interested. The government stopped him from dismantling the stockade for the seasoned lumber it contained, but in 1875 he succeeded in selling the United States 120 acres surrounding the cemetery for $3,390.40, thus clearing his title to the rest of the land.[97]

A series of superintendents and Quartermaster Department officers maintained the graves, installing the remains of nearly a thousand more bodies from all over Georgia—men who had died in Stoneman's raid, in the occupation force, or on the road to Millen, Blackshear, or Thomasville. One civil engineer proposed a vast new cemetery with trees and shrubbery, but the frail skeletons in the serried graves had moldered too far for such ambitious reinterment. For all that engineer's effort, the dead of Andersonville lie today just where Colonel Griffin found them in the spring of 1865.[98]

During the long litigation over the prison land, Deputy Sheriff William Turner's widow and children migrated from Sumter County to Arkansas, and former slaves set up more permanent housekeeping on their late plantation. Ben Dykes rented the freedmen some of his own land after he retrieved it from the government, and a black tenant farmer tilled the plateau and the gentler slopes of what had once been the prison. One by one he laid the stockade logs down and split them into fence rails, and then the visitors began to arrive, seeking relatives in the graveyard and souvenirs from the rotting palisade—dragging it off by "carloads," said one witness, for canes and relic splinters. When a new superintendent took over the cemetery in 1883 he found barely a dozen feet of the inside wall still standing: by then all the prison buildings had disappeared.[99]

With the unseen, unheard tumbling of these last logs, interest in the site subsided for a time. Scrub oak and vines began to reclaim the ground where forty thousand men had spent their last or longest summer, but finally some of the veterans began to find heart enough to return to the scene of their misery. Clad in broadcloth and bowlers, they groped— often fruitlessly—for the exact site where their shebangs had stood thirty years before, or for the spot where some well-remembered friend had died. Wives and children sometimes stood by with sympathetic patience, bearing box cameras and parasols, as middle-aged men churned the underbrush for memories. While they poked about with their walking sticks, an incongruously melodious chorus of cooing, clacking, and trilling challenged them from above as birds and squirrels examined another party of those strange, blatant, gregarious creatures who had so greedily and brutally devoured their ancestors' forest in a distant, forgotten time.[100]

Notes

ABBREVIATIONS

ANHS:	Andersonville National Historic Site
CHS:	Chicago Historical Society
CMH:	*Confederate Military History*
CnHS:	Connecticut Historical Society
CV:	*Confederate Veteran*
DC:	Mark H. Dunkelman Collection
DU:	Duke University
HLH:	Houghton Library, Harvard University
HMBL:	Historical Museum of D. R. Barker Library
IHS:	Indiana Historical Society
IIHS:	Illinois Historical Society
KSHS:	Kansas State Historical Society
LC:	Library of Congress
LSU:	Louisiana State University
M:	Microfilm Publication (National Archives)
MassHS:	Massachusetts Historical Society
MHS:	Minnesota Historical Society
NHHS:	New Hampshire Historical Society
OHS:	Ohio Historical Society
OR:	*War of the Rebellion: A Compilation of the Official Records of the Union and Confederate Armies.* 128 vols. Washington, D.C.: Government Printing Office, 1880–1901. (Unless otherwise indicated, citations to this source are to series 2.)
RG:	Record Group (National Archives)
RNBP:	Richmond National Battlefield Park
RU:	Rutgers University
SHC:	Southern Historical Collection, University of North Carolina
SHSI:	State Historical Society of Iowa
SHSP:	*Southern Historical Society Papers*
SHSW:	State Historical Society of Wisconsin
T:	Microfilm Publication (National Archives)
UG:	University of Georgia
UK:	University of Kentucky
USAMHI:	U.S. Army Military History Institute
UV:	University of Vermont
VHS:	Vermont Historical Society

WRHS: Western Reserve Historical Society
YUL: Yale University Library

CHAPTER ONE

1. Dostoevsky, *Reminiscences*, xxix, 433; Nevins and Thomas, *Strong Diary*, 3:407; Kendall, *Monet by Himself*, 19–20; *Harper's Weekly*, December 12, 1863; descriptive roll of Company F, 1st Wisconsin Cavalry, Knud Hanson military service record, RG94.

2. Nevins and Thomas, *Strong Diary*, 3:373.

3. *OR* series 1, 31(2):647.

4. Casualty sheet, George M. Shearer military service record, RG94; Whitten diary (SHSI), November 25, 1863.

5. *Sumter Republican*, August 29, November 21, December 12, 1862, March 20, August 14, and November 13, 1863; *Georgia Journal and Messenger*, January 27, 1864.

6. *Trial*, 357, 360; Eighth U.S. Census, Chatham County, Ga. (M-653, reel 115:79), RG29; Mark H. Blandford to James A. Seddon, May 19, 1864, and W. H. S. Taylor to Samuel Cooper, February 8, 1865, "Letters Received by the Confederate Adjutant and Inspector General, 1861–65" (M-474, reel 98, item B-3473, and reel 162, item S-235), RG109.

7. Ambrose Spencer to Samuel Cooper, December 26, 1861, and to Judah P. Benjamin, February 9, 1862, "Letters Received by the Confederate Secretary of War" (M-437, reel 21, item 9393, and reel 28, item 11510), RG109; the "Index to Letters Received by the Confederate Adjutant and Inspector General" (M-409), RG109, describes a now-missing letter in which Spencer applied for a direct commission in 1861; *Sumter Republican*, March 21–August 22 and December 5–26, 1862; Sumter County Deeds, Book N:651–52.

8. Shepherd G. Pryor to Penelope Pryor, October 20 and November 10, 1863, Shepherd Green Pryor Collection, UG; *OR* series 1, 27(2):582.

9. Ray, *Diary of a Dead Man*, 19; *OR* series 1, 27(1):650, and 29(1):794.

10. *OR* series 1, 29(1):887; *CMH* 8:433–34.

11. Child, *History of the Fifth Regiment*, 236–37; *OR* 8:993; Rix, "Lisbon, N.H., Families" (NHHS), 2:87; Eighth U.S. Census, Grafton County, N.H. (M-653, reel 670:150), RG29; Marriages, Births, and Deaths, 1850–1876, Lisbon Town Hall; volunteer enlistment certificates, Hiram Jefferson military service record, RG94. Apparently because of Hiram's illiteracy, he did not object when army officials made his papers out in the name of "Jefferson."

12. Little, *Seventh New Hampshire*, 193–94; Eighth U.S. Census, Hillsborough County, N.H. (M-653, reel 676:216), RG29; Hadley, *History of Goffs-*

town, 2:142; muster rolls and final statement, Aaron Elliott military service record, RG94.

13. Enlistment certificate and prisoner-of-war memorandum, Thomas Genzardi military service record, RG94; Seventh U.S. Census, Middlesex County, Mass. (M-432, reel 322:185), RG29; Peter "Ginzardi" pension file, certificate #136344, RG15; Kansas Adjutant General, *Military History of Kansas*, 181–84, 199–201; *OR* series 1, 30(1):174, 532.

14. *OR* series 1, 30(1):786–87; prisoner-of-war memoranda, Thomas Herburt and Patrick Delany military service records, RG94; *Trial*, 135, 149.

15. Prisoner-of-war memoranda and notations from regimental descriptive book and company muster-out roll, George Albert military service record, RG94.

16. *OR* 6:438–40; *Trial*, 650; Jones, *A Rebel War Clerk's Diary*, 183, 338.

17. *OR* 6:455–56, 502, 527–28, 888–90; Whitten diary, December 8, 1863.

18. *CMH* 1:630; John H. Winder to Thomas Jesup, November 1, 1839, Jules P. Gareché to Winder, March 5, 1861, and Winder to Lorenzo Thomas, April 30, 1861, John Henry Winder Papers, SHC. For an account of Winder's life, see Blakey, *Winder*.

19. Lieutenant Colonel Winder's pass, Colonel Winder's appointment, and General Winder's commission, all in the Winder Papers; *OR* series 1, 51(2):146, 351; Jones, *A Rebel War Clerk's Diary*, 39, 53, 69–71, 91, 438.

20. *Trial*, 421; Seventh U.S. Census, Baltimore, Md., (M-432, reel 282:31), RG29; *OR* 6:558. For the location of Winder's office, see Blakey, *Winder*, 149.

21. *OR* 6:558; John H. Winder to Braxton Bragg, July 24, 1864, Frederick M. Dearborn Collection, HLH; Spencer, *Andersonville*, 18–19. Spencer, who had no way of knowing but who evidently wished to smear the Confederate government as much as he could, claimed that the site below Albany was vetoed because there were too many wealthy, influential citizens there who might resist the placement of a prison in their midst. Winder's July letter to Bragg reveals the real reason: Jefferson Davis's concern over a raid from coastal Yankees.

22. Testimony of Uriah B. Harrold, Isaac Turner case, Congressional Jurisdiction Case Files, RG123.

23. Ibid.; Jervey, "Prison Life among the Rebels," 31; Eighth U.S. Census, Sumter County, Ga. (M-653, reel 136: scattered pages), RG29; *OR* 8:593; most issues of the *Sumter Republican* carried the train schedule. Spencer, *Andersonville*, 16, claimed that the village was named Anderson after a Savannah citizen, but was renamed Andersonville by the U.S. Post Office. Citing records in RG28 of the National Archives, Bearss's "Historic Resource Study and Base Map" (UG, 16) dates the change of the village's name from an 1856 decision by the U.S. Post Office. If that date was not a typographical error, however, local citizens ignored the change for a full decade. It appears clear that the settlement

was called Anderson through most of the war by those who lived in or near it, and came to be known as Andersonville only as the natural result of that appellation being persistently applied by Confederate officers and Union prisoners (see, for instance, *The Martyrs*, 8).

24. Ninth U.S. Census, Sumter County, Ga. (M-593, reel 174:60), RG29; Benjamin B. Dykes to Edwin M. Stanton, February 1, 1866, Consolidated Correspondence, Entry 225, RG92; Sumter County Deeds, Book M:95, and Grantor Index, 1830–1917.

25. Testimony of Uriah Harrold, Cynthia Gray, Thomas J. Hardin, and Emma Darby, Isaac Turner case, Congressional Jurisdiction Case Files, RG123; Sumter County Deeds, Book O:65–66; *Sumter Republican*, November 28, 1862, and November 13, 1863.

26. *Georgia Journal and Messenger*, December 23, 1863; *Sumter Republican*, December 4, 1863.

27. *Trial*, 359, 372; *OR* 7:546. The prison's ultimate dimensions are taken from the report of Captain James Moore, who made measurements during his assignment at the prison cemetery in the summer of 1865; that report is included in his introduction to *The Martyrs*, 8. Since the only dimension that was changed during the life of the stockade was its length, Winder's intention to build it in a square implies a run of 750 feet per side.

28. Blakey, *Winder*, genealogical chart; Seventh U.S. Census, Accomack County, Va. (M-432, reel 965:312), and Eighth U.S. Census, Accomack County, Va. (M-653, reel 1330:156), RG29; *OR* series 1, 9:138–39, 51(2):241–42, 454, and series 2, 4:911.

29. John Winder to Samuel Cooper, November 14, 1863, "Letters Received by the Confederate Adjutant and Inspector General, 1861–65" (M-474, reel 89, item 2076), RG109; *OR* 8:730; *Trial*, 359.

30. *OR* 8:731–32; Richard B. Winder to "Major" [F. W. Dillard], August 12, 1864, R. B. Winder Letterbook, RG153; *Macon Daily Telegraph*, February 27, 1864; *Augusta Weekly Constitutionalist*, January 27, 1864. For evidence of one Confederate soldier's opposition to the placement of the prison in his home county, see Joseph J. Felder to Calvin W. Felder, December 15, 1863, Joseph Jackson Felder Papers, Georgia State Archives, quoted in Futch, *Andersonville*, 4.

31. *Sumter Republican*, January 22, 1864; *OR* 6:965, 7:541, and 8:731; testimony of Emma Darby, Isaac Turner case, Congressional Jurisdiction Case Files, RG123. Though Winder spelled the mechanic's name "Hays," the Sumter County family spelled it "Heys." In *Andersonville*, 4, 123, Futch apparently cites Sheppard family tradition that C. C. Sheppard was overseer of the stockade construction, but no such Sheppard appears in prison correspondence.

32. *OR* 7:546 and 8:595; testimony of Emma Darby and L. P. Clarke, Isaac Turner case, Congressional Jurisdiction Case Files, RG123.

33. *The Martyrs*, 8; *Trial*, 113, 160; Crosby diary (VHS), May 22, 1864. Various sources describe the guard platforms as four feet square and six by four: photographs taken in August of 1864 indicate their width was greater than their depth, and a six-foot breadth would have more easily accommodated the occasional need to double the guards. A reputed eyewitness sketch of the stockade gate can be found on page 454 of *Century* for July, 1890, and another of the entire compound appears on page 612 of the August, 1890, issue.

34. W. S. Winder to John H. Winder, January 24, 1864, John Hunt Morgan Papers, SHC, quoted in Blakey, *Winder*, 176; biographical notes, Isaiah White Papers, DU; *OR* series 1, 35(2):393–96, and series 2, 6:885–86, 965; *Sumter Republican*, various dates between July 31, 1863, and July 1, 1864; Richard B. Winder to John H. Winder, February 15, 1864, and to Charles J. Harris, March 31, 1864, R. B. Winder Letterbook, RG153. The man who had been conscripted was William Milton Pickett, who became one of Winder's most dependable suppliers of goods and equipment, and who is generally misidentified in Andersonville literature as "Mr. Piggott."

35. *Sumter Republican*, February 26, 1864; *OR* 6:914, 962, 1000.

36. *OR* 6:965, 1054, and 8:732.

37. Ibid., 6:925.

38. Ibid., series 1, 53:279, and series 2, 6:797, 925, 966; Ninth U.S. Census, Bibb County, Ga. (M-593, reel 136:628), RG29.

39. *Trial*, 99, 456; *OR* 6:966, 993. Persons's orders for all three commands were dated February 26, but for a few days previously he had charge only of the remnant of his regiment, Sid Winder retaining command of the post (*Trial*, 455).

40. *Trial*, 456; *OR* 6:966, 972–73, 976–77, 1000, and 8:731.

41. *OR* 6:498, 544–46, 587–88; Whitten diary, December 20 and 25, 1863, and January 16, 28, 1864; *Richmond Enquirer*, February 2, 1864; *Trial*, 654.

42. Prisoner-of-war memorandum, Thomas Genzardi military service record, RG94; *OR* 6:888–90.

43. *Richmond Examiner*, February 8, 1864; Moore, *Rebellion Record*, 8:450–53; Domschcke, *Zwanzig Monate*, 77, 88.

44. *OR* series 1, 33:178–223. According to his schoolteacher, who was also the captain of his Local Defense company, it was thirteen-year-old William Littlepage who found Dahlgren's papers. See the statement of Edward W. Halbach in Jones, "The Kilpatrick-Dahlgren Raid," 546–47.

45. *OR* series 1, 33:1133–34, 1176, and series 2, 6:925–26.

46. *Richmond Dispatch*, February 17, 1864; Jones, *A Rebel War Clerk's Diary*, 338; Whitten diary, February 17–19, 1864; *OR* series 1, 33:1176, and series 2, 6:925–26. See also H. L. Clay to George E. Pickett, February 9, 1864, and to Edward O'Neal, February 16, 1864, Box 1, Records Relating to Confederate Prisons and Union Prisoners, Entry 464, RG109.

47. No contemporary accounts of that first contingent appear to have survived. This itinerary is taken from McElroy, *Andersonville*, 119–20, a generally unreliable source, using only those particulars corroborated by the manuscript diaries of Michael Dougherty (ANHS), Eseck G. Wilber (USAMHI), W. H. Rinehart (ANHS), and John Whitten, who all followed the same route within the next four weeks. McElroy recorded that four hundred men were squeezed into only four cars, but railroad cars of the early 1860s were smaller than when McElroy first wrote his memoir: diarists on the spot described some cars as uncomfortably crowded with only forty-six men in them (see, for example, Gibson diary [LC], April 29, 1864). Michael Dougherty complained of having sixty men in his car on March 4, and even when Confederate rolling stock became especially scarce, in the last six months of the war, guards forced only seventy-four men into each car, which a Pennsylvanian pronounced "well packed" (Yeakle diary [ANHS], October 31, 1864). Besides, the first shipment of prisoners on February 17 seems not to have exceeded two hundred men; given McElroy's recollection that he left for Andersonville on February 18, he may not have been among that first lot, as he claimed: a memorandum from prisoner-of-war records in Adam Swarner's military service record indicates he was sent from Belle Isle to Andersonville on February 17, for instance. Those who had been prisoners longest appear to have been sent first, and Swarner had been captured a couple of months before McElroy, who belonged to the 16th Illinois Cavalry; other members of McElroy's regiment, such as Leroy L. Key and Ivory H. Pike, were not forwarded to Andersonville until March, according to their service records.

48. *OR* 6:972–73, 976–77, 985, 1000.

49. Ibid., 4:266–68, 6:996.

50. Ibid., 4:449, 6:78–79.

51. Ibid., series 1, 24(3):470, and series 2, 6:279–80, 528, 595–97.

52. Ibid., 6:709, 996.

53. McElroy, *Andersonville*, 120; Whitten diary, February 5 and 14, and March 20–22, 1864; *Sumter Republican*, January 1, 1864.

54. This passage, too, relies upon the collective experience of future arrivals: see, for instance, the notebook of Charles M. Colvin (CHS), who reached the prison on March 22, and the diaries of Michael Dougherty, March 3–10, 1864, Eseck Wilber, March 6, 1864, W. H. Rinehart, March 14–21, 1864, and John Whitten, March 21–22, 1864. In *Andersonville*, 120–21, McElroy recounts the story of marching into the prison at night between rows of blazing bonfires, apparently taking his romantic cue from Kellogg, *Life and Death in Rebel Prisons*, 55. While it may have been logical for Confederate authorities to use the abundant pine slash for such a purpose, they appear not to have had enough surplus labor at that time to distribute such pyres the length of the road to the prison.

Like guards at other stops along the way, Camp Sumter sentries probably took the easier option of simply confining the prisoners to the cars when they arrived at night, at least in the beginning. McElroy claimed he was among the first trainload to enter the prison, and that he arrived in the darkness of February 25, but the first page of the Andersonville hospital register clearly indicates that twenty-five prisoners came into the stockade early enough on February 24 to be admitted as patients that day. At least one witness at Henry Wirz's trial also testified that he arrived on February 24. See Register of Federal Prisoners Admitted to the Hospital at Andersonville, Georgia, Entry 113, RG249, 1; *Trial,* 687.

55. *Macon Daily Telegraph,* February 27, 1864; Colvin notebook, undated and May 31, 1864; *Trial,* 96, 100–101, 457, 687; Crosby diary, May 22, 1864. Charles Colvin's notebook describes the standing trees and brush in the prison's early days (though he did not reach there until March 22); John Whitten's diary for March 25, 1864, records that three pines still stood inside the stockade on that date, and a photograph taken on August 16 shows those three in the southwest corner. In his "diary" for March 16 (53), John Ransom described the stockade as still unfinished, with cannon yawning through the gap. He thereby makes two revealing errors simultaneously, for on the one hand the stockade was finished very early in March, while on the other Colonel Persons had no artillery at Andersonville until late in April. Ransom's published diary, the original of which he claimed later to have lost in a fire, contains so many inconsistencies as to raise a serious doubt whether any original ever existed; few of the messmates whose deaths he records, for instance, appear on any of the death or burial registers, although the dead from that period were nearly all identified. Richard Winder's purchase of 160 skillets early in Andersonville's occupation corroborates a former prisoner's testimony (*Trial,* 687) that he issued these implements to the first arrivals: see Winder's abstract of purchases at Andersonville up to March 31, 1864, Box 18, Tabular Statements, Entry 208, RG109 (boxes 18 and 19 from this entry are obviously misfiled from elsewhere, but they are cited here as they are now found in the National Archives); by March 13 supplies of such cookware had long since run out (Dougherty diary, March 13, 1864).

56. Richard B. Winder to Charles R. Armstrong, February 17, 1864, R. B. Winder Letterbook, RG153; *Trial,* 94; Register of Federal Prisoners Admitted to the Hospital at Andersonville, Entry 113, RG249, 1; prisoner-of-war memoranda, Adam Swarner military service record, RG94.

57. Whitten diary, February 19, 1864; Page, *True Story of Andersonville,* 60–61; *OR* 6:993; Register of Federal Prisoners Admitted to the Hospital at Andersonville, Entry 113, RG249, 1. Futch (*Andersonville,* 12–13) has Colonel Persons taking command February 29, apparently on the basis of Special Order 49 of that date, which assigned him as post commander and gave Major Elias

Griswold command of the actual prison. Special Order 49 merely modified Special Order 47, of February 26, which had put Persons in charge of the post, the troops, and the prison; it appears certain the colonel was on hand at least during the last week of February, if not earlier: see *OR* 6:966, 993, and 1042–43. Surgeon White's presence at the prison from its opening is confirmed by his special requisition for a hospital register on February 18, 1864, in Box 19, Tabular Statements, Entry 208, RG109.

58. Requisitions and vouchers for muskets and accoutrements dated February 27, 1864, Alexander W. Persons military service record, "Compiled Service Records of Confederate Soldiers Who Served in Organizations from the State of Georgia" (M-266, reel 532), RG109.

CHAPTER TWO

1. *Sumter Republican,* January 15, 1864; *OR* series 1, 35(1):276–77, 284–85, 321–22.

2. *CMH* 16:54–55; *OR* series 1, 35(1):325–26.

3. *OR* series 3, 3:88–89; Ayling, *Register,* 355–401.

4. *OR* series 1, 35(1):285–88.

5. Ibid., 310–11, 326–28, 331.

6. Little, *Seventh New Hampshire,* 220–24; *OR* series 1, 35(1):303–4, 311, 315–16.

7. *OR* series 1, 35(1):288–90, 328, 332–33; Ayling, *Register,* 368; *Trial,* 326; casualty sheet, Aaron Elliott military service record, RG94.

8. *OR* series 1, 35(1):488, 643.

9. Ibid., series 2, 6:996, 1015; *Trial,* 100, 458.

10. *OR* 6:1000, 1017–18, 1043; Richard Winder to J. N. Sessions, April 21, 1864, R. B. Winder Letterbook, RG153.

11. *Trial,* 355, 438, 444, 446.

12. *OR* series 1, 25(2):745, 51(2):815, series 2, 3:795, and 6:1041–43; *Trial,* 455.

13. *Trial,* 483, 496; Lew Wallace to "My dear Wife," August 25, Lew Wallace Papers, IHS; *The Demon of Andersonville,* 118; unidentified newspaper clipping dated November 11, 1865, Louis Manigault scrapbook, SHC; Familienregister der Stadt Zürich, Zivilstandsamt der Stadt Zürich, Familie Wirz, 71; *Verzeichniss der Stadtbürger von Zürich auf das Jahr 1851,* 263–66; "Passenger Arrival Lists for the Port of New York" (M-237, reel 78), RG36; Seventh U.S. Census (M-432), Christian County, Ky. (reel 196:427), and New Orleans, La. (reel 237:199), RG29. In his early days in Hopkinsville, Dr. Webber gave his first

name as "Augustine" (Christian County, Ky., Deeds, 10:113, 165, 203, 204, 206, etc.), but thirteen years later he had Anglicized it to "Augustus." According to Wirz's own jailhouse interview a few hours before his execution (from the Manigault clipping), he was born November 25, 1823, and when he arrived in New York on April 23, 1849, he gave his age as twenty-five, but eleven months later a New Orleans census taker put him down as twenty-nine; in June of 1860 another enumerator recorded him as thirty-eight. A tedious search of passenger arrival lists for Boston, New York, and New Orleans reveals that the only Swiss Wirz to arrive in 1849 was "A. Wirz," but his age and origin jibe with Henry Wirz's recollection. (Apparently because of the Gothic German script, the "A" looked more like a "D" to the purser who transcribed it.) Wirz's tale of working in a Massachusetts textile mill and bathhouse until 1851 does not, however, stand up to scrutiny: the name Henry Wirz appears in no census from any eastern state in 1850, but a Swiss-born Henry "Wertz" is found on the New Orleans census under the date of March 15, 1850. August Heinrich Wirz, a cousin, also came to America a few years later; he landed in Philadelphia, where he applied for American citizenship on April 9, 1857 (U.S. Court of Common Pleas, Philadelphia, citizenship application #9312).

14. Newspaper clipping, Manigault scrapbook; Seventh U.S. Census (M-432), Louisville, Ky. (reel 206:154) and Trigg County, Ky. (reel 219:319), RG29; Trigg County Marriage Docket, 1820–1857:159; Trigg County Wills, Book F:72–73; Perrin, *Counties of Christian and Trigg*, 2:98; Judith Ann Maupin, "Trigg County Cemeteries," UK, 234–35.

15. Eighth U.S. Census, Madison Parish, La. (M-653, reel 413:5), RG29; *OR* 3:711.

16. *CMH* 13:322c; *OR* 3:711; *Trial*, 700; Merrell, *Five Months in Rebeldom*, 30–32.

17. *OR* 4:865; *Trial*, 529–30, 556; Otis, *Second Wisconsin*, 193–95, 197–98; newspaper clipping, November 11, 1865, Manigault scrapbook. Wirz's commission, dated June 12, 1862, and the undated citizens' petition are in Wirz's military service record, "Confederate General and Staff Officers and Nonregimental Enlisted Men" (M-331, reel 271), RG109, as is his letter as commandant of the Tuscaloosa prison to Thomas Jordan, May 9, 1862, and his voucher for provisions, May 15, 1862; see also Wirz's endorsements on the statements of E. A. Powell, January 2, 1862, and F. M. Peacock, April–, 1862, "Letters Received by the Confederate Secretary of War, 1861–65" (M-437, reels 27 and 66), RG109. Reel 10 of this last microfilm publication also contains a letter from Captain George C. Gibbs (a man Wirz would also encounter at Andersonville) to John H. Winder dated September 6, 1861, in which Gibbs asks that Wirz be paid the fifty-dollar monthly salary of a government clerk for his "most efficient

service." Though the historian of the 2nd Wisconsin remembered Wirz as a strict disciplinarian, he also detailed Wirz's insistence that his prisoners receive palatable food and adequate quarters when they were available.

18. *OR* 4:865, 871, 901, 925; Wirz's travel vouchers of December 19, 1862, March 24 and April 4, 1863, and his furloughs of December 19, 1862, and March 13, 1863, Henry Wirz military service file, "General and Staff Officers and Nonregimental Enlisted Men" (M-331, reel 271), RG109; newspaper clipping of November 11, 1865, Manigault scrapbook; Perrin, Letter.

19. *Trial*, 99. Wirz's pay vouchers of January 22 and 25, 1864 (in Wirz's military service record), are dated at Wilmington, strongly suggesting he entered through that port at about that time; reports from the Union blockading squadron name only the *A. D. Vance* as having eluded Federal warships in that vicinity in the days immediately preceding (*Official Records of the Union and Confederate Navies*, series 1, 9:413).

20. Colvin notebook (CHS), March 31, 1864; *Trial*, 99, 102; Sparrow diary (UV), July 18, 1864; *OR* 8:66–67 specifically mentions the dead line at Camp Douglas. Prisoners were shot there and at Camp Morton, Indiana; Camp Chase and Johnson's Island, in Ohio; Point Lookout, Maryland; Newport News, Virginia; Fort Delaware, and elsewhere for violating stated bounds, usually to answer the calls of nature. Several Confederate prisoners were shot or bayoneted to death while in the very act of relieving themselves. See *OR* 6:855, 856, 884–85, 7:163–65, 385, 452–54, 1241, 1246, 1252–56, 8:66–67, 115–16, 508–510, 692–93. These incidents do not include uninvestigated shootings or those which may have involved actual escape attempts. John Whitten (diary, SHSI) noted that the dead line had already been established at Andersonville when he arrived on March 22, 1864.

21. *Trial*, 99, 371–72.

22. *Sumter Republican*, April 1, 1864; Whitten diary and Kellogg diary (CnHS), May 7, 1864. On page 27 of his *Andersonville*, Spencer projects a characteristically venomous image of hordes of yokels surrounding the prison day after day, mothers with suckling babes among them, all gaping spellbound and neglecting domestic duties. The Americus editor's felicitous observations, made one month into the prison's history, were probably not that far from the reality of that time.

23. *Sumter Republican*, February 27, 1863; *Macon Daily Telegraph*, March 8, 1864; *Trial*, 94; *The Martyrs*, 223–25. The Plains of Dura is now known simply as Plains, Georgia.

24. Register of the Federal Prisoners Admitted to the Hospital at Andersonville, Georgia, Entry 113, RG249, 2; *The Martyrs*, 223–25; *OR* series 1, 32(1): 411–12, 32(2):296–97, and series 2, 6:1088. By early spring the Knoxville Yan-

kees had carried smallpox into southwest Virginia (Summers, *History of Southwest Virginia*, 533).

25. *OR* 7:89, 548; *Trial*, 45–46, 55, 245, 613; Register of Federal Prisoners Admitted to the Hospital at Andersonville, Georgia, Entry 113, RG249, 92, indicates that William Morris, Company G, 12th U.S. Infantry, was admitted to the pest hospital on June 29 with varioloid, and was returned to the prison from there on August 9. This hospital register is the only evidence for the dates of the pest hospital; on the second page it records the death of "M. Toliver" in that ward on March 12. Other sources identify that first victim as Martin "Poliver," or "Polivar."

26. Little, *Seventh New Hampshire*, 540–42; *Sumter Republican*, April 1, 1864.

27. *OR* 6:145–46.

28. *Trial*, 326–27; *OR* 6:1054; receipt for Major Bogle's money, Confederate States Army Archives Miscellany, DU. During Wirz's trial for mistreating Federal prisoners, his defense counsel presented a letter from Wirz to one of Winder's officers, asking that Bogle be granted an interview in order to present his grievance. Wirz's counsel also asked Bogle if Wirz intimated a desire, but an inability, to help the major further, and the phrasing of the question implies that the answer would have been affirmative; the refusal of that single-minded court to let Bogle respond tends to corroborate that.

29. *OR* series 1, 2:232, and series 4, 3:934–39, 1001, 1002. Cable died July 16, 1864, of "debilitas," a term used for a general wasting away unattributable to any particular diagnosis (*Atwater Report*, 73).

30. *Trial*, 187, 326, 461, 513; Little, *Seventh New Hampshire*, 542; *Sumter Republican*, April 1, 1864.

31. *OR* 7:29–34, 105, 687; Jessie V. Hines to "Dear Ma," March 22, 1864, USAMHI.

32. *OR* 7:62–63.

33. Root diary (HMBL), May 1, 1864.

34. *OR* 7:169. As early as March 27 Wirz was signing receipts for prisoners' personal property: see Confederate States Army Archives Miscellany.

35. Ibid., 170; *Trial*, 502, 507, 520, 523, 529, 544, 556, 657, 700, 803. Wirz was also missing the deltoid muscle on his left shoulder, apparently from an old accident or wound (*Trial*, 803).

36. *OR* 7:63, 169, and 8:599; Hoster diary (ANHS), June 20, 1864.

37. *OR* 7:63, 136–37, 169; *Trial*, 458; Colvin notebook, March 31, 1864. The capacity of the creek has generated some debate. Modern critics in particular have complained that it was patently inadequate for even the original number of prisoners intended for the stockade (see, for instance, Moore, "Poor Administration," 10), but the construction of Georgia Route 49 diverted most of the

drainage that fed it in 1864. A photograph taken in August of that year shows that it was more than six feet wide and knee-deep where prison laborers had channeled it, but personal observations in January and December of 1991 found it a stagnant trickle.

38. Whitten diary, March 28–31, 1864; *OR* 7:40, 136, 169, 207, and 8:731–32; *Trial*, 100.

39. William B. B. Cross to Winder, April 15, 1864, and Winder to F. W. Dillard, April 6 and 25, 1864, to "Major Hallyer," April 6, 1864, to G. W. Cunningham, April 13, 1864, to "Major Bonnell" and A. R. Lawton, April 18, 1864, to John H. Winder, April 26, 1864, and to "Major," June 29, 1864, all in R. B. Winder Letterbook, RG153; *OR* 7:181–82, 402–3; Whitten diary, April 3, 1864; Roe, *Melvin Memorial*, 123; Eliot, "Civil War Diary," 11; Forbes, *Diary*, 20; Hammer, *James Diary*, 81–82; Andrews, *War-Time Journal*, 76–77; Consolidated Morning Reports (April, 1865), Entry 111, RG109. Early correspondence refers to the shoe superintendent as "Mr. Smart," but later cites him as "Mr. Smoot"; the quarterly abstract of September 30, 1864, records a payment of $110 to J. R. Smoot for traveling expenses (Box 18, Tabular Statements, Entry 208, RG109). The would-be recruiter of shoemakers was Francis Carney of the 2nd Massachusetts Heavy Artillery; he died at the prison fifteen weeks after this incident (see Forbes, *Diary*, 20, Keys diary [RU], June 15, 1864, and Massachusetts Adjutant General, *Massachusetts Soldiers, Sailors, and Marines*, 5:713).

40. *OR* 7:137; *Trial*, 432, 450–51, 456, 466–68, 500; George Brown to "Dear Sister," June 28, 1864, Everett Papers, DU.

41. *Trial*, 459, 561.

42. *OR* 6:1117, and 7:63–64, 1041; *Trial*, 355, 459, 500, 503, 508–9, 561. All the pertinent correspondence about the riot is filed with "Letters Received by the Confederate Adjutant and Inspector General, 1861–65" (M-474, reel 134, item O-19), RG109. Selman is variously referred to as James C. Sellman, Jr., James Selman, Jr., and as Mr. Dillman in Andersonville correspondence; he appears to be James W. Selman, Jr., who served for nine months as a lieutenant in Company I, 35th Georgia, and as a private (in the same company as his father) in the Floyd Legion, a state militia unit. See his military service record, "Compiled Service Records of Confederate Soldiers Who Served in Organizations from the State of Georgia" (M-266, reel 421), RG109.

43. *Trial*, 355. McElroy, *Andersonville*, 156, lauds the Alabama troops.

44. *Trial*, 500; *OR* 7:137; Dougherty diary (ANHS), 26. Dougherty's comment about the wood details is dated March 16, but around this time his entries begin slipping further and further out of date—even out of chronological sequence—so although his is an original manuscript diary the citations from this period will be by page number rather than date.

45. *Trial*, 149–51, 252, 434, 469–70, 484, 504; muster rolls and casualty sheet of Company A, 1st Ohio Infantry, Caleb Coplan military service record, RG94; Register of Federal Prisoners Admitted to the Hospital at Andersonville, Georgia, Entry 113, RG249, 25. Andersonville memoirs and the Wirz trial testimony abound with accounts of prisoners shot by guards. Many of them refer to a crazy man, often a German, who was shot while reaching for bread or a bright scrap of cloth (see, for instance, McElroy, *Andersonville*, 141; Ransom, *Diary*, 71; and *Trial*, 320, 370, 372, 394). The only prisoner to die of gunshot wounds until May, however, was Caleb Coplan, who had been wounded and captured at Chickamauga. Admitted to the hospital April 9 with a bullet wound to the left breast, he died April 10; if that had been his original wound, he surely would either have perished from it or recovered long before. Two witnesses at the Wirz trial, Thomas Hall and James Marshall, both testified to seeing a man shot at the north wall in early April, Hall describing the very wound that killed Coplan. Since Marshall took the stand a week after Hall, it is unlikely that he simply regurgitated information he heard while waiting to testify, as seemed to be the case with other witnesses. Nor does it seem probable that Coplan was killed while reaching for food, since the quartermaster issued rations twice that day (Whitten diary, April 9, 1864); the victim everyone remembered reaching for some bread was shot on May 2. Coplan is misidentified as "C. Copeland" in prison hospital records.

46. *Sumter Republican*, April 22, 1864; J. F. Gilmer to Howell Cobb, April 17, 1864, and H. W. Mercer to Cobb, April 19 and 20, 1864, Box 67, Cobb Papers, UG; *OR* series 1, 35(2):433, 447, 456, and series 2, 7:137; Samuel Cooper to Joseph E. Johnston, April 20, 1864, and to Patton Anderson, April 21, 1864, Box 1, Records Relating to Confederate Prisons and Union Prisoners, Entry 464, RG109. Cooper's order to Johnston included the 5th Georgia in the troops directed to Andersonville, but it seems never to have arrived there. Gamble's Florida battery came to Camp Sumter under Lieutenant Charles E. Dyke, who was promptly promoted to captain. On February 10 Gamble's battery was composed of two 6-pounder smoothbores, one 12-pounder Napoleon smoothbore, and one 3-inch rifle, all more or less unserviceable. Immediately after the battle of Olustee one of the 6-pounders was exchanged for a captured 12-pounder Napoleon; by the end of April the other 6-pounder and the 3-inch rifle were gone, replaced by a pair of 10-pounder Parrott rifles also taken from the Federals at Olustee and originally given to John Guerard's Georgia battery: *OR* series 1, 35(1):342, 584, 35(2):464, and series 2, 7:138.

47. *Sumter Republican*, May 6 and 13, 1864.

48. *OR* 7:136–37; Bradd diary (USAMHI), July 30, 1864; Converse diary (KSHS), June 9, 1864; Crosby diary (VHS), May 22, 1864; *Trial*, 498–99, 505, 551. Until March 25 prisoners admitted to the hospital were recorded by straight

numerical squads, 1 through 72. For a week thereafter no squad numbers were listed, and on April 2—the day after massive attempts to "flank" during the reorganization process—their prison designations were listed as 6/2, etc., for sixth detachment, second squad (Register of Federal Prisoners Admitted to the Hospital at Andersonville, Georgia, Entry 113, RG249, 1–25).

49. Homsher diary (LC); Whitten diary, April 1, 1864. Edward Boate, whose testimony on this incident appears in *Trial*, 688, mistakenly remembered the date as March 17; Whitten's on-the-spot diary is not only more reliable, it is corroborated by the change in squad numbers in the hospital register of April 2, cited in the previous note. The Charles Wesley Homsher manuscript consists of an undated series of notations ostensibly made in the prison.

50. *OR* 4:821–22; *Trial*, 379, 478, 659–60; *Sumter Republican*, June 24, 1864. Prison-diary estimates of the weight of Andersonville rations, especially meat, vary wildly.

51. *Trial*, 380–81, 458; Eugene Forbes (see his *Diary*, 19) borrowed such a sieve, several examples of which appear in the photograph of Andersonville relics.

52. *Trial*, 659–61; Consolidated Morning Reports, Entry 111, RG249; Whitten diary, April 20–29, 1864. In the Inquisition-like atmosphere of the Wirz trial Captain Armstrong wisely denied ever having diminished the prison rations until officially ordered to do so on August 9, 1864, but both logic and prisoner diaries suggest that he must have cut individual portions temporarily on several occasions to make his supplies stretch.

53. Consolidated Morning Reports, April 19–28, 1864, Entry 111, RG249; prisoner-of-war memorandum, Thomas Genzardi military service record, RG94; *OR* 7:63.

54. *OR* series 1, 33:92–97, 1101–3.

55. *Official Records of the Union and Confederate Navies*, 9:638–39; *OR* series 1, 33:296–300.

56. Dyer, *Compendium*, 1439, 1608; Sampson diary (SHC), April 21–30, 1864.

57. Sampson diary, April 30 and May 1, 1864; Higginson, *Massachusetts in the Army and Navy*, 2:345; Whitten diary, April 28–30, 1864.

58. Sampson diary, May 1, 1864; Whitten diary, April 30–May 3, 1864; Kellogg diary, May 3 and 4, 1864; *Trial*, 536; *Macon Daily Telegraph*, June 8, 1864; George Z. Pretz to "Provost Marshal, Augusta, Ga.," August 16, 1865, USAMHI. Either Mrs. Leonard or the woman who followed her to Andersonville as the wife of Captain Hunt (Wirz to "Provost Marshal, Augusta, Ga.," May 19, 1864, Letters Sent, Andersonville Prison, Georgia, May, 1864–March, 1865, RG109) may have been the woman who is supposed to have died at the prison camp at Florence, South Carolina, on January 25, 1865 (King, "Death Camp at

Florence," 38). A common-law arrangement could explain the difference in names, if indeed any such person died at Florence: the romance of a woman's death also lingers at Andersonville, to the extent of identifying grave #101 as hers, but that grave is simply the first unknown Andersonville interment. An 1867 visitor claimed that she found the grave of an "unknown lady" who died there on April 6, 1864 (Shearman, "A Visit to Andersonville," 114), but except for two graves filled on April 2 every burial in April was that of an identified soldier. Sergeant Major Robert Kellogg, of the 16th Connecticut, mentioned the bonfires surrounding his first bivouac at Andersonville in his *Life and Death in Rebel Prisons* (55), which he published early in 1865. He did not refer to them in his contemporary diary, but Kellogg lacked John McElroy's romantic proclivities, and because he had no reason to lie about it, his recollection seems believable. The same objectivity does not apply, however, to Kellogg's published account of a threatening Captain Wirz, whom he did not mention at all in his diary during his first ten days of confinement.

59. Prisoner-of-war memoranda, George Albert military service record, RG94; Register of Federal Prisoners Admitted to the Hospital at Andersonville, Georgia, Entry 113, RG249, 36; *Trial*, 370, 372, 394–95.

60. Colvin notebook, April 30, 1864; Kellogg diary, May 3, 1864; Gibson diary (LC), May 20, 1864; Adams diary (CnHS), May 5, 8, 9–12, 20, 27, 31, 1864; Keys diary, June 1, 1864.

61. *Trial*, 560; Hammer, *James Diary*, 80.

62. Gibson diary, July 22 and August 19, 1864; *Trial*, 437, 447, 496; *OR* 7:40, 89; Whitten diary, May 5, 1864. Samuel Henderson, for instance, describes making a meal container from a coat sleeve in his diary entry of June 26, 1864 (ANHS). On an advance inspection for his men, the chief surgeon of the Georgia Reserves announced on May 6 that the cookhouse had just been completed (E. J. Eldridge to Lamar Cobb, May 6, 1864, Box 19, Tabular Statements, Entry 208, RG109).

63. Spencer, *Andersonville*, 48; *Trial*, 305, 371, 494, 679; *OR* 7:1040, and 8:926.

64. *OR* 7:137; Dougherty diary, 33; Dennison, *Diary*, 40.

65. *Atwater Report*; *OR* 7:138.

66. Whitten diary, April 16 and 17, 1864; *OR* 7:40; *Trial*, 459. Probably because his messmates did not report his death until the following morning, John Shuffleton (Whitten's comrade) is recorded as having died on April 17 (*Atwater Report*, 13; *The Martyrs*, 176).

67. *Trial*, 140–41, 171, 257, 260, 261, 295, 298, 316, 319; *Sumter Republican*, May 6, 1864; *Atwater Report*, vi. The forty-seven-year-old Byram, identified by Crandall as "Byron," of the "2nd" Georgia Reserves (*Trial*, 260), was the only man with a similar name on such detached duty at Andersonville: see his military

service record, "Compiled Service Records of Confederate Soldiers Who Served in Organizations from the State of Georgia" (M-266, reel 130), RG109.

68. *Trial*, 36, 50, 140, 172, 462; *OR* 8:600; Vance diary (OHS), June 15, 1864. For a few weeks after the hospital was moved outside the stockade and before Wirz built the deadhouse, in late May and early June, most of the dead seem to have been collected at the gate of the exterior hospital.

69. *Trial*, 128, 140–41, 172, 261.

70. Kennedy diary (MHS), May 4, 5, and 7, 1864; Whitten diary, May 7, 1864.

71. Whitten, Kellogg, and Root diaries, May 7, 1864; Kennedy diary, May 14, 1864; *OR* 7:135.

72. Muster rolls of Company E, 17th Iowa, January–April, 1864, George M. Shearer military service record, RG94; return for March, 1864, Company F, 1st Wisconsin Cavalry, Knud Hanson military service record, RG94; Ray, *Diary of a Dead Man*, 196; Roe, *Melvin Memorial*, 97–98; *OR* series 1, 36(1):553; series 2, 6:1097–1106, and 7:153, 163–65, 385.

CHAPTER THREE

1. *OR* series 1, 32(3):719, and series 4, 3:347–49.

2. The composition of the first four regiments of Georgia Reserves is taken from "Compiled Service Records of Confederate Soldiers Who Served in Organizations from the State of Georgia" (M-266, reels 130–32, 157–59, 173–75, and 190–92), RG109; one of them testified to his equipment in *Trial*, 466.

3. Special Order 98, April 27, 1864, Box 1, Records Relating to Confederate Prisons and Union Prisoners, Entry 464, RG109; *OR* 7:120–21; Braxton Bragg to Cobb, May 3, 1864, Box 67, Cobb Papers, UG.

4. Kennedy diary (MHS), May 4, 1864; Whitten diary (SHSI), May 5 and 6, 1864; Adams diary (CnHS), Gibson diary (LC), and Kellogg diary (CnHS), May 5, 1864; Dougherty diary (ANHS), 33; *Trial*, 62, 371, 457, 507; Root diary (HMBL), May 13, 1864; Forbes, *Diary*, 16; Danker, "Shatzell Diary," 112–13; *OR* 7:137. Sergeant Forbes's posthumously published diary (which was apparently edited) mentioned nearly a hundred men wearing a ball and chain, but after most of the prison had been evacuated Captain Wirz turned over only seven sets to be forwarded to Millen, where most of the inmates had been taken (Wirz to "Colonel" [Henry Forno?], November 9, 1864, Letters Sent, Andersonville Prison, Georgia, May, 1864–March, 1865, RG109). One Illinois private expressed revulsion at witnessing the irons applied to arms and legs of recaptured Southern prisoners at Rock Island: see "Jamey," 133rd Illinois, to unidentified addressee, June 14, 1864, USAMHI.

5. Howell Cobb to Alexander Persons, May 9 and 16, 1864, and Lamar Cobb to Persons, May 30, 1864, all in Box 39, Cobb-Erwin-Lamar Papers, UG; *OR* series 1, 36(2):1011, and 38(4):704; *Trial,* 354, 432; Adams and Kellogg diaries, May 14, 1864; Lucius Gartrell to Howell Cobb, May 11 and 23, 1864, Box 67, Cobb Papers.

6. *Trial,* 62, 78, 149, 254; Kellogg diary, May 15, 1864; Helmreich, "Lee Diary," 17.

7. *Trial,* 114, 137, 711–12; Charles Hancock's receipt of payment for printing the prison rules, dated May 16, 1864, Box 18, Tabular Statements, Entry 208, RG109.

8. *Trial,* 147, 297–98, 373, 516, 711. The U.S. War Department confiscated a big LeMat revolver that allegedly belonged to Wirz, and at least one government witness obligingly testified that Wirz used such a weapon, but even if he did own a LeMat it seems unlikely he would have routinely carried so heavy a piece of armament. Guscetti, the Italian clerk in Wirz's office, testified to the unserviceable revolvers (*Trial,* 519–20), and late in the war Wirz returned them to the Macon quartermaster, describing the same defects named by the clerk: see Wirz to "C. Storekeeper," undated (but March, 1865), Letters Sent, Andersonville Prison, Georgia, May, 1864–March, 1865, RG109.

9. *Trial,* 113, 114, 149, 373, 711; Whitten diary, May 15, 1864. The shooting of "Chickamauga" was the best-remembered incident at the Andersonville dead line. A score of witnesses gave conflicting accounts of it at the Wirz trial, and an entire book has been devoted to it. In that book (Bullard, *Over the Deadline,* 16–17), Private James Kirkpatrick of the 57th Georgia is said to have killed the prisoner. Though a James Kirkpatrick did serve in the 57th Georgia, that regiment was probably on its way to the Army of Tennessee when Herburt was shot, and Kirkpatrick had deserted from it in March or April, never to return: see muster roll memoranda of Company K, 57th Georgia, in James Kirkpatrick's military service record, "Compiled Service Records of Confederate Soldiers Who Served in Organizations from the State of Georgia" (M-266, reel 537), RG109. When it is remembered at all, Herburt's name is recalled as Hubbard, Hulburt, or Hurlbut; he appears on the *Atwater Report,* 6, as D. Hurlburt, and on Captain Moore's list (*The Martyrs,* 102) as D. Hurbert.

10. Affidavit of John P. Chowning, May 4, 1865, and prison memorandum, Thomas W. Herburt military service record, RG94; Register of Federal Prisoners Admitted to the Hospital at Andersonville, Georgia, Entry 113, RG249, 46.

11. "A Letter from Captain Wirz to General Wright," 7; *OR* 7:138–39, 170–71, 386–87, and 8:603–4; Eliot, "Civil War Diary," 7; Bearss, "Historic Resource Study and Base Map," UG.

12. Aldrich diary (DC) and Kennedy diary, May 21, 1864; Gibson diary, May 22, 1864.

13. Danker, "Shatzell Diary," 92; Whitten diary, May 20–26, 1864; Smith, "Lyth Diary," 20; Consolidated Morning Reports, Entry 111, RG249.

14. Gibson and Kellogg diaries, May 22, 1864; Hammer, *James Diary*, 81–82. In his diary entry of September 3, 1864 (USAMHI), James Bradd mentions spending ten cents for a shave and a haircut.

15. Gibson diary, May 27, 1864; Bailey, *Diary*, 69; Forbes, *Diary*, 12; Danker, "Shatzell Diary," 94–95. Shatzell thought the guard had wounded one of the combatants, but no prisoners were treated for gunshot wounds between May 24 and May 30 (Register of Federal Prisoners Admitted to the Hospital at Andersonville, Georgia, Entry 113, RG249).

16. Casualty sheet, regimental returns (88th Pennsylvania), final statement, memoranda from prisoner-of-war records, and Dewitt C. Petus to "Major Constable," January 22, 1863, William Collins military service record, RG94.

17. Muster and descriptive roll dated August 27, 1863, muster roll of Company F, 76th New York, September and October, 1863, and prisoner-of-war memoranda, John Sullivan military service record, RG94; prisoner-of-war memoranda, William Collins military service record, RG94.

18. Sarsfield's name appears on an undated roll of substitutes sent to the 140th New York, with his date of enlistment inadvertently recorded as September 17, "1864"; he also turns up on a similar roll for the 52nd New York, having enlisted in that body on September 1, 1863. These two are both described as Irish-born shoemakers, aged twenty-two, five feet, three and one-half inches tall, and they are obviously the same man. Another John Sarsfield who served in the 94th New York from 1861 until 1863 is evidently someone else. The Andersonville hospital register (Entry 113, RG249) lists the raider merely as "J. Sarsfield, 140th N.Y."

19. Muster rolls of the 5th Rhode Island Heavy Artillery and substitute enrollment certificate, Charles F. Curtis military service record, RG94; muster and descriptive roll of substitutes and drafted men, September 16, 1863, muster roll of Company E, 83rd Pennsylvania for September and October, 1863, and memoranda from prisoner-of-war records, Patrick Delany military service record, RG94.

20. *OR* 7:438; Eighth U.S. Census, Fulton County, Ga. (M-653, reel 122: 753), RG29; muster roll of Company D, 2nd Georgia Reserves, Thomas C. Jackson military service record, "Compiled Service Records of Confederate Soldiers Who Served in Organizations from the State of Georgia" (M-266, reel 158), RG109; Thomas C. Jackson to Josie Jackson, May 13, 1864, Jackson Letters, WRHS; Dougherty diary, 25.

21. *Sumter Republican*, May 21, 1864; *OR* 7:548–49; Cobb to Furlow, May 26, 1864, Box 39, Cobb-Erwin-Lamar Papers; *CMH* 7:667–68.

22. *Macon Daily Telegraph*, May 21, 1864; *OR* 7:167–69.

23. *OR* 7:168.

24. Gibson diary, May 25, 1864; Kellogg diary, May 25–26, 1864; Helmreich, "Lee Diary," 18; Crosby diary (VHS) and Keys diary (RU), May 26, 1864; Forbes, *Diary*, 12. Colonel Persons told the Wirz tribunal he "did not go out" for the attempted escape (*Trial*, 457); since the entire garrison fell out, Colonel Persons must have still been absent.

25. Crosby, Gibson, Kellogg, Kennedy, Keys, and Whitten diaries, May 27, 1864; Forbes, *Diary*, 12–13; Helmreich, "Lee Diary," 18; Danker, "Shatzell Diary," 95; Chapin letter (Chapin's prison diary, posthumously transcribed in a long letter from his mother [VHS], May 27, 1864); *Sumter Republican*, May 28, 1864. This was the same day the raiders attacked the new men near the dead line, which may explain why the doubly cautious sentry fired into the melee.

26. *Sumter Republican*, May 28, 1864.

27. Whitten diary, May 28–31, 1864; Gibson diary, May 28, 29, 1864; Danker, "Shatzell Diary," 95; Forbes, *Diary*, 13; Consolidated Morning Reports, Entry 111, RG249. Forbes and Shatzell both mentioned the artillery fire, but the nearest guns in action at 4:00 A.M. on May 28 would have been a few near Dallas, over a hundred miles due north.

28. Roe, *Melvin Memorial*, 98–104; Shaw diary (USAMHI), May 18, 1864. On March 27, 1864, Wirz signed a receipt for money belonging to several prisoners, heading it "Camp Winder, Ga" (Confederate States Army Archives Miscellany, DU); on March 15, 1864, Dick Winder had also dated a letter at "Camp Winder" (*OR* 6:1054), which perhaps indicates an early intention to change the designation of the post. According to Eugene Forbes (*Diary*, 14), the sinks were constructed at the end of May, at the same time the top of the stockade was being clamped.

29. Roe, *Melvin Memorial*, 104; *Atwater Report*, 18–23.

30. Forbes, *Diary*, 19–23; Danker, "Shatzell Diary," 92–104; Kennedy diary, May 27–June 22, 1864.

31. Kennedy diary, June 1, 3, 6, and 14, 1864; Gibson diary, June 3, 1864; Danker, "Shatzell Diary," 97, 101; Bailey, *Diary*, 70–72; Basile, *Stearns Diary*, 64, 66; Hammer, *James Diary*, 80–81; Burdick diary (SHSW), June 1, 1864; Adams diary, June 1 and 6, 1864.

32. Forbes, *Diary*, 14, 18; Basile, *Stearns Diary*, 64, 66; Danker, "Shatzell Diary," 97; Coulter, "Starr Diary," 185–86; Roe, *Melvin Memorial*, 106, 109; Gibson diary, June 4, 25, 1864; Kellogg diary, May 31, 1864.

33. Basile, *Stearns Diary*, 63, 68; Crosby diary, May 30 and 31, 1864; Forbes, *Diary*, 23; Coulter, "Starr Diary," 185–87; Gibson diary, May 30, June 25, 1864; Consolidated Morning Reports, Entry 111, RG249; Dougherty diary, 49–50; Special Order 21, Box 1, Records Relating to Confederate Prisons and Union Prisoners, Entry 464, RG109; Knight diary (USAMHI), June 19, 1864; Helmreich, "Lee Diary," 18–20.

34. Dougherty diary, 59; Sparrow diary (UV), July 18, 1864; Eliot, "Civil War Diary," 8; Coulter, "Starr Diary," 184–85; Keys diary, July 30, 1864.

35. *Trial*, 369, 371; Whitten diary, May 19, 1864; *Sumter Republican*, July 1, 1864; Crosby diary, June 4, 1864.

36. *Trial*, 487, 687; Danker, "Shatzell Diary," 97–98; Forbes, *Diary*, 15, 16, 22; Trelease, "Letter from a Soldier"; Roe, *Melvin Memorial*, 112, 121; Gibson diary, June 5 and 6, 1864; Chapin letter (August 1, 1864); Vance diary (OHS), July 6, 1864. The Crosby diary entries of July 23 and 31, 1864, recount the construction—and ultimate failure—of one earthen oven.

37. *OR* 7:207; *Trial*, 458, 474; Wirz's voucher for 450 buckets, dated June 11, 1864, Box 18, Tabular Statements, Entry 208, RG109; Helmreich, "Lee Diary," 19.

38. Roe, *Melvin Memorial*, 104; S. J. Gibson to Rachel A. Gibson, June 12, 1864, LC; W. R. Worth to "Dear Father," July 8, 1864, Bringier Papers, LSU; Burdick diary, June 24, 1864; Whitten diary, June 23, 1864; Henry H. Lewis to Erasmus Lewis, July 14, 1864, VHS. Several letters from Wirz, representing the forwarding of thousands of prisoners' letters, are in Letters Sent, Andersonville Prison, Georgia, May, 1864–March, 1865, RG109. Later in the life of the prison, letter writers dared be more critical: see, for instance, Washington Keys Latimer to "Dear Father," November 14, 1864, MHS, and James T. Harnit to Albert R. Kelly, November 15, 1864, OHS.

39. Roe, *Melvin Memorial*, 104; S. J. Gibson to Rachel A. Gibson; Forbes, *Diary*, 12, 18, 20; Dennison, *Diary*, 59; Bailey, *Diary*, 79; *Trial*, 489–90.

40. *Trial*, 500, 536, 547, 586; *OR* 8:603; Kellogg diary, July 30, 1864; Forbes, *Diary*, 16.

41. Consolidated Morning Reports, Entry 111, RG249; Colvin notebook (CHS), April 30 and May 31, 1864; Cobb to Alexander Persons, May 9, 1864, Box 39, Cobb-Erwin-Lamar Papers; *OR* 7:167.

42. *Trial*, 456; Cobb to Furlow, May 26, 1864, and Cobb to Persons, June 9, 1864, Box 39, Cobb-Erwin-Lamar Papers; Colvin notebook, May 31, 1864; Kellogg diary, May 23, 1864; Helmreich, "Lee Diary," 18.

43. Ray, *Diary of a Dead Man*, 196.

44. *OR* series 1, 36(1):375–76; muster rolls of Company C, 5th New Hampshire, May–June and November–December, 1864, and memoranda from prisoner-of-war records, Hiram Jepperson pension application, claim #1138032, RG15.

45. Ray, *Diary of a Dead Man*, 137; memoranda from prisoner-of-war records, Hiram Jepperson pension application, claim #1138032, RG15, and Thomas Genzardi military service record, RG94.

46. *OR* 7:170; Cobb to Samuel Cooper, May 2, 1864, Box 39, Cobb-Erwin-Lamar Papers; Cobb and William Browne to Jefferson Davis, June 2, 1864,

"Letters and Telegrams Sent by the Confederate Adjutant General and Inspector General" (M-627, reel 5:366), RG109.

47. Cooper to Winder, June 3 and 6, 1864, "Letters and Telegrams Sent by the Confederate Adjutant and Inspector General" (M-627, reel 5:372), RG109; W. S. Winder to "Friend George," June 6, 1864, CHS.

48. Forbes, *Diary*, 19; *Sumter Republican*, June 17, 1864; *OR* 7:377; W. S. Winder to "Friend George," June 6, 1864, CHS.

49. *OR* 7:378, 381; Cooper to Winder, June 23, 1864, Box 1, Records Relating to Confederate Prisons and Union Prisoners, Entry 464, RG109; Smith, "Lyth Diary," 20.

50. *OR* 7:378, 381, 396; Dennison, *Diary*, 39; Consolidated Morning Reports, Entry 111, RG249.

51. Consolidated Morning Reports, Entry 111, RG249; *OR* 7:386–87; Forbes, *Diary*, 13, 19; Danker, "Shatzell Diary," 101; Whitten diary, June 16, 1864; *Trial*, 55, 105.

52. *Atwater Report*, iii; Register of Federal Prisoners Admitted to the Hospital at Andersonville, Georgia, Entry 113, RG249, 128; Whitney diary (DC), June 29, 1864. Unlike *The Martyrs*, which was compiled by Captain James Moore for the quartermaster general, Atwater's list contains the causes of death. Generalizations about mortality have been based on both Atwater's published list and on the manuscript hospital register, in the National Archives.

53. *OR* 7:386, 392, 410; Winder to Cooper, June 21, 1864, and Cooper to Winder, June 23, 1864, Box 1, Records Relating to Confederate Prisons and Union Prisoners, Entry 464, RG109; Cooper to Winder, June 21, 23, and July 6, 1864, "Letters and Telegrams Sent by the Confederate Adjutant and Inspector General" (M-627, reel 5:415, 419, 450), RG109; James Seddon to Howell Cobb, May 20, 1864, Box 67, Cobb Papers.

54. *Sumter Republican*, June 24 and July 1, 1864; Knight diary, June 29, 1864; Helmreich, "Lee Diary," 20; Forbes, *Diary*, 34; Coulter, "Starr Diary," 187; Styple and Fitzpatrick, *Hopkins Diary*, 104; *OR* 7:546–47.

55. Myers, *Children of Pride*, 1190, 1204; *OR* 7:393; Forbes, *Diary*, 21, 22; Smith, "Lyth Dairy," 20; Danker, "Shatzell Diary," 104; Coulter, "Starr Diary," 187; Roe, *Melvin Memorial*, 111; Basile, *Stearns Diary*, 67; Whitten and Vance diaries, June 21, 1864; Gibson diary, June 21, 22, 1864; Kennedy diary, June 22, 1864. The drillmaster was Lieutenant James Dunwoody Jones. Darius Starr identified the wounded man as a member of the 118th Pennsylvania, but a search of the various death registers shows no member of that regiment who died between June 10 and July 2, nor does any prisoner seem to have died of wounds in June except Ernst Damkoehler of the 26th Wisconsin, who succumbed June 26 to wounds received at Resaca (memoranda from prisoner-of-war records, Ernst Damkoehler military service record, RG94).

56. *OR* 7:403-4; muster rolls of Company F, 1st Georgia Reserves, for April 26–August 1 and September 1–October 31, 1864, J. E. Anderson military service record, "Compiled Service Records of Confederate Soldiers Who Served in Organizations from the State of Georgia" (M-266, reel 130), RG109. The original of Anderson's letter is preserved in the manuscript proceedings of the Henry Wirz tribunal, Box 1269, MM2975, RG153.

57. Special Order 136, June 11, 1864, Box 1, Records Relating to Confederate Prisons and Union Prisoners, Entry 464, RG109; Samuel Cooper to John H. Winder, July 13, 1864, "Letters and Telegrams Sent by the Confederate Adjutant and Inspector General" (M-627, reel 5:469), RG109.

58. Forbes, *Diary*, 31; *Cattaraugus Freeman*, August 18, 1864.

59. Forbes, *Diary*, 22, 23, 31; *Trial*, 64; *OR* 7:411.

60. Colvin notebook, May 31, 1864; Gibson diary, May 21 and June 19, 1864; Forbes, *Diary*, 21; Smith, "Lyth Diary," 20; *Trial*, 176, 540, 604. Private William Erick, Company H, 9th Illinois, is listed as having died "in quarters" on June 20 of asphyxia (Register of Federal Prisoners Admitted to the Hospital at Andersonville, Georgia, Entry 113, RG249, 82).

61. *Trial*, 186-87, 515, 540, 558, 604; Kellogg diary, May 31, June 9, 10, 1864.

62. *Trial*, 23, 26, 452, 485, 543; muster roll of Company G, 1st Georgia Reserves, April 28–August 1, 1864, Edward C. Turner military service record, "Compiled Service Records of Confederate Soldiers Who Served in Organizations from the State of Georgia" (M-266, reel 132), RG109; *Daily Sun*, March 4, 1864; vouchers for "Driscoll" and Turner through September 15, 1864, and quarterly abstract of expenditures, September 30, 1864, Box 18, Tabular Statements, Entry 208, RG109. B. Driskill and T. Driskill, both of Company G, 3rd Georgia Reserves, served on detached duty under Captain Wirz that summer; Turner's assistant was one of these two, and both may have worked with him: see their military service records, "Compiled Service Records of Confederate Soldiers Who Served in Organizations from the State of Georgia" (M-266, reel 173), RG109. The Consolidated Morning Reports (Entry 111, RG249) indicate that forty-seven men escaped in June, while forty-four were recaptured. Thirty-five of those escapes occurred between June 14 and 21.

63. Consolidated Morning Reports, Entry 111, RG249; *OR* 7:381; Whitten diary, June 19, 21, and 24, 1864; Danker, "Shatzell Diary," 104-5; Kennedy diary, June 27, 1864; Keys diary, June 17, 1864; Forbes, *Diary*, 24; Basile, *Stearns Diary*, 67.

64. *Sumter Republican*, May 6, 1864; Gibson diary, May 4, 5, and 10, 1864; Kellogg diary, May 3, 1864; Bradd diary, August 3–September 5, 1864; *OR* 8:599-600; Whitney diary, May 20, 1864; *Trial*, 622. Eugene Forbes's mess did not run out of soap until June 1 (*Diary*, 15). David Kennedy also used the

analogy of rotten sheep in his diary entry of July 12, as did James Dennison on August 9 (*Diary*, 58) and Amos Yeakle in his of September 23 (ANHS).

65. Burdick diary, June 13, July 4 and 7, 1864; Foust diary (ANHS), June 22, 1864; Forbes, *Diary*, 14; Roe, *Melvin Memorial*, 105, 110; Keys diary, June 18, 20, and August 1, 1864; Adams diary, July 2 and 7, 1864; Converse diary (KSHS), July 7, 1864; Kellogg diary, May 8, 19, and 27, 1864.

66. Keys diary, June 10, 11, and 28, 1864; Register of Federal Prisoners Admitted to the Hospital at Andersonville, Georgia, Entry 113, RG249, 80−82; *OR* 7:558; Roe, *Melvin Memorial*, 122.

CHAPTER FOUR

1. *Official Records of the Union and Confederate Navies*, series 1, 15:474−506, and series 2, 1:237.

2. Ibid., series 1, 15:482; muster roll of the U.S.S. *Water Witch*, October 3, 1863, RG24; Forbes, *Diary*, 17; Hammer, *James Diary*, 81. Since the only crewmen on duty were the four seamen on watch and the engine crew, and all on watch were killed or wounded, it must be assumed that Seaman Muir was off duty and (after one o'clock in the morning) in his hammock.

3. Keys diary (RU), June 29, 1864; Forbes, *Diary*, 24; Kellogg diary (CnHS), May 10, 1864.

4. Danker, "Shatzell Diary," 98; Kellogg diary, May 6, 14, 22, 27, and June 21, 1864; Crosby diary (VHS), June 26, 1864; Forbes, *Diary*, 18−20, 22; Basile, *Stearns Diary*, 66.

5. Kennedy diary (MHS), June 13, 1864; Forbes, *Diary*, 21, 24; Gibson diary (LC), June 18, 1864; *New York Times*, December 11, 1864.

6. Eighth U.S. Census, McLean County, Ill. (M-653, reel 204:658), RG29; muster-in roll of Company M, 16th Illinois Cavalry, Leroy L. Key military service record, RG94; discharge certificate dated January 30, 1863, and declaration of Amanda Jackson Key, January 22, 1881, widow's application #285269 and minor's certificate of pension #372853, RG15.

7. *New York Times*, December 11, 1864. McElroy gives a much more embellished version of this story (*Andersonville*, 228−29).

8. Forbes, *Diary*, 25; Kellogg and Keys diaries, June 29, 1864; Knight diary (USAMHI), June 30, 1864.

9. Whitten diary (SHSI), June 30, 1864; Adams diary (CnHS), Keys diary, and Vance diary (OHS), June 29, 1864; Forbes, *Diary*, 25−26.

10. Hoster diary (ANHS), June 29, 1864; *Trial*, 437; Danker, "Shatzell Diary," 106; *OR* 7:426. McElroy (*Andersonville*, 227) says Sergeant Key was as-

sisted by one "Limber Jim," of the 67th Illinois, and other sources identify him as Jim Laughlin, but "Limber Jim" was almost certainly Key's own nickname. In his diary for June 30, 1864, Robert Kellogg identifies "Limber Jim" as the chief of the police, as does the generally unreliable Ransom, who noted that "Limber Jim" died in the winter of 1880 after fifteen years of failing health (*Diary*, 106, 246): Leroy Key died in the winter of 1880, after fifteen years of failing health. While "Limber Jim" might have been an unusual sobriquet for anyone else, it would not have been uncommon for a wagonmaker, and Key had been a wagonmaker. No James Laughlin ever served in the 67th Illinois, either, nor did any of the James Laughlins who did enlist from Illinois ever serve time at Andersonville. In corroboration, one Pennsylvania cavalryman who was imprisoned at Andersonville remembered after the war—contrary to the myth propagated by McElroy—that Key was also known as "Limber Jim" (Bachman memoir, RNBP, 59).

11. Forbes, *Diary*, 25; Root diary (HMBL), and Crosby, Hoster, and Kellogg diaries, June 29, 1864; Danker, "Shatzell Diary," 106; "Diary of a Prisoner," 1; Colvin notebook (CHS), June 30, 1864; *Trial*, 438.

12. Forbes, *Diary*, 25–26; Gibson diary, June 30, 1864; Hammer, *James Diary*, 83–84; Dennison, *Diary*, 42–43; Converse diary (KSHS) and Foust diary (ANHS), June 29, 1864 (Foust also recorded having received an extremely large ration on June 28). McElroy (*Andersonville*, 229–32) put too much emphasis on the part played by the regulators in bringing down the raiders, describing a spectacular pitched battle between the two forces—completely forgetting the guard detail that began the purge and backed up the prisoners' police force. In his 1879 account McElroy mistakenly dated the incident July 3; supposedly writing from original diaries two years later, John Ransom copied both that error and the exaggerated story of the battle royal (*Diary*, 105–6).

13. Foust and Vance diaries, June 30, 1864; "Diary of a Prisoner," 1; *Trial*, 271.

14. Forbes, *Diary*, 26; Danker, "Shatzell Diary," 107; Burdick diary (SHSW), June 30, 1864; *Trial*, 437–38, 697.

15. *New York Times*, December 11, 1864; *Trial*, 697; "Diary of a Prisoner," 1; Converse, Crosby, Kellogg, and Vance diaries, June 30, 1864. In April of 1899 the remains of two men were recovered from the stockade grounds (Burial Register of Andersonville [ANHS], 417), but they were probably the victims of the mid-winter cave-in of a burrow. Captain Moore, who said his burial detail found no graves inside the prison, was not allowed to finish a remark he made at Henry Wirz's trial, in which he implied that at least one man had already been reinterred from within the stockade. Another witness at the same trial said two men had been buried inside the stockade, one of them near the raiders' tent site: one of those two appears to have been Corporal Henry Brown, 41st Ohio, whose entry in the hospital register includes the notation that he was "buried in the stockade."

16. *Trial*, 438, 697. The Andersonville hospital register lists all the condemned correctly except Delany, whose first initial is mistakenly recorded as "J.," and Curtis, who gave his name as Seaman W. R. Rickson of the U.S. Navy. For some reason the headstone for "Rickson" at Andersonville National Cemetery is placed over Sullivan's grave, instead of Curtis's, and Curtis has a stone of his own. See Register of Federal Prisoners Admitted to the Hospital at Andersonville, Georgia, Entry 113, RG249, 110.

17. *Trial*, 428, 438.

18. Consolidated Morning Reports, Entry 111, RG249. One inspector judged the swamp to be over three acres in area (*OR* 7:546). Averaging the depth of the dead line at seventeen feet results in a deduction of nearly two more acres; the original enclosure was about sixteen and one-half acres in area.

19. Converse diary, June 20, 21, 1864; Crosby diary, June 21, 1864; Kellogg diary, July 1, 1864; "Diary of a Prisoner," 1.

20. Forbes, *Diary*, 26; Hunter, "Ferguson Diaries," 216; Converse, Kellogg, and Keys diaries, July 1, 1864; Foust diary, June 29 and July 1, 1864; Coulter, "Starr Diary," 187–88; Hammer, *James Diary*, 86.

21. Converse and Keys diaries, July 1, 1864; Coulter, "Starr Diary," 188; Forbes, *Diary*, 26.

22. *Trial*, 279, 572; Foust and Keys diaries, July 1, 1864.

23. Forbes, *Diary*, 27; Burdick diary, July 2, 1864; Foust diary, June 11, 12, and July 3, 1864; Vance diary, July 4, 1864; Kellogg diary, July 9, 1864; Danker, "Shatzell Diary," 108–9.

24. Foust diary, July 1, 1864; Kellogg diary, July 2, 1864; Forbes, *Diary*, 26; Hammer, *James Diary*, 88; Dennison, *Diary*, 45; Dougherty diary (ANHS), 61; Danker, "Shatzell Diary," 108; Helmreich, "Lee Diary," 20; Colvin notebook, "June 30," 1864. Colvin's notes were dated at the end of each month, and he may have spent several days jotting them down. Some of his anachronisms are more difficult to explain, however. For instance, on March 31, 1864, he noted that the first man to die at Andersonville was Jacob Swarner, of the 2nd New York Cavalry. The first victim was actually that man's brother, Adam Swarner of the same regiment, and although Jacob did eventually die there he was still alive when Colvin supposedly made that curious entry. Colvin also pointedly avoided the common criticism of Abraham Lincoln over the refusal to exchange prisoners, instead directing his anger at Grant, whom no other prisoner blames in an original diary: that would suggest that at least some of the notes were made subsequent to Lincoln's virtual canonization on April 15, 1865, although the entries appear in a contemporary—albeit undated—diary.

25. *OR* 7:480; Kellogg diary, August 13, 1864.

26. Kellogg diary, June 27 and 28, 1864.

27. *Trial*, 62, 652.

28. *Trial*, 505, 508; Adams, Foust, Keys, and Kellogg diaries, July 23, 1864; "Diary of a Prisoner," 2.

29. *Trial*, 505-6; Kellogg and Keys diaries, July 3 and 4, 1864; Adams diary, July 3, 1864; Gibson and Knight diaries, July 4, 1864; Forbes, *Diary*, 27; Coulter, "Starr Diary," 188; "Diary of a Prisoner," 2; Basile, *Stearns Diary*, 69; Dennison, *Diary*, 45; Burdick diary, July 2-4, 1864; Danker, "Shatzell Diary," 108.

30. Muster and descriptive roll, casualty sheet, and prisoner-of-war memorandum, James Babb military service record, RG94; *Laconia Democrat*, October 2, 30, and November 6, 1863; Roe, *Melvin Memorial*, 115; Dennison, *Diary*, 45; Dougherty diary, 61-62; Hoster diary, July 4, 1864. Forbes (*Diary*, 27) claims two men were shot between July 2 and July 4, as does David Kennedy (diary, July 4, 1864), and Forbes insists the man shot July 2 died the next day, but no Andersonville prisoner's death is attributed to wounds between June 26 and July 13. Two men admitted for wounds on July 3 died, but both had arrived wounded from the Shenandoah Valley the day before: Thomas Johns, a fifty-two-year-old Welshman captured at New Market on May 15, and William Fowkes, a West Virginian taken in the retreat from Lynchburg. Johns died July 27 and Fowkes August 15. Babb, however, had been a prisoner for over four months and ought to have either recovered or died from his Olustee knee wound by now; this new injury—also in the knee, by Hoster's account—killed him on August 7. The hospital clerk erroneously recorded him as a member of the 115th New York, another regiment engaged at Olustee, and his service record refers to confusion with "James Bolt, 115th New York," but no such man existed. The error may have resulted from an inability to understand "Babb's" English. See Register of Federal Prisoners Admitted to the Hospital at Andersonville, Georgia, Entry 113, RG249, 98.

31. Burdick diary, July 4, 1864; Coulter, "Starr Diary," 108.

32. Adams, Kellogg, Kennedy, Keys, and Whitten diaries, July 4, 1864; Coulter, "Starr Diary," 108; Forbes, *Diary*, 27; Basile, *Stearns Diary*, 69; Dennison, *Diary*, 45.

33. Converse, Gibson, and Keys diaries, July 4, 1864; *Trial*, 77, 79, 136, 165, 170, 171. Some of the witnesses may have referred to their diaries for the number of foodless days, only to have been misled by their own notations. Albert Shatzell of the 1st Vermont Cavalry, for instance, recorded on July 5 that he drew his first rations in three days at 8:00 A.M. (Danker, "Shatzell Diary," 109). No rations were withheld the afternoon of July 2, so he must have drawn some then, and his morning issue of July 5 consisted of his July 4 allotment, twelve hours late. Presumably he received another ration that evening, so although he was given no food for sixty hours he missed only one day's supply. It is noteworthy, too, that Shatzell mentioned eating "a little grub" on July 3, the fasting day.

34. Knight diary, July 2, 1864; Kellogg diary, July 3, 1864; *Sumter Republican*, July 1, 1864. Winder's desire to keep "ten" days' rations on hand (*OR* 7:499) was

so clearly impossible to satisfy as to raise the question of an error in transcription: "two" days' rations would have been more reasonable, and poor penmanship could render the two words indistinguishable.

35. *Sumter Republican,* July 9, 1864; Winder to Cooper, July 25, 1864, Box 1, Records Relating to Confederate Prisons and Union Prisoners, Entry 464, RG109 (this correspondence published in *OR* 7:499).

36. *Trial,* 111, 176, 209; George Brown to "Dear Sister," June 28, 1864, Everett Papers, DU; Crosby diary, June 4, 1864; *Sumter Republican,* July 23, 1864.

37. *Trial,* 558, 572–73, 684–85; Keys diary, August 25, 1864. George Fechnor's name does not appear on the 1850 census of Ohio, where he said he lived then, though the rest of the family he described is on the Cincinnati census: Seventh U.S. Census, Hamilton County, Ohio (M-432, reel 690:980), RG29.

38. *Trial,* 560–61, 566, 572–73; Root diary, July 15, 1864.

39. *Trial,* 561; Gibson diary, June 21, 1864; Forbes, *Diary,* 11, 22, 23, 35; "Diary of a Prisoner," 3; Burdick diary, September 3, 1864; Peabody diary (USAMHI), August 14, 1864.

40. Kellogg diary, June 27, 1864; *Melvin Memorial,* 106, 112.

41. Forbes, *Diary,* 12, 18–19, 23, 37; *Trial,* 559.

42. *Trial,* 574. At the end of August one prisoner noted that Selman's business had dropped off sharply (Styple and Fitzpatrick, *Hopkins Diary,* 126). By the end of September Mr. Selman closed up shop and went home (*OR* 7:1041), and within a few months Captain Wirz observed that Selman's replacement could squeeze no greenbacks out of the prisoners at all, especially at the government rate of exchange (Wirz to G. W. McPhail, February 26, 1865, Letters Sent, Andersonville Prison, Georgia, May, 1864–March, 1865, RG109).

43. Bradd diary (USAMHI), September 3, 1864; Whitten diary, August 6, 1864; Styple and Fitzpatrick, *Hopkins Diary,* 93, 103; *Trial,* 560, 574–75.

44. Colvin notebook, May 31, 1864.

45. *Sumter Republican,* April 1, 1864; *Trial,* 290, 513, 522, 550; Foust diary, June 28, 1864; *OR* 7:622; *New York Times,* August 30, 1864. Many Union regiments that provided Andersonville with reluctant representatives—the 9th Ohio and 26th Wisconsin, for instance—were so thoroughly German that their histories were compiled and published in that language.

46. Keys diary, May 27, 1864; statement of Surgeon E. D. Eilund regarding Dr. A. W. Barrows, September 7, 1864, roll 940, Miscellaneous Rolls, Entry 107, RG249; George Gibbs to Samuel Cooper, June 5, 1864, with J. A. Campbell's endorsement of July 26, 1864, Box 1, Records Relating to Confederate Prisons and Union Prisoners, Entry 464, RG109; Futch, "Burdick Diary," 290; Kellogg diary, May 16 and June 2, 1864; Danker, "Shatzell Diary," 121; *Atwater Report,* 73–74; *Trial,* 696. One of the women was Mrs. Herbert Hunt, whose husband captained a vessel owned by the government wood contractor, John Morris

(Wirz to "Provost Marshal, Augusta, Ga.," May 19, 1864, Letters Sent, Andersonville Prison, Georgia, May, 1864–March, 1865, RG109); the other lady was the wife of J. W. Leonard of the 85th New York; he died at Andersonville September 16, 1864 (*Macon Daily Telegraph*, June 8, 1864; George Z. Pretz to "Provost Marshal, Augusta, Ga.," August 16, 1864, USAMHI; *The Martyrs*, 119).

47. Keys diary, May 24, 1864; Forbes, *Diary*, 19, 21, 36; Dougherty diary, 25; Baer diary (ANHS), August 6, 1864; Peabody diary, July 8, 1864; Thomas C. Jackson to Josie Jackson, May 13, 1864, Jackson Letters, WRHS; Gibson diary, July 14, 1864.

48. Roe, *Melvin Memorial*, 110, 119; Forbes, *Diary*, 12; Danker, "Shatzell Diary," 93; Peabody diary, June 7, 10, 26, 27, and September 1, 1864; Gibson diary, July 28 and August 12, 1864; Bailey, *Diary*, 82; Stephen, *Diary*, 27; Dennison, *Diary*, 60; Howard diary (VHS), August 16, 1864; Stone diary (USAMHI), July 29, 1864.

49. Kellogg diary, May 11, 1864; Hammer, *James Diary*, 86, 88; Gibson diary, June 26, July 8 and 9, and August 8, 1864; "Diary of a Prisoner," 2.

50. Foust diary, July 6, 1864; Converse diary, June 26, 1864; Forbes, *Diary*, 16; "Diary of a Prisoner," 3; Helmreich, "Lee Diary," 19–20; Gibson diary, June 8 and September 2, 1864; Kellogg diary, May 19 and August 25, 1864. The modern museum at Andersonville National Historic Site displays numerous delicate artifacts carved by prisoners.

51. Burdick diary, June 21 and August 21, 1864; Danker, "Shatzell Diary," 100; Keys diary, May 29, 1864; Roe, *Melvin Memorial*, 118.

52. Kellogg diary, May 9 and 26, 1864; Helmreich, "Lee Diary," 23; Forbes, *Diary*, 13, 23; Keys diary, June 24, 1864; Danker, "Shatzell Diary," 95; Gibson diary, May 18, 1864; Chapin letter ([VHS], July 4 and 5, 1864).

53. *Sumter Republican*, April 15, 1864; Forbes, *Diary*, 28, 31; Burdick diary, July 9, 1864; Adams and Foust diaries, July 17, 1864; Hunter, "Ferguson Diaries," 215; Gibson diary, July 18, 1864; Dennison, *Diary*, 50; Kellogg diary, July 28 and 31, 1864.

54. Helmreich, "Lee Diary," 22–23; Kellogg diary, July 5, 28, and 31, August 28 and 31, 1864, and January 1, 1865.

55. *Trial*, 287, 290, 293, 426, 430; Robbins, *Diary of Rev. H. Clavreul*, 8–12.

56. Forbes, *Diary*, 18; *Trial*, 290, 426–31; Kellogg diary, July 5, 1864. Kellogg expressed a wish that "clergymen of orthodox denominations" were as devoted and kind as Whelan. John McElroy, one of those who misunderstood that Whelan was the only minister who ever ventured into the prison, also confused him with Father Hamilton (*Andersonville*, 216). Father Whelan turned very ill in 1866, and died early in 1871. The only independent study of his life is Father Peter J. Meaney's "The Prison Ministry of Father Peter Whelan, Georgia Priest and Confederate Chaplain."

57. *Trial*, 428, 698; Forbes, *Diary*, 28. Henry Wirz's counsel tried to offer the higher-level approval of the raiders' sentences as mitigating evidence at his court-martial, but, like all information prejudicial to the government's case, it was not allowed.

58. Danker, "Shatzell Diary," 110–11; Hoster and Keys diaries, July 11, 1864; "Diary of a Prisoner," 3; Root diary, July 11, 1864; Hammer, *James Diary*, 88; *New York Times*, December 11, 1864.

59. *New York Times*, December 11, 1864; "Diary of a Prisoner," 3.

60. Whitten diary, July 11 and 17, 1864.

61. Consolidated Morning Reports, Entry 111, RG249; Foust diary, July 11, 1864.

62. Coulter, "Starr Diary," 188–89; Converse and Burdick diaries, July 11, 1864; Forbes, *Diary*, 29; *Trial*, 428.

63. *Trial*, 428; James Buckley diary (IIHS), and Hoster, Kellogg, and Whitten diaries, July 11, 1864; Forbes, *Diary*, 29; Danker, "Shatzell Diary," 111; Chapin letter (July 12, 1864).

64. Forbes, *Diary*, 29; James Buckley, Hoster, and Whitten diaries, July 11, 1864; Danker, "Shatzell Diary," 111; *New York Times*, December 11, 1864; *Trial*, 428. McElroy, Ransom, and others embellish all these last words—and the whole hanging episode, for that matter—but John Whitten said some of the condemned had something to say while others did not. Reliance upon the firsthand evidence of diaries and Father Whelan's testimony yields this account.

65. James Buckley, Burdick, Hoster, and Whitten diaries, July 11, 1864; Forbes, *Diary*, 29; Coulter, "Starr Diary," 189; Chapin letter (July 12, 1864); *New York Times*, December 11, 1864.

66. James Buckley and Stone diaries, July 11, 1864; Gibson, Kennedy, and Keys diaries, July 12, 1864; *Trial*, 428.

67. James Buckley diary, July 11, 1864; *New York Times*, December 11, 1864; Forbes, *Diary*, 29; Knight diary, July 12, 1864.

68. *New York Times*, December 11, 1864; *Trial*, 557–58, 606–7, 652, 684–85; Baer diary, August 9, 1864; Hunter, "Ferguson Diaries," 221. According to several former prisoners, one of the first men to succeed Sergeant Key as police chief was A. R. Hill of the 100th Ohio. First Sergeant Alfred R. Hill, Company F, 100th Ohio, was a prisoner at Andersonville throughout the summer of 1864. He was thirty years old, above average height at five feet, ten and three-quarter inches, and apparently in robust health, for (unlike most Andersonville prisoners) he returned to his regiment early in 1865 and fought in the final campaigns; such physical qualifications would have been necessary for any of the regulators, but especially for their chief.

69. Forbes, *Diary*, 31; Whitten diary, July 19, 1864.

70. "Diary of a Prisoner," 3; Forbes, *Diary*, 29; Dennison, *Diary*, 47, 50;

Vance and Knight diaries, July 13, 1864; Peabody diary, July 14, 1864; descriptive list of deserters and memorandum from prisoner-of-war records, Francis G. Devendorf military service record, RG94. Devendorf, who appears on the hospital register as "T. Denorf," was mistakenly diagnosed as having died of acute diarrhea (Register of Federal Prisoners Admitted to the Hospital at Andersonville, Georgia, Entry 113, RG249, 112), but Atwater recorded his cause of death as wounds (*Atwater Report*, 33).

71. Knight diary, July 14, 1864; Forbes, *Diary*, 30; Converse, Foust, Kellogg, and Keys diaries, July 14, 1864; *Trial*, 689. Forbes mentions Wirz having cited the expiring enlistments as the ulterior motive behind the Federal government's obstinacy, and Samuel J. Gibson's July 16 diary entry implies that Wirz referred to the difference over black prisoners, too.

72. Bailey, *Diary*, 75; Forbes, *Diary*, 30; Kellogg diary, July 14, 1864; *Savannah Daily Morning News*, July 26, 1864; Danker, "Shatzell Diary," 112.

73. Danker, "Shatzell Diary," 112-13; Crosby diary, July 16, 1864; Forbes, *Diary*, 31; Bailey, *Diary*, 75-76; Vance diary, July 17, 1864; Foust, Hoster, Keys, and Knight diaries, July 18, 1864; Helmreich, "Lee Diary," 21. Hoster's, Vance's, and Foust's diaries, as well as Colvin's notebook, all corroborate the 1887 recollection of Luther B. Harris (USAMHI) that the informer was tattooed by a sailor wielding needle and ink, rather than "branded," as Forbes and Keys recorded.

74. Forbes, *Diary*, 31.

75. Kennedy diary, May 9, 20, June 9, 24, and 25, 1864; Gibson diary, July 2 and 16, 1864; Howard diary, August 3 and September 2, 1864; Colvin notebook, "April 30," 1864; Keys diary, August 22, 29, 31, 1864. The morning report for August 29, the day on which Keys heard that 125 deaths had been recorded by 11:00 A.M., shows 105 deaths during the entire day (Consolidated Morning Reports, Entry 111, RG249).

76. Peabody diary, July 16, 1864; Whitten diary, June 20 and July 17, 1864; *OR* 8:603; Keys diary, September 1 and 4, 1864. On July 26 Samuel Melvin noted in his journal (Roe, *Melvin Memorial*, 123) "it is the duty of the Gov. to release me, and if they don't do something for me, I must try and do something for myself." His enlistment had run out three weeks before, and he was attempting to go outside on parole, which some prisoners considered treasonable. For other instances of prisoners' outrage with their government, see Anonymous diary (ANHS), August 15, 19, and 31, 1864; Crosby diary, July 23, 1864; Colvin notebook, April 30, 1864; and Stone diary, July 16 and August 8, 1864.

77. *Diary of Gideon Welles*, 2:169-70.

78. Forbes, *Diary*, 31; *Melvin Memorial*, 120; Keys diary, July 16, 19, 1864; Stone diary, July 19, 1864.

79. "Diary of a Prisoner," 3-4; *New York Times*, August 30, 1864; *Trial*, 691.

80. Joseph P. Brainerd epitaph, Greenwood Cemetery, Saint Albans, Vermont.

CHAPTER FIVE

1. *Georgia Journal and Messenger,* June 29, 1864; *Sumter Republican,* July 1 and 30, 1864; *CV* 21:84 (February, 1913) and 27:426 (November, 1919); *CMH* 7:668; *OR* series 1, 25(1):969, 27(2):583, and series 2, 7:552.

2. *OR* series 1, 38(2):904-9.

3. Cooper to John Winder, July 17, 1864, "Letters and Telegrams Sent by the Confederate Adjutant and Inspector General" (M-627, reel 5:474), RG109; R. B. Winder to E. Griswold, July 18, 1864, R. B. Winder Letterbook, RG153; Hood to Cobb, July 18, 1864, Box 67, Cobb Papers, UG; *OR* series 1, 52(2): 709-11, and series 4, 3:538, 542-43.

4. Converse diary (KSHS), Foust diary (ANHS), and Whitten diary (SHSI), July 19, 1864; Danker, "Shatzell Diary," 113; Roe, *Melvin Memorial,* 121; Futch, "Burdick Diary," 289.

5. *OR* 7:483; Foust diary, Pennington diary (ANHS), and Vance diary (OHS), July 19, 1864; Crosby diary (VHS), July 20, 1864; Bailey, *Diary,* 76; Forbes, *Diary,* 32; "Diary of a Prisoner," 4.

6. *OR* 7:590; Forbes, *Diary,* 32.

7. Kennedy diary (MHS), Stone diary (USAMHI), Vance, and Whitten diaries, July 20, 1864; Roe, *Melvin Memorial,* 121; Forbes, *Diary,* 32.

8. Forbes, *Diary,* 32; Danker, "Shatzell Diary," 113; *OR* 7:480; Knight diary (USAMHI), July 20, 1864; Stone diary, July 21, 1864; Consolidated Morning Reports, Entry 111, RG249.

9. Crosby diary, July 17, 18, and 20, 1864; Sparrow diary (UV), July 18, 1864; Forbes, *Diary,* 32; Kellogg diary (CnHS), Converse, and Kennedy diaries, July 21, 1864.

10. Lawton to Cobb, July 27, 1864, Box 67, Cobb Papers; *OR* series 2, 7:476, and series 4, 3:542; John H. Winder to Samuel Cooper, July 25, 1864, Box 1, Records Relating to Confederate Prisons and Union Prisoners, Entry 464, RG109; Destler, "Ross Diary," 235; Chadwick diary (MHS), July 26, 1864.

11. Danker, "Shatzell Diary," 114.

12. R. B. Winder to George W. Rice, July 20, 1864, and to F. W. Dillard, undated (but early August, 1864) and August 12, 1864, all in R. B. Winder Letterbook, RG153.

13. Knight diary, memorandum; *Trial,* 176-77, 280; Wirz to H. A. M. Henderson, June 5, 1864, and to J. W. Rhea, undated, Letters Sent, Andersonville

Prison, Georgia, May, 1864–March, 1865, RG109. Atwater's report inadvertently lists at least two white men, members of the 16th and 17th U.S. Infantry, as "negro" (71). One black soldier who claimed to have been whipped also exaggerated wildly about Confederate treatment of prisoners in general (*Trial*, 408–10), describing officers' wives gleefully burning prisoners' letters while Surgeon White boasted over drinks how many Yankees he had poisoned that day. Forbes mentioned a black from "the sailor crowd" who was whipped on July 18 (*Diary*, 31), and another of the imaginative witnesses at the Wirz trial identified that man as one Hawkins, 8th U.S. Colored Infantry (*Trial*, 174), claiming he took 250 lashes. Apparently the best-known black prisoner at Andersonville was Sergeant Isaac Hawkins, Company D, 54th Massachusetts, who served for a time on the burial detail (see Gardiner Tufts to Edwin M. Stanton, July 24, 1865, Consolidated Correspondence File, Entry 225, RG92). Not until the secretary of war ordered him to do so, in October of 1864, did Captain Wirz offer to release a pair of alleged slave brothers to their supposed Alabama owner if he could prove they were his (Wirz to S. S. Cooper, October 16, 1864, Letters Sent, Andersonville Prison, Georgia, May, 1864–March, 1865, RG109). "Proving" the case, in antebellum parlance, might have meant as little as signing an affidavit, since the alleged slaves' word was legally worthless. There is no evidence the Alabama man ever came for the pair, and the geographical origins of the Colored Troops represented at Andersonville would seem to preclude the attachment of any runaways from an Alabama plantation.

14. Knight diary, June 16–19 and July 4–21, 1864; Basile, *Stearns Diary*, 72, 81; Forbes, *Diary*, 33; Stone diary and Hoster diary (ANHS), July 22, 1864; Vance diary, July 23, 1864; *Trial*, 200; Register of Federal Prisoners Admitted to the Hospital at Andersonville, Georgia, Entry 113, RG249, 124–25.

15. Danker, "Shatzell Diary," 114; Kellogg diary, May 13, 23, July 6 and 30, 1864; Keys diary (RU), July 25 and 26, 1864; Forbes, *Diary*, 33–34; "Diary of a Prisoner," 5.

16. Keys diary, July 21, 25, and August 24, 1864; Chapin letter ([VHS], August 7 and 14, 1864); Forbes, *Diary*, 34.

17. Forbes diary (YUL), Hoster, Keys, and Sparrow diaries, July 27, 1864; Chapin letter (July 28, 1864); Danker, "Shatzell Diary," 115; Forbes, *Diary*, 34; Roe, *Melvin Memorial*, 124; "Diary of a Prisoner," 5; *Atwater Report*, 44–50. The hospital register shows no admissions for wounds on July 27, and the only man who died of wounds on that day was Thomas Johns, of the 54th Pennsylvania, who was hospitalized July 3 (see Register of Federal Prisoners Admitted to the Hospital at Andersonville, Georgia, Entry 113, RG249, 98, 129–30). The only unknown man who died July 27 was one who was buried July 28 (and who was consequently recorded as having died on that day), who lies in grave #4184. Captain Moore's 1865 quartermaster detail recorded grave #4184 as unknown

apparently because of inability to read the name, but Atwater lists it as containing the body of W. Urndragh, Company B, 4th Pennsylvania (*Atwater Report*, 59). That man is obviously William Unversagt (as he spelled it), Company B, 4th Pennsylvania Cavalry, who was captured near Warrenton on October 12, 1863. He had been treated for a touch of scurvy and diarrhea a couple of weeks before his death, and the hospital register records his death as due to that last ailment, but by early 1865 an exchanged prisoner reported to his company commander that Unversagt died of wounds (memorandum from prisoner-of-war records and muster rolls of Company B, 4th Pennsylvania Cavalry, September and October, 1863, and January and February, 1865, William "Unverzhdt" military service record, RG94). Eugene Forbes believed the man shot on July 27 was one of the newcomers, but none of those men appears to have died on either that date or the next.

18. Danker, "Shatzell Diary," 115; *Trial*, 433–34, 444, 504; Forbes, *Diary*, 34; Kellogg diary, June 21, 1864.

19. *OR* series 1, 38(1):75–76, and 38(3):688, 953. The telegraph line reached only as far as Fort Valley, thirty miles short of Andersonville, at the time of this raid (*OR* 7:549).

20. *OR* 7:503–4; Danker, "Shatzell Diary," 116.

21. *OR* series 1, 38(3):953; Forbes, *Diary*, 34; James Buckley diary (IIHS), and Converse, Hoster, and Kellogg diaries, July 28, 1864. It was probably Wirz's threats to open with canister on any apparent escape attempt that led to the postwar fiction that General Winder ordered his artillery to fire on the prisoners as soon as Stoneman's cavalry approached within a certain distance of Andersonville. The myth, known as Order Number 13, appears to have originated with an 1887 speech by a member of the Federal Ex-Prisoners Association (*Baltimore Herald*, September 23, 1887, and Davis, *Escape of a Confederate Officer*, 36–42).

22. Forbes, *Diary*, 34; Kellogg diary, August 4, 1864; Helmreich, "Lee Diary," 22.

23. *OR* series 1, 38(3):953. The original of Brown's proclamation is reproduced in William Harris Bragg's article, "The Union General Lost in Georgia," 19.

24. *OR* series 1, 38(3):955–57, 972.

25. Ibid., series 2, 8:620; Forbes, *Diary*, 34–35.

26. Forbes, *Diary*, 34; Danker, "Shatzell Diary," 115–16; Kellogg diary, July 30, 1864.

27. Bailey, *Diary*, 77; Forbes, *Diary*, 34–35; Kellogg diary, July 30 and 31, 1864; Keys diary, July 30, 1864; Foust and Vance diaries, July 31, 1864; "Diary of a Prisoner," 5; Destler, "Ross Diary," 236. Dyke's battery of four guns originally constituted the camp's entire heavy ordnance, but an August 1 inspection found sixteen guns on the post, most of them not yet positioned (*OR* 7:549).

Richard Winder finally located his shoe shop in nearby Oglethorpe, and, despite the disapprobation of some prisoners who saw such work as aiding the enemy, he was able to procure enough workmen. Others, including a couple of Massachusetts artillerymen whose enlistments had run out, saw no harm in applying for shoemaking jobs but failed to secure them (*OR* 7:762; Kellogg diary, July 30, 1864; Roe, *Melvin Memorial,* 123).

28. Forbes, *Diary,* 35; Converse diary, July 31, 1864; Vance diary, August 1, 1864; Danker, "Shatzell Diary," 116; Styple and Fitzpatrick, *Hopkins Diary,* 105.

29. Kennedy and Whitten diaries, August 2, 1864; "Diary of a Prisoner," 5; Danker, "Shatzell Diary," 116; Forbes, *Diary,* 35.

30. Adams diary (CnHS), Converse, and Vance diaries, August 2, 1864; Forbes, *Diary,* 35; Keys diary, August 3 and 4, 1864; Kellogg diary, July 27, 1864; Carley diary (SHSI), August 5 and 6, 1864; Smith, "Lyth Diary," 20–21; *Trial,* 470, 517. Some prisoners later charged that these Federal cavalrymen were thrown into the stockade in their drawers, having been stripped of even shirts and pants, but most diary references to "stripped" cavalry seem to describe those relieved of equipment, rather than clothing. The most extreme on-the-spot observation was that of a Vermont sergeant who said the last of Stoneman's men "had everything taken, even coats off their backs" (Howard diary [VHS], August 9, 1864).

31. Forbes, *Diary,* 36.

32. *OR* series 1, 38(3):601–3, 609–10.

33. Bradd diary (USAMHI), July 22–29, 1864; *Georgia Journal and Messenger,* July 27, 1864.

34. Bradd diary, July 29, August 8, 18, 28, and 29, 1864.

35. *Trial,* 609, 658, 669. At least six men named Bass lived in Sumter County, all of whom gave their occupations as farmers. They all appear to have been sons of a man who moved to Georgia from North Carolina just prior to 1830: Eighth U.S. Census, Sumter County, Ga. (M-653, reel 136:72, 75, 95, 108, 109), RG29.

36. *Trial,* 609–10.

37. Ibid., 610–11; Foust diary, August 1, 1864. Reverend Duncan's visit earned widespread mention, indicating that he did not greatly exaggerate his estimate of the attendance. See Forbes, *Diary,* 35; Adams and Keys diaries and Daniel Buckley diary (IlHS), August 1, 1864; Vance diary, August 1 and 2, 1864; Basile, *Stearns Diary,* 73; Dennison, *Diary,* 57.

38. *OR* series 1, 35(2):212–13, and series 2, 7:378, 475–76; Cooper to Winder, July 22, 1864, "Letters and Telegrams Sent by the Confederate Adjutant and Inspector General" (M-627, reel 5:491), RG109.

39. Consolidated Morning Reports, Entry 111, RG249; *Trial,* 691–92. The morning report for August 9 shows 33,006 men still inside the stockade and hospital, and more than 5,000 had died by that date.

40. *OR* 1:99, 6:24–26, 36–37, 413, 640, 7:1156, and 8:528.

41. Ibid., 8:527.

42. Ibid., 7:546–51; *Trial,* 241; Forbes, *Diary,* 35; Kellogg diary, August 1, 1864.

43. *OR* 7:551–52. Chandler's comments about Winder seemed to provide the script for a number of dubious witnesses at Henry Wirz's trial who claimed they heard Winder voice the very remarks Chandler implied.

44. Ibid., 7:548; muster rolls of the field and staff, 55th Georgia, December, 1862–August, 1863, statements of charges, petition of T. J. Ball et al., December 14, 1862, Harkie to T. J. Ball et al., December 14, 1862, Harkie to James Seddon, December 16, 1862, and Special Order 94, all in Cyrus B. Harkie military service record, "Compiled Service Records of Confederate Soldiers Who Served in Organizations from the State of Georgia" (M-266, reel 530), RG109; Special Order 143, Box 1, Records Relating to Confederate Prisons and Union Prisoners, Entry 464, RG109.

45. *OR* 7:548–49, 754–55.

46. Resignation dated September 23, 1864, and memorandum from Register of Patients, Ocmulgee Hospital, March 7 and 20, 1865, Cyrus B. Harkie military service record, "Compiled Service Records of Confederate Soldiers Who Served in Organizations from the State of Georgia" (M-266, reel 530), RG109.

47. On July 28 Winder ordered Surgeon T. L. Hopkins to inspect the prison and the hospital. Hopkins filed his report the same day Colonel Chandler arrived, advising the removal of 15,000 prisoners, the boarding of the stream channel and filling of the swamp (which was already underway), the immediate erection of barracks, and the production of a vegetable garden by paroled prisoners, among other improvements; that report is preserved in "Inspection Reports and Related Records Received by the Inspection Branch in the Confederate Adjutant and Inspector General's Office" (M-935, reel 7, item H-53), RG109. Besides those in the hospital, the Consolidated Morning Reports, Entry 111, RG249, show 29,851 men in the stockade at dawn of August 2; that day and the next another 1,119 arrived, which (were it not for nearly 900 hospital admissions) would have put 30,970 inside the palisade. The greatest number of men ever held inside the stockade itself was 30,392, on the evening of August 13.

48. Kennedy diary, July 30, 1864; Destler, "Ross Diary," 236; *OR* 7:524–25; Keys and Kellogg diaries, August 2, 1864; "Diary of a Prisoner," 5; Forbes, *Diary,* 35; Danker, "Shatzell Diary," 116; Vance diary, August 2 and 3, 1864; Roe, *Melvin Memorial,* 125; Basile, *Stearns Diary,* 73–74.

49. "Diary of a Prisoner," 5–6; Forbes, *Diary,* 35–36; Roe, *Melvin Memorial,* 125; Gibson diary (LC) and Kellogg diary, August 3–5, 1864; Burdick diary (SHSW), Converse, and Keys diaries, August 3–4, 1864; Root diary (HMBL), August 3–13, 1864; Adams diary, August 4–5, 1864; Consolidated Morning

Reports, Entry 111, RG249. The daily mortality was recorded each morning, so the sudden increase in deaths noted on August 5 and 6 likely represented men who had died on August 4 and 5, the hottest days. On July 9 Robert Kellogg recorded another immense sick call that lasted all day, in which men too weak to walk lay without water in the heat—despite the immediate presence of twenty-five thousand of their own comrades who might easily have ministered to them. Kellogg guessed that thirty of those men died on July 9, and indeed there is a corresponding surge in the daily death totals: forty-two were counted on the morning of July 9 (most of whom died July 8), fifty-six on July 10 (July 9), and only thirty-eight on July 11 (July 10).

50. Roe, *Melvin Memorial*, 125–26; Gibson diary, August 3, 4, and 12, 1864; Whitten diary, August 4, 6, and 24, 1864; Forbes, *Diary*, 36–38; Foust diary, August 13, 1864; Destler, "Ross Diary," 237; Keys diary, August 15, 1864.

51. Adams diary, August 12–15, 18, 23, 24, 30, 31, September 5, October 8 and 20, 1864; Kellogg diary, August 23, 1864.

52. *OR* 7:542; Forbes, *Diary*, 37, 40; Keys diary, August 10, 1864; Roe, *Melvin Memorial*, 128; Kellogg diary, August 19 and 26, 1864; Basile, *Stearns Diary*, 77; Bradd diary, August 22 and 23, 1864. Charles Whitney, a nineteen-year-old boy from western New York, noticed the first signs of scurvy as early as June 29. The stiffness in his legs worsened until, by July 12, he could not walk, but Whitney enjoyed beans and molasses fairly often from July 17 onward, and a five-dollar gift from his uncle allowed him to buy a few onions and potatoes: although the leg troubled him for months, Whitney lived until 1923 (Whitney diary [DC], June 29, 1864–April 16, 1865, with the 1956–57 notations of his granddaughter).

53. *OR* 7:547; Danker, "Shatzell Diary," 117.

54. *OR* 7:760; *Trial*, 55, 104–5, 336, 381; Foust diary, June 11 and 12, 1864; Kellogg diary, July 9, 1864; Keys diary, August 16, 1864.

55. Forbes, *Diary*, 36; Dennison, *Diary*, 57; Bradd diary, August 4, 1864; *Trial*, 386; *Record of Service of Connecticut Men*, 626. In the hospital register the two men were identified as "H. Burk" of the 16th Connecticut and J. Ryan of the 22nd New York Cavalry (Register of Federal Prisoners Admitted to the Hospital at Andersonville, Georgia, Entry 113, RG249, 158, 160).

56. Aldrich diary (DC), Daniel Buckley, Kellogg, and Vance diaries, August 6, 1864; Keys diary, August 7, 1864; Forbes, *Diary*, 36; Dennison, *Diary*, 57; "Diary of a Prisoner," 6; Smith, "Lyth Diary," 21. The identity of this victim is not known, probably because he was so new to the prison. The only man recorded as having died of wounds that day, Henry Crow, had been admitted to the hospital four days previously; the August 6 casualty appears to have been one of the twelve unknown men buried that day (Register of Federal Prisoners Ad-

mitted to the Hospital at Andersonville, Georgia, Entry 113, RG249, 130, 142). Prescott Tracy, who left for exchange with the petition committee on August 9, later testified that he saw a man named "Roberts" shot through the head as he bent to drink at the stream "in the fore part of August" (*Trial*, 212–13), but Tracy dated the incident on a Wednesday; the only August Wednesday Tracy spent at the prison was August 3, and no one was shot by a guard on that day. Another witness, who said he helped keep the hospital register, claimed the man killed August 6 was buried with the unknown dead (*Trial*, 159, 161). The wounded man whose death was recorded on the day of his burial, August 6, was identified in the hospital register as H. Crow, Company C, 5th Vermont, and in both Captain Moore's and Atwater's lists he is cited as N. Crouse, Company C, 5th Vermont; this man was obviously Henry Crow, of Company C, 5th Vermont, who had been captured in the Wilderness; Crow had been admitted to the hospital August 2 (see Peck, *Revised Register of Vermont Volunteers*, 154). The failure of the two published burial records to identify him correctly led the Vermont adjutant general to leave his name out of the list of Vermonters buried in Andersonville's cemetery.

57. Smith, "Lyth Diary," 21–22; Chipman, *Tragedy of Andersonville*, 460; *Trial*, 4–5, 439, 497; Keys diary, June 19, July 17, 1864; Kellogg diary, June 19, 1864; Kennedy diary, August 2, 1864; Forbes, *Diary*, 21, 36, 43; Dennison, *Diary*, 58.

58. The *OR* reveal that at least fifty-five Confederate prisoners were shot by their Union guards. See 6:156, 410–13, 650–51, 854–56, 868, 884–85, 892–93, 946–47, 1097–98, 1109–10, 7:163–65, 383, 385, 398–99, 452–54, 474–75, 595–97, 813–14, 897, 911–12, 915–16, 1037–40, 1241, 1246, 1252–56, 8:66– 67, 107–8, 115–16, 291–92, 508–10, 692–93. The men killed by guards at Andersonville included Caleb Coplan, shot April 9; George "Albert," May 3; Thomas Herburt, May 15; James Babb, July 4; Otis Knight, July 22; William Unversagt, July 27; the unknown man of August 6; another unidentified man who crossed the dead line August 25 as a means of committing suicide; Maurice Printibill, September 5; August Lohmaer, November 30; and Christian Konold, January 1, 1865.

59. *OR* 8:508–10, 692–93, 1001–2.

60. *Trial*, 522, 553, 696.

61. Ibid., 514, 541, 673; Forbes, *Diary*, 38.

62. Kennedy diary, August 9, 1864; Hammer, *James Diary*, 93; Styple and Fitzpatrick, *Hopkins Diary*, 124.

63. *Trial*, 437, 459, 502, 520, 544, 803; Vance diary, August 9 and 17, 1864; Keys diary, August 17, 1864. Samuel B. Davis said he replaced Wirz as commandant August 13 or 14 (*Escape of a Confederate Officer*, 22), but the Vance

diary and the testimony of a Georgia Reserve colonel (*Trial*, 437) indicate Wirz went on sick leave prior to August 9. Wirz's apartment is described in a list of quarters commutations in Box 18, Tabular Statements, Entry 208, RG109.

64. Davis, *Escape of a Confederate Officer*, 5–16; *CMH* 4:831–32; *CV* 23:176 (April, 1915); *OR* 7:518. The portion of Lieutenant Davis's military service records collected under "Confederate Staff Officers and Nonregimental Enlisted Men" (M-331, reel 73), RG109, confuses him with an older Samuel Boyer Davis who served in Texas as a staff captain and field officer, and their documents are intermixed.

65. *Trial*, 179; Forbes, *Diary*, 36; Kellogg and Keys diaries, August 8, 1864.

66. Danker, "Shatzell Diary," 118; Foust and Chadwick diaries, August 9, 1864; Adams diary, August 4–9, 1864.

67. Mendenhall diary (IHS) and Bradd diary, August 9, 1864; Forbes, *Diary*, 37; Danker, "Shatzell Diary," 118. George Bailey remarked upon having to move his tent to make room for this first barracks building (*Diary*, 78).

68. Howard, Adams, Forbes, Foust, Kellogg, and Whitney diaries, August 9, 1864; "Diary of a Prisoner," 6; Danker, "Shatzell Diary," 118.

69. "Diary of a Prisoner," 6; *OR* 7:589; Kellogg diary, August 9, 1864.

70. *OR* 7:589; Forbes, *Diary*, 37; Howard diary, August 9, 1864; Whitten diary, May 27 and August 6, 1864; Danker, "Shatzell Diary," 118; Anonymous diary (ANHS), August 2, 1864; Futch, "Burdick Diary," 290. The morning report for August 9 shows that four men "escaped" that day, and only one had been recaptured three days later (Consolidated Morning Reports, Entry 111, RG249). Given the difficulty of reaching Federal lines, it seems unlikely that all three of the others did so.

71. *OR* 7:589; Kellogg and Gibson diaries, August 9, 1864; "Diary of a Prisoner," 6.

72. Burdick, Gibson, Kellogg, and Keys diaries, August 9, 1864; "Diary of a Prisoner," 6; Danker, "Shatzell Diary," 118.

73. Foust, Gibson, and Mendenhall diaries, August 10, 1864; Anonymous diary, August 11, 1864; Kellogg diary, August 10–12, 1864; Forbes, *Diary*, 37–38. The lumber in question—scantling that connected the uprights on either side of the sinks—was still missing in photographs taken on August 16.

74. *OR* 7:586, 589; "Diary of a Prisoner," 6; Forbes, *Diary*, 38.

75. *Trial*, 589. Ironically, while this spring still flows, its waters are posted as unfit for human consumption.

76. Park, "The 'Rebel Prison Pen,'" 529–30; "Henry Wirz. The True Story of Andersonville Prison," 18; *Trial*, 589. In his diary entry of June 21, 1864, William Keys mentions a spring.

77. Consolidated Morning Reports, Entry 111, RG249; *OR* 7:586, 589.

CHAPTER SIX

1. T. L. Hopkins to Winder, August 1, 1864, "Inspection Reports and Related Records Received by the Inspection Branch in the Confederate Adjutant and Inspector General's Office" (M-935, reel 7, item H-53), RG109; Cooper to Winder, July 14 and August 12, 1864, "Letters and Telegrams Sent by the Confederate Adjutant and Inspector General" (M-627, reel 5:468, 537), RG109; John H. Winder to Braxton Bragg, July 24, 1864, Frederick M. Dearborn Collection, HLH; *OR* 7:501, 565.

2. While several Northern photographers traveled with portable darkrooms on modified wagons, there is no evidence that A. J. Riddle did, and circumstantial evidence suggests that he did not. Georgia's roads were in far worse shape than the turnpikes of the Mid-Atlantic states, and Confederate impressment officers hungered so for horses (and vehicles, at Andersonville) that anyone venturing near a Southern camp might have risked losing his rig. Had Riddle owned such a conveyance he might have used it to record at least the early stages of the Atlanta campaign, but he does not seem to have done so. One other outdoor military image attributed to him (Davis, *Image of War*, 2:82) is that of a gunboat on the Georgia coast, too distant from Macon to reach by any other practical means than the railroad: therefore it must have been feasible for him to move all his equipment by rail, which was the preferred mode of travel between Macon and Andersonville.

3. Eighth U.S. Census, Floyd County, Ga. (M-653, reel 121:199), RG29; Ninth U.S. Census, Bibb County, Ga. (M-593, reel 136:873), RG29. The 1860 census taker caught Riddle and his family in Rome, Georgia, but a graduate student uncovered newspaper evidence that his studio was in Columbus from 1853 until 1860 (Koch, "A History of the Arts" [UG], 165). At least one image of a Maryland Confederate taken during the first half of the war has surfaced with a backmark advertising Riddle's gallery at 151 Main Street, Richmond, while the backmark of Riddle's portrait of General Winder—probably made during the visit to Andersonville—identifies Riddle as "Chief Photographer, Division of the West." Both pictures appear in *Military Images* 10:5 (March–April, 1989): 7, 21. Yet another portrait of a Confederate captain, apparently Wirz himself, bears the same backmark as Winder's (David Mark to the author, July 20, 1992). In the August 22, 1871, issue of the Macon *Telegraph and Messenger*, Riddle indicated that he had been studying daguerreotype photography for twenty-five years; in the April 10, 1872, edition of the same paper he announced his departure from that city, mentioning that he had been in Macon for "six" years, yet Macon appears to have been his base at least since the summer of 1864. The only A. J. Riddle who served in the Confederate army was an Alaba-

mian several years younger than the photographer. "Compiled Service Records of Confederate Soldiers Who Served in Organizations from the State of Alabama" (M-311, reel 443), RG109.

4. All the Riddle photographs in the National Archives and the U.S. Army Military History Institute are marked August 17, 1864, which was the date Riddle printed on those he published in New York in the summer of 1865, but that conflicts with Robert Kellogg's diary entry for August 16 (CnHS), which begins "Some artists from Macon have been taking pictures of our misery from posts around the stockade"; Kellogg's diary entries are otherwise regular and accurate, appearing to have been made during each evening, and in 1922 he confirmed the accuracy of the entry for the state librarian of Connecticut (Kellogg to George S. Godard, February 23, 1922, Kellogg letters, CnHS). If the series was shot in a single day, which seems likely, the photographic evidence also leans slightly toward August 16. While the only rain on August 16 came at dark, a shower would have interrupted Riddle's work on the afternoon of August 17—but no trace of such a shower appears in the afternoon pictures. The shadows in those later studies also seem too distinct for the clouding-up and rain that some diarists described on August 17. See Converse diary (KSHS), August 15, 1864; Danker, "Shatzell Diary," 119; Basile, *Stearns Diary*, 75; Hammer, *James Diary*, 93; Kennedy diary (MHS) and Shaw diary (USAMHI), August 17, 1864. If Riddle did come by train, that offers still more evidence of an August 16 visit, since troop movements monopolized the railroad from late on August 16 until the afternoon of August 17. There is no reason to give nearly as much weight to Riddle's date, which he may have recorded from memory, as to that scribbled on the spot by a methodical diarist and corroborated by him decades later. For evidence of Wirz's collapse on August 16, see Keys diary (RU) and Vance diary (OHS), August 17, 1864, and Bailey, *Diary*, 79–80.

5. Riddle's failure to begin at the nearby south gate further argues for a date of August 16, for only the tremendous sick call of that day (and the traffic between that place and the hospital) would have made it inconvenient to record that advantageous view.

6. Keys diary, August 16, 1864; Danker, "Shatzell Diary," 119–20; Forbes, *Diary*, 38. The recumbent prisoner appears in the middle foreground of this photo, partially obscured by a post and header of the latrine. Twelve days later J. A. Mendenhall (diary, IHS) mentioned "a number of men" who had collapsed near the sinks, unable to return to whatever shelters they may have had, and on September 3 he referred to their filthy condition ("making stoolls in their pants"), which discouraged anyone from taking steps to help them. The visible evidence of the crowded surgeons' call also hints at an August 16 date for at least this view, for no source indicates that the sick call of August 17 was any more than moderate.

7. Foust diary (ANHS), August 16, 1864. The two surviving views mentioned in this paragraph appear as a composite in the illustration section.

8. Shelter halves and blankets tied directly to the dead line in this photo belied the postwar legend that so much as touching that boundary meant instant and inevitable death—although at least a few men were shot for minor violations.

9. Shaw diary, August 13, 1864; Forbes, *Diary*, 38–39.

10. Shaw diary, August 13, 1864; Bradd diary (USAMHI), August 16, 1864; Forbes, *Diary*, 40–41; Dennison, *Diary*, 61; Smith, "Lyth Diary," 23.

11. *Trial*, 257.

12. Burial Register of Andersonville Prison, ANHS, 178–80; Peck, *Revised Register of Vermont Volunteers*, 413–14. The 1st Vermont Heavy Artillery was originally the 11th Vermont Infantry, and some of its members are buried under that regimental designation. Farnham's brother, Sergeant Lorenzo D. Farnham of the same company, died three days after Riddle took this picture; he is buried three rows away (Destler, "Ross Diary," 237–38). It is evident from this photograph that the gravediggers are beginning a new trench along a short but deep swale in the ground. The burials of August 16 are all in Section E of today's Andersonville National Cemetery, just under half of them in row 1 and the rest in row 2. If the Riddle photos are indeed of August 16 vintage, this one shows the beginning of row 2, and the four bodies correspond to grave numbers 5848 through 5851. Section F of the cemetery is visible in the background. John Younker testified (*Trial*, 319) that he carried the bodies into the mass graves on a broken-down litter, which is visible in the photo. A descriptive list pegs Younker as the lighter-haired and taller of the two prisoners standing in the trench: "Register of Enlistments in the U.S. Army, 1798–1914" (M-233, reel 28, 57:329), RG94. Ten months later Riddle would be peddling these pictures in New York (Robert Kellogg to George S. Godard, February 23, 1922, Kellogg Collection).

13. *OR* series 1, 38(5):530; Converse diary, August 16, 1864; Forbes, *Diary*, 38.

14. F. A. Shoup to Cobb, August 15, 1864, Box 67, Cobb Papers, UG; *OR* series 1, 38(5):969, 972; Forbes, *Diary*, 38; Keys and Vance diaries, August 17, 1864; *Trial*, 466–68.

15. Cobb to Winder, August 11 and 17, 1864, Box 39, Cobb-Erwin-Lamar Papers, UG; *OR* series 1, 38(5):985.

16. *OR* series 1, 38(5):556, 969.

17. Forbes, *Diary*, 39; Vance diary, August 17, 1864; Danker, "Shatzell Diary," 120; *Savannah Daily Morning News*, August 23, 1864. On August 5 the 3rd Reserves counted 609 men present for duty out of 2,282 in the overall garrison (*OR* 7:552).

18. *OR* series 1, 35(1):427–33, 439; David C. Barrow to Howell Cobb, August 22, 1864, Box 67, Cobb Papers; Foust diary, August 17–19 and 21, 1864;

Howard diary (VHS), August 18, 1864; Stone diary (USAMHI), August 17, 20, and 22, 1864; Basile, *Stearns Diary*, 77; Hammer, *James Diary*, 93; Bradd diary, August 17–22, 1864; Helmreich, "Lee Diary," 23.

19. Converse diary, August 23, 1864; Basile, *Stearns Diary*, 77; Peabody diary (USAMHI), August 23, 1864; Hammer, *James Diary*, 93–94; Coulter, "Starr Diary," 190; Chapin letter ([VHS], August 24–30, 1864); Destler, "Ross Diary," 238; *Atwater Report*, 72. In his diary entry for August 23 John Melvin Converse noted that he had finally drawn full rations again, and that entry is decorated with what must be one of the earliest examples of the symbol now known as a "happy face." Andersonville authorities, including Henry Wirz (*OR* 7:522) and the post commissary, Captain Armstrong (*Trial*, 659), insisted that the prisoners received the same rations as Confederate soldiers. For much contemporary evidence that Southern troops suffered from the same short, monotonous rations and from unbolted cornmeal that played havoc with their digestive systems, see Daniel, *Soldiering in the Army of Tennessee*, 51–63; the only advantage the Confederate soldier enjoyed was the opportunity to forage, and this alone seems to have prevented a greater instance of scurvy. Former guards of the Georgia Reserves also testified that their government rations at Andersonville were very small (*Trial*, 451). One Federal prisoner later corroborated the physical privations of Confederates at Andersonville—particularly the surgeons (Boate, "The True Story," 28), and another prisoner who returned to the front in 1865 noted that Confederate deserters were "all most starved now, a hafe pint of corn meal and a small pease of pork a day is all they get to eat." This observer wrote as though he considered such rations worse than his own fare at Andersonville (Paul Renno to R. Whittier, March 8, 1865, HLH).

20. *Trial*, 206, 491, 494; *Sumter Republican*, August 27, 1864; Stone diary, August 26–29, 1864; Basile, *Stearns Diary*, 77; Kellogg diary, August 23, 1864; Whitten diary (SHSI), August 24, 1864. General Winder blamed "the impossibility of procuring a sufficiency of vegetable food" for the greater part of the mortality at Andersonville (*OR* 7:955–56).

21. Mendenhall diary, August 28, 1864; Bradd diary, August 17–27, 1864; Forbes, *Diary*, 44; Vance diary, August 26; Smith, "Lyth Diary," 23. Despite his pessimism, Bradd survived Andersonville; the identity of the suicidal soldier remains unknown, but he is evidently buried in grave #6939.

22. Bailey, *Diary*, 80; Hunter, "Ferguson Diaries," 219; Anonymous diary (ANHS), August 24, 1864; Chadwick diary (MHS), August 27, 1864; Gibson diary (LC), August 25–28, 1864.

23. Forbes diary (YUL), July 29 and 30, 1864; Basile, *Stearns Diary*, 64, 74–75.

24. Whitten diary, August 24, 1864; Yeakle diary (ANHS), September 14–30 and October 7–9, 1864.

25. Forbes, *Diary*, 40; Danker, "Shatzell Diary," 121; Dennison, *Diary*, 61; Kellogg and Vance diaries, August 24, 1864; *Trial*, 569; Consolidated Morning Reports, Entry 111, RG249. New Yorker John Burdick mistook those fortunate prisoners for officers who had "passed themselves off for privates when they were captured" (Futch, "Burdick Diary," 290), and the belief persists that many officers deliberately misrepresented themselves in order to share the misery of their men. Most diarists appear to have understood the true nature of the August 24 exchanges, however, and there is no reliable evidence of any officers volunteering for Andersonville under such altruistic motives. Until Castle Reed was set aside to house officers during the last fifteen weeks of the war, the only duly mustered officers in the prison seem to have been a few Colored Troops officers whose status the Confederates refused to recognize.

26. Danker, "Shatzell Diary," 122; Mendenhall diary, August 22, 1864; Vance diary, August 27, 1864; Carley diary (SHSI), August 24–25 and 29–31, 1864.

27. *OR* 7:605–7.

28. *OR* series 1, 38(2):858–59, and 38(5):985.

29. Forbes, *Diary*, 42; *OR* 8:595.

30. Converse diary, August 8, 22, and September 4, 1864; Crosby diary (VHS), August 19, 1864; Bailey, *Diary*, 80; Forbes, *Diary*, 39–40; *Trial*, 270, 338, 480; Richard B. Winder to F. W. Dillard, undated (but August, 1864), R. B. Winder Letterbook, RG153; *OR* 7:624, 830; Carley diary, August 16, 19, and 20, 1864. In his inspection report Dr. Joseph Jones, who visited the camp in September, described the barracks as two-story and unsided (*OR* 8:603).

31. Goodyear diary (YUL), August 29, 1864; John H. Winder to Samuel Cooper, "August 1" [September 1], 1864, "Letters Received by the Confederate Adjutant and Inspector General, 1861–1865" (M-474, reel 151, item W-1754), RG109; *Trial*, 483, 519, 544, 656; Vance diary, August 17, 1864; Keys diary, August 18, 1864.

32. *Trial*, 363–64. Not until at least August 24 did Winder send the requested militia to Macon, and the 3rd Reserves would have been sent back to Andersonville within a few days of that (R. B. Winder to Virgil Powers, August 23, 1864, R. B. Winder Letterbook, RG153).

33. *Sumter Republican*, August 27, 1864.

34. *Trial*, 538; Smith, "Lyth Diary," 23; Dennison, *Diary*, 61; Forbes, *Diary*, 40–41; Vance diary, August 27, 1864.

35. *Trial*, 358, 362.

36. *OR* 7:837, 841, and 8:733; *Trial*, 519, 642, 656. Lieutenant James H. Wright, who was quartermaster of the 55th Georgia at the time, confirmed that Captain Reed cursed at Dr. Head and refused to give the provisions to the prisoners (*Trial*, 406–7).

37. Spencer to Samuel Cooper, June 23, 1864, W. H. S. Taylor to Cooper,

February 8, 1865, and Mark H. Blandford to Cooper, May 19, 1864, all in "Letters Received by the Confederate Adjutant and Inspector General" (M-474, reel 143, item S-1942, reel 162, item S-235, and reel 98, item B-3473), RG109; *Sumter Republican*, September 10, 1864.

38. *OR* 7:473, 762.

39. Ibid., 711, 830–32.

40. Ibid., series 1, 38(3):696, and (5):669, 990, 993, 997, 1011–14.

41. Ibid., 38(5):1018, 1021, 52(2):728, and series 2, 7:706–8, 713, 755; Register of Federal Prisoners Admitted to the Hospital at Andersonville, Georgia, Entry 113, RG249, 219–21; Carley diary, September 3, 1864; Forbes, *Diary*, 43; Danker, "Shatzell Diary," 123; Special Order 209, September 5, 1864, Box 1, Records Relating to Confederate Prisons and Union Prisoners, Entry 464, RG109.

42. Hoster diary (ANHS), September 1, 1864; Consolidated Morning Reports, Entry 111, RG249; John H. Winder to Samuel Cooper, September 1, 1864, "Letters Received by the Confederate Adjutant and Inspector General, 1861–1865" (M-474, reel 151, item W-1754), RG109; Forbes, *Diary*, 43; Keys diary, September 5, 1864; Yeakle diary, September 3, 1864; Stone diary, September 5, 1864; Styple and Fitzpatrick, *Hopkins Diary*, 140; Bailey, *Diary*, 82; *Trial*, 349, 386. The dead man was identified by one prisoner as Morris Prindiville, 7th Maryland, who is buried in grave #7981 (*Trial*, 349). Apparently because of orthographic error, the unit is mistaken: both William Farrand Keys (diary, September 5) and John B. Walker (*Trial*, 349) correctly labeled the victim a member of the 7th Indiana. His real name was Maurice Printibill, and he had arrived at Andersonville in the spring, with a wound incurred in the Wilderness. His death is registered on September 6, the day he was buried, which indicates that the rising death toll had put burial crews a full day behind (War Department notation and muster-out roll, Maurice Printibill military service record, RG94).

43. The original of this telegram is in Box 1, Records Relating to Confederate Prisons and Union Prisoners, Entry 464, RG109.

44. *OR* series 1, 38(5):1025; Adams diary (CnHS), September 5 and 6, 1864; F. A. Shoup to Cobb, September 6, 1864, Box 67, Cobb Papers; Cobb to Winder, September 6, 1864, Box 39, Cobb-Erwin-Lamar Papers.

45. Burdick diary (SHSW) and Adams, Carley, Foust, Howard, Kellogg, Keys, Vance, Whitten, and Yeakle diaries, September 6, 1864; Forbes, *Diary*, 44; Danker, "Shatzell Diary," 123; Destler, "Ross Diary," 239; Bailey, *Diary*, 83.

46. Carley diary, September 7–9, 1864; Gibson diary, September 7, 1864; *Trial*, 502; Keys diary, September 12, 1864.

47. "Diary of a Prisoner," 6; Hoster diary, September 8, 1864; *Sumter Republican*, September 10, 1864; Keys diary, September 12, 1864; Forbes, *Diary*, 44–45; Yeakle diary, September 11 and 12, 1864; Bradd diary, September 10–11, 1864.

48. Forbes, *Diary*, 44–45.

49. Ibid.; Kellogg diary, September 9–10, 1864; Adams diary, September 10 and October 20, 1864; Braun, *Andersonville*, v–vi.

50. Burdick diary, September 11, 1864; Gibson diary, September 10–11, 1864.

51. Danker, "Shatzell Diary," 125; Bradd, Kennedy, and Keys diaries, September 12, 1864; Forbes, *Diary*, 46; Thomas W. Horan to unnamed relative, March 27, 1865, IHS; Stone diary, September 14, 1864.

52. *OR* 7:793, 818; prisoner-of-war memorandum, Leroy L. Key military service record, RG94; Carley diary, November 20–30, 1864; Paul Renno to R. Whittier, March 8, 1865, HLH.

53. Forbes, *Diary*, 48–68; Danker, "Shatzell Diary," 125; Converse diary, October 4 and 5, 1864; Burdick diary, September 18, November 21–23, 1864, and January 8, 1865; Adams diary, October 8–20, 1864; Kennedy diary, September 13–16, 1864.

54. Consolidated Morning Reports, Entry 111, RG249; Converse and Stone diaries, September 13, 1864; Chapin letter (September 19, 1864); Basile, *Stearns Diary*, 80; Dougherty diary (ANHS), 82; *Trial*, 656; Roe, *Melvin Memorial*, 132.

55. Roe, *Melvin Memorial*, 132–33; Smith, "Lyth Diary," 23–24; *Trial*, 656.

56. Between the night of September 8 and the morning of September 13, sixty-six prisoners escaped from Andersonville; nineteen were recaptured between September 10 and 16. Six more got away on September 18 and 19, but all six were returned to the prison on September 26. See Consolidated Morning Reports, Entry 111, RG249.

57. *Trial*, 143, 176, 179, 262, 296, 298, 318; muster roll of Company F, 1st Georgia Reserves, September and October, 1864, W. W. Byram military service record, "Compiled Service Records of Confederate Soldiers Who Served in Organizations from the State of Georgia" (M-266, reel 130), RG109; *Atwater Report*, 74; *The Martyrs*, 197–205. Until September 10 nearly 8,400 bodies were buried, with only 99 marked "unknown"; between that date and October 24, 343 were so listed. Captain James Moore's 1865 cemetery detail added 9 more unknowns to the total as a result of errors or illegible records.

58. Chapin letter (September 12, 1864); Mendenhall diary, September 8, 1864; Whitten diary, September 11 and October 22–27, 1864; Dennison, *Diary*, 70; Forbes, *Diary*, 45.

59. Whitten diary, September 11 and 12, 1864; Forbes, *Diary*, 45; Consolidated Morning Reports, Entry 111, RG249.

60. Register of Federal Prisoners Admitted to the Hospital at Andersonville, Georgia, Entry 43, RG249; *Trial*, 171. The dead man was Corporal Henry Brown, Company A, 41st Ohio. The death register gives his date of death as September 13, but it is not clear whether that was the day his body was first

discovered or the day his remains were reinterred in the prison cemetery: a stone bearing his name sits in proper chronological order among the dead who were buried September 13.

61. Consolidated Morning Reports, Entry 111, RG249.

62. Joseph Jones diary, LSU (this diary is unpaginated, and all but two entries are undated); *Trial*, 641; *OR* 8:508–9, 619; "Remarks Concerning Andersonville," Manigault scrapbook, SHC.

63. Jones diary; *OR* 8:586, 603–4; Whitten diary, September 13, 1864.

64. *OR* 8:589. Louis Manigault's sketch and description of their Andersonville campsite is pasted into his scrapbook.

65. *Trial*, 88, 180, 640; Jones diary, September 17, 1864; "Remarks Concerning Andersonville," Manigault scrapbook; *OR* 8:599–600.

66. Manigault to Mrs. Manigault, September 18, 1864, Manigault scrapbook.

67. *OR* 8:617–18, 625; *Trial*, 641, Jones diary, September 19, 1864. Again, see Daniel, *Soldiering in the Army of Tennessee*, 51–63, for accounts of Confederate privation. Scurvy also affected many Confederate prisoners confined at Hart's Island, New York, in the weeks after Appomattox, but Union authorities deliberately avoided the purchase of fresh vegetables to save money, reasoning that the victims would probably be released soon, anyway (*OR* 8:646).

68. *OR* 8:608, 611, 614–15.

69. Ibid., 626–27; Yeakle diary, September 23, 1864.

70. *OR* 8:618–19, 626–28, 630.

71. Galloway, *One Battle Too Many*, 313, 316, 322–32; Aldrich diary (DC), August 11, 1864; Imholte, "Burch Diary" (USAMHI), 121; *Atwater Report*, 36.

72. *OR* 8:628–29; *Atwater Report*, 29.

73. *OR* 8:620; muster rolls of Company H, 3rd Georgia Reserves, September 1 and October 31, 1864, Thomas J. Cole military service record, "Compiled Service Records of Confederate Soldiers Who Served in Organizations from the State of Georgia" (M-266, reel 173), RG109.

74. Twelfth U.S. Census, Butts County, Ga. (T-623, reel 182, Enumeration District 37, sheet 3), RG29; *OR* 8:620–21.

75. *OR* 8:620–21; Mary Jones to Susan M. Cumming, September 29, 1864, published in Myers, *Children of Pride*, 1208.

76. *OR* 8:640.

77. C. E. McGregor and Lafayette McLaws to Howell Cobb, September 13, 1864, Box 67, Cobb Papers; *OR* 7:837; Consolidated Morning Reports, Entry 111, RG249; Forbes, *Diary*, 48.

78. *OR* series 1, 39(1):805, and 39(2):844.

79. Ibid., 7:837, 841.

80. Ibid., series 1, 39(2):844; Consolidated Morning Reports, Entry 111,

RG249; Foust and Vance diaries, September 16 and 19, 1864; Dennison, *Diary*, 67, 70; Destler, "Ross Diary," 239.

81. Destler, "Ross Diary," 240; *OR* 7:1041.

82. *OR* 8:733; *Trial*, 405–6, 669; Stephen, *Diary*, 22; Vance diary, September 27, 1864; Foust diary, September 27, 29, 30, October 2 and 6, 1864; Dennison, *Diary*, 71; Chapin letter (October 27 and November 11, 1864).

CHAPTER SEVEN

1. *Trial*, 270–71, 452, 454, 466, 503, 511, 588; *OR* 7:761, 869; R. B. Winder to F. W. Dillard, July 13, August 1, and undated (but August), 1864, R. B. Winder Letterbook, RG153. Not until January of 1865 did the Confederate guards receive any regular-issue clothing (*Trial*, 511).

2. *OR* 7:869; Consolidated Morning Reports, Entry 111, RG249; Ray, *Diary of a Dead Man*, 202; Foust and Yeakle diaries (both ANHS), September 27–October 2, 1864; *Atwater Report*, 50, 53.

3. *OR* 7:755–62, 869, 881, 909, 923.

4. *Sumter Republican*, October 8, 1864.

5. *OR* 7:960; Gibbs to John H. Winder, September 16, 1861, "Letters Received by the Confederate Secretary of War, 1861–5" (M-437, reel 10, item 5530), RG109; Register of Roster of Commissioned Officers, Register of C.S.A. General Hospital Number 4, Wilmington, N.C., Gibbs's resignation, Gibbs to Cooper, December 30, 1863, H. L. Clay to Mr. Holt, July 13, 1864, and surgeon's certificates dated August 13 and October 27, 1864, all in George C. Gibbs military service record, "Compiled Service Records of Confederate Soldiers Who Served in Organizations from the State of North Carolina" (M-270, reel 421), RG109; Stevenson, *The Southern Side*, 29.

6. Muster rolls of Company A, 2nd Georgia Reserves, and Camp Sumter returns, James Ormand military service record, "Compiled Service Records of Confederate Soldiers Who Served in Organizations from the State of Georgia" (M-266, reel 158), RG109; Ninth U.S. Census, Fulton County, Ga. (M-593, reel 151:127), RG29.

7. Winder to Cobb, October 12, 1864, Cobb Papers, UG; *OR* 7:993–94. An officer of the 3rd Georgia Reserves who had served in the Army of Northern Virginia testified that the Reserves had little discipline: "I should not call it discipline at all, myself," said Lieutenant John F. Heath (*Trial*, 449).

8. Thomas C. Jackson to Josie Jackson, October 18, 1864, Jackson Letters, WRHS.

9. Anonymous diary (ANHS), October 8, 9, and 11, 1864; Destler, "Ross

Diary," 240–41; Foust diary, October 8–13, 1864; Hart diary (ANHS), October 14, 1864; Yeakle diary, October 9–13 and 20, 1864. The historical base map of Andersonville drawn for the 1970 National Park Service Study, as well as the official park maps, show the dispensary between the two hospitals outside the stockade. Samuel Foust's diary entry of October 13, however, describes the construction of the dispensary beside the barracks inside the stockade, and his entries of October 11 and 12 indicate the surgeons were turning those barracks into a hospital, too. This would explain late-September accounts of only four buildings against the north wall, and postwar recollections of five (*OR* 8:600; *Trial*, 270, 338). The confusion apparently originates with the coincidence that other hospital barracks were under construction outside the stockade at the same period.

10. Thomas C. Jackson to Josie Jackson, October 18, 1864, Jackson Letters; Whitten diary (SHSI), September 30, 1864; Foust diary, October 14, 24, and 25, 1864; Chapin letter ([VHS], October 27, 1864). Surgeon R. Randolph Stevenson was later accused (by an admittedly hostile physician detailed from the militia ranks) of stealing $100,000 from the hospital funds, and a senior army surgeon found a major discrepancy between Commissary Armstrong's accounts and those of the hospital, but the surgeon testified that Stevenson denied having received the money (*Trial*, 381–82, 474–75). It should be remembered that Captain Armstrong appeared to duck Daniel Chandler's audit in August. Even if Stevenson did embezzle the missing $100,000 in hospital money, it seems unlikely he would have stooped to the less profitable and more cumbersome task of skimming and selling the perishable and unpalatable hospital rations, and another Andersonville doctor said he had to organize an informal detective network to catch Union nurses and patients who were stealing from their more defenseless comrades (*Trial*, 666). One Vermonter who lay dying of scurvy in the hospital paid a nurse in advance for six raw potatoes that he never received: Chapin letter (October 11 and 12, 1864).

11. *Atwater Report*, 18, 46, 71; Whitten diary, September 14, 16, October 10, 11, and 21–27, 1864.

12. Destler, "Ross Diary," 241; Hart diary, October 4–12, 1864; *OR* series 1, 39(1):812; prisoner-of-war memoranda, George M. Shearer military service record, RG94.

13. Anonymous diary, October 15, 1864; Hart diary, October 14, 1864; Yeakle diary, October 19, 1864; Whitten diary, October 22–27, 1864; Foust diary, October 14, 1864; Destler, "Ross Diary," 243; *Trial*, 427, 589, 680.

14. *OR* 7:1040–42; Destler, "Ross Diary," 241; Hart diary, October 13, 1864; Yeakle diary, October 11 and 19, 1864. Hart and most of the fresh prisoners from northern Georgia were reenlisted veterans, and presumably they carried a

portion of their regular or bonus pay on their persons; Hart bought extra food as late as November, indicating that he brought a fair amount of cash.

15. Destler, "Ross Diary," 242–43; Foust diary, October 29, 1864; Stevenson to Winder, October 4, 1864, Box 19, Tabular Statements, Entry 208, RG109; Whitten diary, October 30 and November 2, 1864; Yeakle diary, October 31, 1864; Chapin letter (November 1, 1864); Consolidated Morning Reports, Entry 111, RG249.

16. Consolidated Morning Reports, Entry 111, RG249.

17. *Sumter Republican*, October 8, 1864; Thomas C. Jackson to Josie Jackson, October 28, 1864, Jackson Letters; "Son John" to "Dear Pa," and to "My Dear Wife" (for "Uncle Osker"), August 31, 1864, Confederate States Army Archives Miscellany, DU.

18. Special Orders 215, October 13, 1864, and General Order 90, November 5, 1864, White Papers, DU; Wirz to R. B. Thomas, November 27, 1864, Letters Sent, Andersonville Prison, Georgia, May, 1864–March, 1865, RG109.

19. Wirz to Ormand, November 9, 1864, Letters Sent, Andersonville, Prison, Georgia, May, 1864–March, 1865, RG109; Foust diary, October 7 and 26–27, 1864; Whitten diary, October 30 and November 2, 1864.

20. Whitten diary, November 11–12, 1864; Consolidated Morning Reports, Entry 111, RG249.

21. *Trial*, 176, 405, 408, 669; Consolidated Morning Reports, Entry 111, RG249; Wirz to S. S. Cooper, October 16, 1864, Letters Sent, Andersonville Prison, Georgia, May, 1864–March, 1865, RG109.

22. *OR* series 1, 44:858; Consolidated Morning Reports, Entry 111, RG249; W. K. Latimer to "dear Father," November 14, 1864, MHS; James T. Harnit to Albert Kelly, November 15, 1864, OHS; Whitten diary, November 16, 1864; Destler, "Ross Diary," 244.

23. *Trial*, 326–27; Wirz to Henry Forno, November 18, 1864, Letters Sent, Andersonville Prison, Georgia, May, 1864–March, 1865, RG109. As published in *Trial*, 327, the letter bears an erroneous date of November 28, 1864.

24. *OR* series 1, 42(3):1225, and 45(1):1217; Taylor, *Destruction and Reconstruction*, 210–11.

25. *OR* series 1, 44:363, 414–15.

26. *OR* 7:869, 1145, 1148, 1155; Carley diary (SHSI), November 19–22, 1864; Ames diary (SHSI), November 21–24, 1864; Whitten diary, November 21–25, 1864; *Atlas to Accompany the Official Records*, pl. 145. Although the prisoners left for exchange at Savannah would have been the sickest in Winder's immediate custody, the Federal exchange agent remarked (*OR* 7:1149) that "their physical condition is rather better than I expected." Yankee Town appears to be the site of modern Waycross, Georgia.

27. The nickname "Galvanized Yankee" was ultimately applied to six regiments of U.S. Volunteers composed of former Confederate soldiers who enlisted from military prison camps. Originally, however, the term was used to denote Federal prisoners who joined the Confederate service. As early as December 18, 1864, Amos Yeakle made a diary reference to such turncoats at the Florence prison as "galvanized yankees," and on March 5, 1865, General Grenville Dodge specifically defined the expression in that manner when he used it to describe the very men mentioned in this paragraph (*OR* 8:358–59). When recaptured by Union forces, these men exchanged allegiances again and enlisted in the 5th U.S. Volunteers, and their denomination as "Galvanized Yankees" appears to have been extended to include all the U.S. Volunteers, thus reversing the meaning. The earlier derivation certainly seems more analogical, since the galvanizing process coats the original metal—blued steel, for instance—with zinc, which eventually fades to a dull grey.

28. John Blair Hoge to Garnett Andrews, September 24, 1864, Box 1, Records Relating to Confederate Prisons and Union Prisoners, Entry 464, RG109; Wirz to George C. Gibbs, October 17, 1864, and to "Capt. Gayore," October 26, 1864, Letters Sent, Andersonville Prison, Georgia, May, 1864–March, 1865, RG109.

29. Consolidated Morning Reports, Entry 111, RG249.

30. Prisoner-of-war memoranda, Hiram Jefferson military service record, RG94; Roll of Prisoners of War Received at Alton Military Prison from January 15–20, 1865, Rolls of Federal Prisoners of War Who Enlisted in the Confederate Army, Entry 34, RG249; *OR* 8:124, 358–59. To save their necks, Jepperson and the other Egypt Station prisoners reenlisted in the 5th U.S. Volunteers and went west to fight Indians. Many of them deserted there, but Jepperson was honorably discharged at Fort Kearny, Nebraska, in October, 1866. He spent the rest of his life in Iowa, Minnesota, South Dakota, Washington, and Oregon, where he died in 1926. For reasons that he carried to his grave, Jepperson lived most of the intervening years under the alias of Thomas Mulvey, the name of a comrade in the 5th U.S. Volunteers who deserted that regiment; all Jepperson's attempts to obtain a pension were foiled because he did not reenlist in Federal service until March of 1865, two months too late, under the pertinent Act of Congress, to redeem his earlier desertion. See company muster-out roll, Company C, 5th U.S. Volunteers, Hiram Jefferson military service record, RG94; assorted affidavits, Hiram Jepperson original pension application #1138032, RG15; Twelfth U.S. Census, Carroll County, Iowa (T-623, reel 421, Enumeration District 44, sheet 1, line 85), RG29; death certificate of Thomas Mulvey, October 12, 1926, Oregon State Health Division.

31. Muster rolls of Company K, 35th Ohio, casualty sheet, and prisoner-of-war memoranda, August Lohmaer military service record, RG94; *Atwater Report*, 47; *Trial*, 84; Consolidated Morning Reports, Entry 111, RG249.

32. James Moore to Montgomery Meigs, November 4, 1865, Consolidated Correspondence File, Entry 225, RG92; Dykes to Gibbs, October 26, 1864, and R. B. Winder to Dykes, October 30, 1864, Box 19, Tabular Statements, Entry 208, RG109.

33. *Trial*, 101, 480, 490, 493; R. J. Hallett to Persons, December 10 and 12, 1864, Box 39, Cobb-Erwin-Lamar Papers, UG.

34. Consolidated Morning Reports, Entry 111, RG249.

35. *OR* 7:1204.

36. Whitten diary, November 25 and December 5–6, 1864; Ames diary, December 5–6, 1864; Hart diary, December 10–12, 1864; *OR* series 1, 44:992, and series 2, 7:1204.

37. Whitten diary, December 6, 1864.

38. Cooper to John Winder, December 16 and 18, 1864, "Letters and Telegrams Sent by the Confederate Adjutant and Inspector General" (M-627, reel 6:277, 283), RG109; Winder to Cooper, December 17, 1864, Box 1, Records Relating to Confederate Prisons and Union Prisoners, Entry 464, RG109.

39. Thomas W. Horan to unnamed relative, March 27, 1865, IHS; Shearer diary (SHSI), Ames and Hart diaries, December 19–23, 1864; Whitten diary, December 19–23 and 26, 1864; Andrews, *War-Time Journal*, 59–60, 64. Except for the lack of deliberate brutality, the sixty-mile trek from Thomasville to Albany bears an uncomfortable resemblance to the Bataan Death March, and the Thomasville prisoners were already far more malnourished and unfit at the start of their ordeal than the Philippine captives (see Knox, *Death March*, 118–52).

40. Whitten diary, December 23, 1864.

41. Ibid., December 23–25, 1864; Consolidated Morning Reports, Entry 111, RG249; Ames and Shearer diaries, December 24–26, 1864. Two skeletons unearthed from the stockade site on April 28, 1899 (Burial Register of Andersonville, ANHS, 417) more likely belonged to the victims of a cold-spell cave-in from this period than to men killed by the raiders, especially since the remains were so interlocked—as though embracing for warmth—that they were reinterred in a single casket: they lie in grave #13718 of Andersonville National Cemetery. In fact, the two were probably the very men mentioned in the Ames and Shearer diaries as having been asphyxiated Christmas night, for no diaries describe fatal cave-ins on any other date, and no such deaths appear in the hospital register of that period. No contemporary source mentions the Christmas victims being exhumed at all, and doubts expressed by Ames and Shearer about a third body inside the collapsed burrow further suggest the remains were not immediately recovered—and that would explain the lack of documentation in the hospital register.

42. Consolidated Morning Reports, Entry 111, RG249; *Trial*, 276; Gibbs to Samuel Cooper, December 8, 1864, and January Return for Camp Sumter, Box

1, Records Relating to Confederate Prisons and Union Prisoners, Entry 464, RG109; Shearer diary, December 25, 1864; Ames and Hart diaries, December 26, 1864; Stephen, *Diary*, 28.

43. *Trial*, 386; Register of Federal Prisoners Admitted to the Hospital at Andersonville, Georgia, Entry 113, RG249, 337. The details of the shooting were supplied by the Wirz trial testimony of J. Everett Allen, 4th Vermont, whose accounts of shootings by the guards prove remarkably consistent with both Confederate documents and prisoner diaries. Konold is buried under the name "S. Connor" (*The Martyrs*, 46), but his hospital entry is "Z. Connor." Both these sources list him as a member of Company H, 112th Pennsylvania, but according to the records of the adjutant general's office no S. Connor or Z. Connor from Pennsylvania died at Andersonville. The 112th Pennsylvania took the field as the 2nd Pennsylvania Heavy Artillery—without a man in its ranks by either name—but Company H did include Christian Konold, and "C. Konold" might well have been misinterpreted as "Z. Connor" if it were given to the clerk orally. Konold's military service record includes a prisoner-of-war memorandum that he was captured at Chapin's Farm, Virginia, September 29, 1864, and that he died at the Salisbury, North Carolina, military prison on February 10, 1865, but such memoranda are frequently mistaken, or are corrupted as a result of such tactics as "flanking out" of detachments during removals to different prisons. The cemetery at Salisbury is, in fact, credited with containing the remains of this man under both incarnations: a recent compilation of the Salisbury dead includes both "Z. Conner," a private in Company H of the 112th Pennsylvania who died January 1, 1865—the same day as the Andersonville shooting victim—and Christian Konold, a private in Company H of the "7th" Pennsylvania Heavy Artillery, who perished February 10, 1865. The historian of Salisbury prison acknowledged that Salisbury's burial records are far less accurate than Andersonville's (Brown, *Salisbury Prison*, 142, 290, 302).

44. Ames diary, January 4, 1865; Stephen, *Diary*, 27-28.

45. William H. Noble to "My Darling Wife," January 4 and February 12, 1865, Noble Papers, USAMHI; *OR* series 1, 44:824-25, and 47(2):1006; Hunt, *Brevet Brigadier Generals*, 449. Noble's letter collection includes a drawing of Castle Reed alongside the railroad tracks.

46. William H. Noble to "My Dearest Wife," January 4 and February 12, 1865, George C. Gibbs to Noble, March 10, 1865, and Gibbs to "Dear Fred," March 18, 1865, Noble Papers.

47. *Trial*, 607-8.

48. Wirz to R. B. Thomas, January 9, 1865, Letters Sent, Andersonville Prison, Georgia, May, 1864-March, 1865, RG109. Possibly Wirz mistook the woman's name. She may have been Mrs. Ambrose Spencer, whose husband's loyalties vacillated so: the 1860 census indicates that these two were parents of a

daughter born in the Midwest about 1840, which might explain the acquaintanceship with an Iowan: Eighth U.S. Census, Chatham County, Ga. (M-653, reel 115:79), RG29.

49. Wirz to R. B. Thomas, January 17, 1865, Letters Sent, Andersonville Prison, Georgia, May, 1864–March, 1865, RG109.

50. Thomas Jackson to Josie Jackson, February 8, 1865, Jackson Letters; *OR* 8:111; *Sumter Republican,* January 21 and 28, 1865; Andrews, *War-Time Journal,* 72; Whitten diary, February 10, 1865; *Trial,* 270, 338; Shearer diary, February 11, 1865; Stephen, *Diary,* 32.

51. Excerpt of Special Order 8, January 16, 1865, Rolls of Federal Prisoners of War Who Enlisted in the Confederate Army, Entry 34, RG249; Consolidated Morning Reports, Entry 111, RG249; Shearer and Whitten diaries, January 23–25, 1865; Ames diary, January 21–23, 1865.

52. Thomas C. Jackson to Josie Jackson, "January" 1 [February 1?] and February 8, 1865, Jackson Letters; Shearer diary, January 20, 1865; *Sumter Republican,* February 11, 1865.

53. Consolidated Morning Reports, Entry 111, RG249; *Trial,* 85; Shearer diary, January 14 and 26, 1865; *Sumter Republican,* July 3 and November 20, 1863, September 10, 1864–March 18, 1865.

54. Wirz to G. W. McPhail, February 26, 1865, Letters Sent, Andersonville Prison, Georgia, May, 1864–March, 1865, RG109; Shearer diary, February 3, 1865; *Trial,* 173, 494, 681–82.

55. *OR* series 1, 44:977–79. General Order 84, signed by General Winder and dated November 21, 1864, reiterated the curious command structure at Andersonville and reminded higher-ranking troop commanders to accede to the requests of the post or prison commanders for guards. A copy of the order survives in the Isaiah White Papers.

56. Wirz to R. B. Thomas, March 5, 1865, Letters Sent, Andersonville Prison, Georgia, May, 1864–March, 1865. It was not for lack of trying that George Gibbs failed to sew a general's stars on his collar: learning that John Imboden, the new chief of prisons in Georgia, Alabama, and Mississippi, intended to ask for a return to field command, Gibbs hinted to his congressman that if the Florida delegation supported him he might get the promotion himself. See Gibbs to [Samuel St. George] Rogers, March 29, 1865, Gibbs military service record, "Compiled Service Records of Confederate Soldiers Who Served in Organizations from the State of North Carolina" (M-270, reel 421), RG109.

57. *Sumter Republican,* February 4, 1865; Thomas C. Jackson to Josie Jackson, February 8, 1865, Jackson Letters; *Georgia Journal and Messenger,* March 1, 1865; Whitten diary, February 18–26, and March 2–15, 1865; Ames diary, February 18, 22, 25, 27–28, and March 1–12, 1865; *OR* 8:123, 170, 1000; Consolidated Morning Reports, Entry 111, RG249.

58. Ames and Whitten diaries, March 8, 1865.

59. Ames and Whitten diaries, March 18, 1865; *Trial*, 383; Consolidated Morning Reports, Entry 111, RG249; Horan to unnamed relative, March 27, 1865; *OR* 8:170, 425–26.

60. Consolidated Morning Reports, Entry 111, RG249; *Trial*, 173; Ames diary, March 22 and 24–27, 1865; Whitten diary, March 22–27, 1865.

61. D. A. Johnston to Abby E. Stafford, April 9, 1865, Stafford Papers, and Dr. J. G. Thomas to Robert Ould, July 31, 1868, Isaac H. Carrington Papers, both DU. Dr. Thomas said he saw hundreds of Confederates "in every stage of scurvy," and with the flesh of their feet, legs, and hands "sloughing off produced by frostbite."

62. *OR* 8:427, 436, 445; Gideon Pillow to John C. Breckinridge, March 28, 1865, David Homer Bates Papers, reel 1 of Alfred W. Stern Collection of Lincolniana, LC; Ames diary, March 29, 30, and April 1–4, 1865; Stephen, *Diary*, 34–35.

63. Whitten diary, April 4, 1865; Andrews, *War-Time Journal*, 130–31. In his *Sable Arm*, Dudley Cornish noted that no black prisoners were returned until the war was over, despite the resumption of exchanges. That may not be strictly true, as the April 4 release of more than a score at Andersonville suggests, but for all the Federal government's earlier insistence upon that point it does appear to have resumed exchanges without assurance that all black soldiers would be included. Cornish supposes that the policy changed because the sheer number of Confederate prisoners was "burdensome" (172).

64. Consolidated Morning Reports, Entry 111, RG249; Ames and Whitten diaries, April 4–6, 1865; Stephen, *Diary*, 35.

65. Whitten diary, April 6–8, 1865; Stephen, *Diary*, 35.

66. *OR* 8:465, 470; Whitten diary, April 8, 1865; Stephen, *Diary*, 35.

67. Whitten diary, April 9–13, 1865; Ames diary, April 11, 1865; Stephen, *Diary*, 35; Consolidated Morning Reports, Entry 111, RG249; Register of Federal Prisoners Admitted to the Hospital at Andersonville, Georgia, Entry 113, RG249, 363–66.

68. Ames diary, April 11, 1865; Whitten diary, April 13–16, 1865.

69. Ames and Whitten diaries, April 17–28, 1865; Stephen, *Diary*, 35–36; *OR* series 1, 49(1);364–65; Consolidated Morning Reports, Entry 111, RG249; prisoner-of-war memoranda, George W. Shearer military service record, RG94.

70. Consolidated Morning Reports, Entry 111, RG249; prisoner-of-war memorandum, Aaron Elliott military service record, RG94; Hadley, *History of Goffstown*, 2:142. Some records give Aaron Elliott's date of death as April 24 (Ayling, *Register*, 368), but the sequence of grave numbers makes it clear that he died April 21, 1865.

71. Consolidated Morning Reports, Entry 111, RG249; prisoner-of-war memoranda, Knud Hanson military service record, RG94.

72. Whitten diary, undated notation; prisoner-of-war memoranda, Amos Ames, James Dennison, Robert Kellogg, and George Shearer military service records, RG94; Forbes, *Diary*, 68; List of Names of Paroled Prisoners Who Died at Jacksonville, Florida, 1865, Roll 456 of Miscellaneous Rolls, Entry 107, RG249. Consolidated morning reports indicate that Andersonville held 7,160 prisoners on April 1, 1864, while the burial register shows that 304 had already perished by that date. From April until November another 32,630 were received, for a total of 40,094. Of the 12,097 received from December until the close of the prison, only about 1,000 were actually new prisoners, while the balance were duplicate, triplicate, or even quadruplicate entries as a result of the evacuation of Millen, Blackshear, and Thomasville or the frustrated exchange attempts of April, 1865: the morning report for April 20, for instance, carried a notation of 3,102 prisoners received from the loaded trains returning from Macon, although only 14 prisoners actually climbed down from the cars; the other 3,088 appear elsewhere on that same report as "sent to other posts."

73. Thomas W. Horan to "Brother Vick," April 18, 1865, Horan Letters, USAMHI; D. A. Johnston to Abby E. Stafford, April 24, 1865, Stafford Papers; *OR* series 1, 48(1):210–26; prisoner-of-war memorandum, Thomas W. Horan military service record, RG94. For a detailed account of the *Sultana* disaster, see Potter, *The Sultana Tragedy*.

74. Consolidated morning reports, Entry 111, RG249; *OR* series 1, 49(2): 580; *Trial*, 19.

75. Consolidated Morning Reports, Entry 111, RG249; *OR* 8:532.

76. Stapleton, *The Cambridge Guide to English Literature*, 485, 984; Horan, *C.S.S. Shenandoah*, 155–57; Harte and Twain, *The California Sketches*, 166–79; *OR* series 1, 48(2):317, 389; Nevins and Thomas, *Strong Diary*, 3:595; Winkler, *Incredible Carnegie*, 90.

77. Consolidated Morning Reports, Entry 111, RG249. It seems fairly certain that these two bodies were carried to the cemetery and deposited alongside Knud Hanson, either at the time of their deaths or shortly thereafter. Looters had just taken all the teams, so it would have been difficult to carry the bodies half a mile to the gravesite, but other prisoners had borne their dead comrades nearly that far the previous summer. The quartermaster captain who tidied up the cemetery in August reported "of those who were buried last the graves were not marked, and we were unable to identify them" (*Trial*, 315). Since that quartermaster did identify Hanson's grave, (*The Martyrs*, 89), his testimony clearly implies that at least two bodies lay buried just south of Hanson's grave; the first caretaker of the cemetery said he found the last graves there "somewhat offen-

sive" when he assumed his duties, late in May, adding that two bodies were exposed (*Trial*, 384). For all of that, Knud Hanson is still cited by park officials as the last prisoner to die at Andersonville (Mark Ragan to the author, August 30, 1991).

78. Consolidated Morning Reports, Entry 111, RG249; assorted pay vouchers, Henry Wirz military service record, "Confederate General and Staff Officers and Nonregimental Enlisted Men" (M-331, reel 271), RG109; commutation vouchers for quarters and cordwood, Box 18, Tabular Statements, Entry 208, RG109.

79. *Trial*, 19–20; *OR* 8:537–38, 586. Susan J. Wolf, Mrs. Wirz's oldest daughter, would have been eighteen years old by then, and evidently she had left the home (Eighth U.S. Census, Madison County, La., M-653, reel 413:5), RG29.

80. *OR* series 1, 49(2):829–30, 1054; *Trial*, 314–15, 384; James Moore to Montgomery Meigs, November 4, 1865, Consolidated Correspondence File, Entry 225, RG92; *The Martyrs*, 6.

81. *Trial*, 314–15; Barton diary, Clara H. Barton Papers, LC, July 12, 22, 25, and 27, 1865.

82. *Trial*, 314–15. The bodies Moore referred to may have been the two men who died on May 4.

83. Barton diary, July 26–August 14, 1865. The Maine doctor was Augustus C. Hamlin, whose *Martyria* was published in 1866.

84. Barton diary, August 12–17, 1865; *The Martyrs*, 7.

85. *Sumter Republican*, August 5, 1865; Register of Prisoners Who Reported Under General Order 104, George C. Gibbs military service record, "Compiled Service Records of Confederate Soldiers Who Served in Organizations from the State of North Carolina" (M-270, reel 421), RG109; *Trial*, 371, 384; N. P. Chipman to Ambrose Spencer, August 17, 1865, Box 652, Record and Pension Office Document File, Entry 501, RG94.

86. George Merryweather to "My Dear Parents," December 17, 1864, CHS; *Harper's Weekly*, June 17, 1865; *Burlington Free Press*, June 17, 1865; DeLabaume broadside, DU.

87. Kellogg diary (CnHS), August 26, 1865; Lew Wallace to Mrs. Wallace, August 21, 1865, Lew Wallace Collection, IHS; *The Demon of Andersonville*, 118. Military courts such as the one that tried Wirz were declared unconstitutional in the case of *Ex Parte Milligan* in 1866.

88. *Trial*, 2–78, 108, 136, 142, 153, 155–56, 163–69, 181, 189, 193, 195, 278, 295, 323, 325, 329, 398. Ramon Marus of Memphis, Tennessee, owns a first-model LeMat revolver, serial number 189, that reputedly belonged to Wirz (Marus to the author in a telephone conversation, March 29, 1992), and some trial testimony suggests that that was the weapon he carried: the LeMat fired nine .42 caliber pistol balls and a tenth charge of buckshot. According to Al-

baugh, Benet, and Simmons, *Confederate Handguns*, 120, the War Department did claim to have recovered that LeMat from Wirz, but the testimony from government witnesses may have been tailored to correspond with that fact, for most of the more outrageous witnesses had obviously been coached. If the government had such a weapon in its possession, however, it is strange the prosecutor did not produce it as evidence. A witness less hostile to Wirz, the translator Guscetti (*Trial*, 519), referred to two navy revolvers Wirz kept for his own use, one of which had a broken spring while the other "flashed over" dangerously, firing multiple chambers; just before the war's end Wirz returned two pistols with those very defects to the Confederate storekeeper at Macon. See undated letter (but March, 1865), Letters Sent, Andersonville Prison, Georgia, May, 1864–March, 1865, RG109.

89. *Trial*, 282–87, 355–62, 371–72; *New York Daily Tribune*, November 26, 1865; muster roll of Company B, 7th New York, for January and February, 1862, Felix Oeser military service record, RG94; prisoner-of-war memoranda, Felix DeLabaume military service record, RG94; Dykes to Edwin Stanton, February 1, 1866, Consolidated Correspondence File, Entry 225, RG92; *Macon Daily Telegraph*, September 28, 1865.

90. *Trial*, 155–56; muster roll of Company G, 4th New York Cavalry, September and October, 1863, Oliver Fairbanks military service record, RG94; muster roll of Company F, 2nd New Jersey, November and December, 1863, and prisoner-of-war memoranda, Richard Fairclough military service record, RG94; affidavit of Richard Fairclough, Box 1269, Manuscript Transcript of Henry Wirz Court-Martial, MM2975 (part 15:1021), RG153; Chipman, *Tragedy of Andersonville*, 337. The similarity between Fairclough's and Fairbanks's last names was purely coincidental; Fairclough's relationship as Fairbanks's stepfather is established by his widow's application for a pension (claim #81045, RG15) and by the Eighth U.S. Census, Passaic County, N.J. (M-653, reel 706: 807), RG29.

91. Kean, *Inside the Confederate Government*, 228–30; *Trial*, 266, 292–93, 327, 415, 427, 518, 529–30, 533, 546, 593, 605, 695–96. It did not help Wirz's case that one of his witnesses, George Fechnor, was also a perjurer, but the prosecution sinned far worse in that regard.

92. *Harper's Weekly*, September 16, October 7 and 21, 1865; Kellogg diary, October 5–12, 1865; *Hutchinson's Washington and Georgetown Directory*, 282; Wirz to "Miss Carrie," October 24, 1865, George W. Dutton Papers (MassHS); *Trial*, 803–8.

93. Wirz to "My Dearest Wife and Children," November 10, 1865, Long notes, LC; untitled Charleston newspaper clipping, Manigault scrapbook, SHC; *The Demon of Andersonville*, 119; *OR* 8:794. The eyewitness description of Wirz wearing a black robe casts doubt on at least two separate claims (one by an

individual and one by the War Library of Philadelphia) to ownership of an army blanket that Wirz is purported to have worn over his shoulders as he emerged from his cell. An autopsy corroborated the examination of surgeons who saw Wirz just prior to sentencing, finding the scars of old ulcers that were presumed to be scorbutic, and it revealed not only the deep scar on his shoulder but "pleuritic adhesions" and "aortic insufficiency." Most interesting of all, however, was the discovery that the bones of the damaged forearm "had not been fractured or resected": see *Medical and Surgical History*, 1(2):400. Originally Wirz was buried beside George Atzerodt on the grounds of the old Washington Arsenal, but in 1869 his bones were delivered to his former attorney, who had them buried in Washington's Mount Olivet Cemetery according to the family's wishes (Adjutant General F. C. Ainsworth to Anna Roberts, January 21, 1911, and telephone memorandum of January 20, 1911, Box 652, Record and Pension Office Document File, Entry 501, RG94). Ironically enough, the site of Wirz's hanging—the final and most deliberate injustice associated with Andersonville—is now occupied by the United States Supreme Court building.

94. Stevenson, *The Southern Side*, 287; Davis to Isaac H. Carrington, April 2, 1868, Carrington Papers; *OR* 8:887–88, 926–28, 976–79.

95. Clara Barton to D. C. Pavey, January 13, 1911, USAMHI.

96. Shearman, "A Visit to Andersonville," 410–13.

97. Dykes to Montgomery Meigs, October 5, 1865, and to Edwin M. Stanton, February 1, 1866, James Moore to Meigs, November 4, 1865, and to Stanton, February 16, 1866, Consolidated Correspondence File, Entry 225, RG92; Dykes to Andrew Johnson, December 19, 1865, *Papers of Andrew Johnson*, 9:522; Deed Book Q:293, Sumter County Courthouse.

98. Union Soldiers Buried in the Vicinity of Macon, Clinton, and Sunshine, Ga., and Whose Bodies Were Collected and Removed to Andersonville, Roll 907, Miscellaneous Rolls, Entry 107, RG249; reports of A. W. Corliss dated January 27, April 3, and April 6, 1868, Correspondence and Reports of National and Post Cemeteries, Entry 576, RG92. The remains of those Confederate guards who were originally buried at Andersonville have been reinterred in the public cemetery in Americus.

99. Testimony of David G. Sumner, Jerus M. Bryant, and L. P. Clarke, Isaac Turner case, Congressional Jurisdiction Case Files, RG123.

100. The Georgia Department of the Grand Army of the Republic bought part of the prison site in 1890, and in 1896 the Women's Relief Corps took it over and added to it, eventually deeding it to the United States (Averill, *Andersonville Prison Park*, 9–16).

Bibliography

MANUSCRIPTS

Andersonville National Historic Site, Andersonville, Ga.
  Anonymous member of Company E, 87th Pennsylvania, diary (typescript)
  John A. Baer diary (typescript)
  Burial Register
  Michael Dougherty diary (photocopy)
  Samuel L. Foust diary
  Chester F. Hart diary
  Samuel Henderson diary
  John A. Hoster diary (typescript)
  George W. Pennington diary (typescript)
  W. H. Rinehart diary
  Henry H. Stone diary
  Amos A. Yeakle diary (typescript)
Carley, Curtis J., Albuquerque, N.M.
  Lawson H. Carley diary (typescript)
Chicago Historical Society, Chicago, Ill.
  Charles M. Colvin notebook
  George Merryweather letter
  W. S. Winder letter
Christian County Courthouse, Hopkinsville, Ky.
  Deed Books
  Marriage Bonds
Connecticut Historical Society, Hartford, Conn.
  Henry H. Adams diary
  Robert Hale Kellogg diary and letters
Duke University, Durham, N.C.
  Isaac H. Carrington Papers
  Confederate States Army Archives Miscellany
  Felix DeLabaume broadside
  Patience Everett Papers
  Samuel Henderson diary (transcript)
  Abby E. Stafford Papers
  Isaiah White Papers
Dunkelman, Mark H., Providence, R.I.
  Thomas R. Aldrich diary (photocopy of a transcript owned by Patricia
    Wilcox of Fairport, N.Y.)

Charles E. Whitney diary (photocopy of a transcript owned by the late
  Elizabeth Maher of Mayville, N.Y.)
Georgia State Archives, Atlanta, Ga.
  Joseph Jackson Felder Papers
Harvard University, Cambridge, Mass.
  Houghton Library
    Autograph File
      Paul Renno letter
    Frederick M. Dearborn Collection
      John H. Winder letter
Historical Museum of the D. R. Barker Library, Fredonia, N.Y.
  Asa W. Root diary (typescript)
Illinois Historical Society, Springfield, Ill.
  Daniel and James H. Buckley diaries (typescripts)
Indiana Historical Society, Indianapolis, Ind.
  W. H. Smith Memorial Library
    James Anderson Papers
    Thomas W. Horan letter
    J[ohn] A. Mendenhall diary
    George W. Parsons letter
    Lew Wallace Papers
Kansas State Historical Society, Topeka, Kan.
  John Melvin Converse diary
Library of Congress, Washington, D.C.
  Clara H. Barton Papers
  S[amuel] J. Gibson diary and letter
  Charles W. Homsher diary (transcript)
  [E. B. Long], Bruce Catton notes, Doubleday & Co.
  Alfred W. Stern Collection
    David Homer Bates Papers
Lisbon Town Hall, Lisbon, N.H.
  Marriages, Births, and Deaths, 1850–1876
Louisiana State University, Baton Rouge, La.
  LSU Libraries
    Lower Mississippi Valley Collections
      Louis A. Bringier Papers
      Joseph Jones diary
      W. R. Worth letter
Massachusetts Historical Society, Boston, Mass.
  George W. Dutton Papers
    Henry Wirz letter

Minnesota Historical Society, St. Paul, Minn.
  Ransom Chadwick diary (typescript)
  David Kennedy diary (typescript)
  Washington Keys Latimer letter (typescript)
National Archives, Washington, D.C.
  (Within record groups, records are arranged by microfilm publication or entry
    numbers; unnumbered collections are listed at the end of record groups)
  Records of the Pension Office (VA), Record Group 15
    Pension Applications
  Records of the Bureau of Naval Personnel, Record Group 24
    Muster Rolls of the U.S.S. *Water Witch*
  Records of the Post Office Department, Record Group 28
    "Records of Appointments of Postmasters," M-841
  Records of the Bureau of the Census, Record Group 29
    Seventh U.S. Census, M-432
    Ninth U.S. Census, M-593
    Eighth U.S. Census, M-653
    Twelfth U.S. Census, T-623
  Records of the Bureau of Customs, Record Group 36
    "Passenger Arrival Lists for the Port of New York," M-237
  Records of the Quartermaster General, Record Group 92
    Consolidated Correspondence, Entry 225
    Correspondence and Reports of National and Post Cemeteries, Entry 576
  Records of the Adjutant General, Record Group 94
    "Register of Enlistments in the U.S. Army, 1798–1914," M-233
    Record and Pension Office Document File, Entry 501
    Compiled Service Records of Union Soldiers
  Records of the United States Secretary of War, Record Group 107
    "Letters Received by the Secretary of War," M-22
  War Department Collection of Confederate Records, Record Group 109
    Tabular Statements Regarding Confederates Confined in Union Prisons,
      Entry 208
    Confederate Compiled Service Records
      "Compiled Service Records of Confederate Soldiers Who Served in
        Organizations from the State of Georgia," M-266
      "Compiled Service Records of Confederate Soldiers Who Served in
        Organizations from the State of North Carolina," M-270
      "Compiled Service Records of Confederate Soldiers Who Served in
        Organizations from the State of Alabama," M-311
      "Compiled Service Records of Confederate Soldiers Who Served in
        Organizations from the State of Louisiana," M-320

"Confederate General and Staff Officers and Nonregimental Enlisted Men," M-331

"Index to Letters Received by the Confederate Adjutant and Inspector General," M-409

"Letters Received by the Confederate Secretary of War," M-437

Records Relating to Confederate Prisons and Union Prisoners, Entry 464

"Letters Received by the Confederate Quartermaster General," M-469

"Letters Received by the Confederate Adjutant and Inspector General, 1861–65," M-474

"Letters and Telegrams Sent by the Confederate Adjutant and Inspector General, 1861–65," M-627

"Inspection Reports and Related Records Received by the Inspection Branch in the Confederate Adjutant and Inspector General's Office," M-935

Letters Sent, Andersonville Prison, Georgia, May, 1864–March, 1865

Records of the United States Court of Claims, Record Group 123

Congressional Jurisdiction Case Files, 1884–1943

Isaac Turner case, claim #11496

Records of the Adjutant General, Record Group 153

Manuscript Transcript of Henry Wirz Court-Martial, MM2975

R. B. Winder Letterbook

Records of the Commissary General of Prisoners, Record Group 249

Rolls of Federal Prisoners of War Who Enlisted in the Confederate Army, Entry 34

Register of Deceased Federal Prisoners of War Confined at Andersonville, Georgia (alphabetical list), Entry 42

Registers of Federal Prisoners of War Admitted to the Hospital at Andersonville, Georgia (alphabetical list), Entry 43

Statements of Money Claimed by Federal Prisoners of War at Andersonville, Entry 82

Miscellaneous Rolls, Entry 107

Consolidated Morning Reports of Prisoners at Andersonville, Entry 111

Name Index to Register of Federal Prisoners Admitted to the Hospital at Andersonville, Entry 112

Register of Federal Prisoners Admitted to the Hospital at Andersonville, Georgia (chronological list), Entry 113

Register of Deaths and Burials at Andersonville Prison, Entry 114

Register of Deceased Prisoners at Andersonville Prison (chronological list), Entry 115

New Hampshire Historical Society, Concord, N.H.

George S. Rix, "Lisbon, N.H. Families" (unpublished typescript)

Ohio Historical Society, Columbus, Ohio
    James T. Harnit letter
    James W. Vance diary (typescript)
Oregon State Health Division, Portland, Ore.
    Thomas Mulvey Death Certificate
Richmond National Battlefield Park, Richmond, Va.
    "Memoir of Aaron E. Bachman" (typescript)
Rutgers University, New Brunswick, N.J.
    Alexander Library Special Collections
        William Farrand Keys diary
State Historical Society of Iowa, Des Moines and Iowa City, Iowa
    Des Moines branch
        Amos H. Ames diary (typescript)
        John Whitten diary (typescript)
    Iowa City branch
        Lawson H. Carley diary
        George Marion Shearer diary (typescript)
State Historical Society of Wisconsin, Madison, Wis.
    Alfred D. Burdick diary (handwritten transcript)
Sumter County Courthouse, Americus, Ga.
    Registry of Deeds
    Registry of Probate
Trigg County Courthouse, Cadiz, Ky.
    Marriage Docket, 1820–1857
    Wills
U.S. Army Military History Institute, Carlisle Barracks, Pa.
    Clara Barton letter
    James H. Bradd diary
    John and Leo Faller Papers
    Luther B. Harris, "A Prison Diary" (typescript)
    John Q. Imholte, "The Civil War Diary and Related Sources of Corporal
        Newell Burch" (unpublished manuscript)
    "Jamey," 133rd Illinois, letter
    Jessie Hines letter
    Thomas W. Horan Letters
    Otis Knight diary
    William H. Noble Papers
    William T. Peabody diary
    George Z. Pretz letter
    Francis M. Shaw diary

Henry Stone diary (transcript)
Benjamin W. Thompson Papers
Eseck G. Wilber diary (transcript)
U.S. Court of Common Pleas, Philadelphia, Pa.
August Heinrich Wirz citizenship application #9312
University of Georgia, Athens, Ga.
Edwin C. Bearss, "Andersonville National Historic Site Historic Resource Study and Base Map"
Cobb-Erwin-Lamar Papers
Howell Cobb Papers
Mary Levin Koch, "A History of the Arts in Augusta, Macon, and Columbus, Georgia, 1800–1860," Master's Thesis, 1983
Elizabeth Leonard Parker, "The Civil War Career of Henry Wirz and Its Aftermath," Master's Thesis, 1948
Shepherd Green Pryor Collection
University of Kentucky, Lexington, Ky.
Judith Ann Maupin, "Trigg County Cemeteries"
University of North Carolina, Chapel Hill, N.C.
Southern Historical Collection, Wilson Library
Louis Manigault scrapbook
John Hunt Morgan Papers
Ira B. Sampson diary
John Henry Winder Papers
University of Vermont, Burlington, Vt.
Bradford Sparrow diary
Vermont Historical Society, Montpelier, Vt.
Charles B. Chapin letter
George R. Crosby diary
Kendrick R. Howard diary
Henry H. Lewis letter
Western Reserve Historical Society, Cleveland, Ohio
William P. Palmer Collection
Thomas C. Jackson Letters
Yale University, New Haven, Conn.
Sterling Memorial Library
Ira Emory Forbes diary (original and transcript)
Francis Wilbur Goodyear diary (original and transcript)
Henry Wirz letter (photostat, deaccessioned sometime since 1964; transcript in E. B. Long notes, Library of Congress)
Zivilstandsamt der Stadt Zürich (city hall), Zurich, Switzerland
Familienregister der Stadt Zürich

NEWSPAPERS

Augusta Weekly Constitutionalist, Augusta, Ga.
Baltimore Herald
Burlington Free Press, Burlington, Vt.
Cattaraugus Freeman, Ellicottville, N.Y.
Daily Sun, Columbus, Ga.
Georgia Journal and Messenger, Macon, Ga.
Harper's Weekly
Laconia Democrat, Laconia, N.H.
Macon Daily Telegraph
New York Daily Tribune
New York Times
Richmond Dispatch
Richmond Enquirer
Savannah Daily Morning News
Sumter Republican, Americus, Ga.
Telegraph and Messenger, Macon, Ga.
Whig and Rebel Ventilator, Knoxville, Tenn.

PUBLISHED SOURCES

Abbott, A[llen] O. *Prison Life in the South*. New York: Harper & Brothers, 1865.
Albaugh, William A., III, Hugh Benet, Jr., and Edward H. Simmons.
   Confederate Handguns. York, Pa.: George Shumway, 1967.
Andrews, Eliza Frances. *The War-Time Journal of a Georgia Girl, 1864–1865*.
   Edited by Spencer Bidwell King, Jr. Macon: Ardivan Press, 1960.
Atlas to Accompany the Official Records of the Union and Confederate Armies.
   Washington, D.C.: Government Printing Office, 1891–95.
[Atwater, Dorence.] *The Atwater Report: List of Prisoners Who Died in 1864–65
   at Andersonville Prison*. Andersonville, Ga.: National Society of
   Andersonville, 1981.
Averill, James P. *Andersonville Prison Park: A Report of Its Purchase and
   Improvement*. Atlanta: Andersonville Prison Property Advisory Board, n.d.
Ayling, Augustus D. *Revised Register of the Soldiers and Sailors of New Hampshire
   in the War of the Rebellion, 1861–1866*. Concord, N.H.: Ira C. Evans, 1895.
Bailey, George W. *The Civil War Diary of George W. Bailey*. Colleyville, Tex.:
   Privately published, 1990.
Basile, Leon, ed. *The Civil War Diary of Amos E. Stearns, a Prisoner at
   Andersonville*. Rutherford, N.J.: Fairleigh Dickinson University Press, 1981.

Blakey, Arch Fredric. *General John H. Winder, C.S.A.* Gainesville, Fla.: University of Florida Press, 1990.

Boggs, S[amuel] S. *Eighteen Months a Prisoner under the Rebel Flag.* Lovington, Ill.: The author, 1887.

Boate, Edward Wellington. "The True Story of Andersonville Told by a Federal Prisoner." *SHSP* 10 (1882): 25–32.

Bragg, William Harris. "The Union General Lost in Georgia." *Civil War Times Illustrated* 24:4 (June, 1985): 16–23.

Braun, Herman A. *Andersonville: An Object Lesson in Protection, A Critical Sketch.* Milwaukee: C. D. Fahsel, 1892.

Breeden, James O. *Joseph Jones, M.D.: Scientist of the Old South.* Lexington: University Press of Kentucky, [1975].

Brown, Daniel Patrick. *The Tragedy of Libby and Andersonville Prison Camps: A Study of Mismanagement and Inept Logistical Policies at Two Southern Prisoner-of-War Camps.* Ventura, Calif.: Golden West Historical Publications, 1980.

Brown, Louis A. *The Salisbury Prison: A Case Study of Confederate Military Prisons 1861–1865.* Wilmington, N.C.: Broadfoot Publishing, 1992.

Bullard, K. C. *Over the Deadline, or Who Killed Poll Parrot?* New York: Neale, 1909.

Cherry, Peterson H. *Prisoner in Blue, Memories of the Civil War after 70 Years.* Los Angeles: Wetzel, 1931.

Child, William. *A History of the Fifth Regiment, New Hampshire Volunteers, in the American Civil War, 1861–1865.* Bristol, N.H.: R. W. Musgrove, 1893.

Chipman, N. P. *The Tragedy of Andersonville.* San Francisco: The author, 1911.

Clapp, E. L. *Andersonville: Six Months a Prisoner of War.* Milwaukee: Daily Wisconsin Steam Printing House, 1865.

Confederate Military History, 19 vols. Wilmington, N.C.: Broadfoot Publishing, 1987.

Cornish, Dudley Taylor. *The Sable Arm: Negro Troops in the Union Army, 1861–1865.* New York: W. W. Norton, 1966.

Coulter, E. Merton, ed. "From Spotsylvania Courthouse to Andersonville: A Diary of Darius Starr." *Georgia Historical Quarterly* 41 (1957): 176–90.

Daniel, Larry J. *Soldiering in the Army of Tennessee: A Portrait of Life in the Confederate Army.* Chapel Hill: University of North Carolina Press, 1991.

Danker, Donald F. "Imprisoned at Andersonville: The Diary of Albert Henry Shatzell, May 5, 1864–September 12, 1864." *Nebraska History* 38:2 (June, 1957): 81–125.

Daskom, Hiram S. *The Adventures of an Escaped Andersonville Prisoner.* Hammond, Ind.: C. B. Harrold, n.d.

Davidson, H. M. *Fourteen Months in Southern Prisons.* Milwaukee: Daily Wisconsin Printing House, 1865.

Davis, Samuel Boyer. *Escape of a Confederate Officer from Prison. What He Saw at Andersonville.* Norfolk, Va.: Landmark Publishing Company, 1892.

Davis, William C., ed. *The Image of War*, 6 vols. Garden City, N.Y.: Doubleday, 1981–84.

The Demon of Andersonville, or The Trial of Henry Wirz. Philadelphia: Barclay, 1865.

Dennison, James H. *Dennison's Andersonville Diary.* Kankakee, Ill.: Kankakee County Historical Society, 1957.

Destler, Chester McArthur. "A Vermonter in Andersonville: Diary of Charles Ross, 1864." *Vermont History* 25:3 (July, 1957): 229–45.

Diary of Gideon Welles, 3 vols. Boston: Houghton Mifflin, 1911.

"Diary of a Prisoner." *Historical Magazine* 9:1 (second series), (January, 1871): 1–6.

Domschcke, Bernhard. *Zwanzig Monate im Kriegs-Gefangenschaft.* Milwaukee: Druck und Verlag, 1865.

Dostoevsky, Anna. *Dostoevski Reminiscences.* New York: Liveright, 1975.

Dougherty, Michael. *Prison Diary of Michael Dougherty, Late of Co. B, 13th Pa. Cavalry.* Bristol, Pa.: Chas. A. Dougherty, 1908.

Dufur, S. M. *Over the Dead Line, or Tracked by Blood-Hounds.* Burlington, Vt.: Free Press Association, 1902.

Dyer, Frederick H. *A Compendium of the War of the Rebellion.* Dayton, Ohio: Press of Morningside Bookshop, 1978.

Eckcl, Alexander. *Andersonville: Seven Months Experience of Two Tennessee Boys in Andersonville and Five Other Rebel Prisons.* Knoxville: Stubley Printing, n.d.

Eliot, Ellsworth. "A Civil War Diary." *Yale University Library Gazette* 16:1 (July, 1941): 3–13.

Empson, W. H. *A Story of Rebel Military Prisons: Over Nineteen Months a Guest of the So-Called Southern Confederacy.* Lockport, N.Y.: Press of Roberts Brothers, 1895.

Forbes, Eugene. *Diary of a Soldier, and Prisoner of War in the Rebel Prisons.* Trenton, N.J.: Murphy & Bechtel, printers, 1865.

Fosdick, Charles. *Five Hundred Days in Rebel Prisons.* Blythe Dale, Mo.: The author, 1887.

Futch, Ovid L. *History of Andersonville Prison.* [Gainesville]: University of Florida Press, 1968.

——, ed. "The Andersonville Journal of Sergeant J. M. Burdick." *Georgia Historical Quarterly* 45:3 (September, 1961): 287–94.

Galloway, Richard P., ed. *One Battle Too Many: Writings of Simon Bolivar Hulbert, Co. E, 100th N.Y.* N.p.: Richard P. Galloway, 1987.

Goss, Warren Lee. *The Soldier's Story of His Captivity at Andersonville, Belle Isle, and Other Rebel Prisons.* Boston: L. N. Richardson, 1873.

Grigsby, Melvin. *The Smoked Yank*. Chicago: Regan Printing, 1891.

Hadley, George P. *History of the Town of Goffstown, 1733–1920*, 2 vols. Goffstown, N.H.: George P. Hadley, 1924.

Hamlin, Augustus C. *Martyria; or, Andersonville Prison*. Boston: Lee and Shepard, 1866.

Hammer, Jefferson J., ed. *Frederic Augustus James's Civil War Diary, Sumter to Andersonville*. Rutherford, N.J.: Fairleigh Dickinson University Press, 1973.

Harris, Joseph K. "A Soldier's Narrative." *Civil War Times Illustrated* 27:3 (May, 1988): 36–41.

Harrold, John. *Libby, Andersonville, Florence: The Capture, Imprisonment, and Rescue of John Harrold*. Philadelphia: Wm. B. Selheimer, 1870.

Harte, Bret, and Mark Twain. *The California Sketches*. New York: Dover Publishing, 1991.

Helmreich, Paul C. "The Diary of Charles G. Lee in the Andersonville and Florence Prison Camps, 1864." *Connecticut Historical Society Bulletin* 41:1 (January, 1976): 12–28.

"Henry Wirz. The True Story of Andersonville Prison." *Miss Rutherford's Scrap Book* (June, 1924): 18.

Hesseltine, William Best. *Civil War Prisons*. New York: Frederick Ungar, 1964.

Higginson, Thomas Wentworth. *Massachusetts in the Army and Navy during the War of 1861–65*, 2 vols. Boston: Wright & Potter, 1895.

Horan, James D. *C.S.S. Shenandoah: The Memoirs of Lieutenant Commanding James I. Waddell, C.S.N.* New York: Crown, 1960.

Hunt, Roger D., and Jack R. Brown. *Brevet Brigadier Generals in Blue*. Gaithersburg, Md.: Olde Soldier Books, 1990.

Hunter, William A., ed. "The Civil War Diaries of Leonard C. Ferguson." *Pennsylvania History* 14:3 (July, 1947): 196–224, and 14:4 (October, 1947): 289–313.

Hutchinson's Washington and Georgetown Directory. Washington, D.C.: Hutchinson & Brother, 1863.

Hyde, Solon. *A Captive of War*. New York: McClure, Phillips, 1900.

Jervey, Edward D. "Prison Life among the Rebels: Recollections of a Union Chaplain." *Civil War History* 34:1 (March, 1988): 22–38.

Jones, J. Wm. "The Kilpatrick-Dahlgren Raid against Richmond." *SHSP* 13 (1885):515–60.

Jones, John B. *A Rebel War Clerk's Diary*. New York: Sagamore Press, 1958.

Kansas Adjutant General's Office. *Military History of Kansas Regiments during the War for the Suppression of the Great Rebellion*. Leavenworth: W. J. Burke, 1870.

Kean, Robert G. H. *Inside the Confederate Government: The Diary of ——*. Edited by Edward Younger. New York: Oxford University Press, 1957.

Kellogg, Robert H. *Life and Death in Rebel Prisons.* Hartford: L. Stebbins, 1865.

Kendall, Richard, ed. *Monet by Himself.* London: MacDonald, 1989.

King, G. Wayne. "Death Camp at Florence." *Civil War Times Illustrated* 12:9 (January, 1974): 34–42.

King, Spencer B., Jr. "Yankee Letters from Andersonville Prison." *Georgia Historical Quarterly* 38:1 (December, 1954): 394–98.

Knox, Donald. *Death March: The Survivors of Bataan.* New York: Harcourt Brace Jovanovich, 1981.

"A Letter from Captain Wirz to General Wright." *Historical Magazine* 9:1 (second series), (January, 1871): 7.

Little, Henry F. W. *The Seventh New Hampshire Volunteers in the War of the Rebellion.* Concord, N.H.: Ira C. Evans, 1896.

Long, Lessel. *Twelve Months in Andersonville.* Huntington, Ind.: Thad & Mark Butler, 1886.

McElroy, John. *Andersonville, A Story of Rebel Prisons.* Washington, D.C.: National Tribune, 1899.

Mann, T. H. "A Yankee in Andersonville." *Century* (July, 1890): 447–61, and (August, 1890): 606–22.

The Martyrs Who, for Our Country, Gave up Their Lives in the Prison Pens in Andersonville, Ga. Washington, D.C.: Government Printing Office, 1866.

Marvel, William. "Stampede at Olustee." *Blue & Gray Magazine* (March, 1986): 46–47.

Massachusetts Adjutant General. *Massachusetts Soldiers, Sailors, and Marines in the Civil War,* 8 vols. Norwood, Mass.: 1931–35.

Meaney, Peter. "The Prison Ministry of Father Peter Whelan, Georgia Priest and Confederate Chaplain." *Georgia Historical Quarterly* 71:1 (Spring, 1987): 1–24.

The Medical and Surgical History of the War of the Rebellion (1861–65), 3 vols. Washington, D.C.: Government Printing Office, 1870–88.

Merrell, W[illiam] H[oward]. *Five Months in Rebeldom; or Notes from the Diary of a Bull Run Prisoner, at Richmond.* Rochester, N.Y.: Adams & Dabney, 1862.

Military Images 10:5 (March–April, 1989): 7, 21.

Miller, James M. *The Story of Andersonville and Florence.* Des Moines, Iowa: Welch, the Printer, 1900.

Moore, Benjamin G. "Poor Administration from Start to Finish." *Color Bearer* 1:3 (October, 1992): 9–11.

Moore, Frank, ed. *The Rebellion Record,* 12 vols. New York: G. P. Putnam, 1861–68.

Mott, Valentine, et al. *Narrative of Privations and Sufferings of United States Officers and Soldiers While Prisoners of War, Report of a Commission of Inquiry*

Appointed by the United States Sanitary Commission. Boston: Littell's Living Age, 1864.

Murray, George W. *A History of George W. Murray.* Northampton, Mass.: Trumbull & Gere, n.d.

Myers, Robert Manson. *The Children of Pride: A True Story of Georgia and the Civil War.* New Haven: Yale University Press, 1972.

Nevins, Allan, and Milton Halsey Thomas, eds. *The Diary of George Templeton Strong,* 4 vols. New York: Macmillan, 1952.

Northrop, John Worrell. *Chronicles from the Diary of a War Prisoner in Andersonville and Other Military Prisons in the South in 1864.* Witchita, Kan.: The author, 1904.

Official Records of the Union and Confederate Navies in the War of the Rebellion, 30 vols. Washington, D.C.: Government Printing Office, 1894–1922.

Otis, George H. *The Second Wisconsin Infantry.* Dayton, Ohio: Morningside Press, 1984.

Page, James Madison. *The True Story of Andersonville Prison: A Defense of Major Henry Wirz.* New York: Neale Publishing, 1908.

The Papers of Andrew Johnson, 10 vols. Knoxville: University of Tennessee Press, 1967–92.

Park, L. M. "The 'Rebel Prison Pen' at Andersonville, Ga." *Southern Magazine* (May, 1874): 528–37.

Peck, Theodore S., ed. *Revised Roster of Vermont Volunteers and Lists of Vermonters Who Served in the Army and Navy of the United States during the War of the Rebellion, 1861–66.* Montpelier: Watchman Publishing, 1892.

Perrin, Mrs. J. S. (Cora Wirz). Letter. *Confederate Veteran* 14 (December, 1906): 539.

Perrin, William Henry, ed. *Counties of Christian and Trigg, Kentucky.* Chicago: F. A. Batley Publishing, 1884.

Potter, Jerry O. *The Sultana Tragedy: America's Greatest Maritime Disaster.* Gretna, La.: Pelican Publishing, 1992.

Ransom, John L. *John Ransom's Diary.* New York: Paul S. Eriksson, 1963.

Ray, Jean P. *The Diary of a Dead Man.* N.p.: Acorn Press, 1979.

Record of Service of Connecticut Men in the Army and Navy of the United States during the War of the Rebellion. Hartford: Case, Lockwood, & Brainard, 1889.

Robbins, George, ed. *Diary of Rev. H. Clavreul.* Waterbury, Conn.: Connecticut Association of Ex-Prisoners of War, 1910.

[Roe, Alfred S.] *The Melvin Memorial.* Cambridge, Mass.: Riverside Press, 1910.

Shearman, Mary A. "A Visit to Andersonville." *Hours at Home* (September, 1867): 409–15.

Smith, Lester W., ed. "The Andersonville Diary of Private Alfred Lyth."
     Niagara Frontier 8:1 (Spring, 1961): 14, 19–24.

Smith, W. B. *On Wheels and How I Came There*. New York: Hunt & Eaton,
     1893.

Spencer, Ambrose. *A Narrative of Andersonville*. New York: Harper & Brothers,
     1866.

Stapleton, Michael. *The Cambridge Guide to English Literature*, 5th ed.
     Cambridge: Cambridge University Press, 1983.

Stephen, Asberry C. *The Civil War Diary of Asberry C. Stephen*. Bloomington,
     Ind.: Monroe County Historical Society, 1973.

Stevenson, R. Randolph. *The Southern Side, or Andersonville Prison*. Baltimore:
     Turnbull Brothers, 1876.

Styple, William B., and John J. Fitzpatrick, eds. *The Andersonville Diary and
     Memoirs of Charles Hopkins, 1st New Jersey Infantry*. Kearny, N.J.: Belle
     Grove Publishing, 1988.

Summers, Lewis Preston. *History of Southwest Virginia, 1746–1786, Washington
     County, 1777–1870*. Baltimore: Genealogical Publishing Company, 1966.

Taylor, Richard. *Destruction and Reconstruction*. New York: D. Appleton, 1879.

T[release], E[dgar] H. "Letter from a Soldier." *Harper's Weekly* 9 February 11,
     1865): 93–94.

Trial of Henry Wirz. House Executive Document 23, 40th Congress, 2nd
     session.

Urban, John W. *In Defense of the Union, or, Through Shot and Shell and Prison
     Pen*. Chicago and Philadelphia: Monarch Book Co., 1887.

Vaughter, John B. *Prison Life in Dixie*. Chicago: Central Book Concern, 1880.

Verzeichniss der Stadtbürger von Zürich auf das Jahr 1851. Zurich: Die
     Stadtpresse, 1851.

A Voice from Rebel Prisons. Boston: Press of G. C. Rand & Avery, 1865.

*War of the Rebellion: A Compilation of the Official Records of the Union and
     Confederate Armies*, 128 vols. Washington, D.C.: Government Printing
     Office, 1880–1901.

Winkler, John K. *Incredible Carnegie*. New York: Vanguard Press, 1931.

Sources and Acknowledgments

Few Civil War novels are so captivating—so to speak—as Mackinlay Kantor's *Andersonville*, and perhaps none has done quite so much to distort the history of a particular event. Kantor's research was impressive, for a novelist, but for a historian it was painfully superficial: he consulted only the most untrustworthy accounts, swallowed them whole, and left a picture of deliberate brutality that was almost entirely incorrect. A few years later Ovid Futch produced a somewhat more scholarly study of the prison, but his work received nowhere near the circulation of the novel, and Kantor's misjudgment prevails.

Like its fictional counterpart, Futch's history suffers from an unhealthy reliance upon dubious sources (of which Andersonville produced more than its share), most notably John McElroy's *Andersonville, A Study of Rebel Military Prisons* and John Ransom's *Andersonville Diary*. McElroy wrote his highly embellished memoir fifteen years after the fact; Ransom represented his book as an "edited" version of his wartime diary, but so wildly inaccurate were many of his dates and observations that if any such diary existed he must have failed to consult it during the editing process.

Scores of other former prisoners scribbled their bitter recollections of Andersonville in the half century after the war, most of them casting John Winder, Henry Wirz, and all other Andersonville Confederates in the most diabolical light, although a couple of them did actually try to vindicate Wirz. Like Ransom, many purported to write from original diaries, but even those who did own such journals suffered no qualms about embroidering them. Michael Dougherty's published diary, for instance, bears little resemblance to the one he kept at Andersonville, and borrows heavily from exaggerated passages in works already published. Several such postwar accounts appear in the bibliography, and they range from fairly unreliable to perfectly ridiculous. Dozens of manuscript memoirs also survive in archives across the country, most of them too preposterous to attract even the publishers who specialized in that genre, but only a couple of them are cited in this work, and each is used only to corroborate a single piece of information. As far as possible, the evidence for this history of the war's most deadly prison has been drawn from sources of no later vintage than 1865—principally official documents and contemporary diaries and letters, most of them unpublished. The transcript of Henry Wirz's trial yields a trove of useful information, but it also contains some of the most flagrant falsehoods in the entire Andersonville miscellany. The government's prosecutor coached his witnesses shamelessly, prompting them with information he gleaned from captured paperwork, and all the testimony must be handled with at least one eye open to motives of revenge and self-interest. Had the military commission so viewed it, Wirz would probably have gone free.

The National Archives provided a greater amount of information for this work than any other single agency, so I am particularly indebted to the staff of the Military Reference Branch there—most notably to Michael Musick, who outdid himself to help me find cartloads of documents and the correct citations for certain elusive manuscripts: if my footnotes fall short of perfection, they will do so despite his best efforts. Bill Lind and Michael Meier, of the same office, likewise helped me hunt down some valuable information, and Barry Zerby provided me with the muster rolls of the U.S.S. *Water Witch.*

I am also obliged to numerous archivists and curators for their assistance with manuscript material, including a few whose diligent searches of their repositories yielded nothing useful. Dr. Richard Sommers, David Keough, Pamela Cheney, and Michael Winey of the U.S. Army Military History Institute assisted me most cordially, as usual, and Paul Brockman of the Indiana Historical Society again aided me more than he knew. Others who offered vital assistance include Roberta Zonghi of the Boston Public Library's Special Collections; Susan Halpert of Harvard's Houghton Library; Peter Drummey of the Massachusetts Historical Society; Barney Bloom of the Vermont Historical Society; Jeffrey Marshall of the Special Collections Department at the University of Vermont; Tom DeClos of New York's Capitol Collection, in Albany; Cindy Bendroth of the Rhode Island Historical Society; Martha H. Smart of the Connecticut Historical Society; Judith Ann Schiff, chief research archivist at Yale University Library; Valerie Wingfield, manuscripts specialist with the New York Public Library; Edward Skipworth of Special Collections and Archives at Rutgers University; Archivist Bette Barker of New Jersey's Division of Records Management and Archives; Fred Baumann and Maja Keech, in different departments at the Library of Congress; John Grabowski, curator of manuscripts for the Western Reserve Historical Society; Gary Arnold, head research archivist at the Ohio Historical Society; Archie Motley, at the Chicago Historical Society; Curator Cheryl Schnirring of the Illinois State Historical Library; Becki Peterson of the State Historical Society of Iowa's Des Moines office, and Robert Goerdt of the Iowa City branch; Harold Miller, archivist at the State Historical Society of Wisconsin; Steven Nielsen of the Minnesota Historical Society; Judy Bolton of Louisiana State University's Hill Memorial Library; Frank Wheeler of the Atlanta Historical Society; George Whiteley of the Georgia Department of Archives and History; R. B. Rosenburg of the Andrew Johnson Project at the University of Tennessee; Bill Erwin of Duke University's Special Collections Department; and David Moltke-Hansen of the Southern Historical Collection, in the University of North Carolina's Wilson Library.

Fred Boyles, Superintendent of Andersonville National Historic Site, very kindly arranged for me to peruse the park's manuscript holdings, which rangers Jaqueline Holt, Carlene Petty, and Mark Bollinger all helped to collect for me. Jackie, Mark Bollinger, and Mark Ragan also answered long-distance questions about the prison and cemetery, and Marian Harris of the Lake Blackshear Regional Library in Americus provided me with microfilm copies of period newspapers. To Peer Edwin Ravnan of Macon's Middle Georgia Archives I am indebted for information about Andersonville photographer A. J. Riddle, while David Mark of Linthicum Heights, Maryland, generously gave me copies of rare Riddle photographs. Roger Hunt of Rockville, Maryland, likewise came through in a pinch with two coveted photos.

I was extremely grateful to receive a copy of an obscure, privately published Andersonville diary from Stephen Sears, of Norwalk, Connecticut. Mrs. John Winder III of Winston-Salem cheerfully offered likenesses of Richard and Sidney Winder for recopying, and Curtis Carley sent prints of his great-grandfather's portrait from Albuquerque—as well as a handy typescript of that soldier's diary, the original of which resides with the State Historical Society of Iowa. Mark H. Dunkelman of Providence shared some of the material he accumulated on the 154th New York, while Father Peter Meaney of Morristown, New Jersey, sent me a copy of his monograph on Father Whelan. Dick Winslow of Portsmouth, New Hampshire, forwarded numerous newspaper citations, and Bill Christen of Wyandotte, Michigan, sent an interesting memoir of a former prisoner. Bob Krick, chief historian at Fredericksburg and Spotsylvania National Military Park, provided the memoir that confirmed my suspicions about Leroy Key and the mysterious "Limber Jim." Zelda Long helped me with some long-distance research in Baton Rouge, and I cannot forget my overseas assistant, Manual Aicher, who applied his professional research skills to the mystery of Henry Wirz's early years.

One benefactor did not know he had done me a great service until we bumped into each other at the National Archives. Ed Bearss, whose detailed 1970 survey of the prison site aided me immensely, completed his work just as I bid a not-so-fond farewell to olive drab. Unfortunately, that document was never published for general distribution; without some of the insights provided by Ed's labor, I might not have been able to interpret some of the more esoteric diary references to physical aspects of the prison.

John Winder's biographer, Arch Fredric Blakey, not only helped me to obtain some photographs but shared his own research with me and read my entire first draft, offering excellent suggestions throughout. Burnham B. Davis, as objective a critic as one could hope for, read the fourth draft. Blake Magner has once again come through with wonderfully clear and accurate cartography. Bill Frassanito's knowledgeable criticism of my early notions about the Riddle photographs of Andersonville led me to a valuable reconsideration of the circumstances surrounding those images. The ultimate conclusions—on that topic and others—are still mine, however, as are any mistakes.

I wish to express particular gratitude to Ron Maner and the rest of the editorial staff at the University of North Carolina Press, our stylistic squabbles notwithstanding. Would that all writers could enjoy editing that is simultaneously so thorough, knowledgeable, and sensitive.

This book would have been another year or two in the writing had Keith Baker, of Xenia, Ohio, not lured me away from my old manual typewriter with a generous gift from a world I would not otherwise have visited. Thanks, cousin.

The study of Andersonville showed me one of the seamier sides of the Civil War, and it introduced me to an unpleasant aspect of Civil War scholarship as well. Until now my research inquiries have always seemed to result in an avalanche of information, even from direct competitors who apparently value the pursuit of accuracy more highly than gaining the credit for some new revelation. The subject of Civil War prisons appears to attract a different breed, at least among amateur historians: despite the long list of people who assisted me in this project, my Andersonville research has been attended by a greater number of unfulfilled promises, unreciprocated favors, and refusals to share sources than I have experienced in all my other historical efforts combined. It is as though the topic were somehow accursed, but perhaps that is fitting for such a tragedy-within-a-tragedy.

Index